2003 Krause

stamps & prices

A Concise Catalog of United States Stamps

Edited by Maurice D. Wozniak

Published by

krause publications

700 E. State Street • Iola, WI 54990-0001
Telephone: 715/445-2214

To place an order or receive our free catalog, call 800-258-0929.
For editorial comment and further information,
use our regular business telephone at (715) 445-2214.

Library of Congress Catalog Number: 00-102618
ISBN: 0-87349-402-4

Printed in the United States of America

CONTENTS

A brief introduction to United States stamps 4

Regular Issues 10
Commemoratives 100
Airmails 299
Special Delivery Stamps 309
Airmail/Special Delivery Stamps 310
Parcel Post Stamps 311
Parcel Post/Postage Due Stamps 311
Special Handling Stamps 311
Registration Stamp. 312
Certified Mail Stamp 312
Postage Due Stamps 313
Migratory Bird Hunting Permit Stamps 318

A brief introduction to United States stamps

By Maurice D. Wozniak, Editor

Most collectors trace the history of stamp collecting to 1840, when Great Britain revolutionized postal service by introducing adhesive stamps that signified the sender had paid the fee for delivery. That first stamp featured a portrait of the reigning British monarch, Queen Victoria, and the hobby of stamp collecting commenced almost simultaneously.

The United States followed with its first two postage stamps on July 1, 1847. Issued during the presidency of James K. Polk, the stamps featured two popular figures from the American Revolution – Benjamin Franklin, who had been named the first postmaster general in an age when delivery largely was entrusted to personal couriers or the good will of strangers; and George Washington, the general who became the first president of the republic.

Franklin's picture appeared on the 5¢ stamp, sufficient to carry an ordinary letter up to 300 miles, and Washington's picture was on the 10¢ stamp, used for letters requiring higher postage.

They were the world's first stamps to feature prominent persons of the past, and they set the tone for U.S. stamp-issuing policy. In the first 100 years, especially, portraits of America's heroes were prominent on stamps, which represented the country on mail sent to every country on the globe.

So-called commemorative stamps, issued typically in remembrance of a historical event or to highlight a current event, such as a large stamp exhibition, appeared first in 1893. Those first commemoratives were issued in support of the World's Columbian Exposition in Chicago, Ill., an event designed around the 400th anniversary of the voyage of Christopher Columbus, on which he is credited with the discovery of America.

The 16 stamps in that first commemorative set feature exquisite engravings of paintings of Columbus' voyage. The stamps were enormously popular with the public. In fact, more than 1 billion copies of the dull purple 2¢ stamps, the standard postal value at the time, were printed. That output dwarfs the production of almost all modern U.S. commemorative stamps.

People then could buy a 2¢ stamp as a souvenir of the anniversary and put it away for safekeeping. Many did. Today, you can buy that 2¢ stamp or its companion 1¢ value for less than $20 each. Postally used stamps might cost about 25¢. But the black $5 stamp in the set, which would have placed a strain on the budgets of most Americans at the end of the last century, is now valued at more than $2,500.

While commemoratives helped to sing the praises of America, the workhorse definitives could become dull to most mailers. In fact, for a period of more than 20 years in the early part of the 20th century, familiar portraits of either Washington or Franklin appeared on almost all U.S. stamps. Some collectors today specialize in finding the differences among that array of stamps.

The Presidential Series of definitive stamps, named because it featured profile busts of every deceased president in order of his term in office, extended over 16 years. The Liberty Series, the Prominent American Series, Americana Series, and the Great Americans Series, all of which continued to feature famous people and icons of history, followed it.

Then came the Transportation Series, which added an occasional touch of whimsy to the staid postage stamp. (A Tow Truck in a Transportation Series? An Elevator car?)

Today's regular issues are distinguished by variety – flags in various settings, birds and animals, symbols of culture, even berries.

Meanwhile, commemoratives went through a similar evolution in these changing times. Besides recalling famous people and events of history, U.S. stamps became blatantly political and considerably more expansive.

In the 1930s, they extolled the virtue of the Olympic Games, a Roosevelt administration program that was determined to be unconstitutional two years later, Mothers and Baseball.

Today, they have an obvious "topical" bent – art works, trains, professions, extinct animals, living animals, flowers and movie stars. More and more, they are designed to appeal to stamp collectors and entice more people to become stamp collectors. Some of the most difficult stamps to find today are those in the hands (and mounted on the walls) of non-traditional collectors – those for sports stars and Certified Public Accountants.

It may be a reflection of our democratic national character that the most famous U.S. stamp is an airmail error, the "Inverted Jenny" of 1918, on which the center vignette of an airplane was printed upside-down.

Since 1847, the United States has issued approximately 5,000 different postage stamps, not including stamped envelopes and postal cards. In addition, there have been thousands more stamps to raise revenues and signify other business transactions. All of these attract ardent collectors, and the hobby, which changing, remains popular and arguably more interesting than ever. We hope this mini catalog, a more portable version of the *Krause-Minkus Standard Catalog of® U.S. Stamps,* will enhance your enjoyment.

How to use this catalog

Stamps issued by the United States government are listed in chronological order according to Minkus catalog number. To the right of the number is a space for you to write in numbers assigned by other catalog makers for that stamp, if you wish. A cross-reference guide to the Scott catalog is available free from Krause Publications, Iola, WI 54990-0001.

The date of issue, subject of the stamp image, denomination and color of the stamp are given to help in identification. The prices given for used and unused stamps are based on actual selling prices by dealers or at auction.

Five boxes are provided at the right of each listing for you to customize an inventory of your collection. For example, you might designate the boxes to indicate if you have, in order, a used copy, an unused copy, a mint (never-hinged) copy, a multiple (such as a plate block), and a copy on cover. If you mark the boxes to indicate you have a particular item, you will have a simple, illustrated inventory of your collection that you can carry with you to stamp bourses or stamp club meetings.

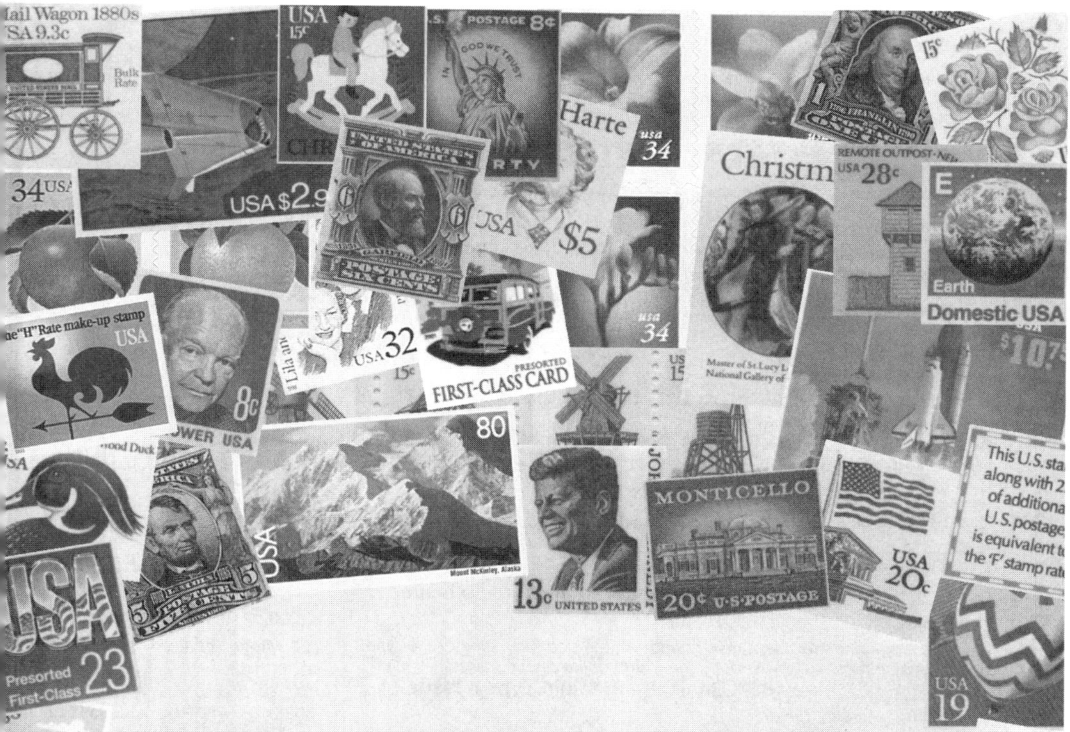

REGULAR ISSUES

UnFVF UseFVF

REGULAR POSTAL ISSUES

1 ________ **1847. Benjamin Franklin Issue**

5¢ **red brown** 6,000.00 600.00 ❑❑❑❑❑

SP1 ________ **1875. Benjamin Franklin Special Printing Issue**

5¢ **red brown** (4,779 copies sold) 800.00 ❑❑❑❑❑

2 ________ **1847. George Washington Issue**

10¢ **black** 27,500.00 1,400.00 ❑❑❑❑❑

NOTE: Government imitations of the 5¢ (in blue) and 10¢ (in Venetian red) were printed in 1947 and are listed as CM290 in the commemorative stamp section.

NOTE: The earliest known use of any U.S. stamp is a pen-canceled pair of No. 2 with a New York City postmark of "July 2," 1847, sent to Indianapolis, Ind.

SP2 ________ **1875. George Washington Special Printing Issue**

10¢ **black** (3,883 copies sold) 1,000.00 ❑❑❑❑❑

3 ________ **1851. Benjamin Franklin Issue**

1¢ **blue** Type I 175,000.00 45,000.00 ❑❑❑❑❑

4 ________ **1857. Benjamin Franklin Type Ia Regular Issue**

1¢ **blue** Type Ia 35,000.00 9,500.00 ❑❑❑❑❑

5 ________ **1851. Benjamin Franklin Type Ib Issue**

1¢ **blue** Type Ib 14,000.00 6,000.00 ❑❑❑❑❑

NOTE: Catalog prices for the above stamp are for nice examples of the type. Stamps with a slightly less complete design at the bottom are worth about one-fourth of the above prices.

6 ________ **1857. Benjamin Franklin Type II Issue**

1¢ **blue** (Plate 1) Type II 1,100.00 150.00 ❑❑❑❑❑

7 ________ **1851. Benjamin Franklin Type III Issue**

1¢ **blue** Type III 11,500.00 2,600.00 ❑❑❑❑❑

8 ________ **1851. Benjamin Franklin Type IIIa Issue**

1¢ **blue** (Plate 1E) Type IIIa 4,250.00 975.00 ❑❑❑❑❑

9 ________ **1852. Benjamin Franklin Type IV Issue**

1¢ **blue** Type IV (recut Type IV) (recut once at top & once at bottom) 750.00 125.00 ❑❑❑❑❑

10 ________ **1851. George Washington Issue**

3¢ **orange brown** Type I 3,000.00 100.00 ❑❑❑❑❑

11 ________

3¢ **Venetian red** Type I 240.00 10.00 ❑❑❑❑❑

12 ________ **1856. Thomas Jefferson Issue**

5¢ **red brown** Type I 17,500.00 1,000.00 ❑❑❑❑❑

13 ________ **1855. George Washington Type I Issue**

10¢ **green** Type I 14,000.00 800.00 ❑❑❑❑❑

14 ________ **1855. George Washington Type II Issue**

10¢ **green** Type II 4,000.00 225.00 ❑❑❑❑❑

15 ________ **1855. George Washington Type III Issue**

10¢ **green** Type III 4,000.00 225.00 ❑❑❑❑❑

16 ________ **1856. George Washington Type IV Issue**

10¢ **green** Type IV (outer line recut at top only) 25,000.00 1,600.00 ❑❑❑❑❑

NOTE: All four types of the 10¢ stamp occur on the same sheet, so that pairs and blocks showing combination of these types exist.

17 ________ **1851. George Washington Type I Issue**

12¢ **black** Type I 5,000.00 325.00 ❑❑❑❑❑

18 ________ **1861. Benjamin Franklin Type I Issue**

1¢ **blue** Type I 1,800.00 600.00 ❑❑❑❑❑

NOTE: The normal setting of the perforating machine was such that perforations cut the design on almost every stamp. Prices quoted are for such copies. Where the perforations do not cut the design No. 18 stamps command very high premiums.

19 ________ **1857. Benjamin Franklin Type Ia Issue**

1¢ **blue** Type Ia 21,000.00 6,250.00 ❑❑❑❑❑

1

1

SP1

2

2

SP2

3, 18

3

4, 19

5

6, 20

7

9

10, 11

10

12

13

13

14

15

16

17

UnFVF	UseFVF	

20 _____ **1857. Benjamin Franklin Type II Issue**
1¢ **blue** (Plate 2) Type II — 1,000.00 — 250.00 ☐☐☐☐☐

21 _____ **1857. Benjamin Franklin Type III Issue**
1¢ **blue** Type III — 12,000.00 — 2,000.00 ☐☐☐☐☐

22 _____ **1857. Benjamin Franklin Type IIIa Issue**
1¢ **blue** (Plate 4) Type IIIa — 1,900.00 — 475.00 ☐☐☐☐☐

23 _____ **1857. Benjamin Franklin Type IV Issue**
1¢ **blue** Type IV recut top and once at bottom — 8,000.00 — 700.00 ☐☐☐☐☐

24 _____ **1857. Benjamin Franklin Type V Issue**
1¢ **blue** Type V — 170.00 — 40.00 ☐☐☐☐☐

25 _____ **1857. George Washington Type I Issue**
3¢ **rose** Type I — 2,250.00 — 85.00 ☐☐☐☐☐
NOTE: Fakes are known of the horizontal pair, imperforate vertically.

26 _____ **1857. George Washington Type II Issue**
3¢ **Venetian red** Type II — 75.00 — 7.00 ☐☐☐☐☐

27 _____ **1857. George Washington Type III Issue**
3¢ **Venetian red** Type III — 225.00 — 55.00 ☐☐☐☐☐

28 _____ **1857. Thomas Jefferson Type I Issue**
5¢ **red brown** Type I — 4,500.00 — 760.00 ☐☐☐☐☐

28A _____
5¢ **henna brown (Indian red)** — 30,000.00 — 3,000.00 ☐☐☐☐☐

29 _____ **1858. Thomas Jefferson Type I Issue**
5¢ **brick red** Type I — 25,000.00 — 1,300.00 ☐☐☐☐☐

30 _____ **1859. Thomas Jefferson Type I Issue**
5¢ **brown** Type I — 2,250.00 — 350.00 ☐☐☐☐☐

31 _____ **1860. Thomas Jefferson Type II Issue**
5¢ **brown** Type II — 1,900.00 — 275.00 ☐☐☐☐☐

32 _____ **1861. Thomas Jefferson Type II Issue**
5¢ **orange brown** Type II — 1,150.00 — 1,100.00 ☐☐☐☐☐

33 _____ **1857. George Washington Type I Issue**
10¢ **green** Type I — 16,500.00 — 850.00 ☐☐☐☐☐

34 _____ **1857. George Washington Type II Issue**
10¢ **green** Type II — 5,000.00 — 275.00 ☐☐☐☐☐

35 _____ **1857. George Washington Type III Issue**
10¢ **green** Type III — 5,000.00 — 275.00 ☐☐☐☐☐

36 _____ **1857. George Washington Type IV Issue**
10¢ **green** Type IV, recut at top — 32,500.00 — 2,250.00 ☐☐☐☐☐

37 _____ **1859. George Washington Type V Issue**
10¢ **green** Type V — 275.00 — 60.00 ☐☐☐☐☐

38 _____ **1857. George Washington Type I Issue**
12¢ **black** Type I — 1,300.00 — 250.00 ☐☐☐☐☐

39 _____ **1859. George Washington Type II Issue**
12¢ **black** Type II — 750.00 — 180.00 ☐☐☐☐☐

40 _____ **1860. George Washington Issue**
24¢ **gray lilac** — 1,600.00 — 350.00 ☐☐☐☐☐

41 _____ **1860. Benjamin Franklin Issue**
30¢ **orange** — 1,850.00 — 450.00 ☐☐☐☐☐

42 _____ **1860. George Washington Issue**
90¢ **deep blue** — 2,750.00 — 6,500.00 ☐☐☐☐☐
NOTE: Many fake cancellations exist on this stamp.

SP3 _____ **1875. Benjamin Franklin Special Printing Issue**
1¢ **brilliant blue** (3,846 copies sold) — 625.00 — ☐☐☐☐☐

SP4 _____ **1875. George Washington Special Printing Issue**
3¢ **bright vermilion** (479 copies) — 3,000.00 — ☐☐☐☐☐

21

23

24

25

26

27

28-30

31, 32

33

33

34

35

36

37

38

39

40

41

42

UnFVF	UseFVF	

SP5 _____ **1875. Thomas Jefferson Special Printing Issue**
5¢ **bright orange brown** (878 copies) — 1,200.00 □□□□□

SP6 _____ **1875. George Washington Special Printing Issue**
10¢ **bluish green** (516 copies) — 2,750.00 □□□□□

SP7 _____ **1875. George Washington Special Printing Issue**
12¢ **greenish black** (489 copies) — 3,250.00 □□□□□

SP8 _____ **1875. George Washington Special Printing Issue**
24¢ **dark violet black** (479 copies) — 3,250.00 □□□□□

SP9 _____ **1875. Benjamin Franklin Special Printing Issue**
30¢ **yellow orange** (480 copies) — 3,250.00 □□□□□

SP10 _____ **1875. George Washington Special Printing Issue**
90¢ **indigo** (454 copies) — 4,500.00 □□□□□

NOTE: *This set is known imperforate.*

43 _____ **1861. Benjamin Franklin Issue**
1¢ **blue** 325.00 32.50 □□□□□

44 _____ **1863. Andrew Jackson Issue**
2¢ **black** 350.00 50.00 □□□□□

45 _____ **1861. George Washington Issue**
3¢ **pink** 7,500.00 750.00 □□□□□

NOTE: *It is almost impossible to describe a "pink" in words, but it should be kept in mind that the inking on a "pink" is rather heavy, and the lines of the design do not stand out as sharply as on the other shades. The color, while not as outstanding as a dull pink ribbon, is nevertheless on that order. It is not any of the shades of brown, dull red, rose red, or brown red so often mistaken for the real pink.*

46 _____ **1861. George Washington Issue**
3¢ **brown carmine** 130.00 2.50 □□□□□

47 _____ **1861. Thomas Jefferson Issue**
5¢ **buff** 20,000.00 800.00 □□□□□

48 _____ **1862. Thomas Jefferson Issue**
5¢ **red brown** 4,500.00 450.00 □□□□□

49 _____ **1863. Thomas Jefferson Issue**
5¢ **brown** 1,200.00 110.00 □□□□□

50 _____ **1861. George Washington Type I Issue**
10¢ **green** Type I 6,750.00 950.00 □□□□□

51 _____ **1861. George Washington Type II Issue**
10¢ **green** Type II 750.00 50.00 □□□□□

52 _____ **1861. George Washington Issue**
12¢ **black** 1,250.00 90.00 □□□□□

53 _____ **1866. Abraham Lincoln Issue**
15¢ **black** 1,750.00 150.00 □□□□□

54 _____ **1861. George Washington Issue**
24¢ **violet** 9,500.00 1,250.00 □□□□□

NOTE: *No. 54 is found only on thin, semi-transparent paper, while Nos. 55 and 56 are on a thicker and more opaque paper.*

55 _____ **1861. George Washington Issue**
24¢ **red lilac** 2,000.00 175.00 □□□□□

56 _____ **1862. George Washington Issue**
24¢ **lilac** 1,200.00 100.00 □□□□□

57 _____ **1861. Benjamin Franklin Issue**
30¢ **orange** 1,600.00 160.00 □□□□□

58 _____ **1861. George Washington Issue**
90¢ **blue** 2,750.00 425.00 □□□□□

SP11 _____ **1875. Benjamin Franklin Special Printing Issue**
1¢ **dark ultramarine** (3,195 copies) 500.00 800.00 □□□□□

SP12 _____ **1875. Andrew Jackson Special Printing Issue**
2¢ **jet black** (979 copies) 2,300.00 4,000.00 □□□□□

43

43

43

44

45

45

45

47

47

47

50

50

51

51

52

52

52

53

54-56

57

58

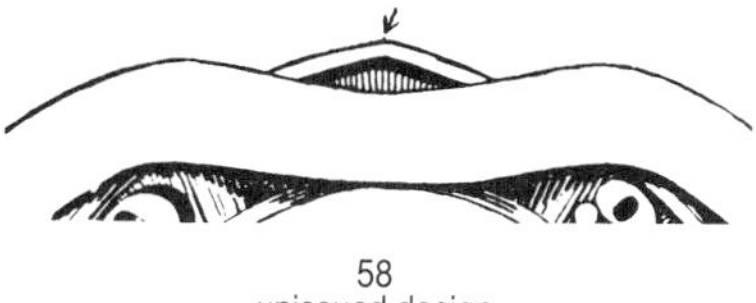
58
unissued design

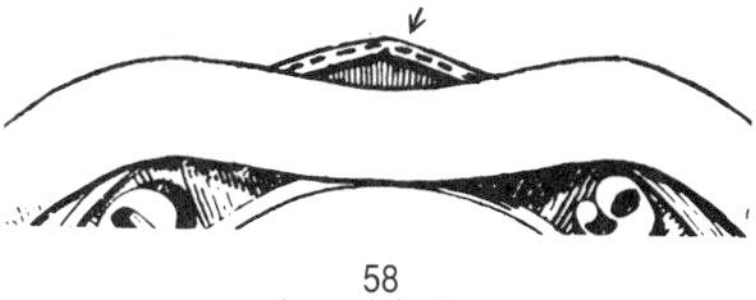
58
issued design

UnFVF	UseFVF	

SP13 _____ **1875. George Washington Special Printing Issue**
 3¢ **brown red** (465 copies) 2,500.00 4,300.00 ☐☐☐☐☐

SP14 _____ **1875. Thomas Jefferson Special Printing Issue**
 5¢ **light yellow brown** (672 copies) 1,850.00 2,300.00 ☐☐☐☐☐

SP15 _____ **1875. George Washington Special Printing Issue**
 10¢ **bluish green** (451 copies) 2,000.00 3,750.00 ☐☐☐☐☐

SP16 _____
 12¢ **deep black** (389 copies) 2,800.00 4,500.00 ☐☐☐☐☐

SP17 _____ **1875. Abraham Lincoln Special Printing Issue**
 15¢ **deep black** (397 copies) 3,250.00 5,500.00 ☐☐☐☐☐

SP18 _____ **1875. George Washington Special Printing Issue**
 24¢ **deep brown violet** (346 copies) 3,250.00 6,000.00 ☐☐☐☐☐

SP19 _____ **1875. Benjamin Franklin Special Printing Issue**
 30¢ **brown orange** (346 copies) 3,500.00 6,000.00 ☐☐☐☐☐

SP20 _____ **1875. George Washington Special Printing Issue**
 90¢ **dark blue** (317 copies) 4,800.00 20,000.00 ☐☐☐☐☐

59 _____ **1867. George Washington w/Grill Issue**
 3¢ **rose** grill A 5,000.00 1,100.00 ☐☐☐☐☐

60 _____ **1867. Thomas Jefferson Grill A Issue**
 5¢ **brown** grill A — 130,000.00 ☐☐☐☐☐

61 _____ **1867. Benjamin Franklin Grill A Issue**
 30¢ **orange** grill A — 60,000.00 ☐☐☐☐☐

61A _____ **1868. George Washington Grill B Issue**
 3¢ **rose** grill B — 175,000.00 ☐☐☐☐☐

62 _____ **1867. George Washington Grill C Issue**
 3¢ **rose** grill C 5,000.00 950.00 ☐☐☐☐☐

NOTE: No. 62 shows rows of grill points, not as heavily impressed as the normal grill, forming a grill whose total area is about 18 x 15mm. Caused by a failure to cut deeply enough into the grill roller when it was being machined, which left a few areas on the roller only "partially erased."

63 _____ **1868. Andrew Jackson w/Grill D Issue**
 2¢ **black** grill D 15,000.00 3,000.00 ☐☐☐☐☐

64 _____ **1868. George Washington Grill D Issue**
 3¢ **rose** grill D 6,000.00 950.00 ☐☐☐☐☐

65 _____ **1868. Benjamin Franklin Z Grill Issue**
 1¢ **blue** grill Z — 935,000.00 ☐☐☐☐☐

66 _____ **1868. Andrew Jackson Grill Z Issue**
 2¢ **black** grill Z 7,000.00 1,100.00 ☐☐☐☐☐

67 _____ **1868. George Washington Grill Z Issue**
 3¢ **rose** grill Z 12,500.00 3,250.00 ☐☐☐☐☐

68 _____ **1868. George Washington Grill Z Issue**
 10¢ **green** grill Z 90,000.00 — ☐☐☐☐☐

69 _____ **1868. George Washington Grill Z Issue**
 12¢ **black** grill Z 11,000.00 1,500.00 ☐☐☐☐☐

69A _____ **1868. Abraham Lincoln Grill Z Issue**
 15¢ **black** grill Z 220,000.00 — ☐☐☐☐☐

70 _____ **1868. Benjamin Franklin Grill E Issue**
 1¢ **blue** grill E 2,750.00 450.00 ☐☐☐☐☐

71 _____ **1868. Andrew Jackson Grill E Issue**
 2¢ **black** grill E 1,400.00 140.00 ☐☐☐☐☐

72 _____ **1868. George Washington Grill E Issue**
 3¢ **rose** grill E 800.00 22.50 ☐☐☐☐☐

73 _____ **1868. George Washington Grill E Issue**
 10¢ **green** grill E 5,000.00 300.00 ☐☐☐☐☐

74 _____ **1868. George Washington Grill E Issue**
 12¢ **black** grill E 4,500.00 350.00 ☐☐☐☐☐

UnFVF	UseFVF	

75 _____ **1868. Abraham Lincoln Grill E Issue**
15¢ **black** grill E — 8,750.00 — 625.00 ☐☐☐☐☐

76 _____ **1868. Benjamin Franklin Grill F Issue**
1¢ **blue** grill F — 1,000.00 — 200.00 ☐☐☐☐☐

77 _____ **1868. Andrew Jackson Grill F Issue**
2¢ **black** grill F — 475.00 — 47.50 ☐☐☐☐☐

78 _____ **1868. George Washington Grill F Issue**
3¢ **rose** grill F — 360.00 — 7.50 ☐☐☐☐☐

79 _____ **1868. Thomas Jefferson Grill F Issue**
5¢ **brown** grill F — 3,000.00 — 750.00 ☐☐☐☐☐

80 _____ **1868. George Washington Grill F Issue**
10¢ **yellow green** grill F — 2,500.00 — 200.00 ☐☐☐☐☐

81 _____
12¢ **black** grill F — 2,800.00 — 225.00 ☐☐☐☐☐

82 _____ **1868. Abraham Lincoln Grill F Issue**
15¢ **black** grill F — 3,250.00 — 300.00 ☐☐☐☐☐

83 _____ **1869. George Washington Grill F Issue**
24¢ **gray lilac** grill F — 5,500.00 — 850.00 ☐☐☐☐☐

84 _____ **1868. Benjamin Franklin Grill F Issue**
30¢ **orange** grill F — 5,500.00 — 700.00 ☐☐☐☐☐

85 _____ **1869. George Washington Grill F Issue**
90¢ **blue** grill F — 10,000.00 — 1,400.00 ☐☐☐☐☐

NOTE: Most of the stamps that bear grills can be found with double grills, triple grills, split grills and quadruple split grills. Double grills are two impressions of the grill on the same stamp, triple grills are three impressions of the grill on the same stamp, split grills are those with about half of a normal grill on each end or on each side of the stamp and quadruple split grills are those that show just a small portion of the grill on each corner of the stamp. The split grill varieties were caused by misplacing the stamps under the grill roller so that the grills were not properly placed on the stamps. Fake grills exist.

86 _____ **1869. Benjamin Franklin Issue**
1¢ **buff** — 750.00 — 160.00 ☐☐☐☐☐

87 _____ **1869. Pony Express Issue**
2¢ **brown** — 700.00 — 75.00 ☐☐☐☐☐

88 _____ **1869. Early Locomotive Issue**
3¢ **ultramarine** — 300.00 — 20.00 ☐☐☐☐☐

59

62

65

86

87

88

		UnFVF	UseFVF	
89 ____________	**1869. George Washington Issue**			
6¢ **ultramarine**		2,750.00	210.00	❑❑❑❑❑
90 ____________	**1869. Shield and Eagle Issue**			
10¢ **yellow**		2,000.00	140.00	❑❑❑❑❑
91 ____________	**1869. Steamship Adriatic Issue**			
12¢ **green**		2,250.00	150.00	❑❑❑❑❑
92 ____________	**1869. Landing of Columbus Type I Issue**			
15¢ **brown & blue** Type I		7,500.00	650.00	❑❑❑❑❑
93 ____________	**1869. Landing of Columbus Type II Issue**			
15¢ **brown & blue** Type II		3,250.00	250.00	❑❑❑❑❑
94 ____________	**1869. Signing of the Declaration of Independence Issue**			
24¢ **green & violet**		7,000.00	750.00	❑❑❑❑❑
95 ____________	**1869. Shield, Eagle and Flags Issue**			
30¢ **blue & carmine**		7,000.00	550.00	❑❑❑❑❑
96 ____________	**1869. Abraham Lincoln Issue**			
90¢ **carmine & black**		9,250.00	2,400.00	❑❑❑❑❑
SP21 ____________	**1875. Benjamin Franklin Special Printing Pictorial Issue**			
1¢ **buff** (approx. 2,750 copies sold)		500.00	325.00	❑❑❑❑❑
SP22 ____________	**1875. Pony Express Special Printing Pictorial Issue**			
2¢ **brown** (4,755 copies)		700.00	475.00	❑❑❑❑❑
SP23 ____________	**1875. Early Locomotive Special Printing Pictorial Issue**			
3¢ **ultramarine** (1,406 copies)		5,250.00	15,000.00	❑❑❑❑❑
SP24 ____________	**1875. George Washington Special Pictorial Issue**			
6¢ **ultramarine** (2,226 copies)		1,600.00	1,700.00	❑❑❑❑❑
SP25 ____________	**1875. Shield and Eagle Special Printing Pictorial Issue**			
10¢ **yellow** (1,947 copies)		2,100.00	1,750.00	❑❑❑❑❑
SP26 ____________	**1875. Steamship Adriatic Special Printing Pictorial Issue**			
12¢ **bright green** (1,584 copies)		2,750.00	2,750.00	❑❑❑❑❑
SP27 ____________	**1875. Landing of Columbus Special Printing Pictorial Issue**			
15¢ **brown & blue** Type III (1,981 copies)		2,000.00	1,000.00	❑❑❑❑❑
SP28 ____________	**1875. Declaration of Independence Special Printing Pictorial Issue**			
24¢ **deep green & violet** (2,091 copies)		2,250.00	1,400.00	❑❑❑❑❑
SP29 ____________	**1875. Shield, Eagle and Flags Special Printing Pictorial Issue**			
30¢ **bright blue & carmine** (1,356 copies)		3,000.00	2,500.00	❑❑❑❑❑
SP30 ____________	**1875. Abraham Lincoln Special Printing Pictorial Issue**			
90¢ **carmine & black** (1,356 copies)		5,000.00	5,500.00	❑❑❑❑❑
SP31 ____________	**1880. Benjamin Franklin Special Printing Pictorial Issue**			
1¢ **buff** without gum (approx. 2,500 copies)		325.00	200.00	❑❑❑❑❑
97 ____________	**1870. Benjamin Franklin Issue**			
1¢ **ultramarine** grill H		2,000.00	140.00	❑❑❑❑❑
98 ____________	**1870. Andrew Jackson Issue**			
2¢ **red brown** grill H		1,200.00	70.00	❑❑❑❑❑
99 ____________	**1870. George Washington Issue**			
3¢ **green** grill H		725.00	19.00	❑❑❑❑❑
100 ____________	**1870. Abraham Lincoln Issue**			
6¢ **carmine** grill H		4,250.00	525.00	❑❑❑❑❑
101 ____________	**1871. Edwin Stanton Issue**			
7¢ **vermilion** grill H		3,000.00	425.00	❑❑❑❑❑
102 ____________	**1871. Thomas Jefferson Issue**			
10¢ **brown**		4,750.00	650.00	❑❑❑❑❑
103 ____________	**1872. Henry Clay Issue**			
12¢ **pale violet**		21,000.00	3,000.00	❑❑❑❑❑
104 ____________	**1870. Daniel Webster Portrait Issue**			
15¢ **orange**		5,500.00	1,200.00	❑❑❑❑❑

89

90

91

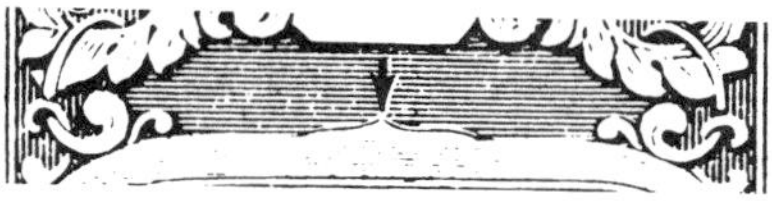
92

92

93 inverted center

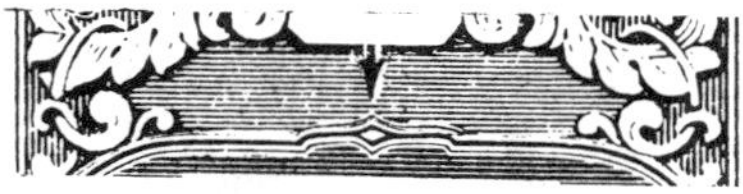
93

94

95

96

97, 108

97, 108

98, 109

98, 109

99, 110

99, 110

100, 111

100, 111

101, 112

101, 112

102, 113

102, 113

103, 114

103, 114

104, 115

104, 115

		UnFVF	UseFVF	
105 ______ 24¢ purple	**1870. Gen. Winfield Scott Issue**	—	6,500.00	❑❑❑❑❑
106 ______ 30¢ black	**1870. Alexander Hamilton Issue**	14,000.00	2,400.00	❑❑❑❑❑
107 ______ 90¢ carmine	**1870. Oliver Perry Issue**	13,500.00	1,600.00	❑❑❑❑❑
108 ______ 1¢ ultramarine	**1870. Benjamin Franklin Issue**	475.00	15.00	❑❑❑❑❑
109 ______ 2¢ red brown	**1870. Andrew Jackson Issue**	325.00	9.00	❑❑❑❑❑
110 ______ 3¢ green	**1870. George Washington Issue**	300.00	1.50	❑❑❑❑❑
111 ______ 6¢ carmine	**1870. Abraham Lincoln Issue**	675.00	25.00	❑❑❑❑❑
112 ______ 7¢ vermilion	**1871. Edwin Stanton Issue**	850.00	90.00	❑❑❑❑❑
113 ______ 10¢ brown	**1870. Thomas Jefferson Issue**	725.00	20.00	❑❑❑❑❑
114 ______ 12¢ pale violet	**1870. Henry Clay Issue**	1,750.00	160.00	❑❑❑❑❑
115 ______ 15¢ orange	**1870. Daniel Webster Issue**	1,900.00	160.00	❑❑❑❑❑
116 ______ 24¢ purple	**1870. Gen. Winfield Scott Issue**	1,500.00	140.00	❑❑❑❑❑
117 ______ 30¢ black	**1871. Alexander Hamilton Issue**	5,000.00	190.00	❑❑❑❑❑
118 ______ 90¢ carmine	**1872. Oliver Perry Issue**	4,000.00	300.00	❑❑❑❑❑
119 ______ 1¢ ultramarine	**1873. Benjamin Franklin Issue**	225.00	3.75	❑❑❑❑❑
120 ______ 2¢ brown	**1873. Andrew Jackson Issue**	375.00	17.50	❑❑❑❑❑
121 ______ 2¢ vermilion	**1875. Andrew Jackson Issue**	400.00	10.00	❑❑❑❑❑
122 ______ 3¢ green	**1873. George Washington Issue**	130.00	.50	❑❑❑❑❑
123 ______ 5¢ Prussian blue	**1875. Zachary Taylor Issue**	550.00	20.00	❑❑❑❑❑
124 ______ 6¢ dull Venetian red	**1873. Abraham Lincoln Issue**	425.00	17.50	❑❑❑❑❑
125 ______ 7¢ vermilion	**1873. Edwin Stanton Issue**	1,100.00	80.00	❑❑❑❑❑
126 ______ 10¢ brown	**1873. Thomas Jefferson Issue**	700.00	18.00	❑❑❑❑❑
127 ______ 12¢ blackish violet	**1874. Henry Clay Issue**	1,800.00	95.00	❑❑❑❑❑
128 ______ 15¢ yellow orange	**1873. Daniel Webster Issue**	2,100.00	110.00	❑❑❑❑❑
129 ______ 24¢ light purple	**1874. Gen. Winfield Scott Issue**	—	400,000.00	❑❑❑❑❑
130 ______ 30¢ gray black	**1874. Alexander Hamilton Issue**	2,500.00	100.00	❑❑❑❑❑

NOTE: The 30¢ Continental and 30¢ National are identical except in shade.

105, 116, 129

106, 117

107

119, 132

119

120, 121, 133

120

122, 134

122

123, 136

124, 137

124

125

125

126, 139

126

127

127

128, 140

128

132

133

		UnFVF	UseFVF	
131 ______________	**1874. Oliver Perry Issue**			
90¢	**rose carmine**	2,750.00	250.00	❑❑❑❑❑

NOTE: The 90¢ Continental and the 90¢ National are identical except in shade.

		UnFVF	UseFVF	
SP32 ______________	**1875. Benjamin Franklin Special Printing of the 1873 Pictorial Issue**			
1¢	**bright ultramarine**	10,500.00		❑❑❑❑❑
SP33 ______________	**1875. Andrew Jackson Special Printing Pictorial Issue**			
2¢	**blackish brown**	4,750.00		❑❑❑❑❑
SP34 ______________	**1875. Andrew Jackson Special Printing Pictorial Issue**			
2¢	**carmine vermilion**	30,000.00		❑❑❑❑❑
SP35 ______________	**1875. George Washington Special Pictorial Issue**			
3¢	**bluish green**	12,500.00		❑❑❑❑❑
SP36 ______________	**1875. Zachary Taylor Special Printing Pictorial Issue**			
5¢	**bright blue**	50,000.00		❑❑❑❑❑
SP37 ______________	**1875. Abraham Lincoln Special Printing Pictorial Issue**			
6¢	**pale rose**	11,500.00		❑❑❑❑❑
SP38 ______________	**1875. Edwin Stanton Special Printing Pictorial Issue**			
7¢	**scarlet vermilion**	2,850.00		❑❑❑❑❑
SP39 ______________	**1875. Thomas Jefferson Special Printing Pictorial Issue**			
10¢	**yellow brown**	11,500.00		❑❑❑❑❑
SP40 ______________	**1875. Henry Clay Special Printing Pictorial Issue**			
12¢	**black violet**	4,250.00		❑❑❑❑❑
SP41 ______________	**1875. Daniel Webster Special Printing Pictorial Issue**			
15¢	**bright orange**	11,500.00		❑❑❑❑❑
SP42 ______________	**1875. Winfield Scott Special Printing Pictorial Issue**			
24¢	**dull purple**	2,900.00		❑❑❑❑❑
SP43 ______________	**1875. Alexander Hamilton Special Printing Pictorial Issue**			
30¢	**greenish black**	8,500.00		❑❑❑❑❑
SP44 ______________	**1875. Oliver Perry Special Printing Pictorial Issue**			
90¢	**violet carmine**	10,500.00		❑❑❑❑❑
132 ______________	**1879. Benjamin Franklin Issue**			
1¢	**dark ultramarine**	300.00	3.50	❑❑❑❑❑
133 ______________	**1879. Andrew Jackson Issue**			
2¢	**vermilion**	130.00	3.00	❑❑❑❑❑
134 ______________	**1879. George Washington Issue**			
3¢	**green**	100.00	.60	❑❑❑❑❑
135 ______________	**1887. George Washington Issue**			
3¢	**vermilion**	80.00	60.00	❑❑❑❑❑
136 ______________	**1879. Zachary Taylor Issue**			
5¢	**blue**	500.00	12.00	❑❑❑❑❑
137 ______________	**1879. Abraham Lincoln Issue**			
6¢	**dull pink**	950.00	20.00	❑❑❑❑❑
138 ______________	**1879. Thomas Jefferson Issue**			
10¢	**brown** like No. 102, but no secret mark	2,250.00	25.00	❑❑❑❑❑
139 ______________	**1879. Thomas Jefferson Issue**			
10¢	**brown** like No. 126, with secret mark	1,750.00	25.00	❑❑❑❑❑
140 ______________	**1879. Daniel Webster Issue**			
15¢	**orange**	350.00	22.50	❑❑❑❑❑
141 ______________	**1882. Alexander Hamilton Issue**			
30¢	**black**	1,100.00	55.00	❑❑❑❑❑
142 ______________	**1888. Alexander Hamilton Issue**			
30¢	**orange brown**	450.00	110.00	❑❑❑❑❑
143 ______________	**1880. Oliver Perry Issue**			
90¢	**carmine**	2,250.00	275.00	❑❑❑❑❑
144 ______________	**1880. Oliver Perry Issue**			
90¢	**dark red violet**	1,300.00	250.00	❑❑❑❑❑

UnFVF	UseFVF

SP45 _____ **1880. Special Printing of the 1879-88 Issue of 1879.**
 1¢ deep ultramarine — 25,000.00 — ☐☐☐☐☐
SP46 _____ **1880. Special Printing of the 1879-88 Issue of 1879.**
 2¢ blackish brown — 10,000.00 — ☐☐☐☐☐
SP47 _____ **1880. Special Printing of the 1879-88 Issue of 1879.**
 2¢ scarlet vermilion — 26,000.00 — ☐☐☐☐☐
SP48 _____ **1880. Special Printing of the 1879-88 Issue of 1879.**
 3¢ bluish green — 32,500.00 — ☐☐☐☐☐
SP49 _____ **1880. Special Printing of the 1879-88 Issue of 1879.**
 5¢ deep blue — 45,000.00 — ☐☐☐☐☐
SP50 _____ **1880. Special Printing of the 1879-88 Issue of 1879.**
 6¢ pale rose — 17,000.00 — ☐☐☐☐☐
SP51 _____ **1880. Special Printing of the 1879-88 Issue of 1879.**
 7¢ scarlet vermilion — 3,500.00 — ☐☐☐☐☐
SP52 _____ **1880. Special Printing of the 1879-88 Issue of 1879.**
 10¢ deep brown — 17,000.00 — ☐☐☐☐☐
SP53 _____ **1880. Special Printing of the 1879-88 Issue of 1879.**
 12¢ black purple — 5,000.00 — ☐☐☐☐☐
SP54 _____ **1880. Special Printing of the 1879-88 Issue of 1879.**
 15¢ orange — 17,000.00 — ☐☐☐☐☐
SP55 _____ **1880. Special Printing of the 1879-88 Issue of 1879.**
 24¢ blackish violet — 5,000.00 — ☐☐☐☐☐
SP56 _____ **1880. Special Printing of the 1879-88 Issue of 1879.**
 30¢ greenish black — 12,500.00 — ☐☐☐☐☐
SP57 _____ **1880. Special Printing of the 1879-88 Issue of 1879.**
 90¢ pale carmine — 14,000.00 — ☐☐☐☐☐
145 _____ **1881-82. Re-Engraved Designs of 1873 Issue**
 1¢ ultramarine — 80.00 — .90 ☐☐☐☐☐
146 _____ **1881. George Washington Issue**
 3¢ blue green — 80.00 — .55 ☐☐☐☐☐
147 _____ **1882. Abraham Lincoln Issue**
 6¢ rose — 525.00 — 80.00 ☐☐☐☐☐
148 _____ **1882. Thomas Jefferson Issue**
 10¢ brown — 160.00 — 6.00 ☐☐☐☐☐
149 _____ **1887. Benjamin Franklin Issue**
 1¢ ultramarine — 110.00 — 1.75 ☐☐☐☐☐
150 _____ **1883. George Washington Issue**
 2¢ red brown — 50.00 — .60 ☐☐☐☐☐

147

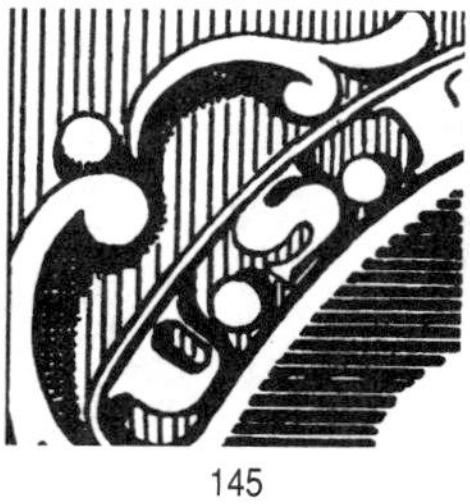

145

146

148

UnFVF	UseFVF	

151 _____ 1887. George Washington Issue
2¢ green — 50.00 | .40 ☐☐☐☐☐

152 _____ 1883. Andrew Jackson Issue
4¢ deep bluish green — 275.00 | 17.50 ☐☐☐☐☐

SP59 _____ 1883. Special Printing Issue
2¢ red brown — 500.00 | ☐☐☐☐☐

SP60 _____ 1883. Special Printing Issue
4¢ blue green — 27,500.00 | ☐☐☐☐☐

153 _____ 1889. Andrew Jackson Issue
4¢ carmine — 225.00 | 20.00 ☐☐☐☐☐

154 _____ 1882. James Garfield Issue
5¢ olive brown — 275.00 | 8.00 ☐☐☐☐☐

SP58 _____ 1882. James Garfield Special Printing Issue
5¢ light brownish gray (2,463 sold) — 28,500.00 | ☐☐☐☐☐

155 _____ 1888. James Garfield Issue
5¢ indigo — 240.00 | 14.00 ☐☐☐☐☐

156 _____ 1890. Benjamin Franklin Issue
1¢ dull blue — 27.50 | .50 ☐☐☐☐☐

157 _____ 1890. George Washington Issue
2¢ lake — 250.00 | 1.00 ☐☐☐☐☐

158 _____
2¢ carmine — 22.50 | .45 ☐☐☐☐☐

159 _____ 1890. Andrew Jackson Issue
3¢ dark lilac — 80.00 | 7.50 ☐☐☐☐☐

160 _____ 1890. Abraham Lincoln Issue
4¢ dark brown — 90.00 | .75 ☐☐☐☐☐

161 _____ 1890. Ulysses S. Grant Issue
5¢ chocolate — 80.00 | 2.75 ☐☐☐☐☐

162 _____ 1890. James Garfield Issue
6¢ brown red — 85.00 | 20.00 ☐☐☐☐☐

163 _____ 1890. W. T. Sherman Issue
8¢ purple brown — 60.00 | 13.00 ☐☐☐☐☐

164 _____ 1890. Daniel Webster Issue
10¢ deep bluish green — 250.00 | 20.00 ☐☐☐☐☐

149 150 152 154 156

157, 158 159 160 161 162

UnFVF	UseFVF

165 _____ **1890. Henry Clay Issue**

 15¢ **indigo** 250.00 20.00 ☐☐☐☐☐

166 _____ **1890. Thomas Jefferson Issue**

 30¢ **black** 375.00 30.00 ☐☐☐☐☐

167 _____ **1890. Oliver Hazard Perry Issue**

 90¢ **orange** 550.00 125.00 ☐☐☐☐☐

NOTE: Stamps of all values of the 1890 issue exist imperforate. They are considered finished proofs.

168 _____ **1894. Benjamin Franklin Issue**

 1¢ **ultramarine** 32.50 4.50 ☐☐☐☐☐

169 _____

 1¢ **blue** 67.50 2.25 ☐☐☐☐☐

170 _____ **1894. George Washington Issue**

 2¢ **pink** triangle I 27.50 3.25 ☐☐☐☐☐

171 _____

 2¢ **carmine lake** triangle I 145.00 3.00 ☐☐☐☐☐

172 _____

 2¢ **carmine** triangle I 30.00 1.20 ☐☐☐☐☐

173 _____

 2¢ **carmine** triangle II 275.00 6.00 ☐☐☐☐☐

174 _____

 2¢ **carmine** triangle III 120.00 6.00 ☐☐☐☐☐

175 _____ **1894. Andrew Jackson Issue**

 3¢ **dark lilac** 105.00 9.00 ☐☐☐☐☐

176 _____ **1894. Abraham Lincoln Issue**

 4¢ **dark brown** 135.00 4.25 ☐☐☐☐☐

177 _____ **1894. Ulysses S. Grant Issue**

 5¢ **chocolate** 100.00 6.00 ☐☐☐☐☐

163

164

165

166

167

168, 169, 187, 188

170-174, 189-192

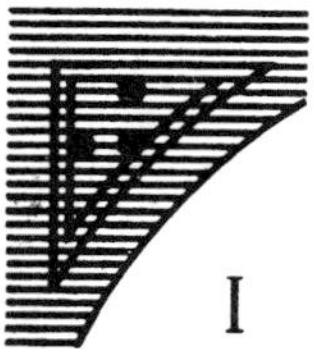

I

170-72, 189

II

173, 190

III

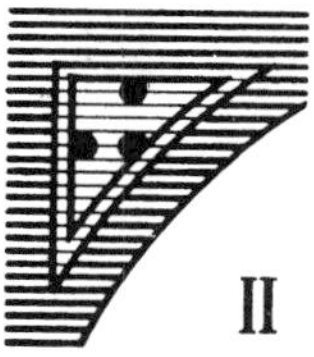

174, 191-192

175, 193

176, 194, 195

177, 196, 197

178, 198, 199

179, 200

UnFVF	UseFVF	

178 _____ **1894. James Garfield Issue**

| 6¢ | red brown | 150.00 | 22.50 | ☐☐☐☐☐ |

179 _____ **1894. William T. Sherman Issue**

| 8¢ | purple brown | 140.00 | 16.00 | ☐☐☐☐☐ |

180 _____ **1894. Daniel Webster Issue**

| 10¢ | blue green | 250.00 | 11.00 | ☐☐☐☐☐ |

181 _____ **1894. Henry Clay Issue**

| 15¢ | indigo | 300.00 | 55.00 | ☐☐☐☐☐ |

182 _____ **1894. Thomas Jefferson Issue**

| 50¢ | orange | 475.00 | 120.00 | ☐☐☐☐☐ |

183 _____ **1894. Oliver Hazard Perry Issue**

| $1 | black Type I | 1,000.00 | 350.00 | ☐☐☐☐☐ |

184 _____

| $1 | black Type II | 2,300.00 | 450.00 | ☐☐☐☐☐ |

185 _____ **1894. James Madison Issue**

| $2 | dark blue | 3,100.00 | 1,100.00 | ☐☐☐☐☐ |

186 _____ **1894. John Marshall Issue**

| $5 | dark green | 4,500.00 | 2,250.00 | ☐☐☐☐☐ |

187 _____ **1895-1898. Bureau of Engraving and Printing Portrait Designs on Watermarked Paper Issue**

| 1¢ | deep blue | 6.50 | .30 | ☐☐☐☐☐ |

188 _____

| 1¢ | deep green | 9.00 | .20 | ☐☐☐☐☐ |

189 _____

| 2¢ | carmine Type I | 30.00 | 1.50 | ☐☐☐☐☐ |

190 _____

| 2¢ | carmine Type II | 30.00 | 3.25 | ☐☐☐☐☐ |

191 _____

| 2¢ | carmine Type III | 5.50 | .20 | ☐☐☐☐☐ |

192 _____

| 2¢ | red Type IV | 9.00 | .20 | ☐☐☐☐☐ |

193 _____

| 3¢ | dark red violet | 37.50 | 1.00 | ☐☐☐☐☐ |

194 _____

| 4¢ | dark brown | 27.50 | 1.50 | ☐☐☐☐☐ |

195 _____

| 4¢ | chocolate | 22.50 | .90 | ☐☐☐☐☐ |

196 _____

| 5¢ | dark orange brown | 27.50 | 1.65 | ☐☐☐☐☐ |

197 _____

| 5¢ | dark blue | 25.00 | .75 | ☐☐☐☐☐ |

198 _____

| 6¢ | red brown | 55.00 | 4.00 | ☐☐☐☐☐ |

199 _____

| 6¢ | lake | 35.00 | 2.25 | ☐☐☐☐☐ |

200 _____

| 8¢ | purple brown | 50.00 | 1.25 | ☐☐☐☐☐ |

201 _____

| 10¢ | dark green Type I | 50.00 | 1.25 | ☐☐☐☐☐ |

202 _____

| 10¢ | brown Type I | 135.00 | 2.50 | ☐☐☐☐☐ |

203 _____

| 10¢ | orange brown Type II | 75.00 | 2.00 | ☐☐☐☐☐ |

204 _____

| 15¢ | indigo | 150.00 | 9.00 | ☐☐☐☐☐ |

UnFVF	UseFVF	
205 _____				
15¢	**olive green**	115.00	7.50	☐☐☐☐☐
206 _____				
50¢	**orange**	200.00	20.00	☐☐☐☐☐
207 _____				
$1	**black** Type I	450.00	55.00	☐☐☐☐☐
208 _____				
$1	**black** Type II	900.00	125.00	☐☐☐☐☐
209 _____				
$2	**dark blue**	775.00	250.00	☐☐☐☐☐
210 _____				
$5	**dark green**	1,600.00	375.00	☐☐☐☐☐
211 _____ **1902-03. Regular Issue**				
1¢	**deep bluish green**	9.00	.20	☐☐☐☐☐
212 _____				
2¢	**carmine**	12.00	.20	☐☐☐☐☐

180, 201-203

181, 204, 205

182, 206

183, 194, 207, 208

183, 184, 207

184, 207

185, 209

186, 210

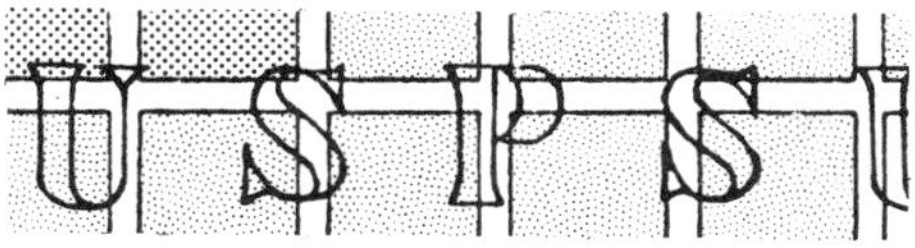

Double-line watermark 187

201, 202

203

211, 225, 228, 230

			UnFVF	UseFVF
213				
	3¢	**dark red violet**	52.50	2.25 ❑❑❑❑❑
214				
	4¢	**brown**	57.50	1.00 ❑❑❑❑❑
215				
	5¢	**deep blue**	57.50	1.15 ❑❑❑❑❑
216				
	6¢	**brown red**	70.00	2.00 ❑❑❑❑❑
217				
	8¢	**violet black**	42.50	1.60 ❑❑❑❑❑
218				
	10¢	**pale red brown**	60.00	1.15 ❑❑❑❑❑
219				
	13¢	**black brown**	42.50	6.50 ❑❑❑❑❑
220				
	15¢	**olive green**	150.00	4.50 ❑❑❑❑❑
221				
	50¢	**orange**	425.00	20.00 ❑❑❑❑❑
222				
	$1	**black**	750.00	45.00 ❑❑❑❑❑
223				
	$2	**dark blue**	1,075.00	140.00 ❑❑❑❑❑
224				
	$5	**dark green**	2,800.00	525.00 ❑❑❑❑❑
225		**1906-08. Regular Issues of 1902-03**		
	1¢	**deep bluish green**	20.00	17.50 ❑❑❑❑❑
226				
	4¢	**brown**	30,000.00	25,000.00 ❑❑❑❑❑
227				
	5¢	**blue**	375.00	475.00 ❑❑❑❑❑

NOTE: Please exercise caution in buying singles of this stamp, particularly used copies. Certification by respected authorities recommended.

228		**1908. Coil Stamp 1902-03 Series Issue**		
	1¢	**blue green** pair	68,500.00	— ❑❑❑❑❑
229				
	5¢	**blue** pair	9,000.00	— ❑❑❑❑❑

NOTE: Perforated 12 vertically.

230				
	1¢	**blue green** pair	6,000.00	— ❑❑❑❑❑
231		**1903. Two-Cent Shield Issue**		
	2¢	**carmine** Type I	4.00	.20 ❑❑❑❑❑
232				
	2¢	**lake** Type II	7.50	.50 ❑❑❑❑❑
233		**1903. Two-Cent Shield Coil Issue**		
	2¢	**carmine** Type II	20.00	15.00 ❑❑❑❑❑
234				
	2¢	**lake** Type II	50.00	40.00 ❑❑❑❑❑
235				
	2¢	**carmine** Type I pair	95,000.00	100,000.00 ❑❑❑❑❑

NOTE: Perforated 12 vertically.

236				
	2¢	**scarlet** Type II pair	7,000.00	4,250.00 ❑❑❑❑❑
237		**1908-09 Washington & Franklin Issue**		
	1¢	**green**	6.00	.20 ❑❑❑❑❑

UnFVF	UseFVF	
238					
	2¢	**carmine**	6.00	.20	☐☐☐☐☐
239		**1908. George Washington Type I Issue**			
	3¢	**violet** Type I	27.50	2.50	☐☐☐☐☐
240					
	4¢	**orange brown**	30.00	1.00	☐☐☐☐☐
241					
	5¢	**blue**	40.00	2.00	☐☐☐☐☐
242					
	6¢	**red orange**	47.50	5.00	☐☐☐☐☐
243					
	8¢	**olive green**	37.50	2.50	☐☐☐☐☐
244					
	10¢	**yellow**	55.00	1.50	☐☐☐☐☐

212

213

214, 226

215, 227, 229

216

217

218

219

220

221

222

223, 365

224, 366

226

231-236

237

239

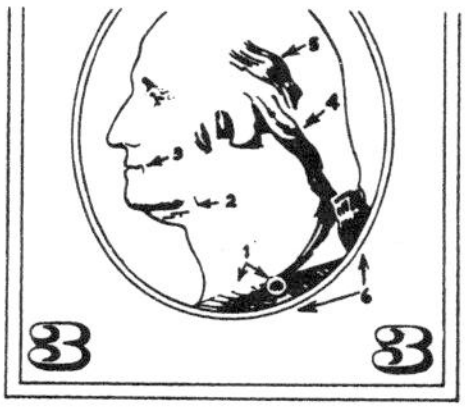

239

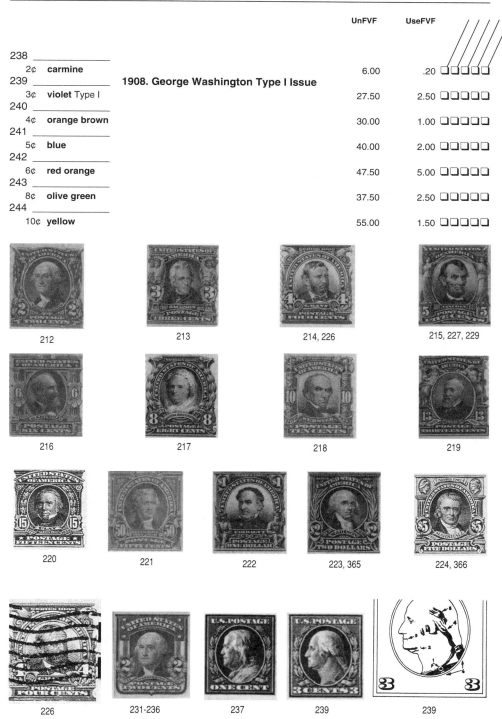

239 *George Washington. Type I: All stamps of this design and perforated 12 are Type I. Top line of toga from front of neck to top of button is very weak, as are upper parts of five lines of shading that join top line; line between the lips is thin.*

UnFVF	UseFVF	

245 _____
13¢ **blue green** — 37.50 — 20.00 ☐☐☐☐☐

246 _____
15¢ **gray blue** — 50.00 — 6.00 ☐☐☐☐☐

247 _____
50¢ **gray lilac** — 250.00 — 17.50 ☐☐☐☐☐

248 _____
$1 **violet brown** — 375.00 — 75.00 ☐☐☐☐☐

1908. Washington & Franklin Type I Issue

249 _____
1¢ **green** — 6.00 — 4.00 ☐☐☐☐☐

250 _____
2¢ **carmine** — 7.50 — 3.00 ☐☐☐☐☐

251 _____
3¢ **violet** Type I — 17.50 — 20.00 ☐☐☐☐☐

252 _____
4¢ **brown** — 27.50 — 22.50 ☐☐☐☐☐

253 _____
5¢ **blue** — 42.50 — 30.00 ☐☐☐☐☐

1908-10. Washington & Franklin Coil Issue

254 _____
1¢ **green** — 22.50 — 12.50 ☐☐☐☐☐

255 _____
2¢ **carmine** — 37.50 — 8.00 ☐☐☐☐☐

256 _____
4¢ **brown** — 85.00 — 70.00 ☐☐☐☐☐

257 _____
5¢ **blue** — 100.00 — 85.00 ☐☐☐☐☐

1908-10. Washington & Franklin Coil Issue

258 _____
1¢ **green** — 50.00 — 30.00 ☐☐☐☐☐

259 _____
2¢ **carmine** — 47.50 — 7.50 ☐☐☐☐☐

260 _____
4¢ **brown** — 115.00 — 55.00 ☐☐☐☐☐

261 _____
5¢ **blue** — 125.00 — 75.00 ☐☐☐☐☐

262 _____
10¢ **yellow** — 1,750.00 — 850.00 ☐☐☐☐☐

1909. Washington & Franklin Issue

263 _____
1¢ **green** — 85.00 — 85.00 ☐☐☐☐☐

264 _____
2¢ **carmine** — 75.00 — 70.00 ☐☐☐☐☐

265 _____
3¢ **deep violet** Type I — 1,600.00 — 1,600.00 ☐☐☐☐☐

266 _____
4¢ **orange brown** — 15,000.00 — — ☐☐☐☐☐

267 _____
5¢ **blue** — 3,500.00 — 3,750.00 ☐☐☐☐☐

268 _____
6¢ **red orange** — 1,150.00 — 1,000.00 ☐☐☐☐☐

269 _____
8¢ **olive green** — 16,000.00 — — ☐☐☐☐☐

270 _____
10¢ **yellow** — 1,400.00 — 1,150.00 ☐☐☐☐☐

271 _____
13¢ **blue green** — 2,350.00 — 1,450.00 ☐☐☐☐☐

No.	Denomination	Color	Issue	UnFVF	UseFVF
272	15¢	**pale ultramarine**		1,150.00	1,000.00
273	1¢	**green**	**1910-14. Washington & Franklin Issue**	6.00	.20
274	2¢	**carmine**		5.75	.20
275	3¢	**violet** Type I		15.00	1.50
276	4¢	**brown**	**1911. George Washington Issue**	22.50	.75
277	5¢	**blue**		22.50	.75
278	6¢	**red orange**		30.00	.85
279	7¢	**black**		70.00	8.50
280	8¢	**light olive green**		95.00	12.50
281	10¢	**yellow**		85.00	4.00
282	15¢	**pale ultramarine**		225.00	15.00
283	1¢	**green**	**1910. George Washington Issue**	3.00	2.75
284	2¢	**carmine**		5.50	3.00
285	1¢	**green**	**1910. Washington & Franklin Coil Issue**	22.50	12.50
286	2¢	**carmine**		37.50	17.50
287	1¢	**green**		85.00	37.50
288	2¢	**carmine**		575.00	250.00
289	3¢	**deep violet** Type I	**1910. George Washington Orangeburg Coil Issue**	28,500.00	7,000.00
290	1¢	**green**	**1910. Washington & Franklin Coil Issue**	4.50	5.00
291	2¢	**carmine**		30.00	12.50
292	1¢	**green**		20.00	20.00
293	2¢	**carmine**		40.00	10.00

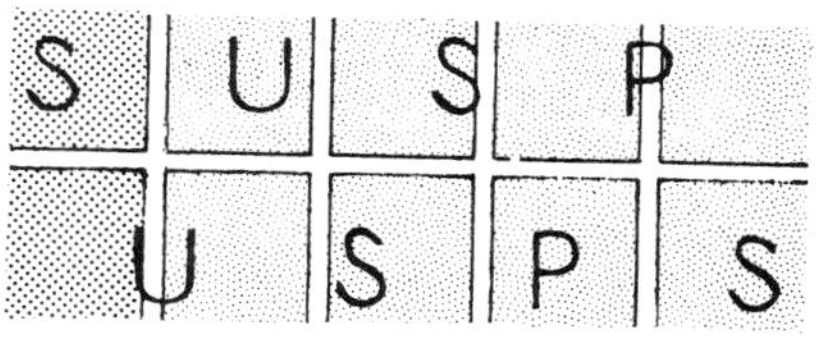

273

275-262

276

297

UnFVF	UseFVF	

294 _____
3¢ **violet** Type I — 50.00 — 50.00 ☐☐☐☐☐

295 _____
4¢ **brown** — 50.00 — 50.00 ☐☐☐☐☐

296 _____
5¢ **blue** — 50.00 — 50.00 ☐☐☐☐☐

297 _____ **1912. Modified George Washington Issue**
1¢ **green** — 5.00 — .20 ☐☐☐☐☐

298 _____
2¢ **carmine** Type I — 4.50 — .20 ☐☐☐☐☐

299 _____
1¢ **green** — 1.25 — .60 ☐☐☐☐☐

300 _____
2¢ **carmine** Type I — 1.30 — .60 ☐☐☐☐☐

301 _____ **1912. George Washington Modified Design Coil Issue**
1¢ **green** — 5.50 — 4.50 ☐☐☐☐☐

302 _____
2¢ **carmine** Type I — 7.50 — 4.50 ☐☐☐☐☐

303 _____
1¢ **green** — 22.50 — 6.25 ☐☐☐☐☐

304 _____
2¢ **carmine** Type I — 35.00 — 1.25 ☐☐☐☐☐

305 _____ **1912-14. Benjamin Franklin Redesigned Issue**
8¢ **pale olive green** — 30.00 — 1.25 ☐☐☐☐☐

306 _____
9¢ **salmon pink** — 45.00 — 12.50 ☐☐☐☐☐

307 _____
10¢ **orange yellow** — 32.50 — .50 ☐☐☐☐☐

308 _____
12¢ **chocolate** — 40.00 — 4.25 ☐☐☐☐☐

309 _____
15¢ **gray black** — 65.00 — 4.00 ☐☐☐☐☐

310 _____
20¢ **gray blue** — 150.00 — 17.50 ☐☐☐☐☐

311 _____
30¢ **orange red** — 115.00 — 17.50 ☐☐☐☐☐

312 _____
50¢ **violet** — 350.00 — 20.00 ☐☐☐☐☐

313 _____
50¢ **violet** — 225.00 — 20.00 ☐☐☐☐☐

298

298

298 *George Washington, Type I. The following detailed description is provided, although any 2¢ that fits Point 1 is a Type I. 1. The line from the front of the neck to tand over the top of the button is very weak. The shading lines that run into this line (top of toga) are thin in the area above the cross hatching lines. 2. One shading line in the first (upper) curve of the ribbon above the left numeral and one line in the second (middle) curve above the right numeral. 3. There is a white dash below the ear. 4. The shading lines of the face terminate in front of the ear and are not joined with each other. 5. The lock of hair behind the ear is formed at the bottom by two lines of shading, the lower one being considerably shorter than the other. 6. The hair lines above the ear and slightly to the right form an arrowhead. 7. The shading lines just to the left of the ear form a fairly solid color.*

UnFVF	UseFVF	

314 _____
$1 **violet brown** 425.00 65.00 ☐☐☐☐☐

315 _____ **1914-15. Washington & Franklin Issue**
1¢ **green** 2.75 .20 ☐☐☐☐☐

316 _____
2¢ **rose red** Type I 2.25 .20 ☐☐☐☐☐

317 _____
3¢ **violet** Type I 12.50 2.00 ☐☐☐☐☐

318 _____
4¢ **brown** 30.00 .75 ☐☐☐☐☐

319 _____
5¢ **blue** 27.50 .70 ☐☐☐☐☐

320 _____
6¢ **red orange** 45.00 2.00 ☐☐☐☐☐

321 _____
7¢ **black** 75.00 5.00 ☐☐☐☐☐

322 _____
8¢ **yellow olive** 30.00 1.25 ☐☐☐☐☐

323 _____
9¢ **salmon** 35.00 2.00 ☐☐☐☐☐

324 _____
10¢ **orange yellow** 40.00 .40 ☐☐☐☐☐

325 _____
11¢ **deep bluish green** 20.00 9.00 ☐☐☐☐☐

326 _____
12¢ **maroon** 23.00 4.25 ☐☐☐☐☐

NOTE: So-called vertical pair, imperforate between, really have at least one perforation hole between the stamps.

327 _____
15¢ **gray black** 110.00 8.50 ☐☐☐☐☐

328 _____
20¢ **pale ultramarine** 175.00 4.50 ☐☐☐☐☐

329 _____
30¢ **orange red** 225.00 20.00 ☐☐☐☐☐

330 _____
50¢ **violet** 600.00 22.50 ☐☐☐☐☐

331 _____ **1914-15. Benjamin Franklin Issue**
$1 **violet black** 725.00 85.00 ☐☐☐☐☐

332 _____ **1915. George Washington Issue**
2¢ **rose red** Type I 100.00 225.00 ☐☐☐☐☐

333 _____ **1914. George Washington Coil Issue**
1¢ **green** 1.25 1.25 ☐☐☐☐☐

334 _____
2¢ **carmine** Type I 8.50 8.00 ☐☐☐☐☐

335 _____ **1914. George Washington Coil Issue**
1¢ **green** 22.50 7.50 ☐☐☐☐☐

305-314 315-321 322-331 333 and 340

UnFVF	UseFVF	

336 _____

 2¢ **carmine** Type I — 32.50 — 1.75 ☐☐☐☐☐

337 _____

 3¢ **violet** Type I — 225.00 — 125.00 ☐☐☐☐☐

338 _____

 4¢ **brown** — 120.00 — 47.50 ☐☐☐☐☐

339 _____

 5¢ **blue** — 47.50 — 32.50 ☐☐☐☐☐

340 _____ **1914-16. Washington & Franklin Rotary Press Coil Issue**

 1¢ **green** — 6.50 — 4.25 ☐☐☐☐☐

341 _____

 2¢ **carmine** Type III — 10.00 — 4.25 ☐☐☐☐☐

342 _____ **1914. Washington Rotary Press Sidewise Coil Issue**

 2¢ **carmine** Type I — 375.00 — 750.00 ☐☐☐☐☐

343 _____ **1914-16. Washington Issue**

 1¢ **green** — 10.00 — 2.50 ☐☐☐☐☐

344 _____

 2¢ **carmine** Type III — 10.00 — 1.15 ☐☐☐☐☐

345 _____

 3¢ **violet** Type I — 225.00 — 115.00 ☐☐☐☐☐

346 _____

 4¢ **yellow brown** — 27.50 — 20.00 ☐☐☐☐☐

347 _____

 5¢ **blue** — 32.50 — 17.50 ☐☐☐☐☐

348 _____ **1916-17. Washington & Franklin Issue**

 1¢ **green** — 6.00 — .50 ☐☐☐☐☐

349 _____

 2¢ **carmine** Type I — 4.00 — .35 ☐☐☐☐☐

350 _____

 3¢ **violet** Type I — 65.00 — 15.00 ☐☐☐☐☐

351 _____

 4¢ **yellow brown** — 42.50 — 2.25 ☐☐☐☐☐

352 _____

 5¢ **blue** — 65.00 — 2.25 ☐☐☐☐☐

353 _____

 5¢ **carmine** — 550.00 — 700.00 ☐☐☐☐☐

NOTE: No. 353 The "Five Cent Red Error" was caused by mistakenly using a 5¢ transfer roll in re-entering three positions on plate 7942, a plate of the 2¢ stamps. Of the 400 positions on the plate, 397 copies were 2¢ and three copies were 5¢. The error was not discovered until a considerable number of sheets were in the post offices, and many of them were picked up by collectors. The errors exist perforated 10 (No. 353), perforated 11 (No. 385), and imperforate (No. 370). The shade actually is carmine, but the stamp commonly is called the "Red Error."

344 Type II. Shading lines in ribbons same as Type I. The top line of toga rope is heavy and the rope is heavily shaded. The shading lines on the face, in front of the ear, are joined by a heavy vertical curved line.

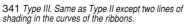

341 Type III. Same as Type II except two lines of shading in the curves of the ribbons.

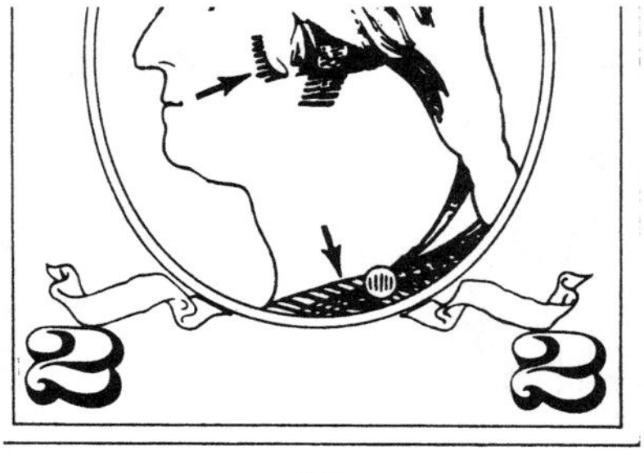

UnFVF	UseFVF	

354 _____

| 6¢ | red orange | 80.00 | 7.50 | ☐☐☐☐☐ |

355 _____

| 7¢ | black | 100.00 | 12.50 | ☐☐☐☐☐ |

356 _____

| 8¢ | yellow olive | 55.00 | 6.50 | ☐☐☐☐☐ |

357 _____

| 9¢ | salmon | 50.00 | 15.00 | ☐☐☐☐☐ |

358 _____

| 10¢ | orange yellow | 95.00 | 1.25 | ☐☐☐☐☐ |

359 _____

| 11¢ | deep bluish green | 35.00 | 22.50 | ☐☐☐☐☐ |

360 _____

| 12¢ | chocolate | 45.00 | 5.50 | ☐☐☐☐☐ |

361 _____

| 15¢ | gray black | 165.00 | 12.50 | ☐☐☐☐☐ |

362 _____

| 20¢ | pale blue | 225.00 | 12.50 | ☐☐☐☐☐ |

362A _____

| 30¢ | orange red | 4,500.00 | — | ☐☐☐☐☐ |

NOTE: No. 362A Two sheets of 100 stamps of the 30¢ denomination were discovered without any trace of watermark, as authenticated by The Philatelic Foundation's expert committee.

363 _____

| 50¢ | light violet | 950.00 | 65.00 | ☐☐☐☐☐ |

364 _____

| $1 | violet black | 625.00 | 20.00 | ☐☐☐☐☐ |

365 _____ **1917. James Madison Issue**

| $2 | dark blue | 325.00 | 45.00 | ☐☐☐☐☐ |

366 _____ **1917. John Marshall Issue**

| $5 | light green | 250.00 | 50.00 | ☐☐☐☐☐ |

367 _____ **1916-1917. George Washington Issue**

| 1¢ | green | 1.15 | 1.00 | ☐☐☐☐☐ |

368 _____

| 2¢ | carmine Type I | 1.40 | 1.30 | ☐☐☐☐☐ |

368A _____

| 2¢ | **deep rose**, Type 1a | | 15,000.00 | ☐☐☐☐☐ |

NOTE: Type Ia is similar to Type I, but lines of the design are stronger. This is particularly noticeable on the toga button, toga rope and rope shading lines, which are heavy. Lines in the ribbons are similar to Type I.

369 _____

| 3¢ | violet Type I | 15.00 | 8.50 | ☐☐☐☐☐ |

370 _____

| 5¢ | carmine | 12,500.00 | | ☐☐☐☐☐ |

NOTE: This stamp commonly is called the "Red Error," but really is carmine. See note with No. 353.

365

366

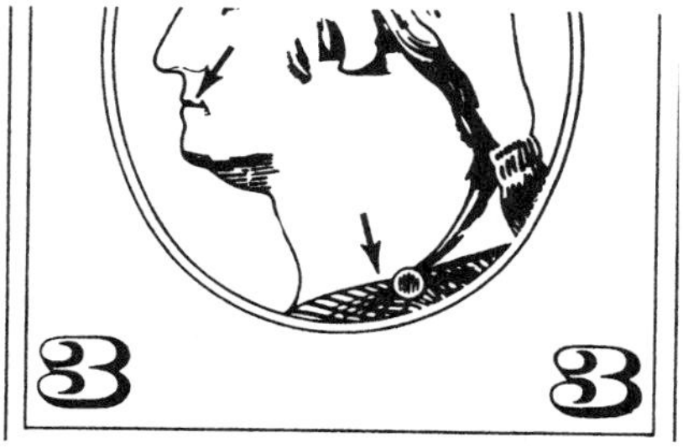

369. 3¢. On Type II the top line of the toga rope is heavy, and the rope shading lines are also heavy and complete. The line between the lips is heavy

369

No.	Value	Color	Issue	UnFVF	UseFVF
371	1¢	**green**	**1916-22. Washington Rotary Press Coil Issue**	.75	.20
372	2¢	**carmine** Type III		3.00	1.75
373	3¢	**violet** Type I		4.50	1.50
374	1¢	**green**	**1916-22. Washington Issue**	.60	.20
375	2¢	**carmine** Type III		8.50	.20
376	3¢	**violet** Type II		11.50	1.25
377	4¢	**yellow brown**		10.50	4.00
378	5¢	**blue**		3.50	1.25
379	10¢	**orange yellow**		19.00	12.50
380	1¢	**green**	**1917-19 Washington & Franklin Issue**	.55	.20
381	2¢	**rose red** Type I		.50	.20
382	3¢	**violet** Type I		12.50	.20
382A	3¢	**violet** Type II		15.00	.40
383	4¢	**yellow brown**		11.50	.30
384	5¢	**blue**		8.50	.25
385	5¢	**carmine**		400.00	500.00

NOTE: This stamp commonly is called the "Red Error" but really is carmine. See note with No. 353.

No.	Value	Color	UnFVF	UseFVF
386	6¢	**red orange**	12.50	.40
387	7¢	**black**	25.00	1.25
388	8¢	**yellow olive**	12.50	1.00
389	9¢	**salmon**	14.00	2.50
390	10¢	**orange yellow**	17.50	.25
391	11¢	**deep bluish green**	9.00	3.00
392	12¢	**brown purple**	9.00	.65
393	13¢	**apple green**	10.50	6.50
394	15¢	**gray black**	37.50	1.25
395	20¢	**pale blue**	47.50	.50
396	30¢	**orange red**	37.50	1.25

UnFVF	UseFVF	

397 _____			
50¢ **reddish violet**	65.00	.90	☐☐☐☐☐
398 _____			
$1 **black purple**	55.00	1.75	☐☐☐☐☐

399 _____ 1917. George Washington Issue

2¢ **carmine**	275.00	450.00	☐☐☐☐☐

400 _____ 1918-20. Benjamin Franklin Issue

$2 **orange & black**	650.00	225.00	☐☐☐☐☐
401 _____			
$2 **carmine & black**	190.00	40.00	☐☐☐☐☐
402 _____			
$5 **deep green & black**	225.00	35.00	☐☐☐☐☐

403 _____ 1918-20. George Washington Issue

1¢ **dull green**	2.00	.75	☐☐☐☐☐
404 _____			
2¢ **rose red** Type VII	17.50	.35	☐☐☐☐☐
404A _____			
2¢ **rose red** Type V	15.00	1.00	☐☐☐☐☐
404B _____			
2¢ **rose red** Type Va	8.00	.35	☐☐☐☐☐
404C _____			
2¢ **rose red** Type VI	45.00	1.50	☐☐☐☐☐
404D _____			
2¢ **rose red** Type IV	25.00	4.25	☐☐☐☐☐

405 _____ 1918. George Washington Issue

3¢ **purple** Type III	3.00	.40	☐☐☐☐☐
405A _____			
3¢ **purple** Type IV	1.25	.20	☐☐☐☐☐

400, 401

402

403

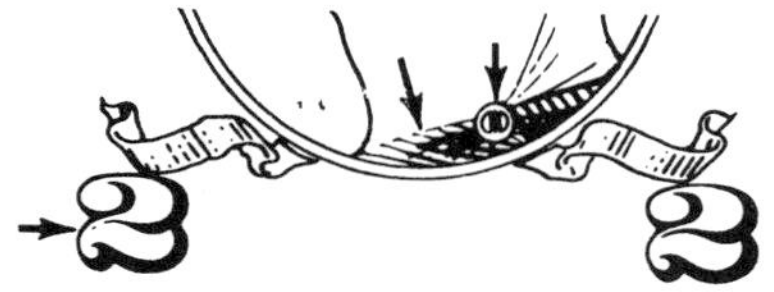

Type IV: Top line of toga rope is broken. Lines inside toga button read "D (reversed) ID." The line of color in the left "2" is very thin and is usually broken.

Type V: Top line of the toga is complete. Five vertical shading lines in toga button. Line of color in left "2" is very thin and usually broken. Shading dots on nose form a triangle with six dots in third row from bottom.

Type Va: Same as Type V except on the shading dots on the nose, in which the third row from the bottom has only four dots instead of six.

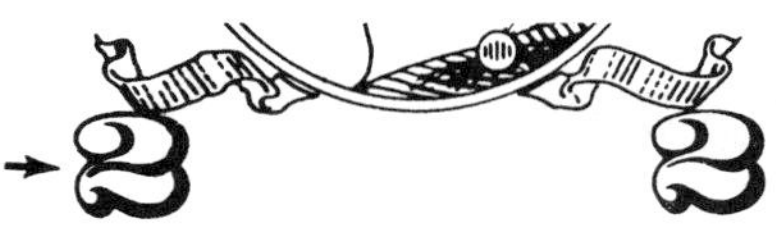

Type VI: Same as Type V but there is a heavy line of color in the left "2".

		UnFVF	UseFVF
406 ______________	**1919-20. George Washington Issue**		
1¢	**dull green**	10.00	8.50 ❑❑❑❑❑
407 ______________			
2¢	**rose red** Type IV	35.00	30.00 ❑❑❑❑❑
407A ______________			
2¢	**rose red** Type V	190.00	85.00 ❑❑❑❑❑
407B ______________			
2¢	**rose red** Type Va	12.50	8.50 ❑❑❑❑❑
407C ______________			
2¢	**rose red** Type VI	35.00	22.50 ❑❑❑❑❑
407D ______________			
2¢	**rose red** Type VII	1,500.00	575.00 ❑❑❑❑❑
408 ______________			
3¢	**violet** Type IV	8.75	6.00 ❑❑❑❑❑
409 ______________	**1919. George Washington Issue**		
1¢	**dull green**	14.00	16.50 ❑❑❑❑❑
410 ______________			
1¢	**green**	8.00	8.00 ❑❑❑❑❑
411 ______________			
2¢	**carmine red** Type II	2,500.00	3,200.00 ❑❑❑❑❑
411A ______________			
2¢	**carmine red** Type III	10.00	9.00 ❑❑❑❑❑
412 ______________			
3¢	**gray lilac** Type II	32.50	35.00 ❑❑❑❑❑
413 ______________	**1920. George Washington Issue**		
1¢	**green**	10.00	1.00 ❑❑❑❑❑

Type VII: The line of color in the left "2" is clear and unbroken, heavier than on Type V or Va but not as heavy as on Type VI. An extra vertical row of dots has been added on the lip, making four rows of three dots instead of two dots. Additional dots have been added to the hair on top of the head.

404-404D →

405

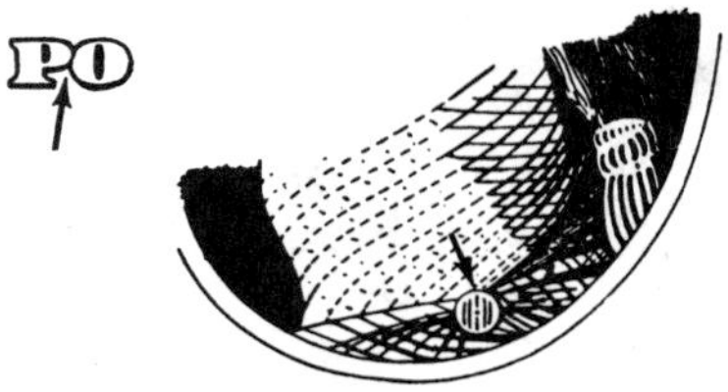

Type III: Top line of toga is strong but the fifth shading line is missing. The center shading line of the toga button consists of two vertical dashes with a dot between them. The "P" and "O" of "POSTAGE" have a line of color between them.

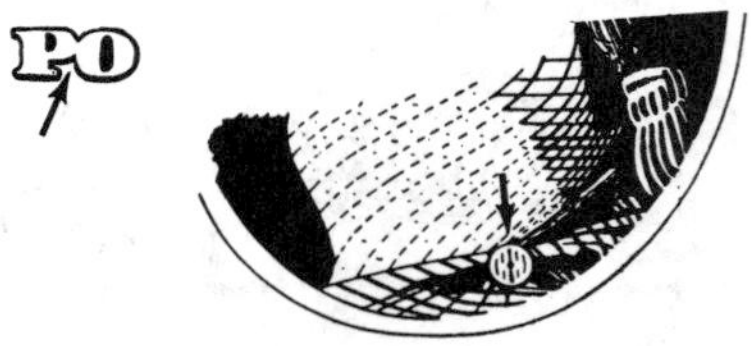

369. 3¢. On Type II the top line of the toga rope is heavy, and the rope shading lines are also heavy and complete. The line between the lips is heavy.

		UnFVF	UseFVF
414 ________	**1921. George Washington Issue**		
1¢ **green**		.55	.20 ❑❑❑❑❑
415 ________	**1922. George Washington Issue**		
1¢ **green**		15,000.00	3,200.00 ❑❑❑❑❑
416 ________	**1921. George Washington Issue**		
1¢ **green**		120.00	130.00 ❑❑❑❑❑
417 ________			
2¢ **carmine** Type III		85.00	115.00 ❑❑❑❑❑
418 ________	**1925. Nathan Hale Issue**		
1/2¢ **olive brown**		.30	.20 ❑❑❑❑❑
419 ________	**1923. Benjamin Franklin Issue**		
1¢ **green**		1.50	.20 ❑❑❑❑❑
420 ________	**1925. Warren Harding Issue**		
1-1/2¢ **yellow brown**		2.50	.25 ❑❑❑❑❑

NOTE: See also CM60-63, a 2¢ black Harding of the same design as 420. Some include it with the 1922-34 Regular Issue Series.

		UnFVF	UseFVF
421 ________	**1923. George Washington Type I Issue**		
2¢ **carmine** Type I		1.25	.20 ❑❑❑❑❑
422 ________	**1923. Abraham Lincoln Issue**		
3¢ **reddish violet**		18.00	.65 ❑❑❑❑❑
423 ________	**1923. Martha Washington Issue**		
4¢ **yellow brown**		20.00	.20 ❑❑❑❑❑
424 ________	**1922. Theodore Roosevelt Issue**		
5¢ **Prussian blue**		20.00	.20 ❑❑❑❑❑

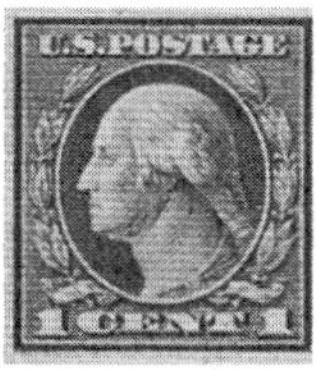
410

411

412

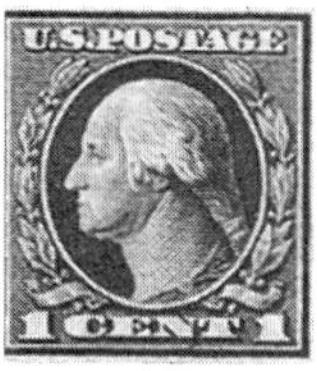
416

417

418, 473

419, 443, 446, 448, 449A, 450,461, 469, 474, 495, 506

420, 444, 451, 462, 470, 472, 475, 496, 507

421, 445, 447, 449, 452, 463, 471, 476, 476A, 497, 508

422, 453, 464, 477, 498,509

423, 454, 465, 478, 499, 510

424, 455, 466, 479, 500, 511

425, 456, 467, 480, 501, 512

426, 457, 481, 502, 513

427, 458, 482, 503, 514

No.	Issue	UnFVF	UseFVF
425	**1922. James Garfield Issue**		
6¢	**red orange**	35.00	.55
426	**1923. William McKinley Issue**		
7¢	**black**	9.00	.35
427	**1923. Ulysses S. Grant Issue**		
8¢	**yellow olive**	50.00	.85
428	**1923. Thomas Jefferson Issue**		
9¢	**carmine rose**	15.00	.75
429	**1923. James Monroe Issue**		
10¢	**orange yellow**	19.00	.25
430	**1922. Rutherford B. Hayes Issue**		
11¢	**turquoise blue**	2.50	.30

NOTE: No. 430 is known in a wide range of color shades between yellow green and light blue.

No.	Issue	UnFVF	UseFVF
431	**1923. Grover Cleveland Issue**		
12¢	**maroon**	6.25	.20
432	**1926. Benjamin Harrison Issue**		
13¢	**green**	10.00	.30
433	**1923. American Indian Issue**		
14¢	**blue**	4.75	.50
434	**1922. Statue of Liberty Issue**		
15¢	**gray black**	25.00	.20
435	**1925. Woodrow Wilson Issue**		
17¢	**black**	12.00	.20
436	**1923. Golden Gate Issue**		
20¢	**carmine red**	22.50	.20
437	**1922. Niagara Falls Issue**		
25¢	**green**	19.00	.50
438	**1923. Bison Issue**		
30¢	**olive brown**	35.00	.50
439	**1922. Arlington Issue**		
50¢	**gray lilac**	57.00	.20
440	**1923. Lincoln Memorial Issue**		
$1	**purple brown**	47.00	.50
441	**1923. U. S. Capitol Issue**		
$2	**blue**	100.00	6.00

428, 459, 483, 504, 515

429, 460, 468, 484, 505, 516

430, 485

431, 486

432, 487

433, 488

434, 489

435, 490

436, 491

UnFVF	UseFVF	

442 _____ **1923. Head of Freedom Issue**

$5 **carmine & blue** — 200.00 — 13.50 ☐☐☐☐☐

443 _____ **1923. Issue**

1¢ **green** — 7.50 — 3.00 ☐☐☐☐☐

444 _____

1-1/2¢ **yellow brown** — 1.50 — 1.00 ☐☐☐☐☐

NOTE: No. 444 exists in a rotary press printing, No. 472.

445 _____

2¢ **carmine** — 1.50 — 1.00 ☐☐☐☐☐

446 _____ **1923-24. Rotary Press Printings**

1¢ **green** — 90.00 — 90.00 ☐☐☐☐☐

447 _____

2¢ **carmine** — 75.00 — 85.00 ☐☐☐☐☐

448 _____ **1923-24. Rotary Press Printing Issue**

1¢ **green** — 15,000.00 — 4,000.00 ☐☐☐☐☐

449 _____

2¢ **carmine** — 285.00 — 300.00 ☐☐☐☐☐

NOTE: Nos. 448 and 449 were made from coil waste. Design 18 1/2 to 19mm wide by 22 1/2mm high.

449A _____

1¢ **green** — — — 42,500.00 ☐☐☐☐☐

450 _____ **1923-26. Rotary Press Printing Issue**

1¢ **green** — 7.50 — 1.00 ☐☐☐☐☐

451 _____

1-1/2¢ **yellow brown** — 3.75 — 1.00 ☐☐☐☐☐

452 _____

2¢ **carmine** — 2.00 — .35 ☐☐☐☐☐

453 _____

3¢ **reddish violet** — 20.00 — 2.50 ☐☐☐☐☐

454 _____

4¢ **yellow brown** — 14.00 — .80 ☐☐☐☐☐

455 _____

5¢ **blue** — 14.00 — .80 ☐☐☐☐☐

456 _____

6¢ **orange** — 6.25 — .75 ☐☐☐☐☐

457 _____

7¢ **black** — 9.00 — 6.50 ☐☐☐☐☐

437, 492

438, 493

439, 494

440

441

442

UnFVF	UseFVF	
458 _____				
8¢	yellow olive	20.00	4.00	☐☐☐☐☐
459 _____				
9¢	red	4.25	2.50	☐☐☐☐☐
460 _____				
10¢	orange yellow	50.00	.45	☐☐☐☐☐
461 _____	**1923-26. Rotary Press Coil Issue**			
1¢	yellow green	.35	.20	☐☐☐☐☐
462 _____				
1-1/2¢	yellow brown	.75	.20	☐☐☐☐☐
463 _____				
2¢	carmine Type I	.45	.20	☐☐☐☐☐
464 _____				
3¢	reddish violet	5.50	.30	☐☐☐☐☐
465 _____				
4¢	yellow brown	3.75	.50	☐☐☐☐☐
466 _____				
5¢	blue	1.75	.20	☐☐☐☐☐
467 _____				
6¢	orange	9.50	.35	☐☐☐☐☐
468 _____				
10¢	orange yellow	3.50	.20	☐☐☐☐☐
469 _____	**1924. Rotary Press Coil Issue**			
1¢	yellow green	.35	.20	☐☐☐☐☐
470 _____				
1-1/2¢	yellow brown	.35	.20	☐☐☐☐☐
471 _____				
2¢	carmine	.35	.20	☐☐☐☐☐
472 _____	**1926. Rotary Press Issue**			
1-1/2¢	yellow brown	2.25	2.00	☐☐☐☐☐
473 _____	**1926-34. Rotary Press Issue**			
1/2¢	olive brown	.25	.20	☐☐☐☐☐
474 _____				
1¢	green	.25	.20	☐☐☐☐☐
475 _____				
1-1/2¢	yellow brown	2.00	.20	☐☐☐☐☐
476 _____				
2¢	carmine red Type I	.25	.20	☐☐☐☐☐
476A _____				
2¢	carmine red Type II	300.00	15.00	☐☐☐☐☐
477 _____				
3¢	reddish violet	.55	.20	☐☐☐☐☐

463 Type 1 (left); Type II (right)

463 Type II

UnFVF	UseFVF	

478 _____
 4¢ yellow brown — 2.75 — .20 ☐☐☐☐☐
479 _____
 5¢ blue — 2.25 — .20 ☐☐☐☐☐
480 _____
 6¢ orange — 2.25 — .20 ☐☐☐☐☐
481 _____
 7¢ black — 2.25 — .20 ☐☐☐☐☐
482 _____
 8¢ yellow olive — 2.25 — .20 ☐☐☐☐☐
483 _____
 9¢ red — 2.00 — .20 ☐☐☐☐☐
484 _____
 10¢ orange yellow — 4.00 — .20 ☐☐☐☐☐
485 _____
 11¢ turquoise green — 2.75 — .20 ☐☐☐☐☐
486 _____
 12¢ brown purple — 6.00 — .20 ☐☐☐☐☐
487 _____
 13¢ yellow green — 2.25 — .20 ☐☐☐☐☐
488 _____
 14¢ blue — 4.00 — .50 ☐☐☐☐☐
489 _____
 15¢ gray black — 8.00 — .20 ☐☐☐☐☐

1931. Rotary Press Issue

490 _____
 17¢ black — 5.50 — .20 ☐☐☐☐☐
491 _____
 20¢ carmine rose — 9.50 — .20 ☐☐☐☐☐
492 _____
 25¢ green — 11.00 — .20 ☐☐☐☐☐
493 _____
 30¢ olive brown — 17.50 — .20 ☐☐☐☐☐
494 _____
 50¢ lilac — 42.50 — .20 ☐☐☐☐☐

1929. Kansas and Nebraska Overprints Issue

495 _____
 1¢ green — 2.00 — 1.50 ☐☐☐☐☐
496 _____
 1-1/2¢ yellow brown — 3.00 — 2.25 ☐☐☐☐☐
497 _____
 2¢ carmine red — 3.00 — 1.00 ☐☐☐☐☐
498 _____
 3¢ reddish violet — 15.00 — 11.00 ☐☐☐☐☐
499 _____
 4¢ yellow brown — 15.00 — 8.50 ☐☐☐☐☐
500 _____
 5¢ blue — 12.50 — 9.00 ☐☐☐☐☐

495-505 502 503 506-516 514

UnFVF	UseFVF	
501 _____				
	6¢ orange	25.00	15.00	☐☐☐☐☐
502 _____				
	7¢ black	25.00	20.00	☐☐☐☐☐
503 _____				
	8¢ yellow olive	70.00	60.00	☐☐☐☐☐
504 _____				
	9¢ salmon	12.50	10.00	☐☐☐☐☐
505 _____				
	10¢ orange yellow	20.00	12.50	☐☐☐☐☐
506 _____				
	1¢ green	2.25	2.00	☐☐☐☐☐
507 _____				
	1-1/2¢ yellow brown	2.25	2.00	☐☐☐☐☐
508 _____				
	2¢ carmine red	2.25	1.00	☐☐☐☐☐
509 _____				
	3¢ reddish violet	11.00	8.00	☐☐☐☐☐
510 _____				
	4¢ yellow brown	15.00	10.00	☐☐☐☐☐
511 _____				
	5¢ blue	12.50	11.50	☐☐☐☐☐
512 _____				
	6¢ orange	35.00	17.50	☐☐☐☐☐
513 _____				
	7¢ black	18.50	12.50	☐☐☐☐☐
514 _____				
	8¢ yellow olive	25.00	17.50	☐☐☐☐☐
515 _____				
	9¢ salmon	30.00	22.50	☐☐☐☐☐
516 _____				
	10¢ orange yellow	85.00	17.50	☐☐☐☐☐

517 _____ **1930-32. Warren G. Harding New Design Issue**

	1-1/2¢ yellow brown		.25	.20 ☐☐☐☐☐

518 _____ **1930-32. George Washington Issue**

	3¢ reddish violet		.25	.20 ☐☐☐☐☐

519 _____ **1930-32 William H. Taft Issue**

	4¢ yellow brown		.90	.20 ☐☐☐☐☐

520 _____ **1930-32. Warren G. Harding New Design Coil Issue**

	1-1/2¢ yellow brown		1.50	.20 ☐☐☐☐☐

521 _____ **1930-32. George Washington Coil Issue**

	3¢ reddish violet		1.75	.20 ☐☐☐☐☐

522 _____ **1930-32. William H. Taft Coil Issue**

	4¢ yellow brown		2.75	.75 ☐☐☐☐☐

516 517, 520 518, 521, 523 519, 522 520 Line Pair

No.	Issue	UnFVF	UseFVF
523	**1930-32. George Washington Coil Issue**		
	3¢ reddish violet	1.00	.75
524	**1938. Benjamin Franklin Issue**		
	1/2¢ red orange	.25	.20
525	**1938. George Washington Issue**		
	1¢ green	.25	.20
526	**1938. Martha Washington Issue**		
	1-1/2¢ yellow brown	.25	.20
527	**1938. John Adams Issue**		
	2¢ rose	.25	.20
528	**1938. Thomas Jefferson Issue**		
	3¢ violet	.25	.20
529	**1938. James Madison Issue**		
	4¢ bright purple	1.15	.20
530	**1938. White House Issue**		
	4-1/2¢ gray	.25	.20
531	**1938. James Monroe Issue**		
	5¢ light blue	.25	.20
532	**1938. John Quincy Adams Issue**		
	6¢ orange	.35	.20
533	**1938. Andrew Jackson Issue**		
	7¢ sepia	.45	.20
534	**1938. Martin Van Buren Issue**		
	8¢ olive green	.45	.20
535	**1938. William Henry Harrison Issue**		
	9¢ rose pink	.50	.20

524

525, 556, 565

526, 557, 566

527, 558, 567

528, 559, 568

529, 560

530, 561

531, 562

532, 563

533

534

535

536, 564

537

538

		UnFVF	UseFVF
536 ______________	**1938. John Tyler Issue**		
	10¢ **Venetian red**	.45	.20 ❑❑❑❑❑
537 ______________	**1938. James Knox Polk Issue**		
	11¢ **cobalt**	.75	.20 ❑❑❑❑❑
538 ______________	**1938. Zachary Taylor Issue**		
	12¢ **light reddish violet**	1.40	.20 ❑❑❑❑❑
539 ______________	**1938. Millard Fillmore Issue**		
	13¢ **blue green**	2.25	.20 ❑❑❑❑❑
540 ______________	**1938. Franklin Pierce Issue**		
	14¢ **blue**	1.15	.20 ❑❑❑❑❑
541 ______________	**1938. James Buchanan Issue**		
	15¢ **slate**	.65	.20 ❑❑❑❑❑
542 ______________	**1938. Abraham Lincoln Issue**		
	16¢ **black**	1.25	.60 ❑❑❑❑❑
543 ______________	**1938. Andrew Johnson Issue**		
	17¢ **rose red**	1.25	.20 ❑❑❑❑❑
544 ______________	**1938. Ulysses S. Grant Issue**		
	18¢ **brown carmine**	2.25	.25 ❑❑❑❑❑
545 ______________	**1938. Rutherford B. Hayes Issue**		
	19¢ **light reddish violet**	2.00	.60 ❑❑❑❑❑
546 ______________	**1938. James A. Garfield Issue**		
	20¢ **blue green**	1.25	.20 ❑❑❑❑❑
547 ______________	**1938. Chester A. Arthur Issue**		
	21¢ **slate blue**	2.25	.20 ❑❑❑❑❑
548 ______________	**1938. Grover Cleveland Issue**		
	22¢ **vermilion**	1.50	.75 ❑❑❑❑❑

539

540

541

542

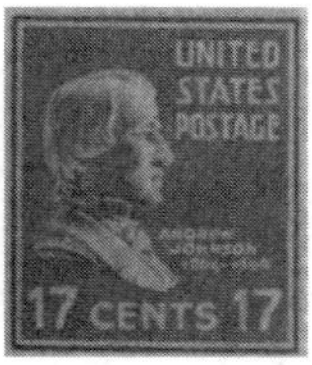

543

544

545

546

547

548

549

550

551

552

553

	UnFVF	UseFVF	
549 ______________ **1938. Benjamin Harrison Issue**			
24¢ **gray green**	4.25	.35	❑❑❑❑❑
550 ______________ **1938. William McKinley Issue**			
25¢ **claret**	1.20	.20	❑❑❑❑❑
551 ______________ **1938. Theodore Roosevelt Issue**			
30¢ **deep ultramarine**	5.00	.20	❑❑❑❑❑
552 ______________ **1938. William Howard Taft Issue**			
50¢ **light red violet**	8.50	.20	❑❑❑❑❑
NOTE: Flat plate printing, perforated 11.			
553 ______________ **1938. Woodrow Wilson Issue**			
$1 **dark purple and black**	10.00	.20	❑❑❑❑❑
NOTE: No. 553a is printed on pre-gummed, whiter and thicker paper. It was printed on "dry" paper; No. 553 was printed on pre-dampened paper.			
554 ______________ **1938. Warren G. Harding Issue**			
$2 **green and black**	27.50	4.75	❑❑❑❑❑
555 ______________ **1938. Calvin Coolidge Issue**			
$5 **carmine and black**	115.00	4.50	❑❑❑❑❑
556 ______________ **1939. Presidential Coil Issue**			
1¢ **green**	.25	.20	❑❑❑❑❑
557 ______________			
1-1/2¢ **yellow brown**	.25	.20	❑❑❑❑❑
558 ______________			
2¢ **rose**	.25	.20	❑❑❑❑❑
559 ______________			
3¢ **violet**	.25	.20	❑❑❑❑❑
560 ______________			
4¢ **bright purple**	7.50	.75	❑❑❑❑❑
561 ______________			
4-1/2¢ **gray**	.75	.50	❑❑❑❑❑
562 ______________			
5¢ **bright blue**	6.00	.50	❑❑❑❑❑
563 ______________			
6¢ **orange**	1.25	.50	❑❑❑❑❑
564 ______________			
10¢ **Venetian red**	12.50	1.25	❑❑❑❑❑
565 ______________ **1939. Presidential Coil Issue**			
1¢ **green**	.75	.25	❑❑❑❑❑
566 ______________			
1-1/2¢ **yellow brown**	1.50	.75	❑❑❑❑❑
567 ______________			
2¢ **rose**	2.50	.75	❑❑❑❑❑
568 ______________			
3¢ **violet**	2.25	.75	❑❑❑❑❑

554

555

569

570, 587

571

MNHFVF	UseFVF

569 _____ 1955. Benjamin Franklin Issue
1/2¢ **vermilion** wet print .25 .20 ☐☐☐☐☐
570 _____ 1954. George Washington Issue
1¢ **dull green** wet print .25 .20 ☐☐☐☐☐
571 _____ 1956. Mount Vernon Issue
1-1/2¢ **brown carmine** dry print .25 .20 ☐☐☐☐☐
572 _____ 1954. Thomas Jefferson Issue
2¢ **rose** dry print .25 .20 ☐☐☐☐☐
NOTE: *Silkote paper was used for only 50,000 stamps. Silkote varieties need expertization.*
573 _____ 1954. Statue of Liberty Issue
3¢ **violet** wet print .25 .20 ☐☐☐☐☐
NOTE: *Type I tagging: mat tagging. The four separate mats used did not cover the entire sheet of 400 stamps and certain untagged areas help to identify this variety.*
NOTE: *Type II tagging: roll tagging. Continuously surfaced rolls replaced the previously used tagging mats. Only the plate number selvage margin is partially tagged, and the plate number blocks have one untagged margin.*
NOTE: *Type III tagging: curved metal plate tagging. Sheet margins are almost fully tagged but a "hot line" of intense phosphor-tagging or untagged narrow gap, 1mm or less in width, can appear on stamps from any position in the pane.*
574 _____ 1954. Abraham Lincoln Issue
4¢ **magenta** wet print .25 .20 ☐☐☐☐☐
575 _____ 1954. James Monroe Issue
5¢ **blue** dry print .25 .20 ☐☐☐☐☐
576 _____ 1955. Theodore Roosevelt Issue
6¢ **rose red** wet print .25 .20 ☐☐☐☐☐
577 _____ 1956. Woodrow Wilson Issue
7¢ **carmine red** dry print .25 .20 ☐☐☐☐☐
578 _____ 1954. Statue of Liberty Issue
8¢ **deep blue & carmine** .25 .20 ☐☐☐☐☐
NOTE: *Flat plate printing, 22.7mm high. See also 591 for Type II.*
578A _____ 1954. Statue of Liberty Issue
8¢ **deep blue and carmine** .40 .20 ☐☐☐☐☐
NOTE: *Rotary press printing, 22.9mm high, slightly taller than No. 578.*
579 _____ 1956. The Alamo Issue
9¢ **rose lilac** dry print .25 .20 ☐☐☐☐☐
580 _____ 1956. Independence Hall Issue
10¢ **brown purple** dry print .25 .20 ☐☐☐☐☐
581 _____ 1956. Monticello Issue
20¢ **bright blue** dry print .50 .20 ☐☐☐☐☐

572, 588 573, 589 574, 590 575 576

577 578 579 580 581

MNHFVF	UseFVF	

582 _____ **1955. Robert E. Lee Issue**

30¢ **black** wet print — 1.50 — .25 ☐☐☐☐☐

583 _____ **1955. John Marshall Issue**

40¢ **brown carmine** wet print — 2.75 — .25 ☐☐☐☐☐

584 _____ **1955. Susan B. Anthony Issue**

50¢ **red violet** wet print — 2.00 — .20 ☐☐☐☐☐

585 _____ **1955. Patrick Henry Issue**

$1 **dark lilac** wet print — 7.00 — .20 ☐☐☐☐☐

586 _____ **1956. Alexander Hamilton Issue**

$5 **black** dry print — 70.00 — 6.50 ☐☐☐☐☐

587 _____ **1954. George Washington Issue**

1¢ **dull green** wet print — .45 — .25 ☐☐☐☐☐

588 _____ **1954. Thomas Jefferson Issue**

2¢ **rose** wet print — .25 — .20 ☐☐☐☐☐

589 _____ **1954. Statue of Liberty Issue**

3¢ **purple** wet print, large holes — .25 — .20 ☐☐☐☐☐

NOTE: No. 589psz1, the so-called "Look Coil," was prepared for Look magazine in coil rolls of 3,000 subjects. All but 99,000 of this issue were affixed to outgoing mail and return addressed envelopes on an automatic labeling machine at Des Moines, Iowa. The earliest known use was Dec. 29, 1966. The common usage was in combination with a 2¢ Jefferson coil (No. 588). The paper on which the stamps were printed is plain, without fluorescent content, and tagging is uniform and brilliant. A special printing was issued, in coils of 500 subjects, to satisfy collector demands (No. 589psz1). The original printing had a sharper, more well-defined design. The reprint has a more intense shade of purple ink. The philatelic examples were on slightly fluorescent paper, the tagging was less intense and on some coils a tagging plate flaw repeats every 24th stamp, both as a "Hot" line and as an untagged line.

590 _____ **1958. Abraham Lincoln Issue**

4¢ **bright purple** wet print (Bureau precancel only) — 29.00 — 1.00 ☐☐☐☐☐

591 _____ **1958. Statue of Liberty Issue**

8¢ **deep blue & carmine** — .25 — .20 ☐☐☐☐☐

592 _____ **1958. John Jay Issue**

15¢ **brown purple** dry print — .75 — .20 ☐☐☐☐☐

593 _____ **1958. Paul Revere Issue**

25¢ **deep blue green** — 1.50 — .20 ☐☐☐☐☐

594 _____ **1959. Bunker Hill Monument Issue**

2-1/2¢ **slate blue** dry print — .25 — .20 ☐☐☐☐☐

595 _____ **1959. Hermitage Issue**

4-1/2¢ **blue green** dry print — .25 — .20 ☐☐☐☐☐

596 _____ **1959. Benjamin Harrison Issue**

12¢ **carmine red** dry print — .30 — .20 ☐☐☐☐☐

NOTE: Type IIa tagging: wide roll tagging. All margins are fully tagged.

597 _____ **1959. Hermitage Coil Issue**

4-1/2¢ **blue green** large holes — 2.00 — 1.25 ☐☐☐☐☐

598 _____ **1959. Bunker Hill Monument Coil Issue**

2-1/2¢ **slate blue** large holes — .25 — .20 ☐☐☐☐☐

599 _____ **1960. Palace of the Governors**

1-1/4¢ **turquoise blue** — .25 — .20 ☐☐☐☐☐

600 _____ **1960. Palace of the Governors Coil Issue**

1-1/4¢ **turquoise blue** large holes — 15.00 — .25 ☐☐☐☐☐

601 _____ **1961. Statue of Liberty Issue**

11¢ **carmine red & blue** — .30 — .20 ☐☐☐☐☐

NOTE: Type OP tagging: Used on multicolor stamps previously designated to be printed on Giori presses.

602 _____ **1961. John J. Pershing Issue**

8¢ **brown** — .25 — .20 ☐☐☐☐☐

NOTE: There is disagreement concerning whether No. 602 is actually part of the Liberty Series. Although printed within the same period, it does not match the design characteristics of other stamps in the series.

			MNHFVF	UseFVF	
603	______	**1962. Evergreen Wreath and Burning Candles Issue**			
	4¢	**green & red**	.25	.20	❑❑❑❑❑
604	______	**1962. George Washington Issue**			
	5¢	**gray blue**	.25	.20	❑❑❑❑❑
605	______	**1962. George Washington Coil Issue**			
	5¢	**gray blue**	.25	.20	❑❑❑❑❑
606	______	**1963. U.S. Flag and White House Issue**			
	5¢	**blue & red**	.25	.20	❑❑❑❑❑
607	______	**1963. Andrew Jackson Issue**			
	1¢	**green**	.25	.20	❑❑❑❑❑
608	______	**1963. Andrew Jackson Coil Issue**			
	1¢	**green**	.25	.20	❑❑❑❑❑
609	______	**1963. Christmas Tree and White House**			
	5¢	**dark blue, indigo & red**	.25	.20	❑❑❑❑❑
610	______	**1964. Holiday Evergreens Issue**			
	5¢	**Holly**	.25	.20	❑❑❑❑❑
611	______				
	5¢	**Mistletoe**	.25	.20	❑❑❑❑❑

582

583

584

585

586

591

592

593, 614

594, 598

595, 597

596

599, 600

601

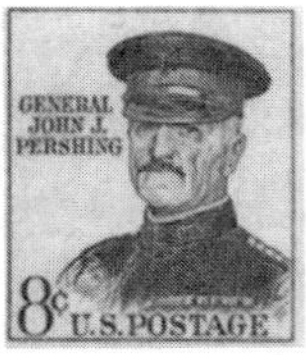

602

603

604, 605

606

607, 608

609

		MNHFVF	UseFVF	
612 ____________				
5¢	**Poinsettia**	.25	.20	❑❑❑❑❑
613 ____________				
5¢	**Conifer sprig**	.25	.20	❑❑❑❑❑
614 ____________	**1965. Paul Revere Coil Issue**			
25¢	**deep blue green** small holes	.45	.25	❑❑❑❑❑
615 ____________	**1965. Angel Gabriel Issue**			
5¢	**red, green & yellow**	.25	.20	❑❑❑❑❑
616 ____________	**1968. Thomas Jefferson Issue**			
1¢	**green** tagged Type II or III	.25	.20	❑❑❑❑❑
617 ____________	**1967. Albert Gallatin Issue**			
1-1/4¢	**light green**	.25	.20	❑❑❑❑❑
618 ____________	**1966. Frank Lloyd Wright Issue**			
2¢	**blue** tagged Type II or III	.25	.20	❑❑❑❑❑
619 ____________	**1967. Francis Parkman Issue**			
3¢	**purple** tagged Type II	.25	.20	❑❑❑❑❑
620 ____________	**1965. Abraham Lincoln Issue**			
4¢	**black**	.25	.20	❑❑❑❑❑
621 ____________	**1965. George Washington Issue**			
5¢	**deep blue**	.25	.20	❑❑❑❑❑
622 ____________	**1966. Franklin D. Roosevelt Issue**			
6¢	**black brown**	.25	.20	❑❑❑❑❑
623 ____________	**1966. Albert Einstein Issue**			
8¢	**violet**	.25	.20	❑❑❑❑❑
624 ____________	**1967. Andrew Jackson Issue**			
10¢	**lavender** tagged Type II or III	.25	.20	❑❑❑❑❑

610-613

615

616, 634

617

618

619, 693

620, 635

621, 636

622

623

624

624A

MNHFVF	UseFVF

624A _____ **1968. Henry Ford Issue**
12¢ **black** tagged Type II .25 .20 ☐☐☐☐☐

625 _____ **1967. John F. Kennedy Issue**
13¢ **brown** tagged Type II or III .25 .20 ☐☐☐☐☐

626 _____ **1968. Oliver Wendell Holmes Issue**
15¢ **maroon** design Type I, tagged Type III .25 .20 ☐☐☐☐☐

NOTE: Type I: crosshatching on tie complete and strong; bottom of necktie just touches coat. Type II: crosshatching on tie (lines running upper left to lower right) very faint; necktie does not touch coat. Type III (know only on booklet pane) overall design smaller and "15¢" closer to head.

626A _____
15¢ **maroon** design Type II, tagged .50 .20 ☐☐☐☐☐

626B _____
15¢ **maroon** design Type III perforated 10 .25 .20 ☐☐☐☐☐

627 _____ **1967. George C. Marshall Issue**
20¢ **olive brown** .35 .20 ☐☐☐☐☐

628 _____ **1967. Frederick Douglass Issue**
25¢ **maroon** .50 .20 ☐☐☐☐☐

629 _____ **1968. John Dewey Issue**
30¢ **purple** .55 .25 ☐☐☐☐☐

630 _____ **1968. Thomas Paine Issue**
40¢ **dark blue** .75 .25 ☐☐☐☐☐

631 _____ **1968. Lucy Stone Issue**
50¢ **maroon** 1.00 .25 ☐☐☐☐☐

632 _____ **1967. Eugene O'Neill Issue**
$1 **dark purple** 2.25 .50 ☐☐☐☐☐

633 _____ **1966. John Bassett Moore Issue**
$5 **dark gray** 10.00 3.00 ☐☐☐☐☐

634 _____ **1968. Thomas Jefferson Coil Issue**
1¢ **green** tagged .25 .20 ☐☐☐☐☐

635 _____ **1966. Abraham Lincoln Coil Issue**
4¢ **black** tagged Type II .25 .20 ☐☐☐☐☐

636 _____ **1966. George Washington Coil Issue**
5¢ **deep blue** tagged Type II .25 .20 ☐☐☐☐☐

637 _____ **1968. Franklin D. Roosevelt Coil Issue**
6¢ **black brown** tagged .25 .20 ☐☐☐☐☐

625

626, 721, 721A

627

628

629

630

631

632, 672

633

644

		MNHFVF	UseFVF	
638 ______________	**1967. Franklin D. Roosevelt Coil Issue**			
6¢	**black brown** tagged	.25	.20	❑❑❑❑❑
NOTE: Nos. 639-643 are not assigned.				
644 ______________	**1966. Traditional Christmas Issue**			
5¢	**multicolored**	.25	.20	❑❑❑❑❑
645 ______________	**1967. Traditional Christmas Issue**			
5¢	**multicolored**	.25	.20	❑❑❑❑❑
646 ______________	**1967. George Washington Issue**			
5¢	**deep blue** tagged, shiny gum	.25	.20	❑❑❑❑❑
647 ______________	**1968. Flag Over White House Issue**			
6¢	**dark blue, green & red** tagged Type OP	.25	.20	❑❑❑❑❑
648 ______________	**1968. Serviceman's Airlift Issue**			
$1	**multicolored**	3.00	2.00	❑❑❑❑❑
649 ______________	**1968. Traditional Christmas Issue**			
6¢	**multicolored** tagged Type B	.25	.20	❑❑❑❑❑
NOTE: Type B tagging: Billet or bar-like shapes designed to register within the limits of a single stamp. Untagged areas surround the design and were intended to register with the perforations.				
650 ______________	**1969. Flag Over White House Coil Stamp Issue**			
6¢	**dark blue, green & red** tagged	.25	.20	❑❑❑❑❑
651 ______________	**1969. Contemporary Christmas Issue**			
6¢	**multicolored** tagged	.25	.20	❑❑❑❑❑
NOTE: Experimental precanceled stamps were sold for use by the public, imprinted, "ATLANTA, GA," "BALTIMORE, MD," "MEMPHIS, TN," and "NEW HAVEN, CT."				
652 ______________	**1970. Dwight D. Eisenhower Issue**			
6¢	**blue** tagged Type II, shiny gum	.25	.20	❑❑❑❑❑
653 ______________	**1970. Dwight D. Eisenhower Coil Issue**			
6¢	**blue** tagged, shiny gum	.25	.20	❑❑❑❑❑

(637), 638

645

646, 747A

647, 650, 654

648

649 ⟵

651

652, 653

		MNHFVF	UseFVF	
654 ______________	**1970. Flag Over White House Issue**			
6¢	**dark blue, green & red** tagged Type B	.25	.20	❑❑❑❑❑
655 ______________	**1970. Contemporary Christmas Issue**			
6¢	**multicolored** tagged	.25	.20	❑❑❑❑❑
656 ______________				
6¢	**multicolored** tagged	.25	.20	❑❑❑❑❑
657 ______________				
6¢	**multicolored** tagged	.25	.20	❑❑❑❑❑
658 ______________				
6¢	**multicolored** tagged	.25	.20	❑❑❑❑❑
659 ______________	**1970. Traditional Christmas Issue**			
6¢	**multicolored** tagged design Type I	.25	.20	❑❑❑❑❑

NOTE: Type I has a slightly blurry impression and no gum breaker ridges. Type II has a shiny surfaced paper, sharper impression, and both horizontal and vertical gum breaker ridges. Type I precancel is gray black; Type II precancel is intense black.

		MNHFVF	UseFVF	
660 ______________	**1971. Ernie Pyle Issue**			
16¢	**brown** tagged	.30	.20	❑❑❑❑❑
661 ______________	**1971. Flag Over White House Issue**			
8¢	**dark blue, red & slate green** tagged Type B	.25	.20	❑❑❑❑❑
662 ______________	**1971. Flag Over White House Coil Issue**			
8¢	**dark blue, red & slate green** tagged Type B	.20	.20	❑❑❑❑❑
663 ______________	**1971. Dwight D. Eisenhower Issue**			
8¢	**black, blue gray & red** tagged Type OP	.25	.20	❑❑❑❑❑
663A ______________	**1971. Dwight D. Eisenhower Booklet Issue**			
8¢	**reddish brown,** shiny gum Type II, in booklet form only	.25	.20	❑❑❑❑❑

NOTE: All these booklet stamps have 1 or 2 straight edges.

		MNHFVF	UseFVF	
664 ______________	**1971. Dwight D. Eisenhower Coil Issue**			
8¢	**reddish brown** tagged	.25	.20	❑❑❑❑❑
665 ______________	**1971. U.S. Postal Service Issue**			
8¢	**multicolored** tagged	.25	.20	❑❑❑❑❑
666 ______________	**1971. Contemporary Christmas Issue**			
8¢	**multicolored** tagged	.25	.20	❑❑❑❑❑
667 ______________	**1971. Traditional Christmas Issue**			
8¢	**multicolored** tagged	.25	.20	❑❑❑❑❑
668 ______________	**1972. Fiorello H. LaGuardia Issue**			
14¢	**dark brown** tagged	.25	.20	❑❑❑❑❑

655-658

659

660

661, 662

663

663A, 664

	MNHFVF	UseFVF
669 ____________ 1972. Benjamin Franklin Issue		
7¢ **light blue** shiny gum, tagged	.25	.20 ☐☐☐☐☐
670 ____________ 1972. Contemporary Christmas Issue		
8¢ **multicolored** tagged	.25	.20 ☐☐☐☐☐
671 ____________ 1972. Traditional Christmas Issue		
8¢ **multicolored** tagged	.25	.20 ☐☐☐☐☐
672 ____________ 1973. Eugene O'Neill Coil Issue		
$1 **dark purple** tagged, shiny gum	2.00	.75 ☐☐☐☐☐
673 ____________ 1973. Amadeo P. Giannini Issue		
21¢ **banknote green** tagged	.40	.25 ☐☐☐☐☐
674 ____________ 1973. Traditional Christmas Issue		
8¢ **multicolored** tagged	.25	.20 ☐☐☐☐☐
675 ____________ 1973. Contemporary Christmas Issue		
8¢ **multicolored** tagged	.25	.20 ☐☐☐☐☐
676 ____________ 1973. Crossed Flags Issue		
10¢ **red & blue** tagged	.25	.20 ☐☐☐☐☐
677 ____________ 1973. Crossed Flags Coil Issue		
10¢ **red & blue** tagged	.40	.25 ☐☐☐☐☐

NOTE: The lines on this issue, which can occur every 4 stamps, are usually incomplete. Full, complete lines sell for a premium.

665

666

667

668

669

670

671

673

674

675

676, 677

678, 679

680

681

682

		MNHFVF	UseFVF
678 ______	**1973. Jefferson Memorial Issue**		
	10¢ **blue** tagged, Type II or III	.25	.20 ❑❑❑❑❑
679 ______	**1973. Jefferson Memorial Coil Issue**		
	10¢ **blue** tagged	.25	.20 ❑❑❑❑❑
680 ______	**1974. ZIP Code Issue**		
	10¢ **multicolored** tagged with small rectangle in center of stamp	.25	.20 ❑❑❑❑❑
681 ______	**1974. Elizabeth Blackwell Issue**		
	18¢ **purple** tagged	.30	.25 ❑❑❑❑❑
682 ______	**1974. Swinging Bell Coil Issue**		
	6.3¢ **brick red** tagged	.25	.20 ❑❑❑❑❑
683 ______	**1974. Contemporary Christmas Issue**		
	10¢ **multicolored** tagged	.25	.20 ❑❑❑❑❑
684 ______	**1974. Dove of Peace Issue**		
	10¢ **multicolored** self-adhesive	.25	.20 ❑❑❑❑❑
NOTE: Two types of rouletting were used on backing paper.			
685 ______	**1974. Traditional Christmas Issue**		
	10¢ **multicolored** tagged	.25	.20 ❑❑❑❑❑
686 ______	**1975. Contemporary Christmas Issue**		
	10¢ **multicolored** tagged	.30	.20 ❑❑❑❑❑
686A ______			
	10¢ **multicolored** tagged	.30	.20 ❑❑❑❑❑
686B ______			
	10¢ **multicolored** tagged	.60	.20 ❑❑❑❑❑
687 ______	**1975. Traditional Christmas Issue**		
	10¢ **multicolored** tagged	.30	.20 ❑❑❑❑❑
688 ______	**1975. Capitol Dome Issue**		
	9¢ **green** on gray paper, tagged	.25	.20 ❑❑❑❑❑

683

684

685

686

687

688, 697, 702, 702A

689

690, 694, 782

691

		MNHFVF	UseFVF	
689 ____________	**1975. Colonial Printing Press Issue**			
	11¢ **orange** on gray paper, tagged	.25	.20	❑❑❑❑❑
690 ____________	**1975. Flag over Independence Hall Issue**			
	13¢ **dark blue & red** tagged	.25	.20	❑❑❑❑❑
691 ____________	**1975. Eagle and Shield Issue**			
	13¢ **multicolored** tagged with eagle-shape untagged area	.25	.20	❑❑❑❑❑
691A ____________				
	13¢ **multicolored** perforated 11 (L-perforation)	40.00	15.00	❑❑❑❑❑
692 ____________	**1975. Old North Church Issue**			
	24¢ **red** on blue paper, tagged	.50	.25	❑❑❑❑❑
693 ____________	**1975. Francis Parkman Coil Issue**			
	3¢ **purple** tagged, shiny gum	.25	.20	❑❑❑❑❑
694 ____________	**1975. Flag over Independence Hall Coil Issue**			
	13¢ **dark blue & red** tagged	.25	.20	❑❑❑❑❑
695 ____________	**1975. Liberty Bell Issue**			
	13¢ **brown** from booklet panes only, tagged	.25	.20	❑❑❑❑❑
696 ____________	**1975. Liberty Bell Coil Issue**			
	13¢ **brown** shiny gum, tagged	.25	.20	❑❑❑❑❑
697 ____________	**1976. Capitol Dome Coil Issue**			
	9¢ **green** on gray paper, shiny gum, tagged	.25	.20	❑❑❑❑❑
698 ____________	**1976. American Eagle and Drum Coil Issue**			
	7.9¢ **red** on canary paper, shiny gum, tagged	.25	.20	❑❑❑❑❑
699 ____________	**1976. Contemporary Christmas Issue**			
	13¢ **multicolored** overall tagged	.40	.25	❑❑❑❑❑
699A ____________				
	13¢ **multicolored** block tagged	.40	.25	❑❑❑❑❑
700 ____________	**1976. Traditional Christmas Issue**			
	13¢ **multicolored** tagged	.40	.25	❑❑❑❑❑
701 ____________	**1976. Saxhorns Issue**			
	7.7¢ **brown** on canary paper, tagged	.25	.20	❑❑❑❑❑
702 ____________	**1977. Capitol Dome Booklet Issue**			
	9¢ **green** tagged, perforated 11 x 10 1/2	1.00	.20	❑❑❑❑❑
702A ____________				
	9¢ **green** tagged	35.00	22.50	❑❑❑❑❑

692

695, 696

697

698

699, 699A

700

701

MNHFVF	UseFVF

703 _____ **1977. Flag over Capitol Booklet Issue**
13¢ **red & blue** tagged .25 .20 ☐☐☐☐☐

703A _____ **1977. Flag over Capitol Issue**
13¢ **red & blue** tagged .75 .50 ☐☐☐☐☐

704 _____ **1977. Rural Mail Box Issue**
13¢ **multicolored** tagged .40 .20 ☐☐☐☐☐

705 _____ **1977. Washington Kneeling At Prayer Issue**
13¢ **multicolored** tagged .40 .20 ☐☐☐☐☐

NOTE: The multicolor Combination Press issue (No. 705) has "floating" plate numbers, a set of five numbers sand-wiched between two or three blanks, so that on a plate strip of 20 there are five numbers and five blanks, six numbers and four blanks, seven numbers and three blanks or eight numbers and two blanks. There are no ZIP or Mail Early slogans.

NOTE: Nos. 706-707 are not assigned.

708 _____ **1977. Contemplation of Justice Issue**
10¢ **purple** on gray paper, shiny gum, tagged .25 .20 ☐☐☐☐☐

709 _____ **1977. Contemplation of Justice Coil Issue**
10¢ **purple** on gray paper, tagged .25 .20 ☐☐☐☐☐

710 _____ **1977. Quill Pen and Inkwell Issue**
1¢ **blue** on green paper, tagged .25 .20 ☐☐☐☐☐

711 _____ **1977. Symbols of Speech Issue**
2¢ **brown** on green paper, shiny gum, tagged .25 .20 ☐☐☐☐☐

711A _____ **1981. Symbols of Speech Issue**
2¢ **brown** on cream paper, matte gum, tagged .25 .20 ☐☐☐☐☐

712 _____ **1977. Ballot Box Issue**
3¢ **olive** on green paper, shiny gum, tagged .25 .20 ☐☐☐☐☐

713 _____ **1977. Reading and Learning Issue**
4¢ **maroon** on cream paper, tagged .25 .20 ☐☐☐☐☐

702, 702A, 703, 703A

704

705

708, 709

710, 742

711, 711A

712

713

714

715, 716

	MNHFVF	UseFVF	
714 ______________ **1978. Indian Head Penny Issue**			
13¢ **brown & blue** on tan paper, tagged	.25	.20	❑❑❑❑❑
715 ______________ **1978. Statue of Liberty Issue**			
16¢ **blue** tagged	.30	.20	❑❑❑❑❑
716 ______________ **1978. Statue of Liberty Coil Issue**			
16¢ **blue** overall tagged	.35	.20	❑❑❑❑❑
716A ______________			
16¢ **multicolored** block tagged, B Press (design slightly narrower than 716, no joint line)	—		❑❑❑❑❑
717 ______________ **1978. Sandy Hook Lighthouse Issue**			
29¢ **blue** on blue paper, shiny gum, tagged	.50	.65	❑❑❑❑❑
718 ______________ **1978. "A" Stamp Issue**			
15¢ **orange** perforated 11, tagged	.30	.25	❑❑❑❑❑
718A ______________ **1978. "A" Stamp Issue**			
15¢ **orange** perforated 11 1/4, tagged	.30	.25	❑❑❑❑❑
719 ______________ **1978. "A" Booklet Stamp Issue**			
15¢ **orange** tagged	.25	.20	❑❑❑❑❑
720 ______________ **1978. "A" Stamp Coil Issue**			
15¢ **orange** tagged	.25	.15	❑❑❑❑❑
721 ______________ **1978. Oliver Wendell Holmes Issue**			
15¢ **maroon,** shiny gum, Type I, tagged	.25	.20	❑❑❑❑❑
721A ______________			
15¢ **maroon** Type II matte gum, tagged	.25	.20	❑❑❑❑❑
NOTE: For booklet pane issued the same date see No. 626B.			
722 ______________ **1978. American Flag Issue**			
15¢ **red, blue & gray** perforated 11, tagged	.30	.20	❑❑❑❑❑
722A ______________ **1978. American Flag Booklet Issue**			
15¢ **red, blue & gray** booklet stamp, perforated 11 x 10 1/2, tagged	.35	.20	❑❑❑❑❑
723 ______________ **1978. American Flag Coil Issue**			
15¢ **red, blue & gray**	.40	.20	❑❑❑❑❑
724 ______________ **1978. American Roses Booklet Issue**			
15¢ **orange, red & green** tagged	.25	.20	❑❑❑❑❑
725 ______________ **1978. Steinway Grand Piano Coil Issue**			
8.4¢ **blue** on canary paper, shiny gum, tagged	.25	.20	❑❑❑❑❑
726 ______________ **1978. Blockhouse Issue**			
28¢ **brown** on blue paper, tagged, shiny gum	.50	.20	❑❑❑❑❑

717

718-720

722, 722A, 723

724

725

726

727

728

729

		MNHFVF	UseFVF	
727 ______________	**1978. Contemporary Christmas Issue**			
	15¢ **multicolored** tagged	.40	.20	❑❑❑❑❑
728 ______________	**1978. Madonna and Child with Cherubim Issue**			
	15¢ **multicolored** tagged	.40	.20	❑❑❑❑❑
729 ______________	**1978. Kerosene Table Lamp Issue**			
	$2 **multicolored** tagged	3.50	1.00	❑❑❑❑❑
730 ______________	**1979. Rush Lamp and Candle Holder Issue**			
	$1 **multicolored** tagged	2.00	.25	❑❑❑❑❑

NOTE: In the spring of 1986, a mail room employee of the United States Central Intelligence Agency, after buying stamps at a post office in the Washington, D.C., suburb of Fairfax, Va., for agency use, discovered he had bought 95 copies of the $1 Rush Lamp and Candle Holder stamp — nearly a full pane of 100 — with an inverted design. He and fellow workers had removed 10 more stamps from the pane to prepare for a mailing before they noticed the disjointed printing.

The Americana Series stamp was printed first in offset for the tan background, the yellow candle and flame and the red halo behind it, and then in intaglio for the engraved candle holder and lettering in dark brown. In this case one sheet of 400 stamps was fed into the intaglio press upside-down so that the two elements did not line up correctly — the brown was inverted.

The finder and some fellow workers each held one copy for themselves, replaced the stamps, and disposed of the remaining error stamps to a dealer. Because of the supersecret nature of the agency's affairs and the fact that the employee used agency money to buy the stamps, controversy erupted over the ownership of the errors. Some employees quit their jobs rather than turn in the stamps they had kept. It has become known as the CIA Invert.

		MNHFVF	UseFVF	
731 ______________	**1979. Railroad Conductor's Lantern Issue**			
	$5 **multicolored** tagged	8.50	2.25	❑❑❑❑❑
732 ______________	**1979. Country Schoolhouse Issue**			
	30¢ **green** on blue paper, tagged	1.00	.30	❑❑❑❑❑
733 ______________	**1979. Iron "Betty" Lamp Issue**			
	50¢ **black, orange & tan** tagged	1.00	.20	❑❑❑❑❑
734 ______________	**1979. Santa Claus Christmas Tree Ornament Issue**			
	15¢ **multicolored** tagged	.40	.20	❑❑❑❑❑
735 ______________	**1979. Traditional Christmas Issue**			
	15¢ **multicolored** tagged	.40	.20	❑❑❑❑❑
736 ______________	**1979. Standard Six-string Guitar Coil Issue**			
	3.1¢ **brown** on canary paper, tagged	.25	.20	❑❑❑❑❑
737 ______________	**1980. Historic Windmills Issue**			
	15¢ **Virginia, brown** on yellow paper, tagged	.30	.20	❑❑❑❑❑
738 ______________				
	15¢ **Rhode Island, brown** on yellow paper, tagged	.30	.20	❑❑❑❑❑
739 ______________				
	15¢ **Massachusetts, brown,** on yellow paper, tagged	.30	.20	❑❑❑❑❑

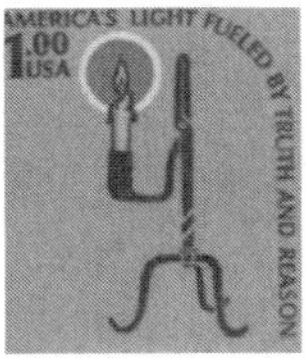

730

731

732

733

734

735

736 ←

737-741 →

MNHFVF	UseFVF

740 _____
15¢ **Illinois, brown** on yellow paper, tagged .30 .20 ☐☐☐☐☐

741 _____
15¢ **Texas, brown** on yellow paper, tagged .30 .20 ☐☐☐☐☐

742 _____ **1980. Quill Pen and Inkwell Coil Issue**
1¢ **blue** on green paper, shiny gum, tagged .25 .20 ☐☐☐☐☐

743 _____ **1980. Dolley Madison Issue**
15¢ **red brown & sepia** tagged .40 .20 ☐☐☐☐☐

744 _____ **1980. Weaver Manufactured Violins Coil Issue**
3.5¢ **purple** on yellow paper, tagged .25 .20 ☐☐☐☐☐

745 _____ **1980. Contemporary Christmas Issue**
15¢ **multicolored** tagged .50 .20 ☐☐☐☐☐

746 _____ **1980. Traditional Christmas Issue**
15¢ **multicolored** tagged .50 .20 ☐☐☐☐☐

747 _____ **1980. Sequoyah Issue**
19¢ **brown** overall tagged .30 .20 ☐☐☐☐☐

747A _____ **1980. Washington Coil Issue**
5¢ **deep blue** tagged .25 .20 ☐☐☐☐☐

748 _____ **1981. Non-Denominated "B" Stamp Issue**
18¢ **purple** tagged .30 .20 ☐☐☐☐☐

749 _____ **1981. Non-Denominated "B" Booklet Issue**
18¢ **purple** tagged .30 .20 ☐☐☐☐☐

750 _____ **1981. Non-Denominated "B" Coil Issue**
18¢ **purple** tagged .40 .20 ☐☐☐☐☐

751 _____ **1981. Freedom Of Conscience Issue**
12¢ **red brown** on beige paper, tagged .25 .20 ☐☐☐☐☐

NOTE: U.S. Postal Service Plate-Numbering Change. *In response to collector complaints that its plate-numbering system resulted in many inconvenient and costly blocks of 10, 12 and 20 stamps, the USPS in January 1981 instituted a new plate number arrangement. Under the new system, most sheets were to contain a single plate number consisting of one (for monocolor stamps) to six digits, each digit representing a given printing plate and color. Thus, under this system, most plate blocks returned to blocks of four.*

Booklet panes hereafter also contain a plate number in the selvage.

In coils, a plate number was incorporated into some stamps in the roll, at various intervals between stamps, depending on the press used.

743

744

745

746

747

748-750

751, 752

753

754

No.	Description	MNHFVF	UseFVF
752	**1981. Freedom of Conscience Coil Issue**		
	12¢ **red brown** on beige paper, tagged	.25	.20 ❑❑❑❑❑
753	**1981. America The Beautiful Issue**		
	18¢ **multicolored** tagged	.30	.20 ❑❑❑❑❑
754	**1981. America The Beautiful Issue**		
	18¢ **multicolored** tagged	.30	.20 ❑❑❑❑❑
755	**1981. America The Beautiful Combination Booklet**		
	6¢ **blue** tagged	.55	.25 ❑❑❑❑❑
756			
	18¢ **multicolored** tagged	.30	.20 ❑❑❑❑❑
757	**1981. George Mason Issue**		
	18¢ **blue** overall tagged	.30	.20 ❑❑❑❑❑
758	**1981. Wildlife Booklet Issue**		
	18¢ **Bighorn sheep, brown,** tagged	.50	.20 ❑❑❑❑❑
759			
	18¢ **Puma, brown,** tagged	.50	.20 ❑❑❑❑❑
760			
	18¢ **Harbor seal, brown,** tagged	.50	.20 ❑❑❑❑❑
761			
	18¢ **Bison, brown,** tagged	.50	.20 ❑❑❑❑❑
762			
	18¢ **Brown bear, brown,** tagged	.50	.20 ❑❑❑❑❑
763			
	18¢ **Polar bear, brown,** tagged	.50	.20 ❑❑❑❑❑
764			
	18¢ **Elk (Wapiti), brown,** tagged	.50	.20 ❑❑❑❑❑

755, 756

758-767

768

769

770

771

757

772-774

775

		MNHFVF	UseFVF
765	18¢ **Moose, brown,** tagged	.50	.20 ❑❑❑❑❑
766	18¢ **White-tailed deer, brown,** tagged	.50	.20 ❑❑❑❑❑
767	18¢ **Pronghorn antelope, brown,** tagged	.50	.20 ❑❑❑❑❑
768	**1981. Surrey Issue** 18¢ **brown** tagged	.35	.20 ❑❑❑❑❑
769	**1981. Rachel Carson Issue** 17¢ **green** overall tagged	.30	.20 ❑❑❑❑❑
770	**1981. Charles R. Drew Issue** 35¢ **gray** overall tagged	.50	.25 ❑❑❑❑❑

NOTE: Plate blocks from plates 3 & 4 carry a premium.

		MNHFVF	UseFVF
771	**1981. Electric Auto Issue** 17¢ **blue** tagged	.35	.20 ❑❑❑❑❑
772	**1981. Non-Denominated "C" Issue** 20¢ **brown** tagged	.35	.20 ❑❑❑❑❑
773	**1981. Non-Denominated "C" Booklet Pane Issue** 20¢ **brown** tagged	.50	.20 ❑❑❑❑❑
774	**1981. Non-Denominated "C" Coil Issue** 20¢ **brown** tagged	.60	.20 ❑❑❑❑❑
775	**1981. Christmas Issue** 20¢ **multicolored** tagged	.50	.20 ❑❑❑❑❑
776	20¢ **multicolored** tagged	.50	.20 ❑❑❑❑❑
777	**1981. Fire Pumper Issue** 20¢ **red** tagged	.40	.20 ❑❑❑❑❑
778	**1981. Mail Wagon Issue** 9.3¢ **dark red** tagged	.25	.20 ❑❑❑❑❑

776

777

778

779-781

783, 783A

784

785

786

787

788

789

790

791

MNHFVF	UseFVF	

779 _____ 1981. Flag Over Supreme Court Issue
20¢ **black, dark blue & red** perforated 11, tagged — .35 — .20 ☐☐☐☐☐

779A _____
20¢ **black, dark blue & red** perforated 11 1/4, tagged — .35 — .20 ☐☐☐☐☐

780 _____ 1981. Flag Over Supreme Court Coil Issue
20¢ **black, dark blue & red** tagged — .35 — .20 ☐☐☐☐☐

781 _____ 1981. Flag Over Supreme Court Issue
20¢ **black, dark red & blue** tagged — .35 — .20 ☐☐☐☐☐

782 _____ 1981. Flag Over Independence Hall Issue
13¢ **dark blue & red** block tagged — .60 — .25 ☐☐☐☐☐

783 _____ 1982. Bighorn Sheep Issue
20¢ **blue** Type I, overall tagged — .50 — .20 ☐☐☐☐☐

783A _____
20¢ **blue** Type II, block tagged, 18 1/2mm wide — .50 — .20 ☐☐☐☐☐
NOTE: Type I is 18 3/4mm wide, Type II is 18 1/2mm wide.

784 _____ 1982. Ralph Bunche Issue
20¢ **maroon** overall tagged — .35 — .20 ☐☐☐☐☐

785 _____ 1982. Crazy Horse Issue
13¢ **light maroon** overall tagged — .35 — .20 ☐☐☐☐☐

786 _____ 1982. Robert Millikan Issue
37¢ **blue** overall tagged — .60 — .20 ☐☐☐☐☐

787 _____ 1982. High Wheeler Bicycle Issue
5.9¢ **blue** tagged — .25 — .20 ☐☐☐☐☐

788 _____ 1982. Hansom Cab Issue
10.9¢ **purple** tagged — .25 — .20 ☐☐☐☐☐

789 _____ 1982. Consumer Education Issue
20¢ **blue** tagged — .50 — .20 ☐☐☐☐☐

790 _____ 1982. Locomotive Issue
2¢ **black** tagged — .25 — .20 ☐☐☐☐☐
NOTE: (For similar design with "2 USA" see No. 873.)

791 _____ 1982. Stagecoach Issue
4¢ **brown** tagged — .25 — .20 ☐☐☐☐☐
NOTE: For similar design with "Stagecoach 1890s" measuring 17mm long. see No. 868.

792 _____ 1982. Christmas Issue
20¢ **Sledding, multicolored,** tagged — .35 — .20 ☐☐☐☐☐

793 _____
20¢ **Building snowman, multicolored,** tagged — .35 — .20 ☐☐☐☐☐

794 _____
20¢ **Skating, multicolored,** tagged — .35 — .20 ☐☐☐☐☐

795 _____
20¢ **Decorating tree, multicolored,** tagged — .35 — .20 ☐☐☐☐☐

792-795

796

797

MNHFVF	UseFVF	

796 _____ **1982. Traditional Christmas Issue**
20¢ **multicolored** tagged — .35 / .20 ☐☐☐☐☐

797 _____ **1982. Kitten and Puppy Issue**
13¢ **multicolored** tagged — .35 / .20 ☐☐☐☐☐

798 _____ **1982. Igor Stravinsky Issue**
2¢ **brown** overall tagged — .25 / .20 ☐☐☐☐☐

799 _____ **1983. Sleigh Issue**
5.2¢ **red** tagged — .25 / .20 ☐☐☐☐☐

800 _____ **1983. Handcar Issue**
3¢ **green** tagged — .25 / .20 ☐☐☐☐☐

801 _____ **1983. Carl Schurz Issue**
4¢ **purple** overall tagged — .20 / .20 ☐☐☐☐☐

802 _____ **1983. Thomas H. Gallaudet Issue**
20¢ **green** overall tagged — .40 / .20 ☐☐☐☐☐

803 _____ **1983. Pearl Buck Issue**
5¢ **red brown** overall tagged — .20 / .20 ☐☐☐☐☐

804 _____ **1983. Henry Clay Issue**
3¢ **olive** overall tagged — .20 / .20 ☐☐☐☐☐

805 _____ **1983. Express Mail Issue**
$9.35 **multicolored** tagged — 25.00 / 20.00 ☐☐☐☐☐

806 _____ **1983. Omnibus Issue**
1¢ **purple** tagged — .20 / .20 ☐☐☐☐☐
NOTE: For similar design with "1 USA" see No. 867.

807 _____ **1983. Dorothea Dix Issue**
1¢ **black** tagged (small block) perforated 11 1/4 — .20 / .20 ☐☐☐☐☐

807A _____
1¢ **black** tagged (small block) perforated 10 3/4 — .20 / .20 ☐☐☐☐☐

808 _____ **1983. Motorcycle Issue**
5¢ **dark green** tagged — .25 / .20 ☐☐☐☐☐

809 _____ **1983. Christmas Issue**
20¢ **multicolored** tagged — .35 / .20 ☐☐☐☐☐

798

799

800

801

802

803

804

805

		MNHFVF	UseFVF	
810 ______________				
	20¢ **multicolored** tagged	.35	.20	❑❑❑❑❑
811 ______________	**1984. Harry S. Truman Issue**			
	20¢ **black** tagged (small block)	.35	.20	❑❑❑❑❑
NOTE: (See also No. 904.)				
812 ______________	**1984. Railroad Caboose Issue**			
	11¢ **red** tagged	.25	.20	❑❑❑❑❑
813 ______________	**1984. Lillian Gilbreth Issue**			
	40¢ **green,** tagged (small block) perforated 11	.60	.20	❑❑❑❑❑
813A ______________				
	40¢ **green** tagged (large block) perforated 11 1/4 (1987)	.60	.20	❑❑❑❑❑
814 ______________	**1984. Baby Buggy Issue**			
	7.4¢ **brown** tagged	.25	.20	❑❑❑❑❑
815 ______________	**1984. Richard Russell Issue**			
	10¢ **blue** tagged (small block)	.25	.20	❑❑❑❑❑
NOTE: Imperforate printer's waste is known to exist, and in one case was used as postage.				
816 ______________	**1984. Frank C. Laubach Issue**			
	30¢ **green** tagged (small block) perforated 11	.75	.20	❑❑❑❑❑
816A ______________				
	30¢ **green** tagged (large block) perforated 11 1/4	.75	.20	❑❑❑❑❑
817 ______________	**1984. Christmas Issue**			
	20¢ **multicolored** tagged	.25	.20	❑❑❑❑❑
818 ______________				
	20¢ **multicolored** tagged	.25	.20	❑❑❑❑❑
819 ______________	**1985. Abraham Baldwin Issue**			
	7¢ **red** tagged (small block)	.25	.20	❑❑❑❑❑
820 ______________	**1985. Non-Denominated "D" Issue**			
	22¢ **green** tagged	.45	.20	❑❑❑❑❑
821 ______________	**1985. Non-Denominated "D" Coil Issue**			
	22¢ **green** tagged perforated 11	.60	.20	❑❑❑❑❑
822 ______________	**1985. Non-Denominated "D" Rate Booklet Issue**			
	22¢ **green** tagged	.40	.20	❑❑❑❑❑
823 ______________	**1985. Alden Partridge Issue**			
	11¢ **blue** overall tagged	.25	.20	❑❑❑❑❑

806

807

808

809

810 →

811

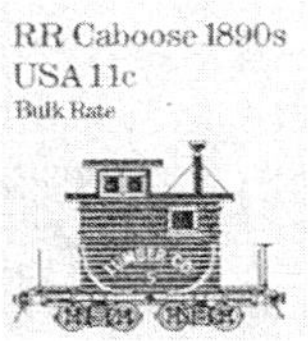

812

813

814

815

MNHFVF	UseFVF	

824 _____ **1985. Chester W. Nimitz Issue**
50¢ **brown** overall tagged, perforated 11, shiny gum | .90 | .20 ☐☐☐☐☐

824A _____
50¢ **brown** tagged (large block) perforated 11 1/4, matte gum | .90 | .20 ☐☐☐☐☐

825 _____ **1985. Grenville Clark Issue**
39¢ **purple** tagged (small block) perforated 11 | .75 | .20 ☐☐☐☐☐

825A _____
39¢ **purple** tagged (large block), perforated 11 1/4 | .75 | .20 ☐☐☐☐☐

826 _____ **1985. Sinclair Lewis Issue**
14¢ **gray** tagged (small block) | .25 | .20 ☐☐☐☐☐

827 _____ **1985. Iceboat Issue**
14¢ **blue** Type I, overall tagged | .25 | .20 ☐☐☐☐☐

827A _____
14¢ **blue** Type II, block tagged | .25 | .20 ☐☐☐☐☐

NOTE: Type I is 17 1/2 mm wide with overall tagging. Type II is 17 1/4 mm wide with block tagging.

828 _____ **1985. Flag over the Capitol Issue**
22¢ **black, blue, & red** tagged | .35 | .20 ☐☐☐☐☐

829 _____ **1985. Flag Over the U.S. Capitol Coil Issue**
22¢ **black, blue, & red** tagged | .40 | .20 ☐☐☐☐☐

NOTE: For similar design with "T" at bottom, see No. 876.

830 _____ **1985. Flag Over the Capitol Booklet Issue**
22¢ **black, blue, & red** tagged | .40 | .20 ☐☐☐☐☐

NOTE: Issued for use in vending machines, and was available with one or two panes.

831 _____ **1985. Stanley Steamer Issue**
12¢ **blue** Type I, tagged | .25 | .20 ☐☐☐☐☐

831A _____
12¢ **blue** Type II, untagged (Bureau precancel: "PRESORTED FIRST-CLASS") | .25 | .20 ☐☐☐☐☐

NOTE: Type I: "Stanley Steamer 1909" is 18mm long;

NOTE: Type II: "Stanley Steamer 1909" is 17 1/2 mm long.

832 _____ **1985. Seashell Booklet Issue**
22¢ **Frilled dogwinkle, black & brown** tagged | .35 | .20 ☐☐☐☐☐

816, 816A 817 818 819 820-822

823 824, 824A 825, 825A 826 827, 827A

	MNHFVF	UseFVF	
833 ______________			
22¢ **Reticulated helmet, black & multicolored** tagged	.35	.20	❑❑❑❑❑
834 ______________			
22¢ **New England neptune, black & brown,** tagged	.35	.20	❑❑❑❑❑
835 ______________			
22¢ **Calico scallop, black & purple** tagged	.35	.20	❑❑❑❑❑
836 ______________			
22¢ **Lightning whelk, multicolored,** tagged	.35	.20	❑❑❑❑❑
NOTE: Mis-registered tagging is common on this issue.			
837 ______________ **1985. Oil Wagon Issue**			
10.1¢ **blue** tagged	.25	.20	❑❑❑❑❑
838 ______________ **1985. Pushcart Issue**			
12.5¢ **olive** tagged	.25	.20	❑❑❑❑❑
839 ______________ **1985. John J. Audubon Issue**			
22¢ **blue** tagged (small block) perforated 11	.40	.20	❑❑❑❑❑
839A ______________			
22¢ **blue** tagged (large block) perforated 11 1/4	.40	.20	❑❑❑❑❑
840 ______________ **1985. Express Mail Issue**			
$10.75 **multicolored** Type I	15.00	9.00	❑❑❑❑❑
NOTE: Type I: overall dull appearance, "$10.75" appears grainy. Type II: more intense colors, "$10.75" smoother, much less grainy.			
841 ______________ **1985. Tricycle Issue**			
6¢ **brown** tagged	.25	.20	❑❑❑❑❑
842 ______________ **1985. Sylvanus Thayer Issue**			
9¢ **green** tagged (small block)	.25	.20	❑❑❑❑❑
843 ______________ **1985. School Bus Issue**			
3.4¢ **green** tagged	.20	.20	❑❑❑❑❑
844 ______________ **1985. Stutz Bearcat Issue**			
11¢ **green** tagged	.25	.20	❑❑❑❑❑
845 ______________ **1985. Ambulance Issue**			
8.3¢ **green** Type I, tagged	.20	.20	❑❑❑❑❑
845A ______________			
8.3¢ **green** Type II, untagged (Bureau precancel: "Blk. Rt./CAR-RT/SORT")	.20	.20	❑❑❑❑❑
NOTE: Type I: "Ambulance 1860s" is 18 1/2mm long. Type II: "Ambulance 1860s" is 18mm long.			
846 ______________ **1985. Buckboard Issue**			
4.9¢ **brown** tagged	.25	.20	❑❑❑❑❑
847 ______________ **1985. Henry Knox Issue**			
8¢ **olive** overall tagged	.25	.20	❑❑❑❑❑
848 ______________ **1985. Walter Lippmann Issue**			
6¢ **orange** tagged (large block)	.25	.20	❑❑❑❑❑
849 ______________ **1985. Envelope Stamp Issue**			
21.1¢ **multicolored** tagged	.35	.20	❑❑❑❑❑
NOTE: Some precanceled stamps are known with light tagging.			
850 ______________ **1985. Contemporary Christmas Issue**			
22¢ **multicolored** tagged	.35	.20	❑❑❑❑❑
851 ______________ **1985. Traditional Christmas Issue**			
22¢ **multicolored** tagged	.35	.20	❑❑❑❑❑
852 ______________ **1985. George Washington & Monument Issue**			
18¢ **multicolored** tagged	.35	.20	❑❑❑❑❑
NOTE: Some precanceled stamps are known with light tagging.			
853 ______________ **1986. Jack London Issue**			
25¢ **blue** tagged (large block) perforated 11	.45	.20	❑❑❑❑❑
NOTE: For booklet panes of 10 and 6, see Nos. 888-889.			
854 ______________ **1986. Hugo L. Black Issue**			
5¢ **deep olive green** tagged (large block)	.25	.20	❑❑❑❑❑

828, 829, 876

830

831, 831A

832-836

837

838

840

839, 839A

841

842

843

844

845, 845A

846

847 ←

848

849

850

851

852

853, 888, 889

		MNHFVF	UseFVF	
855 ________	**1986. William Jennings Bryan Issue**			
	$2 **purple** tagged (large block)	3.25	.75	❑❑❑❑❑
856 ________	**1986. Belva Ann Lockwood Issue**			
	17¢ **blue green** tagged (large block)	.35	.20	❑❑❑❑❑
857 ________	**1986. Margaret Mitchell Issue**			
	1¢ **brown** tagged (large block)	.25	.20	❑❑❑❑❑
858 ________	**1986. Father Flanagan Issue**			
	4¢ **purple** tagged (large block)	.25	.20	❑❑❑❑❑
859 ________	**1986. Dog Sled Issue**			
	17¢ **blue** tagged	.30	.20	❑❑❑❑❑
860 ________	**1986. John Harvard Issue**			
	56¢ **crimson** tagged (large block)	1.10	.20	❑❑❑❑❑
861 ________	**1986. Paul Dudley White Issue**			
	3¢ **blue** tagged (large block), matte gum	.25	.20	❑❑❑❑❑
862 ________	**1986. Bernard Revel Issue**			
	$1 **blue** tagged (large block)	2.00	.25	❑❑❑❑❑
863 ________	**1986. Christmas Issue**			
	22¢ **multicolored** tagged	.50	.20	❑❑❑❑❑
864 ________				
	22¢ **multicolored** tagged	.50	.20	❑❑❑❑❑
865 ________	**1986. Star Route Truck Issue**			
	5.5¢ **maroon** tagged	.25	.20	❑❑❑❑❑
866 ________	**1986. Bread Wagon Issue**			
	25¢ **orange brown** tagged, plates 2, 3, 4	.40	.20	❑❑❑❑❑
867 ________	**1986. Omnibus Issue**			
	1¢ **violet** tagged	.25	.20	❑❑❑❑❑
NOTE: For similar design with "USA 1¢" see No. 806.				
868 ________	**1986. Stagecoach Issue**			
	4¢ **red brown** block tagged	.25	.20	❑❑❑❑❑
869 ________	**1987. Tow Truck Issue**			
	8.5¢ **dark gray** tagged	.50	.20	❑❑❑❑❑
870 ________	**1987. Tractor Issue**			
	7.1¢ **dark red** tagged	.25	.20	❑❑❑❑❑
871 ________	**1987. Julia Ward Howe Issue**			
	14¢ **red** tagged (large block)	.25	.20	❑❑❑❑❑
872 ________	**1987. Mary Lyon Issue**			
	2¢ **blue** tagged (large block)	.25	.20	❑❑❑❑❑
873 ________	**1987. Locomotive Issue**			
	2¢ **black** tagged	.25	.20	❑❑❑❑❑
NOTE: For similar design with "USA 2¢" see No. 790.				
874 ________	**1987. Canal Boat Issue**			
	10¢ **sky blue** block tagged matte gum	.25	.20	❑❑❑❑❑
875 ________	**1987. Flag With Fireworks Issue**			
	22¢ **multicolored** tagged	.35	.20	❑❑❑❑❑
876 ________	**1987. Flag Over Capitol Coil Issue**			
	22¢ **black, blue, & red** with "T" at bottom	.40	.20	❑❑❑❑❑
877 ________	**1987. Red Cloud Issue**			
	10¢ **carmine red** tagged (large block)	.25	.20	❑❑❑❑❑
878 ________	**1987. Bret Harte Issue**			
	$5 **Venetian red** tagged (large block)	8.00	2.00	❑❑❑❑❑
879 ________	**1987. Milk Wagon Issue**			
	5¢ **charcoal** tagged	.25	.20	❑❑❑❑❑
880 ________	**1987. Racing Car Issue**			
	17.5¢ **blue violet** tagged	.30	.20	❑❑❑❑❑

MNHFVF	UseFVF	

881 _____ **1987. Christmas Issue**
22¢ **multicolored** tagged .50 .20 ☐☐☐☐☐
882 _____
22¢ **multicolored** tagged .50 .20 ☐☐☐☐☐
883 _____ **1988. Conestoga Wagon Coil Issue**
3¢ **dark lilac purple** tagged .25 .20 ☐☐☐☐☐
884 _____ **1988. Non-Denominated "E" Issue**
28¢ **multicolored** tagged .50 .20 ☐☐☐☐☐
885 _____ **1988. Non-Denominated "E" Coil Issue**
25¢ **multicolored** tagged .50 .20 ☐☐☐☐☐

854

855

856

857

858

859

860

861

862

863

864

865

866

867

868

869

870

871

872

873

874

875

877

878

879

		MNHFVF	UseFVF	
886 ______________	**1988. Non-Denominated "E" Booklet Issue**			
	25¢ **multicolored** tagged	.50	.20	❑❑❑❑❑
887 ______________	**1988. Pheasant Booklet Issue**			
	25¢ **multicolored** tagged	.50	.20	❑❑❑❑❑
NOTE: Fully imperforate panes were cut from printer's waste.				
888 ______________	**1988. Jack London Booklet Issue**			
	25¢ **blue** tagged (large block) perforated 11	.45	.20	❑❑❑❑❑
889 ______________				
	25¢ **blue** tagged, perforated 10	.50	.20	❑❑❑❑❑
890 ______________	**1988. Flags With Clouds Issue**			
	25¢ **multicolored** tagged	.35	.20	❑❑❑❑❑
890A ______________	**1988. Flags With Clouds Booklet Issue**			
	25¢ **multicolored** tagged	.50	.20	❑❑❑❑❑
891 ______________	**1988. Flag Over Yosemite Issue**			
	25¢ **multicolored** tagged	.40	.20	❑❑❑❑❑
892 ______________	**1988. Owl and Grosbeak Issue**			
	25¢ **multicolored** tagged	.40	.20	❑❑❑❑❑
893 ______________				
	25¢ **multicolored** tagged	.40	.20	❑❑❑❑❑
894 ______________	**1988. Buffalo Bill Cody Issue**			
	15¢ **maroon** tagged (large block)	.30	.20	❑❑❑❑❑
895 ______________	**1988. Harvey Cushing Issue**			
	45¢ **blue** tagged (large block)	1.00	.20	❑❑❑❑❑
NOTE: Nos. 896 and 897 are not assigned.				
898 ______________	**1988. Popcorn Wagon Issue**			
	16.7¢ **dark rose** (Bureau-printed service indicator "Bulk Rate")	.35	.20	❑❑❑❑❑
899 ______________	**1988. Tugboat Issue**			
	15¢ **purple** block tagged	.30	.20	❑❑❑❑❑
900 ______________	**1988. Coal Car Issue**			
	13.2¢ **dark green** (Bureau-printed red service indicator "Bulk Rate")	.30	.20	❑❑❑❑❑
901 ______________	**1988. Wheel Chair Issue**			
	8.4¢ **dark violet** (Bureau-printed red service indicator: "Non-profit")	.30	.20	❑❑❑❑❑
902 ______________	**1988. Railroad Mail Car Issue**			
	21¢ **green** (Bureau-printed red service indicator "Presorted 1st Class")	.35	.20	❑❑❑❑❑
903 ______________	**1988. Carreta Issue**			
	7.6¢ **brown** Bureau-printed red service indicator: "Nonprofit"	.25	.20	❑❑❑❑❑
904 ______________	**1988. Harry S. Truman Issue**			
	20¢ **black** tagged (large block), matte gum	.35	.20	❑❑❑❑❑
NOTE: (See also No. 811)				
905 ______________	**1988. Honeybee Issue**			
	25¢ **multicolored** tagged	.40	.20	❑❑❑❑❑
906 ______________	**1988. Elevator Issue**			
	5.3¢ **black** (Bureau-printed red service indicator: "Nonprofit/Carrier Route Sort")	.25	.20	❑❑❑❑❑
907 ______________	**1988. Fire Engine Issue**			
	20.5¢ **red** (Bureau-printed black service indicator: "ZIP+4 Presort")	.35	.20	❑❑❑❑❑
908 ______________	**1988. Eagle and Moon Issue**			
	$8.75 **multicolored** tagged	25.00	8.00	❑❑❑❑❑
909 ______________	**1988. Christmas Issue**			
	25¢ **multicolored,** tagged	.40	.20	❑❑❑❑❑
910 ______________	**1988. Madonna And Child by Botticelli Issue**			
	25¢ **multicolored** tagged	.40	.20	❑❑❑❑❑
911 ______________	**1988. Chester Carlson Issue**			
	21¢ **blue violet** tagged (large block)	.35	.20	❑❑❑❑❑

		MNHFVF	UseFVF
912 ______________	**1988. Tandem Bicycle Issue**		
	24.1¢ **deep blue violet** (Bureau-printed red service indicator: "ZIP+4")	.40	.20 ❑❑❑❑❑
913 ______________	**1988. Cable Car Issue**		
	20¢ **dark violet,** block tagged	.35	.20 ❑❑❑❑❑
914 ______________	**1988. Police Patrol Wagon Issue**		
	13¢ **black** (Bureau-printed red service indicator: "Presorted First Class")	.30	.20 ❑❑❑❑❑

880

881

882

883

884-886

887

890, 890A

891

892

893

894

895

898

899

900

901

902

903

905

906

907

908

909

910

MNHFVF	UseFVF

915 _____ **1988. Mary Cassatt Issue**
　23¢　**purple** tagged (large block) · · · · · · · · · · .45 · · · .20 ☐☐☐☐☐
916 _____ **1988. H.H. "Hap" Arnold Issue**
　65¢　**dark blue** tagged (large block) · · · · · · · 1.25 · · · .20 ☐☐☐☐☐
NOTE: No. 917 is not assigned.
918 _____ **1989. Johns Hopkins Issue**
　$1　**blackish blue** tagged (large block) matte gum · · · 2.00 · · · .30 ☐☐☐☐☐
919 _____ **1989. Sitting Bull Issue**
　28¢　**green** tagged (large block) · · · · · · · · · .50 · · · .20 ☐☐☐☐☐
920 _____ **1989. Sleigh with Gifts Issue**
　25¢　**multicolored** tagged · · · · · · · · · · · .40 · · · .20 ☐☐☐☐☐
921 _____ **1989. Sleigh with Gifts Booklet Issue**
　25¢　**multicolored** booklet stamp, tagged · · · · · .40 · · · .20 ☐☐☐☐☐
922 _____ **1989. The Dream of St. Alexandria Issue**
　25¢　**multicolored** tagged · · · · · · · · · · · .40 · · · .20 ☐☐☐☐☐
NOTE: No. 923 is not assigned.
924 _____ **1989. Eagle and Shield Self-Adhesive Issue**
　25¢　**multicolored** tagged · · · · · · · · · · · .40 · · · .20 ☐☐☐☐☐
NOTE: No. 925 is not assigned.
926 _____ **1990. Beach Umbrella Issue**
　15¢　**multicolored** booklet stamp, tagged · · · · · .30 · · · .20 ☐☐☐☐☐
927 _____ **1990. Luis Muñoz Marin Issue**
　5¢　**dark rose,** overall tagged · · · · · · · · · .25 · · · .20 ☐☐☐☐☐
928 _____ **1990. Seaplane Issue**
　$1　**dark blue & red** overall tagged, matte gum · · · 1.75 · · · .50 ☐☐☐☐☐
929 _____ **1990. Flag Issue for Automatic Teller Machines**
　25¢　**red & dark blue** tagged · · · · · · · · · · .50 · · · .50 ☐☐☐☐☐
930 _____ **1990. Bobcat Issue**
　$2　**multicolored** tagged · · · · · · · · · · · 4.00 · · 1.25 ☐☐☐☐☐
931 _____ **1990. Circus Wagon Issue**
　5¢　**carmine red** tagged · · · · · · · · · · · .25 · · · .20 ☐☐☐☐☐
NOTE: For stamps of this design inscribed "USA 5¢" see No. 1007 (gravure) or No. 1077 (intaglio).
932 _____ **1990. Claire Lee Chennault Issue**
　40¢　**dark blue** overall tagged, matte gum · · · · · .75 · · · .20 ☐☐☐☐☐
NOTE: Perforated 11
933 _____ **1990. Contemporary Christmas Issue**
　25¢　**multicolored** tagged · · · · · · · · · · · .40 · · · .20 ☐☐☐☐☐
NOTE: Perforated 11 1/2 x 11
934 _____
　25¢　**multicolored** booklet stamp, tagged · · · · · .40 · · · .20 ☐☐☐☐☐
935 _____ **1990. Madonna and Child Issue**
　25¢　**multicolored** tagged · · · · · · · · · · · .40 · · · .20 ☐☐☐☐☐
936 _____
　25¢　**multicolored** booklet stamp, tagged · · · · · .40 · · · .20 ☐☐☐☐☐
NOTE: The booklet version has a much heavier shading in the Madonna's veil where it meets the right frame line.
937 _____ **1991. "F" (Flower) Non-Denominated Issue**
　29¢　**multicolored** tagged · · · · · · · · · · · .50 · · · .20 ☐☐☐☐☐
938 _____ **1991. "F" (Flower) Non-Denominated Booklet Issue**
　29¢　**multicolored** booklet stamp, tagged · · · · · .50 · · · .20 ☐☐☐☐☐
939 _____ **1991. "F" (Flower) Non-Denominated Booklet Issue**
　29¢　**multicolored** booklet stamp, printed by KCS Industries, tagged · · .50 · · · .20 ☐☐☐☐☐
940 _____ **1991. "F" (Flower) Non-Denominated Coil Issue**
　29¢　**multicolored** tagged · · · · · · · · · · · .60 · · · .20 ☐☐☐☐☐
941 _____ **1991. Non-Denominated 4¢ Make Up Issue**
　4¢　**bister & carmine** · · · · · · · · · · · · .25 · · · .20 ☐☐☐☐☐

MNHFVF	UseFVF	

942 _____ **1991. "F" Non-Denominated ATM Flag Issue**
 29¢ **black, dark blue & red** tagged .50 .20 ☐☐☐☐☐
943 _____ **1991. Steam Carriage Issue**
 4¢ **maroon** tagged .25 .20 ☐☐☐☐☐
944 _____ **1991. Fawn Issue**
 19¢ **multicolored** tagged .35 .20 ☐☐☐☐☐

911

912

913

914

915

916

918

919

920, 921

922

924

926

927

928

929

930

931

932

933, 934

935, 936

937-940

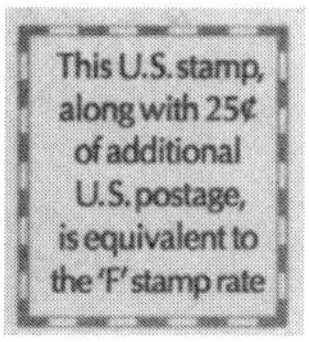

941

942

943

944

		MNHFVF	UseFVF	
945 ______________	**1991. Flag Over Mount Rushmore**			
	29¢ **red, blue, & maroon** tagged	.50	.20	❑❑❑❑❑
945A ______________				
	29¢ **red, blue & brown** color change "Toledo brown" (error), tagged	5.00	—	❑❑❑❑❑

NOTE: For gravure version of this design, see No. 963.

946 ______________	**1991. Dennis Chavez Issue**			
	35¢ **black** phosphored paper, mottled tagging	.75	.20	❑❑❑❑❑
947 ______________	**1991. Flower Issue**			
	29¢ **multicolored** tagged, perforated 11	.40	.20	❑❑❑❑❑
947A ______________	**1991. Flower Issue**			
	29¢ **multicolored** tagged, perforated 12 1/2 x 13	.40	.20	❑❑❑❑❑
948 ______________	**1991. Flower Booklet Issue**			
	29¢ **multicolored** booklet stamp, tagged, perforated 11	.40	.20	❑❑❑❑❑

NOTE: For coil version of the Flower Issue, see Nos. 966 and 982.

949 ______________	**1991. Lunch Wagon Issue**			
	23¢ **blue** tagged, matte gum	.50	.20	❑❑❑❑❑
950 ______________	**1991. Wood Duck Issue**			
	29¢ **multicolored** booklet stamp, black inscription (B.E.P.), tagged	.75	.20	❑❑❑❑❑
951 ______________	**1991. Wood Duck Issue**			
	29¢ **multicolored** booklet stamp, red inscription (KCS Industries), tagged	1.00	.20	❑❑❑❑❑
952 ______________	**1991. U.S. Flag with Olympic Rings Issue**			
	29¢ **multicolored** booklet stamp, tagged	.75	.20	❑❑❑❑❑
953 ______________	**1991. Hot Air Balloon Issue**			
	19¢ **multicolored** booklet stamp, tagged	.30	.20	❑❑❑❑❑
954 ______________	**1991. Tractor Trailer Issue**			
	10¢ **green** (Bureau-printed gray service indicator: "Additional Presort Postage Paid")	.25	.20	❑❑❑❑❑

NOTE: For version with service indicator in black, see No. 1042.

955 ______________	**1991. Canoe Issue**			
	5¢ **brown** (printed gray service indicator: "Additional Nonprofit Postage Paid")	.25	.20	❑❑❑❑❑

NOTE: For gravure version of No. 955 in red, see No. 979.

956 ______________	**1991. Flags on Parade Issue**			
	29¢ **multicolored** tagged	.50	.20	❑❑❑❑❑
957 ______________	**1991. Hubert H. Humphrey Issue**			
	52¢ **purple** phosphored paper (solid tagging) matte gum	1.50	.20	❑❑❑❑❑
958 ______________	**1991. Eagle and Olympic Rings Issue**			
	$9.95 **multicolored** tagged	15.00	7.50	❑❑❑❑❑
959 ______________	**1991. American Kestrel Issue**			
	1¢ **multicolored**	.25	.20	❑❑❑❑❑

NOTE: For versions inscribed "USA 1¢", see No. 1079 (sheet) and No. 1115 (Coil).

960 ______________	**1991. Bluebird Issue**			
	3¢ **Eastern bluebird**	.25	.20	❑❑❑❑❑

NOTE: For version inscribed "USA 3¢" see No. 1123.

961 ______________	**1991. Cardinal Issue**			
	30¢ **multicolored** on phosphored paper	.45	.20	❑❑❑❑❑
962 ______________	**1991. Statue of Liberty Torch Issue**			
	29¢ **black, gold & green** tagged, die cut	.60	.30	❑❑❑❑❑
963 ______________	**1991. Flag Over Mount Rushmore Coil Issue**			
	29¢ **blue, red & brown** tagged	.50	.25	❑❑❑❑❑

NOTE: For intaglio version of the same design, see No. 945.

964 ______________	**1991. Eagle and Olympic Rings Issue**			
	$2.90 **multicolored** tagged	5.00	2.75	❑❑❑❑❑
965 ______________	**1991. Fishing Boat Coil Issue**			
	19¢ **multicolored** Type I, tagged	.40	.20	❑❑❑❑❑

NOTE: Imperforates in this design came from printer's waste. For version with one loop of rope tying boat to piling, see No. 1044.

945, 945A

946

947, 947A, 948, 962

949

950, 951

952

953

954

955

956

957

958

959

960

961

962

963

964

965

966

967

969

971, 972, 972A

973

970

MNHFVF	UseFVF

966 _____ **1991. Flower Coil Issue**
29¢ **multicolored** tagged · .75 · .20 ☐☐☐☐☐
967 _____ **1991. Eagle Over Coastline, Olympic Rings Issue**
$14 **multicolored** tagged · 30.00 · 17.50 ☐☐☐☐☐
NOTE: No. 968 is not assigned.
969 _____ **1991. U.S. Flag Issue**
23¢ **red & blue** printed service indicator: "Presorted First Class" · .65 · .20 ☐☐☐☐☐
970 _____ **1991. USPS Olympic Sponsor Issue**
$1 **multicolored** tagged · 2.75 · .75 ☐☐☐☐☐
971 _____ **1991. Santa Descending a Chimney Issue**
29¢ **multicolored** tagged · .45 · .20 ☐☐☐☐☐
972 _____ **1991. Santa Booklet Issue**
29¢ **multicolored** booklet stamp, Type I, tagged · .45 · .20 ☐☐☐☐☐
972A _____
29¢ **multicolored** booklet stamp, Type II, tagged · .45 · .20 ☐☐☐☐☐
NOTE: Type I has an extra vertical line of brick in the top row of bricks at left; Type II is missing that vertical line of brick.
973 _____
29¢ **multicolored** booklet stamp, tagged · .45 · .20 ☐☐☐☐☐
974 _____
29¢ **multicolored** booklet stamp, tagged · .45 · .20 ☐☐☐☐☐
975 _____
29¢ **multicolored** booklet stamp, tagged · .45 · .20 ☐☐☐☐☐
976 _____
29¢ **multicolored** booklet stamp, tagged · .45 · .20 ☐☐☐☐☐
977 _____ **1991. Traditional Christmas Issue**
29¢ **multicolored** tagged · .45 · .20 ☐☐☐☐☐
NOTE: No. 978 is not assigned.
979 _____ **1991. Canoe Issue**
5¢ **red** (printed service indicator: "Additional Nonprofit Postage Paid") · .25 · .20 ☐☐☐☐☐
NOTE: For intaglio version in brown, see No. 955.
980 _____ **1991. Eagle and Shield Non-Denominated Issue**
10¢ **multicolored** (printed service indicator: "Bulk Rate") · .25 · .20 ☐☐☐☐☐
NOTE: See Nos. 1011 and 1012 for similar stamps printed by the Bureau of Engraving and Printing and Stamp Venturers.
981 _____ **1992. Wendell L. Willkie Issue**
75¢ **maroon** phosphored paper (solid tagging) matte gum · 1.25 · .50 ☐☐☐☐☐
982 _____ **1992. Flower Perforated Coil Issue**
29¢ **multicolored** tagged · .75 · .20 ☐☐☐☐☐
983 _____ **1992. Earl Warren Issue**
29¢ **blue** phosphored paper (mottled tagging) · .50 · .20 ☐☐☐☐☐
984 _____ **1992. Flag Over White House Issue**
29¢ **blue & red** tagged, phosphored paper · .50 · .20 ☐☐☐☐☐
985 _____ **1992. USA Issue**
23¢ **multicolored** (printed service indicator: "Presorted First-Class") · .50 · .20 ☐☐☐☐☐
NOTE: See Nos. 994 and 1010 for similar stamps printed by the Bureau of Engraving and Printing and by Stamp Venturers.
986 _____ **1992. ECA GARD Variable Denominated Issue**
red & blue variable rate, denomination (.01 to 9.99) printed in black, phosphored paper (solid tagging) matte gum · 1.50 · .50 ☐☐☐☐☐
NOTE: For narrow, tall format, see No. 1040.
987 _____ **1992. Pledge of Allegiance Issue**
29¢ **multicolored** black inscription, booklet stamp, tagged · .75 · .20 ☐☐☐☐☐
NOTE: For version with red inscription see No. 1008.
988 _____ **1992. Eagle and Shield Self-Adhesive Issue**
29¢ **multicolored** red inscription, tagged · .45 · .30 ☐☐☐☐☐
NOTE: No. 989 is not assigned.

	MNHFVF	UseFVF	
990 ______________			
29¢ **multicolored** green inscription, tagged	.45	.30	❑❑❑❑❑

NOTE: No. 991 is not assigned.

992 ______________			
29¢ **multicolored** brown inscription, tagged	.45	.30	❑❑❑❑❑

NOTE: No. 993 is not assigned.

994 ______________ **1992. "USA" Issue**

23¢ **multicolored** printed service indicator: "Presorted First-Class," shiny gum	.50	.20	❑❑❑❑❑

NOTE: In this version, "23" is 7mm long. See Nos. 985 and 1010 for versions printed by the American Bank Note Co. or by Stamp Venturers.

995 ______________ **1992. Contemporary Christmas Issue**

29¢ **Locomotive multicolored,** tagged	.45	.20	❑❑❑❑❑
996 ______________			
29¢ **Pony & rider multicolored,** tagged	.45	.20	❑❑❑❑❑
997 ______________			
29¢ **Fire engine multicolored,** tagged	.45	.20	❑❑❑❑❑

974

975

976

977

979

980

981

982

983

984

985

986

987, 1008

988, 990, 992

994

995, 999, 1005 (upper left)
996, 1000 (upper right)
997, 1001 (lower left)
998, 1002 (lower right)

1003

1005

		MNHFVF	UseFVF	
998 ____________				
	29¢ **Steamship multicolored,** tagged	.45	.20	❑❑❑❑❑
999 ____________	**1992. Contemporary Booklet Issue**			
	29¢ **Locomotive multicolored,** booklet single	.45	.20	❑❑❑❑❑
1000 ____________				
	29¢ **Pony & rider multicolored,** booklet single	.45	.20	❑❑❑❑❑
1001 ____________				
	29¢ **Fire engine multicolored,** booklet single	.45	.20	❑❑❑❑❑
1002 ____________				
	29¢ **Steamship multicolored,** booklet single	.45	.20	❑❑❑❑❑
1003 ____________	**1992. Traditional Christmas Issue**			
	29¢ **multicolored** tagged	.45	.20	❑❑❑❑❑
NOTE: No. 1004 is not assigned.				
1005 ____________	**1992. Contemporary Christmas Self-Adhesive ATM Issue**			
	29¢ **multicolored** tagged	.75	.20	❑❑❑❑❑
1006 ____________	**1992. Pumpkinseed Sunfish Issue**			
	45¢ **multicolored** tagged	1.00	.20	❑❑❑❑❑
1007 ____________	**1992. Circus Wagon Issue**			
	5¢ **red** untagged	.25	.20	❑❑❑❑❑
NOTE: For intaglio stamps of this design see No. 931 ("05 USA") and No. 1077 ("USA 5¢").				
1008 ____________	**1993. Pledge of Allegiance Issue**			
	29¢ **multicolored** red inscription, tagged	.75	.20	❑❑❑❑❑
NOTE: For similar stamp with black inscription see No. 987.				
1009 ____________	**1993. Thomas Jefferson Issue**			
	29¢ **indigo** phosphored paper (solid tagging)	.50	.30	❑❑❑❑❑
1010 ____________	**1993. USA Issue**			
	23¢ **multicolored** printed service indicator: "Presorted First-Class"	.75	.20	❑❑❑❑❑
NOTE: In this version, "23" is 8-1/2mm long. See No. 985 and No. 994 for versions printed by the American Bank Note Co. and by the Bureau of Engraving and Printing.				
1011 ____________	**1993. Eagle and Shield Non-Denominated Issue**			
	(10¢) **multicolored** (B.E.P.)	.30	.20	❑❑❑❑❑
1012 ____________				
	(10¢) **multicolored** (Stamp Venturers)	.30	.20	❑❑❑❑❑
NOTE: See No. 980 for similar design printed by the American Bank Note Co.				
1013 ____________	**1993. Futuristic Space Shuttle Issue**			
	$2.90 **multicolored**	6.50	2.50	❑❑❑❑❑
1014 ____________	**1993. Red Squirrel Issue**			
	29¢ **multicolored** from booklet or coil, tagged	.50	.20	❑❑❑❑❑
NOTE: No. 1015 is not assigned.				
1016 ____________	**1993. Rose Issue**			
	29¢ **multicolored** from booklet or coil, tagged	.50	.20	❑❑❑❑❑
NOTE: No. 1017 is not assigned.				
1018 ____________	**1993. African Violet Booklet Issue**			
	29¢ **multicolored** from booklet, tagged	.75	.20	❑❑❑❑❑
1019 ____________	**1993. Contemporary Christmas Issue**			
	29¢ **Jack-in-the-box,** tagged	.50	.20	❑❑❑❑❑
1020 ____________				
	29¢ **Reindeer,** tagged	.50	.20	❑❑❑❑❑
1021 ____________				
	29¢ **Snowman,** tagged	.50	.20	❑❑❑❑❑
1022 ____________				
	29¢ **Toy soldier,** tagged	.50	.20	❑❑❑❑❑
1023 ____________				
	29¢ **Jack-in-the-box,** tagged	.50	.20	❑❑❑❑❑

		MNHFVF	UseFVF	
1024				
	29¢ **Reindeer,** tagged	.50	.20	❑❑❑❑❑
1025				
	29¢ **Snowman,** tagged	.50	.20	❑❑❑❑❑
1026				
	29¢ **Toy soldier,** tagged	.50	.20	❑❑❑❑❑
1027	**1993. Traditional Christmas Issue**			
	29¢ **multicolored** tagged	.50	.20	❑❑❑❑❑
1028				
	29¢ **multicolored** booklet single, tagged	.50	.20	❑❑❑❑❑
1029	**1993. Contemporary Christmas Self-adhesive Issue**			
	29¢ **Jack-in-the-box,** tagged	.50	.20	❑❑❑❑❑
1030				
	29¢ **Reindeer,** tagged	.50	.20	❑❑❑❑❑
1031				
	29¢ **Snowman,** tagged	.50	.20	❑❑❑❑❑
1032				
	29¢ **Toy soldier,** tagged	.50	.20	❑❑❑❑❑

NOTE: Nos. 1033-1036 are not assigned.

1006

1009

1011, 1012

1013

1014

1016

1019, 1023, 1029 (upper left)
1020, 1024, 1030 (upper right)
1021, 1025, 1031 (lower left)
1022, 1026, 1032 (lower right)

1018

1027, 1028

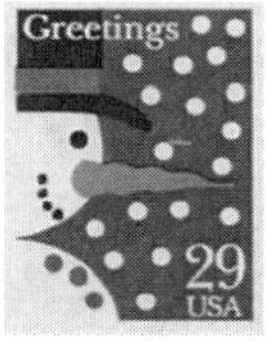

1037

1038

1039

1040

1041

1042

MNHFVF UseFVF

1037 ____________ **1993. Snowman ATM Pane Issue**

29¢ **multicolored,** tagged .75 .25 ☐☐☐☐☐

NOTE: Although the placement is different, the Snowmen depicted on Nos. 1021 and 1031 have three buttons and seven snowflakes beneath the nose. No. 1025 has two buttons and five snowflakes beneath the nose.

1038 ____________ **1993. Pine Cone Issue**

29¢ **multicolored** from booklet or coil, tagged .50 .20 ☐☐☐☐☐

1039 ____________ **1994. Eagle Issue**

29¢ **red, cream & blue** from booklet or coil, tagged .50 .20 ☐☐☐☐☐

1040 ____________ **1994. Postage and Mail Center (PMC) Issue**

(variable rate) red and blue, denomination 20¢-$99.99 printed in black, phosphored paper 1.50 .50 ☐☐☐☐☐

1041 ____________ **1994. Surrender of Burgoyne at Saratoga Issue**

$1 **dark blue** tagged 2.00 .75 ☐☐☐☐☐

1042 ____________ **1994. Tractor Trailer Issue**

10¢ **green** Bureau-printed service indicator (in gray): "Additional Presort Postage Paid" .25 .20 ☐☐☐☐☐

1043 ____________ **1994. Statue of Liberty Issue**

29¢ **multicolored** from booklet or coil, tagged .50 .20 ☐☐☐☐☐

1044 ____________ **1994. Fishing Boat Issue**

19¢ **multicolored** tagged .50 .20 ☐☐☐☐☐

1045 ____________ **1994. Moon Landing Issue**

$9.95 **multicolored** tagged 25.00 10.00 ☐☐☐☐☐

1046 ____________ **1994. Washington and Jackson Issue**

$5 **dark green** tagged 10.00 3.75 ☐☐☐☐☐

1047 ____________ **1994. Contemporary Christmas Issue**

29¢ **multicolored** from sheet or booklet, tagged .50 .20 ☐☐☐☐☐

1048 ____________ **1994. Traditional Christmas Issue**

29¢ **multicolored** shiny gum, tagged .50 .20 ☐☐☐☐☐

1049 ____________

29¢ **multicolored** from booklet, tagged .50 .20 ☐☐☐☐☐

1050 ____________ **1994. Contemporary Santa Claus Booklet Issue**

29¢ **multicolored** from booklet or coil, tagged .50 .20 ☐☐☐☐☐

1051 ____________ **1994. Cardinal in Snow ATM Issue**

29¢ **multicolored** tagged .50 .20 ☐☐☐☐☐

1052 ____________ **1994. Virginia Apgar Issue**

20¢ **brown** phosphored paper grainy tagging .50 .20 ☐☐☐☐☐

1053 ____________ **1994. Postage and Mail Center (PMC) Issue**

(variable rate) red & blue, denomination (.01-9.99) printed in black, phosphored paper (mottled tagging), shiny gum .75 .50 ☐☐☐☐☐

1054 ____________ **1994. Black "G" Sheet Issue**

(32¢) **red, blue, gray & black** tagged .50 .20 ☐☐☐☐☐

1055 ____________ **1994. Red "G" Sheet Issue**

(32¢) **red, blue, gray & black** tagged .75 .20 ☐☐☐☐☐

1056 ____________ **1994. Black "G" Booklet Issue**

(32¢) **red, blue, gray & black** tagged .50 .20 ☐☐☐☐☐

1057 ____________ **1994. Blue "G" Booklet Issue**

(32¢) **red, blue, gray & black** tagged .50 .20 ☐☐☐☐☐

1058 ____________ **1994. Red "G" Booklet Issue**

(32¢) **red, blue, gray & black** tagged .50 .20 ☐☐☐☐☐

1059 ____________ **1994. Black "G" Coil Issue**

(32¢) **red, blue, gray & black** tagged .50 .20 ☐☐☐☐☐

1060 ____________ **1994. Blue "G" Coil Issue**

(32¢) **red, blue, gray & black** tagged .50 .20 ☐☐☐☐☐

1061 ____________ **1994. Red "G" Coil Issue**

(32¢) **red, blue, gray & black** tagged .50 .20 ☐☐☐☐☐

		MNHFVF	UseFVF	
1061A ____________	**1994. Red "G" Coil Issue**			
	(32¢) **red, blue, gray & black** tagged	.50	.20	❑❑❑❑❑
1062 ____________	**1994. "G" Self Adhesive Issue**			
	(32¢) **red, dark blue, light blue, gray & black,** from booklet or coil, tagged	1.00	.35	❑❑❑❑❑
1063 ____________	**1994. "G" Self Adhesive ATM Issue**			
	(32¢) **red, blue & black** tagged	1.00	.35	❑❑❑❑❑
1064 ____________	**1994. "G" First-Class Presort Rate Issue**			
	(25¢) **red, dark blue, gray, black & light blue**	.50	.50	❑❑❑❑❑
1065 ____________	**1994. Black "G" Postcard Rate Issue**			
	(20¢) **red, blue, gray, yellow & black** tagged	.50	.20	❑❑❑❑❑
1066 ____________	**1994. Red "G" Postcard Rate Issue**			
	(20¢) **red, blue, gray, yellow & black,** tagged	.50	.20	❑❑❑❑❑
1067 ____________	**1994. Non-Denominated "Make-Up " Rate Issue**			
	(3¢) **red, bright blue & tan**	.20	.20	❑❑❑❑❑
1068 ____________	**1994. Non-Denominated "Make-Up" Rate**			
	(3¢) **red, dark blue & tan**	.20	.20	❑❑❑❑❑
1069 ____________	**1995. "G" Nonprofit Presort Coil Issue**			
	(5¢) **green & multicolored** untagged	.25	.20	❑❑❑❑❑

NOTE: First-day covers received a Dec. 13, 1994 cancellation although these stamps were not yet available on that date.

1043

1044

1045

1046

1047

1048, 1049

1050

1051

1052

1053

1054-1063

1064

1065, 1066

1067, 1068

1069

1070

		MNHFVF	UseFVF	
1070 ____________	**1995. Butte and "Nonprofit Organization" Issue**			
	(5¢) **yellow, blue & red** untagged	.25	.20	❑❑❑❑❑
1071 ____________	**1995. Car Hood and "Bulk Rate" Issue**			
	(10¢) **black, brown & red brown** untagged	.30	.20	❑❑❑❑❑
1072 ____________	**1995. Tail Fin Presorted First-Class Coil Issue**			
	(15¢) **yellow orange & multicolored** untagged	.40	.30	❑❑❑❑❑
1073 ____________	**1995. Tail Fin Presorted First-Class Coil Issue**			
	15¢ **buff & multicolored** untagged	.40	.30	❑❑❑❑❑
1074 ____________	**1995. Juke Box Presorted First-Class Coil Issue**			
	25¢ **dark red, yellow green & multicolored,** untagged	.65	.40	❑❑❑❑❑
1075 ____________	**1995. Juke Box "Presorted First Class" Coil Issue**			
	25¢ **orange red, bright yellow green & multicolored** untagged	.65	.40	❑❑❑❑❑
1076 ____________	**1995. Flag Over Field ATM Issue**			
	32¢ **multicolored** tagged	1.00	.30	❑❑❑❑❑
1077 ____________	**1995. Circus Wagon Issue**			
	5¢ **red** untagged	.25	.20	❑❑❑❑❑
NOTE: For intaglio & gravure versions of this design inscribed "05 USA" see Nos. 931 & 1007.				
1078 ____________	**1995. Flag Over Porch Self Adhesive Booklet Issue**			
	32¢ **multicolored** from booklet or coil, phosphored paper, large "1995"	.70	.20	❑❑❑❑❑
1079 ____________	**1995. American Kestrel Issue**			
	1¢ **multicolored** tagged	.25	.20	❑❑❑❑❑
NOTE: For version inscribed "USA 01" see No. 959. For coil see No. 1115.				
1080 ____________	**1995. Flag Over Porch Issue**			
	32¢ **multicolored** tagged	.60	.20	❑❑❑❑❑
1081 ____________	**1995. Flag Over Porch Booklet Issue**			
	32¢ **multicolored** tagged	.80	.20	❑❑❑❑❑
1082 ____________	**1995. Flag Over Porch Coil Issue**			
	32¢ **multicolored** tagged, red "1995"	.50	.20	❑❑❑❑❑
1083 ____________	**1995. Flag Over Porch Coil Issue**			
	32¢ **multicolored** tagged, blue "1995"	.75	.20	❑❑❑❑❑
1084 ____________	**1995. Pink Rose Issue**			
	32¢ **pink, green & black** from booklet or coil, phosphored	.80	.30	❑❑❑❑❑
1085 ____________	**1995. Ferryboat Issue**			
	32¢ **deep blue** phosphored paper	.65	.20	❑❑❑❑❑
1086 ____________	**1995. Cog Railway Issue**			
	20¢ **green** phosphored paper	.40	.20	❑❑❑❑❑
1087 ____________	**1995. Blue Jay Issue**			
	20¢ **multicolored** phosphored paper	.45	.20	❑❑❑❑❑
1088 ____________	**1995. Space Shuttle Challenger Issue**			
	$3 **multicolored** phosphored paper	6.00	3.00	❑❑❑❑❑
1089 ____________	**1995. Peaches and Pear Issue**			
	32¢ **multicolored** phosphored paper	.75	.20	❑❑❑❑❑
1090 ____________				
	32¢ **multicolored** phosphored paper	.75	.20	❑❑❑❑❑
1091 ____________	**1995. Peaches and Pear Self-Adhesive Issue**			
	32¢ **multicolored** phosphored paper	.85	.30	❑❑❑❑❑
1091A ____________	**1995. Peaches and Pear Self-Adhesive Coil Issue**			
	32¢ **multicolored**	.85	.30	❑❑❑❑❑
1092 ____________	**1995. Peaches and Pear Self-Adhesive Issue**			
	32¢ **multicolored** phosphored paper	.85	.30	❑❑❑❑❑
1092A ____________	**1995. Peaches and Pear Self-Adhesive Coil Issue**			
	32¢ **multicolored**	.85	.30	❑❑❑❑❑

		MNHFVF	UseFVF	
1093	**1995. Alice Hamilton Issue**			
	55¢ **green** phosphored paper, grainy tagging	1.10	.20	❑❑❑❑❑
1094	**1995. Space Shuttle Endeavor Issue**			
	$10.75 **multicolored** phosphored paper	21.00	8.00	❑❑❑❑❑
1095	**1995. Alice Paul Issue**			
	78¢ **purple** phosphored paper solid tagging	1.75	.25	❑❑❑❑❑
1096	**1995. Milton S. Hershey Issue**			
	32¢ **chocolate brown** phosphored paper solid tagging	.65	.20	❑❑❑❑❑
1097	**1995. Eddie Rickenbacker Issue**			
	60¢ **multicolored** phosphored paper	.75	.20	❑❑❑❑❑

1071

1072

1073, 1133

1074-75, 1134, 1153

1076

1077

1078, 1080-83

1079

1084

1085

1086

1087, 1135-1136

1088

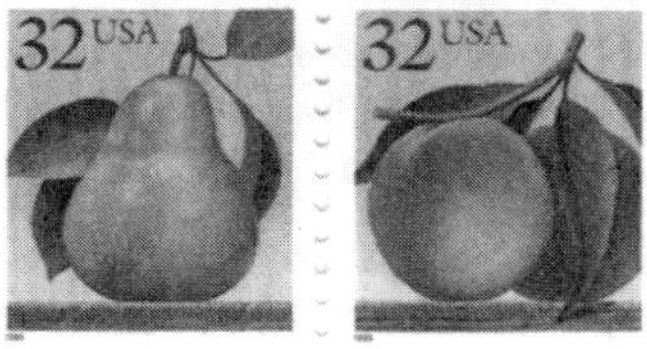

1089, 1091, 1091A (left)
1090, 1092, 1092A (right)

1093

1094

1095

1098, 1102, 1106 (upper left)
1099, 1103, 1107 (upper right)
1100, 1104, 1108 (lower left)
1101, 1105, 1109 (lower right)

1096

1097, 1250

No.	Description	MNHFVF	UseFVF
1098	**1995. Contemporary Christmas Issue**		
	32¢ **Santa on rooftop,** phosphored paper	.60	.20
1099			
	32¢ **Child and jumping jack,** phosphored paper	.60	.20
1100			
	32¢ **Child and tree,** phosphored paper	.60	.20
1101			
	32¢ **Santa in workshop,** phosphored paper	.60	.20
1102	**1995. Contemporary Christmas Coil Issue**		
	32¢ **Santa on rooftop,** phosphored paper	.60	.20
1103			
	32¢ **Child and Jumping Jack,** phosphored paper	.60	.20
1104			
	32¢ **Child and tree,** phosphored paper	.60	.20
1105			
	32¢ **Santa in workshop,** phosphored paper	.60	.20
1106	**1995. Contemporary Christmas Booklet Issue**		
	32¢ **multicolored** phosphored paper	.60	.20
1107			
	32¢ **multicolored** phosphored paper	.60	.20
1108			
	32¢ **multicolored** phosphored paper	.60	.20
1109			
	32¢ **multicolored** phosphored paper	.60	.20
1110	**1995. Midnight Angel Christmas Booklet Issue**		
	32¢ **multicolored** phosphored paper	.60	.20
1110A	**1995. Midnight Angel Christmas Coil Issue**		
	32¢ **multicolored** phosphored paper	.75	.45
1111	**1995. Contemporary Christmas Booklet ATM Issue**		
	32¢ **multicolored** phosphored lacquer on surface of stamps	.75	.45
1112	**1995. Traditional Christmas Issue**		
	32¢ **multicolored** phosphored paper, perforated 11 1/4	.75	.20
1113			
	32¢ **multicolored** phosphored paper, perforated 9 3/4 x 11	.75	.20
1114	**1995. Ruth Benedict Issue**		
	46¢ **carmine** phosphored paper (mottled tagging)	1.00	.25
1115	**1996. American Kestrel Coil Issue**		
	1¢ **multicolored** untagged	.25	.20

NOTE: First printed on the B.E.P. "D" Press with the colors of the plate number in the order of BYCM (black, yellow, cyan, magenta), a second version printed on the Optiforma press was printed in BCYM, and first seen in August 1996.

NOTE: For sheet version see No. 1079. For version inscribed "USA 01" see No. 959.

No.	Description	MNHFVF	UseFVF
1116	**1996. Flag Over Porch Issue**		
	32¢ **multicolored** phosphored paper	.75	.30
1117	**1996. Unisys Variable Denomination Issue**		
	32¢ **red & blue** denomination (.20 to $20.00) printed in black, tagged	.95	.50
1118	**1996. Red-headed Woodpecker Issue**		
	2¢ **multicolored** untagged	.25	.20
1119	**1996. Space Shuttle Challenger Issue**		
	$3 **multicolored** phosphored paper	6.00	3.00
1120	**1996. Jacqueline Cochran Issue**		
	50¢ **multicolored** phosphored paper	1.20	.40
1121	**1996. Mountain Coil Issue**		
	5¢ **purple & multicolored** untagged	.25	.20
1122	**1996. Mountain Coil Issue**		
	5¢ **blue & multicolored** untagged	.25	.20

		MNHFVF	UseFVF	
1123 ____________	**1996. Eastern Bluebird Issue**			
	3¢ **multicolored** untagged	.25	.20	❑❑❑❑❑
NOTE: For version inscribed "USA03" see No. 960.				
1124 ____________	**1996. Cal Farley Issue**			
	32¢ **green** phosphored paper (solid tagging)	.65	.20	❑❑❑❑❑
1125 ____________	**1996. Flag Over Porch Booklet Stamp Issue**			
	32¢ **multicolored** phosphored paper	.75	.30	❑❑❑❑❑
1126 ____________	**1996. Flag Over Porch Coil Stamp Issue**			
	32¢ **multicolored** phosphored paper	1.00	.30	❑❑❑❑❑
1127 ____________	**1996. Flag Over Porch Coil Stamp Issue**			
	32¢ **multicolored** phosphored paper	1.50	.50	❑❑❑❑❑
1128 ____________	**1996. Flag Over Porch Coil Stamp Issue**			
	32¢ **multicolored** phosphored paper	.70	.20	❑❑❑❑❑
NOTE: On this issue, stamps are spaced apart on the 10,000 stamp coil roll.				
1129 ____________	**1996. Eagle and Shield Non-Denominated Self-Adhesive Coil Issue**			
	10¢ **multicolored** untagged	.25	.20	❑❑❑❑❑
1130 ____________	**1996. Butte Coil Issue**			
	5¢ **yellow, blue & red** untagged	.25	.20	❑❑❑❑❑
1131 ____________	**1996. Mountains Coil Issue**			
	5¢ **purple & multicolored** untagged	.25	.20	❑❑❑❑❑

1110,1110A

1111

1112, 1113

1114

1115

1116

1117

1118

1119

1120

1121, 1122

1123

1124

1125-1128

1129

1130

1131

1132

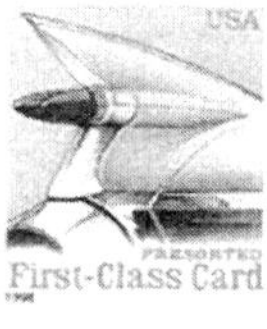

1133

1134

1135, 1136

MNHFVF	UseFVF

1132 _____ **1996. Automobile Coil Issue**
10¢ **black, brown & red brown** untagged .25 .20 ☐☐☐☐☐
1133 _____ **1996. Auto Tail Fin Coil Issue**
15¢ **buff & multicolored** untagged .35 .30 ☐☐☐☐☐
1134 _____ **1996. Juke Box Coil Issue**
25¢ **orange red, bright yellow green & multicolored** untagged .60 .30 ☐☐☐☐☐
1135 _____ **1996. Blue Jay Booklet Issue**
20¢ **multicolored** phosphored paper, serpentine die cut 10 1/2 x 10 3/4
on three sides .45 .25 ☐☐☐☐☐
1136 _____ **1996. Blue Jay Coil Issue**
20¢ **multicolored** phosphored paper .40 .20 ☐☐☐☐☐
1137 _____ **1996. Contemporary Christmas Issue**
32¢ **Family at yule hearth,** phosphored paper .60 .20 ☐☐☐☐☐
1138 _____
32¢ **Family trimming tree,** phosphored paper .60 .20 ☐☐☐☐☐
1139 _____
32¢ **Dreaming of Santa,** phosphored paper .60 .20 ☐☐☐☐☐
1140 _____
32¢ **Holiday shopping,** phosphored paper .60 .20 ☐☐☐☐☐
1141 _____ **1996. Contemporary Self Adhesive Booklet Issue**
32¢ **Family at yule hearth,** phosphored paper .60 .20 ☐☐☐☐☐
1142 _____
32¢ **Family trimming tree,** phosphored paper .60 .20 ☐☐☐☐☐
1143 _____
32¢ **Dreaming of Santa,** phosphored paper .60 .20 ☐☐☐☐☐
1144 _____
32¢ **Holiday shopping,** phosphored paper .60 .20 ☐☐☐☐☐
1145 _____ **1996. Holiday Skaters Booklet ATM Issue**
32¢ **multicolored,** phosphored lacquer on surface of stamps .75 .30 ☐☐☐☐☐
1146 _____ **1996. Traditional Christmas Issue**
32¢ **multicolored** phosphored paper, perforated 11 1/4 .70 .20 ☐☐☐☐☐
1147 _____
32¢ **multicolored** tagged, serpentine die cut 10 .95 .30 ☐☐☐☐☐
NOTE: No. 1148 is not assigned.
1149 _____ **1996. Yellow Rose Issue**
32¢ **yellow & multicolored** phosphored paper .75 .25 ☐☐☐☐☐
1150 _____ **1997. Flag Over Porch Booklet Issue**
32¢ **multicolored** phosphored paper .75 .30 ☐☐☐☐☐
1151 _____ **1997. Flag Over Porch Coil Issue**
32¢ **multicolored** phosphored paper .75 .30 ☐☐☐☐☐
1152 _____ **1997. Mountain Coil Issue**
5¢ **purple & multicolored** untagged .25 .20 ☐☐☐☐☐
1153 _____ **1997. Juke Box Coil Issue**
25¢ **multicolored** untagged .60 .20 ☐☐☐☐☐
1154 _____ **1997. Statue of Liberty Issue**
32¢ **multicolored** phosphored paper .75 .20 ☐☐☐☐☐
1155 _____ **1997. Citron and Insect Issue**
32¢ **multicolored** phosphored paper .75 .20 ☐☐☐☐☐
1156 _____ **1997. Flowering Pineapple Issue**
32¢ **multicolored** phosphored paper .75 .20 ☐☐☐☐☐
1157 _____ **1997. Citron and Insect Booklet Issue**
32¢ **multicolored** phosphored paper .75 .20 ☐☐☐☐☐
1158 _____ **1997. Flowering Pineapple Booklet Issue**
32¢ **multicolored** phosphored paper .75 .20 ☐☐☐☐☐

1137, 1141 (upper left)
1138, 1142 (upper right)
1139, 1143 (lower left)
1140, 1144 (lower right)

1145

1146, 1147

1149, 1163

1150-1151

1152

1153

1154

1155

1156

1157, 1159

1158, 1160

1161

1162

1163

1164

1165

1166, 1167

1168

1169

1170, 1177

1171

1172, 1173, 1248

		MNHFVF	UseFVF	
1159 ____________	**1997. Citron and Insect Booklet Issue**			
	32¢ **multicolored** phosphored paper	1.25	.50	❑❑❑❑❑
1160 ____________	**1997. Flowering Pineapple Booklet Issue**			
	32¢ **multicolored** phosphored paper	1.25	.50	❑❑❑❑❑

NOTE: Nos. 1159-60, which are die cut on all four sides, have a single irregular large serration near the middle of the right side created by die cutting.

		MNHFVF	UseFVF	
1161 ____________	**1997. Juke Box Issue**			
	25¢ **multicolored** untagged	.60	.20	❑❑❑❑❑
1162 ____________	**1997. Flag Over Porch Issue**			
	32¢ **multicolored** phosphored paper	.60	.20	❑❑❑❑❑
1163 ____________	**1997. Rose Issue**			
	32¢ **yellow & multicolored** phosphored paper	.65	.20	❑❑❑❑❑
1164 ____________	**1997. Christmas Issue**			
	32¢ **multicolored** phosphored paper, serpentine die cut 10	.50	.20	❑❑❑❑❑
1165 ____________				
	32¢ **multicolored** phosphored paper, serpentine die cut 11 1/4 x 11 3/4	.50	.20	❑❑❑❑❑
1166 ____________	**1997. Mars Pathfinder Issue**			
	$3 **multicolored** phosphored paper *(15,000,000 printed)*	4.50	2.50	❑❑❑❑❑
1167 ____________	**1998. Mars Pathfinder Press Sheet Issue**			
	$3 **multicolored** phosphored paper (single)	15.00	—	❑❑❑❑❑
1168 ____________	**1998. Henry R. Luce Issue**			
	32¢ **lake** phosphored paper (grainy tagging)	.50	.20	❑❑❑❑❑
1169 ____________	**1998. Swamp Coil Issue**			
	5¢ **multicolored** untagged	.25	.20	❑❑❑❑❑
1169A ____________	**1998. Swamp Self-adhesive Coil Issue**			
	5¢ **multicolored** untagged	.20	.20	❑❑❑❑❑
1170 ____________	**1998. Diner Non-Denominated Coil Issue**			
	25¢ **multicolored** untagged	.40	.20	❑❑❑❑❑
1171 ____________	**1998. Lila and De Witt Wallace Issue**			
	32¢ **blue** phosphored paper (solid tagging)	.50	.20	❑❑❑❑❑
1172 ____________	**1998. Ring-necked Pheasant Coil Issue**			
	20¢ **multicolored** phosphored paper	.40	.20	❑❑❑❑❑
1173 ____________	**1998. Ring-necked Pheasant Booklet Issue**			
	20¢ **multicolored** phosphored paper	.40	.20	❑❑❑❑❑
1174 ____________	**1998. Red Fox Issue**			
	$1 **multicolored** phosphored paper	1.50	.75	❑❑❑❑❑
1175 ____________	**1998. Bicycle Coil Issue**			
	10¢ **multicolored** untagged	.30	.20	❑❑❑❑❑
1176 ____________	**1998. Bicycle Coil Issue**			
	10¢ **multicolored** untagged	.30	.20	❑❑❑❑❑
1177 ____________	**1998. Diner Coil Issue**			
	25¢ **multicolored** untagged	.30	.20	❑❑❑❑❑
1178 ____________	**1998. Traditional Christmas Issue**			
	32¢ **multicolored** phosphored paper	.50	.20	❑❑❑❑❑
1179 ____________	**1998. Contemporary Christmas Issue**			
	32¢ **Traditional wreath,** phosphored paper	.50	.20	❑❑❑❑❑
1180 ____________				
	32¢ **Colonial wreath,** phosphored paper	.50	.20	❑❑❑❑❑
1181 ____________				
	32¢ **Chili wreath,** phosphored paper	.50	.20	❑❑❑❑❑
1182 ____________				
	32¢ **Tropical wreath,** phosphored paper	.50	.20	❑❑❑❑❑
1183 ____________	**1998. Contemporary Christmas Booklet Issue**			
	32¢ **Traditional wreath,** phosphored paper	.50	.20	❑❑❑❑❑

		MNHFVF	UseFVF
1184 ____________			
	32¢ **Colonial wreath,** phosphored paper	.50	.20 ❑❑❑❑❑
1185 ____________			
	32¢ **Chili wreath,** phosphored paper	.50	.20 ❑❑❑❑❑
1186 ____________			
	32¢ **Tropical wreath,** phosphored paper	.50	.20 ❑❑❑❑❑
NOTE: Vending booklet, 21x24mm, serpentine die cut 11 1/4 x 11 1/2.			
1187 ____________			
	32¢ **Traditional wreath**	.50	.20 ❑❑❑❑❑
1188 ____________			
	32¢ **Colonial wreath**	.50	.20 ❑❑❑❑❑
1189 ____________			
	32¢ **Chili wreath**	.50	.20 ❑❑❑❑❑
1190 ____________			
	32¢ **Tropical wreath**	.50	.20 ❑❑❑❑❑
1191 ____________	**1998. "H" Make-up Rate, USA White Issue**		
	1¢ **multicolored**	.25	.20 ❑❑❑❑❑
1192 ____________	**1998. "H" Make-Up Rate, USA Light Blue Issue**		
	1¢ **multicolored**	.25	.20 ❑❑❑❑❑
1193 ____________	**1998. Hat "H" First Class Issue**		
	33¢ **multicolored** tagged	.50	.20 ❑❑❑❑❑
1194 ____________	**1998. Hat "H" First Class Coil Issue**		
	33¢ **multicolored** tagged	.50	.20 ❑❑❑❑❑
1195 ____________	**1998. Hat "H" First Class Booklet Issue**		
	33¢ **multicolored** tagged	.50	.20 ❑❑❑❑❑
1196 ____________			
	33¢ **multicolored** tagged	.50	.20 ❑❑❑❑❑
1197 ____________	**1998. Hat "H" First Class Coil Issue**		
	33¢ **multicolored** tagged	.50	.20 ❑❑❑❑❑
1198 ____________	**1998. Uncle Sam Issue**		
	22¢ **multicolored** tagged	.50	.20 ❑❑❑❑❑
1199 ____________	**1998. Uncle Sam Coil Issue**		
	22¢ **multicolored** tagged	.50	.20 ❑❑❑❑❑

1174

1175, 1176

1178

1179, 1183, 1187 (upper left)
1180, 1184, 1188 (upper right)
1181, 1185, 1189 (lower left)
1182, 1186, 1190 (lower right)

1191

1192

1193-1197

MNHFVF	UseFVF	

1200 _____ **1998. Mary Breckinridge Issue**
77¢ **blue** phosphored paper solid tagging | 1.00 | .20 ☐☐☐☐☐
1201 _____ **1998. Shuttle Landing Issue**
$3.20 **multicolored** tagged | 4.00 | 2.75 ☐☐☐☐☐
1202 _____ **1998. Shuttle Piggyback Transport Issue**
$11.75 **multicolored** tagged | 14.00 | 8.00 ☐☐☐☐☐
1203 _____ **1998. Hat "H" First Class ATM Vending Issue**
33¢ **multicolored** | .50 | .20 ☐☐☐☐☐
1204 _____ **1998. Eagle and Shield Coil Issue**
10¢ **multicolored** | .20 | .20 ☐☐☐☐☐

NOTE: See U.S. Nos. 980 ("Bulk Rate USA"), 1011 and 1012 ("USA Bulk Rate") and 1129 ("USA Bulk Rate").

1205 _____ **1998. Eagle and Shield Coil Issue**
10¢ **multicolored** | .20 | .20 ☐☐☐☐☐
1206 _____ **1999. Flag and Skyscrapers Issue**
33¢ **multicolored,** phosphored paper | .50 | .20 ☐☐☐☐☐
1207 _____ **1999. Flag and Skyscrapers Coil Issue**
33¢ **multicolored,** phosphored paper | .50 | .20 ☐☐☐☐☐
1208 _____ **1999. Flag and Skyscrapers Coil Issue**
33¢ **multicolored,** phosphored paper | .50 | .20 ☐☐☐☐☐
1209 _____ **1999. Flag and Skyscrapers Coil Issue**
33¢ **multicolored,** phosphored paper | .50 | .20 ☐☐☐☐☐
1210 _____ **1999. Flag and Skyscrapers Issue**
33¢ **multicolored,** phosphored paper | .50 | .20 ☐☐☐☐☐
1211 _____ **1999. Flag and Skyscrapers Issue**
33¢ **multicolored,** phosphored paper | .60 | .20 ☐☐☐☐☐
1212 _____ **1999. Flag and Skyscrapers Issue**
33¢ **multicolored,** phosphored paper | .60 | .20 ☐☐☐☐☐
1213 _____ **1999. Flag in Classroom Issue**
33¢ **multicolored,** phosphored lacquer on surface | .50 | .20 ☐☐☐☐☐
1214 _____ **1999. Fruit Berries Issue**
33¢ **Blueberries,** phosphored paper | .50 | .20 ☐☐☐☐☐
1215 _____
33¢ **Raspberries,** phosphored paper | .50 | .20 ☐☐☐☐☐
1216 _____
33¢ **Strawberries,** phosphored paper | .50 | .20 ☐☐☐☐☐
1217 _____
33¢ **Blackberries,** phosphored paper | .50 | .20 ☐☐☐☐☐
1218 _____ **1999. Fruit Berries Issue**
33¢ **Blueberries,** phosphored paper | .50 | .20 ☐☐☐☐☐
1219 _____
33¢ **Strawberries,** phosphored paper | .50 | .20 ☐☐☐☐☐
1220 _____
33¢ **Raspberries,** phosphored paper | .50 | .20 ☐☐☐☐☐
1221 _____
33¢ **Blackberries,** phosphored paper | .50 | .20 ☐☐☐☐☐
1222 _____ **1999. Fruit Berries Coil Issue**
33¢ **Blackberries** | .50 | .20 ☐☐☐☐☐
1223 _____
33¢ **Strawberries** | .50 | .20 ☐☐☐☐☐
1224 _____
33¢ **Blueberries** | .50 | .20 ☐☐☐☐☐
1225 _____
33¢ **Raspberries** | .50 | .20 ☐☐☐☐☐

MNHFVF	UseFVF

1226 _____ **1999. Niagara Falls Issue**
 48¢ **multicolored,** phosphored paper 1.00 .20 ☐☐☐☐☐

NOTE: With this stamp, the USPS began to add the silhouette of a jetliner next to the denomination on some stamps, indicating they paid an international rate for which air service was used. For many years, virtually all letters and cards have been moved by air. The last U.S. stamp to bear an "Airmail" designation was the William T. Piper Issue of 1993 (A132), and Minkus ceased to classify stamps as airmail after that issue. (See Minkus Nos. 1097, 1120 and 1250.)

1227 _____ **1999. Red-headed Woodpecker Issue**
 2¢ **multicolored,** untagged .25 .20 ☐☐☐☐☐

1198, 1199

1200

1201

1202

1203

1204, 05

1214-1217, 1251-1254

1218-1221

1206-1212

1222-1225

1213

1226

1227

1228

MNHFVF	UseFVF	
1228 _____	**1999. Justin S. Morrill Issue**			
55¢	**black,** phosphored paper, (solid tagging)	1.00	.20 ☐☐☐☐☐	
1229 _____	**1999. American Kestrel Coil Issue**			
1¢	**multicolored,** untagged	.25	.20 ☐☐☐☐☐	
1230 _____	**1999. Rio Grande Issue**			
40¢	**multicolored,** phosphored paper	.75	.20 ☐☐☐☐☐	
1231 _____	**1999. Billy Mitchell Issue**			
55¢	**multicolored,** phosphored paper	1.00	.40 ☐☐☐☐☐	
1232 _____	**1999. Coral Pink Rose Issue**			
33¢	**multicolored** phosphored paper	.50	.20 ☐☐☐☐☐	
1233 _____	**1999. Uncle Sam Coil Issue**			
22¢	**multicolored,** phosphored paper	.50	.20 ☐☐☐☐☐	
1234 _____	**1999. Madonna and Child Issue**			
33¢	**multicolored,** phosphored paper	.50	.20 ☐☐☐☐☐	
1235 _____	**1999. Greetings Reindeer Issue**			
33¢	**red** background, phosphored paper	.50	.20 ☐☐☐☐☐	
1236 _____				
33¢	**blue** background, phosphored paper	.50	.20 ☐☐☐☐☐	
1237 _____				
33¢	**violet** background, phosphored paper	.50	.20 ☐☐☐☐☐	
1238 _____				
33¢	**green** background, phosphored paper	.50	.20 ☐☐☐☐☐	
1239 _____	**1999. Greetings Reindeer Booklet Issue**			
33¢	**red** background, phosphored paper	.50	.20 ☐☐☐☐☐	
1240 _____				
33¢	**blue** background, phosphored paper	.50	.20 ☐☐☐☐☐	
1241 _____				
33¢	**violet** background, phosphored paper	.50	.20 ☐☐☐☐☐	
1242 _____				
33¢	**green** background, phosphored paper	.50	.20 ☐☐☐☐☐	
1243 _____	**1999. Greetings Reindeer Vending Booklet Issue**			
33¢	**red** background, phosphored paper	.50	.20 ☐☐☐☐☐	
1244 _____				
33¢	**blue** background, phosphored paper	.50	.20 ☐☐☐☐☐	
1245 _____				
33¢	**violet** background, phosphored paper	.50	.20 ☐☐☐☐☐	

1229, 1247

1230

1231

1232, 1255

1233

1234

1235-1238,
1239-1242, 1243-1246

MNHFVF	UseFVF	

1246 _____

33¢ **green** background, phosphored paper — .50 — .20 ☐☐☐☐☐

1247 _____ **1999. American Kestrel Issue**

1¢ **multicolored,** untagged — .25 — .20 ☐☐☐☐☐

1248 _____ **1999. Ring-necked Pheasant Booklet Issue**

20¢ **multicolored,** phosphored paper, die cut 10 1/2 x 11 — .40 — .20 ☐☐☐☐☐

1249 _____ **2000. Grand Canyon Issue**

60¢ **multicolored,** phosphored paper — 1.20 — .30 ☐☐☐☐☐

1250 _____ **2000. Eddie Rickenbacker Issue**

60¢ **multicolored,** phosphored paper — 1.00 — .30 ☐☐☐☐☐

1251 _____ **2000. Fruit Berries Booklet Issue**

33¢ **Blueberries,** phosphored paper — .60 — .20 ☐☐☐☐☐

1252 _____

33¢ Raspberries, phosphored paper — .60 — .20 ☐☐☐☐☐

1253 _____

33¢ **Strawberries,** phosphored paper — .60 — .20 ☐☐☐☐☐

1254 _____

33¢ **Blackberries,** phosphored paper — .60 — .20 ☐☐☐☐☐

1255 _____ **2000. Coral Pink Rose Booklet Issue**

33¢ **multicolored,** phosphored paper — .60 — .20 ☐☐☐☐☐

1256 _____ **2000. Fruit Berries Vertical Coil Issue**

33¢ **Raspberries,** phosphored paper — .60 — .20 ☐☐☐☐☐

1257 _____

33¢ **Blueberries,** phosphored paper — .60 — .20 ☐☐☐☐☐

1258 _____

33¢ **Strawberries,** phosphored paper — .60 — .20 ☐☐☐☐☐

1259 _____

33¢ **Blackberries,** phosphored paper — .60 — .20 ☐☐☐☐☐

1260 _____ **2000. Joseph W. Stillwell Issue**

10¢ **black and red** — .20 — .20 ☐☐☐☐☐

1261 _____ **2000. Claude Pepper Issue**

33¢ **black and red** — .50 — .20 ☐☐☐☐☐

1262 _____ **2000. The New York Public Library Lion Issue**

(10¢) **multicolored** — .20 — .20 ☐☐☐☐☐

1249

1261

1262

1256-1259 ◄

1260

1263

MNHFVF	UseFVF	

1263 _____ **2000. Blue Kestrel Issue**
 1¢ **multicolored** .20 .20 ☐☐☐☐☐
1264 _____ **2000. Farm Flag Issue**
 (34¢) **multicolored** .50 .20 ☐☐☐☐☐
1265 _____
 (34¢) **multicolored** .50 .20 ☐☐☐☐☐
1266 _____ **2000. Farm Flag Booklet Issue**
 (34¢) **multicolored** .50 .20 ☐☐☐☐☐
1267 _____ **2000. Statue of Liberty Issue**
 (34¢) **multicolored** .50 .20 ☐☐☐☐☐
1268 _____
 (34¢) **multicolored** .50 .20 ☐☐☐☐☐
1269 _____ **2000. Statue of Liberty Booklet Issue**
 (34¢) **multicolored** .50 .20 ☐☐☐☐☐
1270 _____ **2000. Flowers Coil Issue**
 (34¢) **multicolored** 50 .20 ☐☐☐☐☐
1271 _____
 (34¢) **multicolored** .50 .20 ☐☐☐☐☐
1272 _____
 (34¢) **multicolored** .50 .20 ☐☐☐☐☐
1273 _____
 (34¢) **multicolored** .50 .20 ☐☐☐☐☐
1274 _____ **2000. Flowers Booklet Issue**
 (34¢) **Longiflorum lily, purple** background, 10 1/4 x 10 3/4 .50 .20 ☐☐☐☐☐
1275 _____
 (34¢) **Cymbidium orchid, tan,** 10 1/4 x 10 3/4 .50 .20 ☐☐☐☐☐
1276 _____
 (34¢) **Freesia, green,** 10 1/4 x 10 3/4 .50 .20 ☐☐☐☐☐
1277 _____
 (34¢) **Asian hybrid lily, red,** 10 1/4 x 10 3/4 .50 .20 ☐☐☐☐☐
1278 _____
 (34¢) **Longiflorum lily, purple** background, 11 1/2 x 11 3/4 .50 .20 ☐☐☐☐☐
1279 _____
 (34¢) **Cymbidium orchid, tan,** 11 1/2 x 11 3/4 .50 .20 ☐☐☐☐☐
1280 _____
 (34¢) **Freesia, (green,** 11 1/2 x 11 3/4) .50 .20 ☐☐☐☐☐
1281 _____
 (34¢) **Asian hybrid lily, (red,** 11 1/2 x 11 3/4) .50 .20 ☐☐☐☐☐

1264-1266

1267-1269

1274-1277, 1278-1281

1270-1273

No.	Issue / Description	MNHFVF	UseFVF
1282	**2001. Statue of Liberty Coil Issue**		
	34¢ **multicolored**	.65	.20
1283	**2001. Capitol Dome Issue**		
	$3.50 **multicolored**	7.00	3.00
1284	**2001. Washington Monument Issue**		
	$12.25 **multicolored**	24.50	10.00
1285	**2001. Farm Flag Issue**		
	34¢ **multicolored**	.65	.20
1286	**2001. Flowers Coil Issue**		
	34¢ **multicolored**	.65	.20
1287			
	34¢ **multicolored**	.65	.20
1288			
	34¢ **multicolored**	.65	.20
1289			
	34¢ **multicolored**	.65	.20
1290	**2001. Flowers Booklet Issue**		
	34¢ **Longiflorum lily, purple** background	.65	.20
1291			
	34¢ **Cymbidium orchid, tan**	.65	.20
1292			
	34¢ **Freesia, green**	.65	.20
1293			
	34¢ **Asian hybrid lily, red**	.65	.20
1294	**2001. Statue of Liberty Coil Issue**		
	34¢ **multicolored**	.65	.20
1295	**2001. Statue of Liberty Coil Issue**		
	34¢ **multicolored**	.65	.20
1296	**2001. Statue of Liberty Booklet Issue**		
	34¢ **multicolored**	.65	.20
1297	**2001. Hattie Caraway Issue**		
	76¢ **black and red**	1.50	.20
1298	**2001. George Washington Booklet Issue**		
	20¢ **dark carmine**	.40	.20
1299	**2001. George Washington Booklet Issue**		
	20¢ **dark carmine**	.40	.20

1282, 1294-1296

1283

1284

1290-1293

1285, 1306, 1335

1286-1289

MNHFVF	UseFVF	

1300 _____ **2001. Bison Issue**
21¢ multicolored — .40 .20 ☐☐☐☐☐

1301 _____ **2001. Bison Coil Issue**
21¢ multicolored — .40 .20 ☐☐☐☐☐

1302 _____ **2001. Art Deco Eagle Issue**
55¢ multicolored — 1.00 .20 ☐☐☐☐☐

1303 _____ **2001. Apple and Orange Issue**
34¢ multicolored (Apple) — .65 .20 ☐☐☐☐☐

1304 _____
34¢ multicolored (Orange) — .65 .20 ☐☐☐☐☐

1305 _____ **2001. Nine-Mile Prairie Issue**
70¢ multicolored — 1.40 .30 ☐☐☐☐☐

1306 _____ **2001. Farm Flag Issue**
34¢ multicolored — .65 .20 ☐☐☐☐☐

1307 _____ **2001. Mount McKinley Issue**
80¢ multicolored — 1.50 .35 ☐☐☐☐☐

1308 _____ **2001. Apple and Orange Issue**
34¢ multicolored (Apple) — .65 .20 ☐☐☐☐☐

1309 _____
34¢ multicolored (Orange) — .65 .20 ☐☐☐☐☐

1310 _____ **2001. Acadia National Park Issue**
60¢ multicolored — 1.20 .30 ☐☐☐☐☐

1311 _____ **2001. Atlas Statue Coil Issue**
(10¢) multicolored — .20 .20 ☐☐☐☐☐

1312 _____ **2001. Woody Wagon Presorted First Class Coil Issue**
(15¢) mulitcolored — .30 .20 ☐☐☐☐☐

1313 _____ **2001. Bison Issue**
21¢ multicolored — .40 .20 ☐☐☐☐☐

1314 _____ **2001. Bison Convertible Booklet Issue**
21¢ multicolored — .40 .20 ☐☐☐☐☐

1315 _____ **2001. Bison Vending Booklet Issue**
21¢ multicolored — .40 .20 ☐☐☐☐☐

1316 _____ **2001. Art Deco Eagle Issue**
57¢ multicolored — 1.00 .50 ☐☐☐☐☐

1317 _____ **2001. George Washington Issue**
23¢ green — .45 .20 ☐☐☐☐☐

1318 _____ **2001. George Washington Coil Issue**
23¢ green — .45 .20 ☐☐☐☐☐

1319 _____ **2001. Old World Santas Issue**
34¢ multicolored — .65 .20 ☐☐☐☐☐

1320 _____
34¢ multicolored — .65 .20 ☐☐☐☐☐

1321 _____
34¢ multicolored — .65 .20 ☐☐☐☐☐

1322 _____
34¢ multicolored — .65 .20 ☐☐☐☐☐

1323 _____ **2001. Old World Santas Booklet Issue**
34¢ multicolored — .65 .20 ☐☐☐☐☐

1324 _____
34¢ multicolored — .65 .20 ☐☐☐☐☐

1325 _____
34¢ multicolored — .65 .20 ☐☐☐☐☐

1326 _____
34¢ multicolored — .65 .20 ☐☐☐☐☐

		MNHFVF	UseFVF
1327	**2001. Old World Santas Vending Booklet Issue**		
	34¢ **multicolored**	.65	.20 ❑❑❑❑❑
1328			
	34¢ **multicolored**	.65	.20 ❑❑❑❑❑
1329			
	34¢ **multicolored**	.65	.20 ❑❑❑❑❑
1330			
	34¢ **multicolored**	.65	.20 ❑❑❑❑❑
1331	**2001. Madonna and Child (Costa) Issue**		
	34¢ **multicolored**	.65	.20 ❑❑❑❑❑
1332	**2001. United We Stand Issue**		
	34¢ **multicolored**	.65	.20 ❑❑❑❑❑
1333	**2001. United We Stand Coil Issue**		
	34¢ **multicolored**	.65	.20 ❑❑❑❑❑
1334	**2001. United We Stand Coil Issue**		
	34¢ **multicolored**	.65	.20 ❑❑❑❑❑
1335	**2001. Farm Flag ATM Issue**		
	34¢ **multicolored**	.65	.20 ❑❑❑❑❑

1297

1298, 1299

1300, 1301, 1313-1315

1302

1305

1303-1304, 1308-1309

1307

1310

1311

1312

1316

1319-1322, 1323-1326, 1327-1330

1317, 1318

1331

1332-1334

COMMEMORATIVES

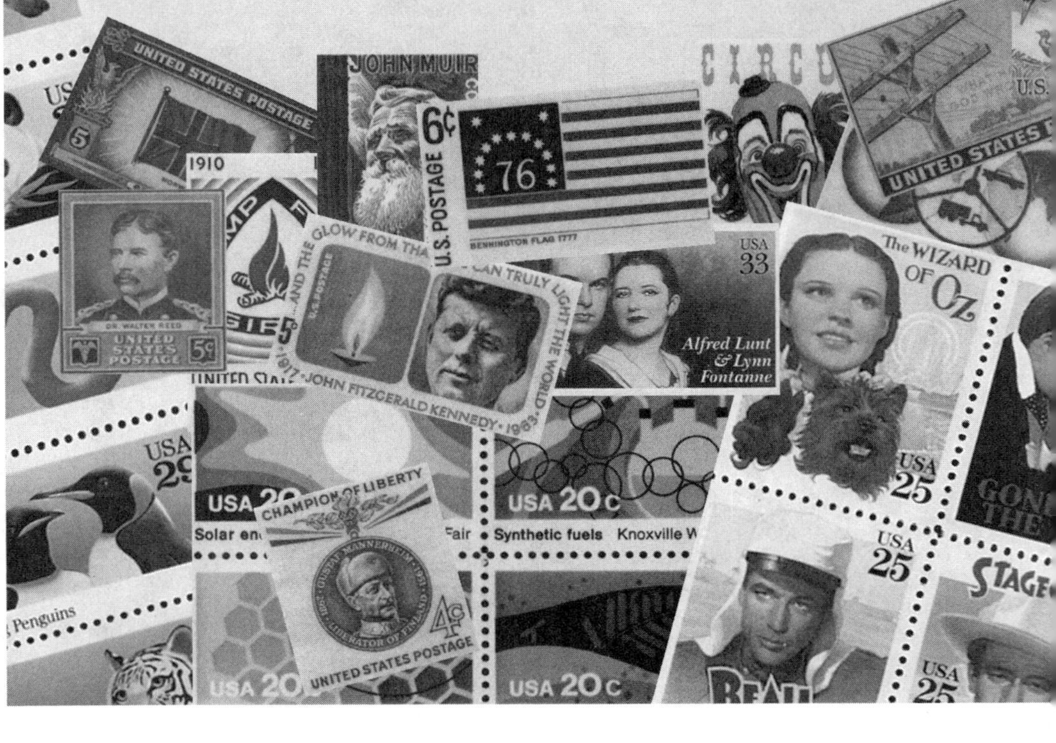

Commemorative Issues

	UnFVF	UseFVF	
CM1 ______________ **1893. Columbian Issues**			
1¢ **deep blue** (449,195,550)	17.50	.35	❑❑❑❑❑
CM2 ______________			
2¢ **dull purple** (1,464,588,750)	17.50	.20	❑❑❑❑❑
NOTE: Imperforate 2¢ Columbians are from printer's waste.			
CM3 ______________			
3¢ **deep bluish green** (11,501,250)	40.00	11.00	❑❑❑❑❑
CM4 ______________			
4¢ **gray blue** (19,181,550)	60.00	5.50	❑❑❑❑❑
CM5 ______________			
5¢ **brown** (35,248,250)	65.00	6.00	❑❑❑❑❑
CM6 ______________			
6¢ **dark lilac** (4,707,550)	60.00	17.50	❑❑❑❑❑
CM7 ______________			
8¢ **brown purple** (10,656,550)	50.00	7.00	❑❑❑❑❑
CM8 ______________			
10¢ **black brown** (16,516,950)	95.00	5.50	❑❑❑❑❑

CM1

CM2

CM3

CM4

CM5

CM6

CM7

CM8

CM9

CM10

CM11

CM12

		UnFVF	UseFVF	
CM9	15¢ **deep bluish green** (1,576,950)	175.00	50.00	❑❑❑❑❑
CM10	30¢ **orange brown** (617,250)	225.00	65.00	❑❑❑❑❑
CM11	50¢ **slate black** (243,750)	350.00	125.00	❑❑❑❑❑
CM12	$1 **Venetian red** (55,050)	1,000.00	450.00	❑❑❑❑❑
CM13	$2 **brown red** (45,550)	1,100.00	400.00	❑❑❑❑❑
CM14	$3 **bronze green** (27,650)	1,700.00	725.00	❑❑❑❑❑
CM15	$4 **deep rose** (26,350)	2,250.00	1,000.00	❑❑❑❑❑
CM16	$5 **black** (27,350)	2,750.00	1,600.00	❑❑❑❑❑

NOTE: For stamps of these designs, but with "1992" instead of "1893" in the top-right corner see Nos. CM1456-61.

1898. Trans-Mississippi Issue

		UnFVF	UseFVF	
CM17	1¢ **green** (70,993,400)	22.50	4.75	❑❑❑❑❑
CM18	2¢ **brown red** (159,720,800)	19.00	1.25	❑❑❑❑❑
CM19	4¢ **orange red** (94,924,500)	100.00	17.50	❑❑❑❑❑
CM20	5¢ **deep blue** (7,694,180)	100.00	17.50	❑❑❑❑❑
CM21	8¢ **chocolate** (2,927,200)	135.00	32.50	❑❑❑❑❑
CM22	10¢ **violet black** (4,629,760)	135.00	17.50	❑❑❑❑❑
CM23	50¢ **bronze green** (530,400)	450.00	130.00	❑❑❑❑❑
CM24	$1 **black** (56,900)	950.00	400.00	❑❑❑❑❑
CM25	$2 **red brown** (56,200)	2,700.00	700.00	❑❑❑❑❑

NOTE: For bicolor versions of the Trans-Mississippi Issue, see Nos. CM1985 and CM1986.

1901. Pan-American Issue

		UnFVF	UseFVF	
CM26	1¢ **emerald & black** (91,401,500)	15.00	2.75	❑❑❑❑❑
CM27	2¢ **rose red & black** (209,759,700)	15.00	1.00	❑❑❑❑❑
CM28	4¢ **orange brown & black** (5,737,100)	70.00	12.50	❑❑❑❑❑
CM29	5¢ **gray blue & black** (7,201,300)	75.00	12.50	❑❑❑❑❑
CM30	8¢ **chocolate & black** (4,921,700)	100.00	45.00	❑❑❑❑❑
CM31	10¢ **yellow brown & black** (5,043,700)	140.00	22.50	❑❑❑❑❑

1904. Louisiana Purchase Exposition Issue

		UnFVF	UseFVF	
CM32	1¢ **green** (79,779,200)	20.00	3.50	❑❑❑❑❑
CM33	2¢ **carmine** (192,732,400)	19.00	1.25	❑❑❑❑❑
CM34	3¢ **dark red violet** (4,542,600)	60.00	25.00	❑❑❑❑❑

CM13

CM14

CM15

CM16

CM17

CM18

CM19

CM20

CM21

CM22

CM23

CM24

CM25

CM26

CM27

CM28

CM29

CM30

CM31

CM32

CM33

		UnFVF	UseFVF	
CM35______				
5¢ **indigo** (6,926,700)		75.00	17.50	❑❑❑❑❑
CM36______				
10¢ **red brown** (4,011,200)		125.00	25.00	❑❑❑❑❑
CM37______	**1907. Jamestown Issue**			
1¢ **deep bluish green** (77,728,794)		17.50	3.00	❑❑❑❑❑
CM38______				
2¢ **rose red** (149,497,994)		22.50	2.75	❑❑❑❑❑
CM39______				
5¢ **indigo** (7,980,594)		85.00	22.50	❑❑❑❑❑
NOTE: Perforated 12.				
CM40______	**1909. Lincoln Memorial Centennial Issue**			
2¢ **carmine** (148,387,191)		5.00	1.75	❑❑❑❑❑
NOTE: Imperforate.				
CM41______				
2¢ **carmine** (1,273,900)		22.50	1,750.00	❑❑❑❑❑
NOTE: Bluish gray paper, perforated 12 (Feb. 1909).				
CM42______				
2¢ **carmine** (637,000)		175.00	195.00	❑❑❑❑❑
NOTE: Perforated 12.				
CM43______	**1909. Alaska-Yukon Issue**			
2¢ **carmine** (152,887,311)		7.00	1.50	❑❑❑❑❑
NOTE: Imperforate.				
CM44______				
2¢ **carmine** (525,400)		30.00	22.50	❑❑❑❑❑
NOTE: Perforated 12.				
CM45______	**1909. Hudson-Fulton Issue**			
2¢ **carmine** (72,634,631)		10.00	3.50	❑❑❑❑❑
NOTE: Imperforate.				
CM46______				
2¢ **carmine** (216,480)		35.00	22.50	❑❑❑❑❑
CM47______	**1913-15. Panama-Pacific Issue**			
1¢ **green** (334,796,926)		15.50	1.25	❑❑❑❑❑
CM48______				
2¢ **rose red** (503,713,086)		20.00	.50	❑❑❑❑❑
CM49______				
5¢ **blue** (29,088,726)		75.00	9.00	❑❑❑❑❑
CM50______				
10¢ **orange yellow** (16,968,365)		125.00	20.00	❑❑❑❑❑
CM51______				
10¢ **orange** (16,968,365) (Aug. 1913)		200.00	15.00	❑❑❑❑❑
CM52______	**1914-15. Panama-Pacific Issue**			
1¢ **green**		22.00	5.25	❑❑❑❑❑
CM53______				
2¢ **rose red**		70.00	1.50	❑❑❑❑❑
CM54______				
5¢ **blue**		160.00	14.50	❑❑❑❑❑
CM55______				
10¢ **orange**		900.00	60.00	❑❑❑❑❑
CM56______	**1919. Victory Issue**			
3¢ **dark lilac** (99,585,200)		7.50	3.00	❑❑❑❑❑
CM57______	**1920. Pilgrim Tercentenary Issue**			
1¢ **green** (137,978,207)		3.50	2.50	❑❑❑❑❑
CM58______				
2¢ **rose red** (196,037,327)		5.25	1.75	❑❑❑❑❑

UnFVF	UseFVF					

CM59_____

5¢ **deep blue** (11,321,607) 35.00 12.50 ☐☐☐☐☐

NOTE: Flat plate printing, perforated 11.

CM60_____ **1923. Harding Memorial Issue**

2¢ **black** (1,459,487,085) .60 20 ☐☐☐☐☐

NOTE: Flat plate printing, imperforate.

CM61_____

2¢ **black** (770,000) 6.50 4.50 ☐☐☐☐☐

NOTE: Rotary press printing, perforated 10.

CM62_____

2¢ **gray black** (99,950,300) 15.00 1.75 ☐☐☐☐☐

NOTE: Rotary press printing, perforated 11.

CM34

CM35

CM36

CM37

CM38

CM39

CM40-42

CM43, CM44

CM45

CM47, CM52

CM48, CM53

CM49, CM54

CM50-51, CM55

CM56

CM57

UnFVF	UseFVF

CM63_____
2¢ gray black 30,000.00 ☐☐☐☐☐

CM64_____ **1924. Huguenot-Walloon Issue**
1¢ **green** (51,378,023) 2.75 2.75 ☐☐☐☐☐

CM65_____
2¢ **carmine red** (77,753,423) 5.00 2.00 ☐☐☐☐☐

CM66_____
5¢ **Prussian blue** (5,659,023) 27.50 14.00 ☐☐☐☐☐

CM67_____ **1925. Lexington-Concord Issue**
1¢ **green** (15,615,000) 2.75 2.50 ☐☐☐☐☐

CM68_____
2¢ **carmine red** (26,596,600) 5.00 3.50 ☐☐☐☐☐

CM69_____
5¢ **Prussian blue** (5,348,800) 25.00 14.00 ☐☐☐☐☐

CM70_____ **1925. Norse-American Issue**
2¢ **carmine & black** (9,104,983) 4.00 3.00 ☐☐☐☐☐

CM71_____
5¢ **indigo & black** (1,900,983) 15.00 12.50 ☐☐☐☐☐

CM72_____ **1926. Sesquicentennial Issue**
2¢ **carmine red** (307,731,900) 2.50 .50 ☐☐☐☐☐

CM73_____ **1926. Ericsson Memorial Issue**
5¢ **slate violet** (20,280,500) 6.00 2.50 ☐☐☐☐☐

CM74_____ **1926. White Plains Issue**
2¢ **carmine red** (40,639,485) 2.00 1.50 ☐☐☐☐☐

CM75_____ **1926. White Plains Philatelic Exhibition Issue**
2¢ **carmine red** (107,398) 400.00 425.00 ☐☐☐☐☐

CM76_____ **1927. Vermont Sesquicentennial Issue**
2¢ **carmine red** (39,974,900) 1.25 1.00 ☐☐☐☐☐

CM77_____ **1927. Burgoyne Campaign Issue**
2¢ **carmine red** (25,628,450) 3.50 2.25 ☐☐☐☐☐

CM78_____ **1928. Valley Forge Issue**
2¢ **carmine red** (101,330,328) 1.00 .50 ☐☐☐☐☐

CM79_____ **1928. Hawaiian Sesquicentennial Issue**
2¢ **carmine** (5,519,897) 4.50 4.50 ☐☐☐☐☐

CM80_____
5¢ **blue** (1,459,897) 12.50 12.50 ☐☐☐☐☐

CM81_____ **1928. Molly Pitcher Issue**
2¢ **carmine** (9,779,896) 1.00 1.25 ☐☐☐☐☐

CM82_____ **1928. Aeronautics Conference Issue**
2¢ **carmine red** (51,342,273) 1.25 1.00 ☐☐☐☐☐

CM83_____
5¢ **Prussian blue** (10,319,700) 5.00 3.00 ☐☐☐☐☐

CM84_____ **1929. George Rogers Clark Issue**
2¢ **carmine & black** (16,684,674) .60 .50 ☐☐☐☐☐
NOTE: Flat press, perforated 11.

CM85_____ **1929. Edison Commemorative Issue**
2¢ **carmine red** (31,679,200) .75 .75 ☐☐☐☐☐
NOTE: Rotary press, perforated 11 x 10 1/2.

CM86_____
2¢ **carmine red** (210,119,474) .75 .25 ☐☐☐☐☐
NOTE: Rotary press coil, perforated 10 vertically.

CM87_____
2¢ **carmine red** (133,530,000) 12.50 1.50 ☐☐☐☐☐

CM88_____ **1929. Sullivan Expedition Issue**
2¢ **carmine red** (51,451,880) .75 .75 ☐☐☐☐☐

CM58

CM59

CM60-63

CM64

CM65

CM66

CM67

CM68

CM69

CM70

CM71

CM72

CM73

CM74

CM76

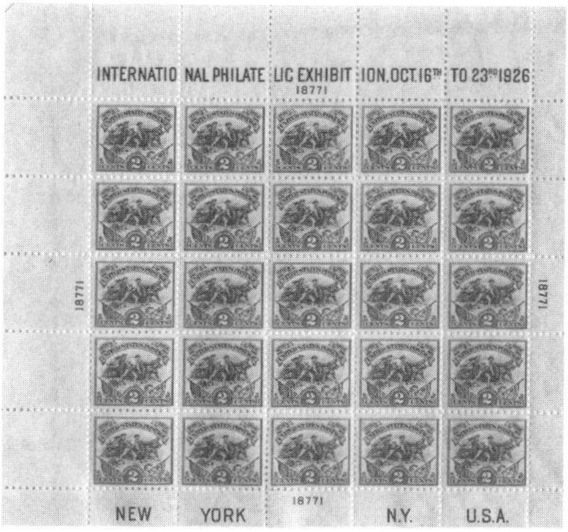

CM75

CM77

CM78

CM79

UnFVF	UseFVF	

CM89_____ **1929. Battle of Fallen Timbers Issue**
2¢ carmine red (29,338,274) — .75 — .75 ☐☐☐☐☐

CM90_____ **1929. Ohio River Canalization Issue**
2¢ carmine red (32,680,900) — .50 — .75 ☐☐☐☐☐

CM91_____ **1930. Massachusetts Bay Colony Issue**
2¢ carmine red (74,000,774) — .75 — .45 ☐☐☐☐☐

CM92_____ **1930. Carolina-Charleston Issue**
2¢ carmine red (25,215,574) — 1.25 — 1.00 ☐☐☐☐☐

CM93_____ **1930. Braddock's Field Issue**
2¢ carmine red (25,609,470) — 1.00 — 1.00 ☐☐☐☐☐

CM94_____ **1930. Von Steuben Issue**
2¢ carmine red (66,487,000) — .50 — .50 ☐☐☐☐☐

CM95_____ **1931. Pulaski Issue**
2¢ carmine red (96,559,400) — .25 — .20 ☐☐☐☐☐

CM96_____ **1931. Red Cross Issue**
2¢ black & scarlet (99,074,600) — .25 — .20 ☐☐☐☐☐

CM97_____ **1931. Yorktown Issue**
2¢ carmine red & black (25,006,400) — .35 — .20 ☐☐☐☐☐

CM98_____ **1932. Washington Bicentennial Issue**
1/2¢ olive brown (87,969,700) — .25 — .20 ☐☐☐☐☐

CM99_____
1¢ yellow green (1,265,555,100) — .25 — .20 ☐☐☐☐☐

CM100_____
1-1/2¢ yellow brown (304,926,800) — .50 — .20 ☐☐☐☐☐

CM101_____
2¢ carmine red (4,222,198,300) — .25 — .20 ☐☐☐☐☐

CM102_____
3¢ slate purple (456,198,500) — .50 — .20 ☐☐☐☐☐

CM103_____
4¢ yellow brown (151,201,300) — .40 — .20 ☐☐☐☐☐

CM104_____
5¢ Prussian blue (170,656,100) — 1.75 — .20 ☐☐☐☐☐

CM105_____
6¢ orange (111,739,400) — 3.50 — .20 ☐☐☐☐☐

CM106_____
7¢ black (83,257,400) — .40 — .20 ☐☐☐☐☐

CM107_____
8¢ bister (96,506,100) — 3.00 — .75 ☐☐☐☐☐

CM108_____
9¢ salmom (75,706,200) — 2.50 — .20 ☐☐☐☐☐

CM109_____
10¢ orange yellow (147,216,000) — 12.50 — .20 ☐☐☐☐☐

CM110_____ **1932. Olympic Winter Games Issue**
2¢ carmine red (51,102,800) — .40 — .25 ☐☐☐☐☐

CM111_____ **1932. Arbor Day Issue**
2¢ carmine red (100,869,300) — .25 — .20 ☐☐☐☐☐

CM112_____ **1932. Olympic Summer Games Issue**
3¢ reddish violet (168,885,300) — 1.50 — .20 ☐☐☐☐☐

CM113_____
5¢ blue (52,376,100) — 2.25 — .30 ☐☐☐☐☐

CM114_____ **1932. William Penn Issue**
3¢ reddish violet (49,949,000) — .35 — .25 ☐☐☐☐☐

CM115_____ **1933. Daniel Webster Issue**
3¢ reddish violet (49,538,500) — .35 — .40 ☐☐☐☐☐

HAWAII
1778 - 1928

CM80

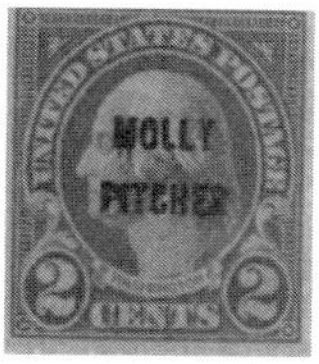

CM81

CM82

CM83

CM84

CM85-87

CM88

CM89

CM90

CM91

CM92

CM93

CM94

CM95

CM96

CM97

CM98

CM99

CM100

CM101

CM102

CM103

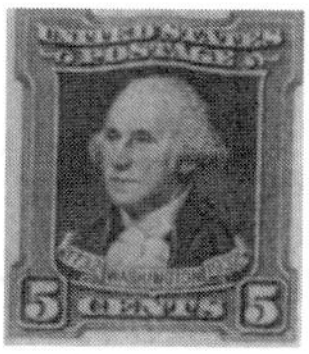

CM104

CM105

CM106

CM107

		UnFVF	UseFVF	
CM116	**1933. Oglethorpe Issue**			
3¢	**reddish violet** (61,719,200)	.35	.25	❑❑❑❑❑
CM117	**1933. Newburgh Issue**			
3¢	**reddish violet** (73,382,400)	.25	.20	❑❑❑❑❑

NOTE: For ungummed stamps (Farley Issue), see CM142.

CM118	**1933. Century of Progress Issue**			
1¢	**yellow green** (348,266,800)	.25	.20	❑❑❑❑❑
CM119				
3¢	**reddish violet** (480,239,300)	.25	.20	❑❑❑❑❑
CM120	**1933. Century of Progress Souvenir Sheets**			
1¢	**yellow green** (456,704)	35.00	32.50	❑❑❑❑❑
CM121				
3¢	**reddish violet** (441,172)	30.00	27.50	❑❑❑❑❑

NOTE: For ungummed stamps (Farley issue) see CM156 & CM157.

CM122	**1933. NRA Issue**			
3¢	**reddish violet** (1,978,707,300)	.25	.20	❑❑❑❑❑
CM123	**1933. Byrd Antarctic Issue**			
3¢	**blue** (5,735,944)	.75	.60	❑❑❑❑❑

NOTE: For ungummed stamps (Farley issue), see CM143.

CM124	**1933. Kosciuszko Issue**			
5¢	**blue** (45,137,700)	.75	.35	❑❑❑❑❑
CM125	**1934. Byrd Souvenir Sheet**			
3¢	**blue** (811,404)	17.50	16.50	❑❑❑❑❑

NOTE: For ungummed stamps (Farley issue), see CM158.

CM126	**1934. Maryland Tercentenary Issue**			
3¢	**carmine red** (46,258,300)	.25	.20	❑❑❑❑❑

NOTE: Rotary press, perforated 11 x 10 1/2.

CM127	**1934. Mother's Day Issue**			
3¢	**reddish violet** (193,239,100)	.25	.20	❑❑❑❑❑

NOTE: Flat press, perforated 11.

CM128				
3¢	**reddish violet** (15,432,200)	.25	.20	❑❑❑❑❑

NOTE: For ungummed stamps (Farley issue), see CM144.

CM129	**1934. Wisconsin Tercentenary Issue**			
3¢	**reddish violet** (64,525,400)	.25	.20	❑❑❑❑❑

NOTE: For ungummed stamps (Farley issue), see CM145.

CM130	**1934. National Parks Issue**			
1¢	**green** (84,896,350)	.25	.20	❑❑❑❑❑
CM131				
2¢	**red** (74,400,200)	.25	.20	❑❑❑❑❑
CM132				
3¢	**reddish violet** (95,089,000)	.25	.20	❑❑❑❑❑
CM133				
4¢	**yellow brown** (19,178,650)	.50	.35	❑❑❑❑❑
CM134				
5¢	**light blue** (30,980,100)	1.00	.75	❑❑❑❑❑
CM135				
6¢	**blue** (16,923,350)	1.25	1.00	❑❑❑❑❑
CM136				
7¢	**black** (15,988,250)	1.00	.75	❑❑❑❑❑
CM137				
8¢	**gray green** (15,288,700)	2.00	1.75	❑❑❑❑❑
CM138				
9¢	**orange red** (17,472,600)	2.00	.75	❑❑❑❑❑

CM108

CM109

CM110

CM111

CM112

CM113

CM114

CM115

CM116

CM117, CM142

CM118

CM120, CM156

CM119

CM122

CM123, CM143

CM124

CM121, CM157

CM125, CM158

		UnFVF	UseFVF	
CM139				
10¢ **gray black** (18,874,300)		3.25	1.25	❑❑❑❑❑

NOTE: For ungummed stamps, (Farley issue), see CM146-CM155.

CM140	**1934. Trans-Mississippi Philatelic Exposition Issue**			
1¢ **green,** sheet of 6 (793,551)		14.00	12.50	❑❑❑❑❑

NOTE: For ungummed stamps, (Farley issue), see CM159.

CM141	**1934. American Philatelic Society Issue**			
3¢ **reddish violet,** sheet of 6 (511,391)		40.00	30.00	❑❑❑❑❑

NOTE: For ungummed stamps (Farley issue), see CM160.

CM142	**1935. Newburgh Farley Issue**			
3¢ **reddish violet** (3,274,556)		.25	.20	❑❑❑❑❑
CM143	**1935. Byrd Farley Issue**			
3¢ **blue** (2,040,760)		.50	.45	❑❑❑❑❑
CM144	**1935. Mother's Day Farley Issue**			
3¢ **reddish violet** (2,389,288)		.60	.60	❑❑❑❑❑
CM145	**1935. Wisconsin Farley Issue**			
3¢ **reddish violet** (2,294,948)		.60	.60	❑❑❑❑❑
CM146	**1935. National Parks Farley Issue**			
1¢ **green** (3,217,636)		.25	.20	❑❑❑❑❑
CM147				
2¢ **red** (2,746,640)		.25	.20	❑❑❑❑❑
CM148				
3¢ **reddish violet** (2,168,088)		.50	.45	❑❑❑❑❑
CM149				
4¢ **yellow brown** (1,822,684)		1.25	1.25	❑❑❑❑❑
CM150				
5¢ **light blue** (1,724,576)		1.75	1.75	❑❑❑❑❑
CM151				
6¢ **blue** (1,647,696)		2.25	2.25	❑❑❑❑❑
CM152				
7¢ **black** (1,682,948)		2.00	1.75	❑❑❑❑❑
CM153				
8¢ **gray green** (1,638,644)		2.00	2.00	❑❑❑❑❑
CM154				
9¢ **orange red** (1,625,224)		2.00	2.00	❑❑❑❑❑
CM155				
10¢ **gray black** (1,644,900)		4.00	3.50	❑❑❑❑❑
CM156	**1935. Century of Progress Souvenir Sheet, Farley Issue**			
1¢ **yellow green** (2,467,800)		22.50	22.50	❑❑❑❑❑
CM157				
3¢ **reddish violet** (2,147,856)		20.00	20.00	❑❑❑❑❑
CM158	**1935. Byrd Souvenir Sheet, Farley Issue**			
3¢ **blue** (1,603,200)		17.50	12.50	❑❑❑❑❑
CM159	**1935. National Parks Souvenir Sheets, Farley Issue**			
1¢ **green** (1,679,760)		10.00	9.00	❑❑❑❑❑
CM160				
3¢ **reddish violet** (1,295,520)		25.00	20.00	❑❑❑❑❑
CM161	**1935. Airmail Special Delivery Farley Issue**			
16¢ **blue** (1,370,560)		2.75	2.50	❑❑❑❑❑
CM162	**1935. Connecticut Tercentenary Issue**			
3¢ **purple** (70,726,800)		.25	.20	❑❑❑❑❑

NOTE: For imperforates, see No. CM168.

CM163	**1935. California-Pacific Issue**			
3¢ **dark lilac** (100,839,600)		.25	.20	❑❑❑❑❑

NOTE: For imperforates, see No. CM168.

CM126

CM127-128, CM144

CM129, CM145

CM130, CM146

CM131, CM147

CM132, CM148

CM134, CM150

CM133, CM149

CM135, CM151

CM139, CM155

CM136, CM152

CM137, CM153

CM138, CM154

CM141, CM160

CM140, CM159

CM162

CM163

CM164

UnFVF	UseFVF

CM164_____ **1935. Boulder Dam Issue**
3¢ **dark lilac** (73,610,650) .25 .20 ☐☐☐☐☐

CM165_____ **1935. Michigan Centennial Issue**
3¢ **dark lilac** (75,823,900) .25 .20 ☐☐☐☐☐

NOTE: For imperforates, see No. CM168.

CM166_____ **1936. Texas Centennial Issue**
3¢ **dark lilac** (124,324,500) .25 .20 ☐☐☐☐☐

NOTE: For imperforates, see No. CM168.

CM167_____ **1936. Rhode Island Tercentenary Issue**
3¢ **dull purple** (67,127,650) .25 .20 ☐☐☐☐☐

CM168_____ **1936. TIPEX Souvenir Sheet**
4x3c **reddish purple** (2,809,039) 2.75 2.50 ☐☐☐☐☐

CM169_____ **1936. Arkansas Centennial Issue**
3¢ **dark lilac** (72,992,650) .25 .20 ☐☐☐☐☐

CM170_____ **1936. Oregon Territory Centennial Issue**
3¢ **dark lilac** (74,407,450) .25 .20 ☐☐☐☐☐

CM171_____ **1936. Susan B. Anthony Issue**
3¢ **reddish purple** (269,522,200) .25 .20 ☐☐☐☐☐

CM172_____ **1936-37. Army Issue**
1¢ **green** (105,196,150) .25 .20 ☐☐☐☐☐

CM173_____
2¢ **rose red** (93,848,500) .25 .20 ☐☐☐☐☐

CM174_____
3¢ **dull purple** (87,741,150) .25 .20 ☐☐☐☐☐

CM175_____
4¢ **slate** (35,794,150) .50 .20 ☐☐☐☐☐

CM176_____
5¢ **gray blue** (36,839,250) .75 .20 ☐☐☐☐☐

CM177_____ **1936-37. Navy Issue**
1¢ **green** (104,773,450) .25 .20 ☐☐☐☐☐

CM178_____
2¢ **rose red** (92,054,550) .25 .20 ☐☐☐☐☐

CM179_____
3¢ **dull purple** (93,291,650) .25 .20 ☐☐☐☐☐

CM180_____
4¢ **slate** (34,521,950) .50 .20 ☐☐☐☐☐

CM181_____
5¢ **gray blue** (36,819,050) .75 .20 ☐☐☐☐☐

CM182_____ **1937. Northwest Ordinance Issue of 1787**
3¢ **dull purple** (84,825,250) .25 .20 ☐☐☐☐☐

CM183_____ **1937. Virginia Dare Issue**
5¢ **light slate blue** (25,040,400) .25 .20 ☐☐☐☐☐

CM184_____ **1937. Society of Philatelic Americans Souvenir Sheet**
10¢ **blue green** (5,277,445) .75 .65 ☐☐☐☐☐

CM185_____ **1937. Constitution Sesquicentennial Issue**
3¢ **bright purple** (99,882,300) .25 .20 ☐☐☐☐☐

CM186_____ **1937. Hawaii Territory Issue**
3¢ **violet** (78,454,450) .25 .20 ☐☐☐☐☐

CM187_____ **1937. Alaska Territory Issue**
3¢ **violet** (77,004,200) .25 .20 ☐☐☐☐☐

CM188_____ **1937. Puerto Rico Territory Issue**
3¢ **light reddish violet** (81,292,450) .25 .20 ☐☐☐☐☐

CM189_____ **1937. Virgin Islands Issue**
3¢ **lilac** (76, 474,550) .25 .20 ☐☐☐☐☐

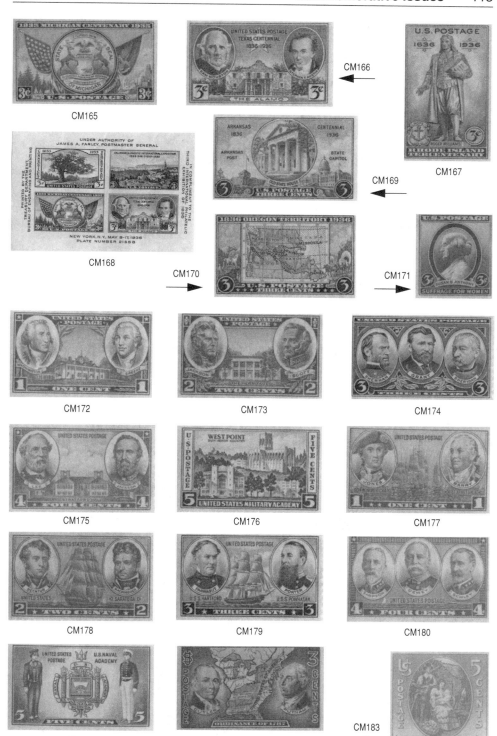

CM165

CM166

CM167

CM168

CM169

CM170

CM171

CM172

CM173

CM174

CM175

CM176

CM177

CM178

CM179

CM180

CM181

CM182

CM183

		UnFVF	UseFVF
CM190	**1938. Constitution Ratification Issue**		
3¢	**violet** (73,043,650)	.50	.20
CM191	**1938. Swedes and Finns Issue**		
3¢	**carmine purple** (58,564,368)	.25	.20
CM192	**1938. Northwest Territory Issue**		
3¢	**light reddish violet** (65,939,500)	.25	.20
CM193	**1938. Iowa Territory Issue**		
3¢	**violet** (47,064,300)	.25	.20
CM194	**1939. Golden Gate Exposition Issue**		
3¢	**light reddish violet** (114,439,600)	.25	.20
CM195	**1939. New York World's Fair Issue**		
3¢	**bluish violet** (101,699,550)	.25	.20
CM196	**1939. Washington Inauguration Issue**		
3¢	**bright purple** (73,764,550)	.25	.20
CM197	**1939. Baseball Centennial Issue**		
3¢	**violet** (81,269,600)	2.25	.20
CM198	**1939. Panama Canal Issue**		
3¢	**deep reddish purple** (67,813,350)	.50	.20
CM199	**1939. Printing Tercentenary Issue**		
3¢	**violet** (71,394,750)	.25	.20
CM200	**1939. Four States Issue**		
3¢	**reddish purple** (66,835,000)	.25	.20

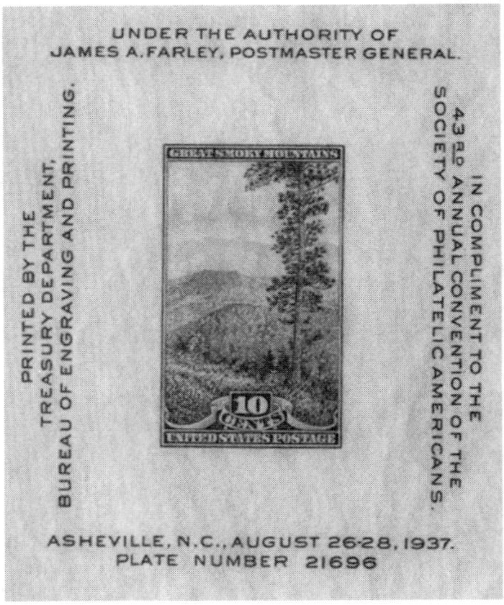

CM184

CM185

CM186

CM187

CM188

CM191

CM189

CM190

CM192

CM193

CM194

CM195

CM196

CM197

CM198

CM200

CM199

CM201

CM202

CM203

CM204

CM205

CM206

CM207

CM208

CM209

CM210

CM211

CM212

CM213

CM214

CM215

CM216

CM217

CM218

	MNHFVF	UseFVF
CM201 **1940. Famous Americans Series**		
1¢ **emerald** (56,348,320)	.25	.20 ❑❑❑❑❑
CM202		
2¢ **carmine** (53,177,110)	.25	.20 ❑❑❑❑❑
CM203		
3¢ **bright purple** (53,260,270)	.25	.20 ❑❑❑❑❑
CM204		
5¢ **gray blue** (22,104,950)	.40	.25 ❑❑❑❑❑
CM205		
10¢ **sepia** (13,201,270)	2.25	1.75 ❑❑❑❑❑
CM206		
1¢ **emerald** (51,603,580)	.25	.20 ❑❑❑❑❑
CM207		
2¢ **carmine** (52,100,510)	.25	.20 ❑❑❑❑❑
CM208		
3¢ **bright purple** (51,666,580)	.25	.20 ❑❑❑❑❑
CM209		
5¢ **gray blue** (22,207,780)	.45	.25 ❑❑❑❑❑
CM210		
10¢ **sepia** (11,835,530)	2.25	1.75 ❑❑❑❑❑
CM211		
1¢ **emerald** (52,471,160)	.25	.20 ❑❑❑❑❑
CM212		
2¢ **carmine** (52,366,440)	.25	.20 ❑❑❑❑❑
CM213		
3¢ **bright purple** (51,636,270)	.25	.20 ❑❑❑❑❑
CM214		
5¢ **gray blue** (20,729,030)	.40	.30 ❑❑❑❑❑
CM215		
10¢ **sepia** (14,125,580)	2.50	1.75 ❑❑❑❑❑
CM216		
1¢ **emerald** (59,409,000)	.25	.20 ❑❑❑❑❑
CM217		
2¢ **carmine** (57,888,600)	.25	.20 ❑❑❑❑❑
CM218		
3¢ **bright purple** (58,273,180)	.25	.20 ❑❑❑❑❑
CM219		
5¢ **gray blue** (23,779,000)	.50	.20 ❑❑❑❑❑
CM220		
10¢ **sepia** (15,112,580)	1.50	1.50 ❑❑❑❑❑
CM221		
1¢ **emerald** (57,322,790)	.25	.20 ❑❑❑❑❑
CM222		
2¢ **carmine** (58,281,580)	.25	.20 ❑❑❑❑❑
CM223		
3¢ **bright purple** (56,398,790)	.25	.20 ❑❑❑❑❑
CM224		
5¢ **gray blue** (21,147,000)	.75	.30 ❑❑❑❑❑
CM225		
10¢ **sepia** (13,328,000)	5.00	2.00 ❑❑❑❑❑
CM226		
1¢ **emerald** (54,389,510)	.25	.20 ❑❑❑❑❑
CM227		
2¢ **carmine** (53,636,580)	.25	.20 ❑❑❑❑❑

CM219

CM220

CM221

CM222

CM223

CM224

CM225

CM226

CM227

CM228

CM229

CM230

CM231

CM232

CM233

CM234

CM235

CM236

CM237

CM238

CM239

CM240

CM241

CM242

CM243

CM244

CM245

		MNHFVF	UseFVF	
CM228______				
3¢ **bright purple** (55,313,230)		.25	.20	❑❑❑❑❑
CM229______				
5¢ **gray blue** (21,720,580)		.75	.30	❑❑❑❑❑
CM230______				
10¢ **sepia** (13,600,580)		2.00	1.75	❑❑❑❑❑
CM231______				
1¢ **emerald** (47,599,580)		.25	.20	❑❑❑❑❑
CM232______				
2¢ **carmine** (53,766,510)		.25	.20	❑❑❑❑❑
CM233______				
3¢ **bright purple** (54,193,580)		.25	.20	❑❑❑❑❑
CM234______				
5¢ **gray blue** (20,264,580)		1.25	.50	❑❑❑❑❑
CM235______				
10¢ **sepia** (13,726,580)		15.00	3.25	❑❑❑❑❑
CM236______	**1940. Pony Express Issue**			
3¢ **chestnut** (46,497,400)		.35	.20	❑❑❑❑❑
CM237______	**1940. Pan-American Union Issue**			
3¢ **lilac** (47,700,000)		.30	.20	❑❑❑❑❑
CM238______	**1940. Idaho Statehood Issue**			
3¢ **light reddish violet** (50,618,150)		.25	.20	❑❑❑❑❑
CM239______	**1940. Wyoming Statehood Issue**			
3¢ **purple brown** (50,034,400)		.25	.20	❑❑❑❑❑
CM240______	**1940. Coronado Expedition Issue**			
3¢ **reddish lilac** (60,943,700)		.25	.20	❑❑❑❑❑
CM241______	**1940. National Defense Issue**			
1¢ **emerald** (6,081,409,300)		.25	.20	❑❑❑❑❑
CM242______				
2¢ **rose** (5,211,708,200)		.25	.20	❑❑❑❑❑
CM243______				
3¢ **light reddish violet** (8,384,867,600)		.25	.20	❑❑❑❑❑
CM244______	**1940. Thirteenth Amendment Issue**			
3¢ **violet** (44,389,550)		.35	.20	❑❑❑❑❑
CM245______	**1941. Vermont Statehood Issue**			
3¢ **violet** (54,574,550)		.25	.20	❑❑❑❑❑
CM246______	**1942. Kentucky Statehood Issue**			
3¢ **reddish violet** (63,558,400)		.25	.20	❑❑❑❑❑
CM247______	**1942. Win the War Issue**			
3¢ **violet** (20,642,793,300)		.25	.20	❑❑❑❑❑
CM248______	**1942. Chinese Commemorative Issue**			
5¢ **Prussian blue** (21,272,800)		.60	.30	❑❑❑❑❑
CM249______	**1943. Allied Nations Issue**			
2¢ **carmine** (1,671,564,200)		.25	.20	❑❑❑❑❑
CM250______	**1943. Four Freedoms Issue**			
1¢ **emerald** (1,227,334,200)		.25	.20	❑❑❑❑❑
CM251______	**1943-44. Overrun Countries Issue**			
5¢ **slate violet, scarlet & black** (19,999,646)		.25	.20	❑❑❑❑❑
CM252______				
5¢ **slate violet, blue, scarlet & black** (19,999,646)		.25	.20	❑❑❑❑❑
CM253______				
5¢ **slate violet, rose red, ultramarine & black** (19,999,616)		.25	.20	❑❑❑❑❑
CM254______				
5¢ **slate violet, rose red, light blue & black** (19,999,646)		.25	.20	❑❑❑❑❑

CM246

CM247

CM248

CM249

CM250

CM251

CM252

CM253

CM254

CM255

CM256

CM257

CM258

CM259

CM260

CM261

CM262

CM263

CM264

MNHFVF	UseFVF

CM255 _____
5¢ slate violet, scarlet, blue & black (19,999,646) .25 .20 ☐☐☐☐☐
CM256 _____
5¢ slate violet, scarlet, greenish yellow & black (19,999,646) .25 .20 ☐☐☐☐☐
CM257 _____
5¢ slate violet, blue, red & black (19,999,648) .25 .20 ☐☐☐☐☐
CM258 _____
5¢ slate violet, pale light blue & black (14,999,646) .50 .20 ☐☐☐☐☐
CM259 _____
5¢ slate violet, blue, rose red & black (14,999,646) .30 .20 ☐☐☐☐☐
CM260 _____
5¢ slate violet, red & black (14,999,646) .30 .20 ☐☐☐☐☐
CM261 _____
5¢ slate violet, red & black (14,999,646) .30 .20 ☐☐☐☐☐
CM262 _____
5¢ slate violet, scarlet & black (14,999,646) .30 .20 ☐☐☐☐☐
CM263 _____
5¢ slate violet, scarlet, bright blue & gray (14,999,646) .30 .20 ☐☐☐☐☐
CM264 _____ **1944. Transcontinental Railroad Issue**
3¢ violet (61,303,000) .30 .20 ☐☐☐☐☐
CM265 _____ **1944. Steamship Issue**
3¢ violet (61,001,450) .25 .20 ☐☐☐☐☐
CM266 _____ **1944. Telegraph Centennial Issue**
3¢ bright purple (60,605,000) .25 .20 ☐☐☐☐☐
CM267 _____ **1944. Corregidor Issue**
3¢ violet (50,129,350) .25 .20 ☐☐☐☐☐
CM268 _____ **1944. Motion Picture Issue**
3¢ violet (53,479,400) .25 .20 ☐☐☐☐☐
CM269 _____ **1945. Florida Centennial Issue**
3¢ bright purple (61,617,350) .25 .20 ☐☐☐☐☐
CM270 _____ **1945. United Nations Conference Issue**
5¢ ultramarine (75,500,000) .25 .20 ☐☐☐☐☐
CM271 _____ **1945-46. Roosevelt Series**
1¢ blue green (128,140,000) .25 .20 ☐☐☐☐☐

CM265

CM266

CM267

CM268

CM269

CM270

CM271

CM272

CM273

CM274

CM275

CM276

CM277

CM278

CM279

CM280

CM281

CM282

CM283

CM284

CM285

CM286

CM287

CM288

CM289

		MNHFVF	UseFVF
CM272			
2¢ **carmine red** (67,255,000)		.25	.20 ❑❑❑❑❑
CM273			
3¢ **lilac** (138,870,000)		.25	.20 ❑❑❑❑❑
CM274			
5¢ **light blue** (76,455,400)		.25	.20 ❑❑❑❑❑
CM275	**1945. Marine Commemorative**		
3¢ **dark yellow green** (137,321,000)		.25	.20 ❑❑❑❑❑
CM276	**1945. Army Commemorative**		
3¢ **brown olive** (128,357,750)		.25	.20 ❑❑❑❑❑
CM277	**1945. Navy Commemorative**		
3¢ **blue** (138,863,000)		.25	.20 ❑❑❑❑❑
CM278	**1945. Coast Guard Commemorative**		
3¢ **blue green** (111,616,700)		.25	.20 ❑❑❑❑❑
CM279	**1946. Merchant Marine Commemorative**		
3¢ **blue green** (135,927,000)		.25	.20 ❑❑❑❑❑
CM280	**1945. Alfred E. Smith Issue**		
3¢ **dark lilac** (308,587,700)		.25	.20 ❑❑❑❑❑
CM281	**1945. Texas Statehood Issue**		
3¢ **Prussian blue** (170,640,000)		.25	.20 ❑❑❑❑❑
CM282	**1946. Honorable Discharge Stamp**		
3¢ **violet** (269,339,100)		.25	.20 ❑❑❑❑❑
CM283	**1946. Tennessee Statehood Issue**		
3¢ **violet** (132,274,500)		.25	.20 ❑❑❑❑❑
CM284	**1946. Iowa Statehood Issue**		
3¢ **Prussian blue** (132,430,000)		.25	.20 ❑❑❑❑❑
CM285	**1946. Smithsonian Institution Issue**		
3¢ **brown purple** (139,209,500)		.25	.20 ❑❑❑❑❑
CM286	**1946. Kearny Expedition Issue**		
3¢ **brown purple** (114,684,450)		.25	.20 ❑❑❑❑❑
CM287	**1947. Thomas A. Edison Issue**		
3¢ **bright purple** (156,540,510)		.25	.20 ❑❑❑❑❑
CM288	**1947. Joseph Pulitzer Issue**		
3¢ **dark lilac** (120,452,600)		.25	.20 ❑❑❑❑❑
CM289	**1947. Postage Stamp Centenary Issue**		
3¢ **blue** (127,104,300)		.25	.20 ❑❑❑❑❑
CM290	**1947. CIPEX Souvenir Sheet**		
15¢ **Complete sheet of 2 stamps** (10,299,600)		.75	.65 ❑❑❑❑❑
CM291	**1947. The Doctors Issue**		
3¢ **brown purple** (132,902,000)		.25	.20 ❑❑❑❑❑
CM292	**1947. Utah Issue**		
3¢ **violet** (131,968,000)		.25	.20 ❑❑❑❑❑
CM293	**1947. U.S. Frigate Constitution Issue**		
3¢ **blue green** (131,488,000)		.25	.20 ❑❑❑❑❑
CM294	**1947. Everglades National Park Issue**		
3¢ **emerald** (122,362,000)		.25	.20 ❑❑❑❑❑
CM295	**1948. George Washington Carver Issue**		
3¢ **bright purple** (121,548,000)		.25	.20 ❑❑❑❑❑
CM296	**1948. California Gold Centennial Issue**		
3¢ **violet** (131,109,500)		.25	.20 ❑❑❑❑❑
CM297	**1948. Mississippi Territory Issue**		
3¢ **brown purple** (122,650,500)		.25	.20 ❑❑❑❑❑
CM298	**1948. Four Chaplains Issue**		
3¢ **black** (121,953,500)		.25	.20 ❑❑❑❑❑

CM290

CM291

CM292

CM293

CM294

CM295

CM296

CM297

CM298

CM299

CM300

CM301

CM302

CM303

CM304

CM305

		MNHFVF	UseFVF	
CM299	**1948. Wisconsin Centennial Issue**			
3¢	**violet** (115,250,000)	.25	.20	❑❑❑❑❑
CM300	**1948. Swedish Pioneers Issue**			
5¢	**blue** (64,198,500)	.25	.20	❑❑❑❑❑
CM301	**1948. The Progress of Women Issue**			
3¢	**violet** (117,642,500)	.25	.20	❑❑❑❑❑
CM302	**1948. William Allen White Issue**			
3¢	**bright purple** (77,649,000)	.25	.20	❑❑❑❑❑
CM303	**1948. United States - Canada Friendship Issue**			
3¢	**blue** (113,474,500)	.25	.20	❑❑❑❑❑
CM304	**1948. Francis Scott Key Issue**			
3¢	**carmine** (120,868,500)	.25	.20	❑❑❑❑❑
CM305	**1948. American Youth Issue**			
3¢	**blue** (77,800,500)	.25	.20	❑❑❑❑❑
CM306	**1948. Oregon Territory Issue**			
3¢	**Venetian red** (52,214,000)	.25	.20	❑❑❑❑❑
CM307	**1948. Harlan Fiske Stone Issue**			
3¢	**bright purple** (53,958,100)	.25	.20	❑❑❑❑❑
CM308	**1948. Palomar Mountain Observatory Issue**			
3¢	**blue** (61,120,010)	.25	.20	❑❑❑❑❑
CM309	**1948. Clara Barton Issue**			
3¢	**carmine** (57,823,000)	.25	.20	❑❑❑❑❑
CM310	**1948. Poultry Industry Centennial Issue**			
3¢	**sepia** (52,975,000)	.25	.20	❑❑❑❑❑
CM311	**1948. Gold Star Mothers Issue**			
3¢	**yellow** (77,149,000)	.25	.20	❑❑❑❑❑
CM312	**1948. Fort Kearny Issue**			
3¢	**violet** (58,332,000)	.25	.20	❑❑❑❑❑
CM313	**1948. Volunteer Fireman Issue**			
3¢	**rose carmine** (56,228,000)	.25	.20	❑❑❑❑❑
CM314	**1948. Indian Centennial Issue**			
3¢	**brown** (57,832,000)	.25	.20	❑❑❑❑❑
CM315	**1948. Rough Riders Issue**			
3¢	**brown purple** (53,875,000)	.25	.20	❑❑❑❑❑
CM316	**1948. Juliette Low Issue**			
3¢	**blue green** (63,834,000)	.25	.20	❑❑❑❑❑
CM317	**1948. Will Rogers Issue**			
3¢	**bright purple** (67,162,200)	.25	.20	❑❑❑❑❑
CM318	**1948. Fort Bliss Centennial Issue**			
3¢	**chestnut** (64,561,000)	.35	.20	❑❑❑❑❑
CM319	**1948. Moina Michael Issue**			
3¢	**rose carmine** (64,079,500)	.25	.20	❑❑❑❑❑
CM320	**1948. Gettysburg Address Issue**			
3¢	**light blue** (63,388,000)	.25	.20	❑❑❑❑❑
CM321	**1948. American Turners Issue**			
3¢	**carmine** (62,285,000)	.25	.20	❑❑❑❑❑
CM322	**1948. Joel Chandler Harris Issue**			
3¢	**bright purple** (57,492,610)	.25	.20	❑❑❑❑❑
CM323	**1949. Minnesota Territory Issue**			
3¢	**blue green** (99,190,000)	.25	.20	❑❑❑❑❑
CM324	**1949. Washington and Lee University Issue**			
3¢	**bright blue** (104,790,000)	.25	.20	❑❑❑❑❑
CM325	**1949. Puerto Rico Election Issue**			
3¢	**dull green** (108,805,000)	.25	.20	❑❑❑❑❑

CM306

CM307

CM308

CM309

CM310

CM311

CM312

CM313

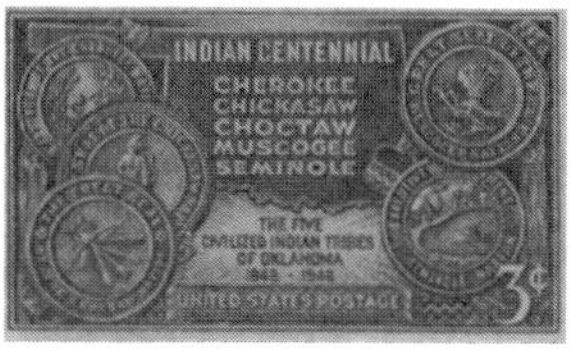

CM314

CM315

CM316

CM317

CM318

CM319

CM320

CM321

CM322

CM323

CM324

CM325

CM326

MNHFVF	UseFVF	

CM326_____ 1949. Annapolis Tercentenary Issue
3¢ turquoise green (107,340,000) .25 .20 ☐☐☐☐☐

CM327_____ 1949. GAR Issue
3¢ carmine (117,020,000) .25 .20 ☐☐☐☐☐

CM328_____ 1949. Edgar Allan Poe Issue
3¢ bright purple (122,633,000) .25 .20 ☐☐☐☐☐

CM329_____ 1950. American Bankers Association Issue
3¢ green (130,960,000) .25 .20 ☐☐☐☐☐

CM330_____ 1950. Samuel Gompers Issue
3¢ bright purple (128,478,000) .25 .20 ☐☐☐☐☐

CM331_____ 1950. National Capital Sesquicentennial Issue
3¢ light blue (132,090,000) .25 .20 ☐☐☐☐☐

CM332_____
3¢ dull green (130,050,000) .25 .20 ☐☐☐☐☐

CM333_____
3¢ bluish violet (131,350,000) .25 .20 ☐☐☐☐☐

CM334_____
3¢ bright purple (129,980,000) .25 .20 ☐☐☐☐☐

CM335_____ 1950. Railroad Engineers Issue
3¢ brown purple (122,315,000) .25 .20 ☐☐☐☐☐

CM336_____ 1950. Kansas City Centennial Issue
3¢ violet (122,170,000) .25 .20 ☐☐☐☐☐

CM337_____ 1950. Boy Scout Issue
3¢ sepia (131,635,000) .25 .20 ☐☐☐☐☐

CM338_____ 1950. Indiana Territory Sesquicentennial Issue
3¢ light blue (121,860,000) .25 .20 ☐☐☐☐☐

CM339_____ 1950. California Statehood Centennial Issue
3¢ yellow (121,120,000) .25 .20 ☐☐☐☐☐

CM340_____ 1951. Confederate Veterans Issue
3¢ gray (119,120,000) .25 .20 ☐☐☐☐☐

CM341_____ 1951. Nevada Centennial Issue
3¢ light olive green (112,125,000) .25 .20 ☐☐☐☐☐

CM342_____ 1952. Detroit Issue
3¢ light blue (114,140,000) .25 .20 ☐☐☐☐☐

CM343_____ 1951. Colorado Statehood Issue
3¢ violet blue (114,490,000) .25 .20 ☐☐☐☐☐

CM344_____ 1951. American Chemical Society Issue
3¢ brown purple (117,200,000) .25 .20 ☐☐☐☐☐

CM345_____ 1951. Battle of Brooklyn Issue
3¢ violet (16,130,000) .25 .20 ☐☐☐☐☐

CM346_____ 1952. Betsy Ross Issue
3¢ carmine red (116,175,000) .25 .20 ☐☐☐☐☐

CM347_____ 1952. 4-H Club Issue
3¢ blue green (115,945,000) .25 .20 ☐☐☐☐☐

CM348_____ 1952. American Railroads Issue
3¢ light blue (112,540,000) .25 .20 ☐☐☐☐☐

CM349_____ 1952. AAA Issue
3¢ blue (117,415,000) .25 .20 ☐☐☐☐☐

CM350_____ 1952. NATO Issue
3¢ violet (2,899,580,000) .25 .20 ☐☐☐☐☐

CM351_____ 1952. Grand Coulee Dam Issue
3¢ blue green (114,540,000) .25 .20 ☐☐☐☐☐

CM352_____ 1952. Lafayette Issue
3¢ bright blue (113,135,000) .25 .20 ☐☐☐☐☐

CM327

CM328

CM329

CM330

CM331

CM332

CM333

CM334

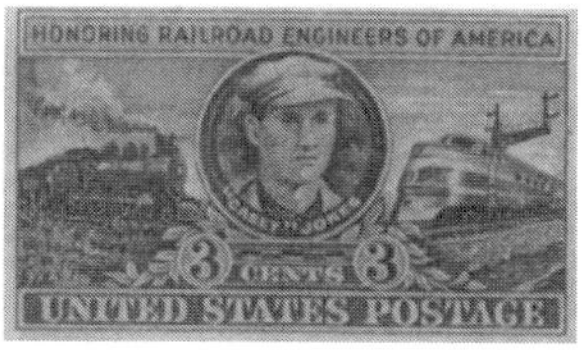

CM335

CM336

CM337

CM338

CM339

CM340

CM341

CM342

CM343

CM344

CM345

		MNHFVF	UseFVF	
CM353	**1952. Mount Rushmore Memorial Issue**			
3¢	**blue green** (116,255,000)	.25	.20	❑❑❑❑❑
CM354	**1952. Engineering Centennial Issue**			
3¢	**ultramarine** (113,860,000)	.25	.20	❑❑❑❑❑
CM355	**1952. Service Women Issue**			
3¢	**blue** (124,260,000)	.25	.20	❑❑❑❑❑
CM356	**1952. Gutenberg Bible Issue**			
3¢	**violet** (115,735,000)	.25	.20	❑❑❑❑❑
CM357	**1952. Newspaperboys of America Issue**			
3¢	**violet** (115,430,000)	.25	.20	❑❑❑❑❑
CM358	**1952. International Red Cross Issue**			
3¢	**ultramarine & scarlet** (136,220,000)	.25	.20	❑❑❑❑❑
CM359	**1953. National Guard Issue**			
3¢	**light blue** (114,894,600)	.25	.20	❑❑❑❑❑
CM360	**1953. Ohio Sesquicentennial Issue**			
3¢	**sepia** (117,706,000)	.25	.20	❑❑❑❑❑
CM361	**1953. Washington Territory Issue**			
3¢	**blue green** (114,190,000)	.25	.20	❑❑❑❑❑
CM362	**1953. Louisiana Purchase Issue**			
3¢	**brown purple** (113,990,000)	.25	.20	❑❑❑❑❑
CM363	**1953. Opening of Japan Issue**			
5¢	**blue green** (89,289,600)	.25	.20	❑❑❑❑❑
CM364	**1953. American Bar Association Issue**			
3¢	**light reddish violet** (114,865,000)	.25	.20	❑❑❑❑❑
CM365	**1953. Sagamore Hill Issue**			
3¢	**green** (115,780,000)	.25	.20	❑❑❑❑❑

CM346

CM347

CM348

CM349

CM350

CM351

CM352

CM353

CM354

CM355

CM356

CM357

CM358

CM359

CM360

CM361

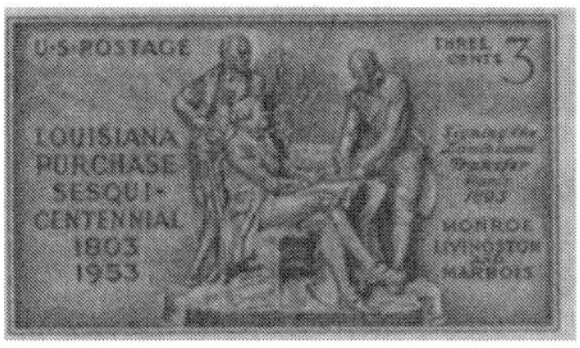

CM362

CM363

CM364

CM365

CM366

CM367

CM368

CM369

CM370

CM371

CM372

		MNHFVF	UseFVF
CM366	**1953. Future Farmers of America Issue**		
3¢	**bright blue** (115,224,600)	.25	.20 ❑❑❑❑❑
CM367	**1953. Trucking Industry Issue**		
3¢	**violet** (123,709,600)	.25	.20 ❑❑❑❑❑
CM368	**1953. General Patton Issue**		
3¢	**bluish violet** (114,789,600)	.25	.20 ❑❑❑❑❑
CM369	**1953. New York City Tercentenary Issue**		
3¢	**bright purple** (115,759,600)	.25	.20 ❑❑❑❑❑
CM370	**1953. Gadsden Purchase Issue**		
3¢	**Venetian red** (115,759,600)	.25	.20 ❑❑❑❑❑
CM371	**1953. Columbia University Issue**		
3¢	**cobalt blue** (118,540,000)	.25	.20 ❑❑❑❑❑
CM372	**1954. Nebraska Territorial Centennial Issue**		
3¢	**violet** (115,810,000)	.25	.20 ❑❑❑❑❑
CM373	**1954. Kansas Territorial Centennial Issue**		
3¢	**salmon** (113,603,700)	.25	.20 ❑❑❑❑❑
CM374	**1954. George Eastman Issue**		
3¢	**brown purple** (121,100,000)	.25	.20 ❑❑❑❑❑
CM375	**1954. Lewis and Clark Expedition Issue**		
3¢	**brown** (116,078,150)	.25	.20 ❑❑❑❑❑
CM376	**1955. Pennsylvania Academy of Fine Arts Issue**		
3¢	**brown purple** (116,139,800)	.25	.20 ❑❑❑❑❑
CM377	**1955. First Land-Grant College Issue**		
3¢	**emerald green** (120,484,800)	.25	.20 ❑❑❑❑❑
CM378	**1955. Rotary International Issue**		
8¢	**deep blue** (53,854,750)	.25	.20 ❑❑❑❑❑
CM379	**1955. The Armed Forces Reserve Issue**		
3¢	**bright purple** (176,075,000)	.25	.20 ❑❑❑❑❑
CM380	**1955. Old Man of the Mountains Issue**		
3¢	**blue green** (125,944,400)	.25	.20 ❑❑❑❑❑
CM381	**1955. Soo Locks Centennial Issue**		
3¢	**blue** (122,284,600)	.25	.20 ❑❑❑❑❑
CM382	**1955. Atoms for Peace Issue**		
3¢	**deep blue** (133,638,850)	.25	.20 ❑❑❑❑❑
CM383	**1955. Fort Ticonderoga Bicentennial Issue**		
3¢	**dark red brown** (118,664,600)	.25	.20 ❑❑❑❑❑
CM384	**1955. Andrew Mellon Issue**		
3¢	**carmine red** (112,434,000)	.25	.20 ❑❑❑❑❑
CM385	**1956. Franklin 250th Anniversary Issue**		
3¢	**carmine** (129,384,550)	.25	.20 ❑❑❑❑❑
CM386	**1956. Booker T. Washington Issue**		
3¢	**deep blue** (121,184,600)	.25	.20 ❑❑❑❑❑
CM387	**1956. FIPEX Issue**		
3¢	**violet** (119,784,200)	.25	.20 ❑❑❑❑❑
CM388	**1956. Fifth International Philatelic Exhibition (FIPEX) Souvenir Sheet**		
11¢	**Complete sheet of 2 stamps** (9,802,025)	2.50	2.00 ❑❑❑❑❑
CM389	**1956. Wild Turkey Issue**		
3¢	**brown purple** (123,159,400)	.25	.20 ❑❑❑❑❑
CM390	**1956. Pronghorn Antelope Issue**		
3¢	**sepia** (123,138,800)	.25	.20 ❑❑❑❑❑
CM391	**1956. King Salmon Issue**		
3¢	**blue green** (109,275,000)	.25	.20 ❑❑❑❑❑
CM392	**1956. Pure Food and Drug Laws Issue**		
3¢	**blue green** (112,932,200)	.25	.20 ❑❑❑❑❑

CM373

CM374

CM375

CM376

CM377

CM378

CM380

CM381

CM379

CM382

CM383

CM384

CM385

CM386

CM387

CM388

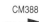

CM389

		MNHFVF	UseFVF	
CM393____________	**1956. Wheatland Issue**			
3¢	**black brown** (125,475,000)	.25	.20	❑❑❑❑❑
CM394____________	**1956. Labor Day Issue**			
3¢	**deep blue** (117,855,000)	.25	.20	❑❑❑❑❑
CM395____________	**1956. Nassau Hall Issue**			
3¢	**black on orange** (122,100,00)	.25	.20	❑❑❑❑❑
CM396____________	**1956. Devils Tower Issue**			
3¢	**lilac** (118,180,000)	.25	.20	❑❑❑❑❑
CM397____________	**1956. Children's Issue**			
3¢	**blue** (100,975,000)	.25	.20	❑❑❑❑❑
CM398____________	**1957. Alexander Hamilton Bicentennial Issue**			
3¢	**rose red** (115,299,450)	.25	.20	❑❑❑❑❑
CM399____________	**1957. Anti-Polio Issue**			
3¢	**bright purple** (186,949,250)	.25	.20	❑❑❑❑❑
CM400____________	**1957. Coast and Geodetic Survey Issue**			
3¢	**deep blue** (115,235,000)	.25	.20	❑❑❑❑❑
CM401____________	**1957. Architects of America Issue**			
3¢	**rose lilac** (106,647,500)	.25	.20	❑❑❑❑❑
CM402____________	**1957. Steel Industry in America Issue**			
3¢	**bright blue** (112,010,000)	.25	.20	❑❑❑❑❑
CM403____________	**1957. International Naval Review Issue**			
3¢	**blue green** (118,399,600)	.25	.20	❑❑❑❑❑
CM404____________	**1957. Oklahoma Statehood Issue**			
3¢	**bright blue** (102,209,500)	.25	.20	❑❑❑❑❑
CM405____________	**1957. Teachers of America Issue**			
3¢	**brown purple** (103,045,000)	.25	.20	❑❑❑❑❑
CM406____________	**1957. American Flag Issue**			
4¢	**deep blue & carmine** (84,054,400)	.25	.20	❑❑❑❑❑
CM407____________	**1957. Virginia of Sagadahock Issue**			
3¢	**violet** (126,266,000)	.25	.20	❑❑❑❑❑
CM408____________	**1957. Ramon Magsaysay Issue**			
8¢	**scarlet, deep ultramarine & ocher** (39,489,600)	.25	.20	❑❑❑❑❑
CM409____________	**1957. Lafayette Issue**			
3¢	**brown purple** (122,990,000)	.25	.20	❑❑❑❑❑
CM410____________	**1957. Whooping Crane Issue**			
3¢	**gray blue, yellow & blue green** (174,372,800)	.25	.20	❑❑❑❑❑
CM411____________	**1957. Flushing Remonstrance Issue**			
3¢	**brown black** (114,365,000)	.25	.20	❑❑❑❑❑
CM412____________	**1958. Garden and Horticultural Issue**			
3¢	**dull green** (122,765,200)	.25	.20	❑❑❑❑❑
CM413____________	**1958. Brussels Universal and International Exhibition Issue**			
3¢	**brown purple** (113,660,200)	.25	.20	❑❑❑❑❑
CM414____________	**1958. James Monroe Issue**			
3¢	**violet** (120,196,580)	.25	.20	❑❑❑❑❑
CM415____________	**1958. Minnesota Statehood Centennial Issue**			
3¢	**emerald green** (120,805,200)	.25	.20	❑❑❑❑❑
CM416____________	**1958. International Geophysical Year Issue**			
3¢	**black & red** (125,815,200)	.25	.20	❑❑❑❑❑
CM417____________	**1958. Gunston Hall Bicentennial Issue**			
3¢	**dull green** (108,415,200)	.25	.20	❑❑❑❑❑
CM418____________	**1958. Mackinac Straits Bridge Issue**			
3¢	**turquoise blue** (107,195,200)	.25	.20	❑❑❑❑❑
CM419____________	**1958. Simon Bolívar Issue**			
4¢	**olive buff** (115,745,280)	.25	.20	❑❑❑❑❑

CM390

CM391

CM392

CM393

CM394

CM395

CM396

CM397

CM398

CM399

CM400

CM401

CM403

CM404

CM402

CM405

CM406

CM407

		MNHFVF	UseFVF	
CM420	**1958. Simon Bolívar Issue**			
8¢	**scarlet, deep ultramarine & deep ocher** (39,743,640)	.25	.20	❑❑❑❑❑
CM421	**1958. Atlantic Cable Centennial Issue**			
4¢	**red violet** (114,570,200)	.25	.20	❑❑❑❑❑
CM422	**1958. Lincoln Douglas Debate Issue**			
4¢	**brown** (114,860,200)	.25	.20	❑❑❑❑❑
CM423	**1958. Lajos Kossuth Issue**			
4¢	**dull green** (120,561,280)	.25	.20	❑❑❑❑❑
CM424	**1958. Lajos Kossuth Issue**			
8¢	**scarlet, deep ultramarine & deep ochre** (44,064,576)	.25	.20	❑❑❑❑❑
CM425	**1958. Journalism and Freedom of the Press Issue**			
4¢	**gray black** (118,390,200)	.25	.20	❑❑❑❑❑
CM426	**1958. Overland Mail Centennial Issue**			
4¢	**orange red** (125,770,200)	.25	.20	❑❑❑❑❑
CM427	**1958. Noah Webster Bicentennial Issue**			
4¢	**magenta** (114,114,280)	.25	.20	❑❑❑❑❑
CM428	**1958. Forest Conservation Issue**			
4¢	**deep green, yellow & brown** (156,600,200)	.25	.20	❑❑❑❑❑
CM429	**1958. Fort Duquesne Bicentennial Issue**			
4¢	**light blue** (124,200,200)	.25	.20	❑❑❑❑❑
CM430	**1959. Lincoln Sesquicentennial Issue**			
1¢	**deep green** (120,400,200)	.25	.20	❑❑❑❑❑
CM431	**1959. Head of Lincoln Issue**			
3¢	**deep plum** (91,160,200)	.25	.20	❑❑❑❑❑
CM432	**1959. Lincoln Statue Issue**			
4¢	**blue** (126,500,000)	.25	.20	❑❑❑❑❑
CM433	**1959. Oregon Statehood Issue**			
4¢	**blue green** (120,740,200)	.25	.20	❑❑❑❑❑
CM434	**1959. José de San Martin Issue**			
4¢	**blue** (113,623,280)	.25	.20	❑❑❑❑❑
CM435				
8¢	**carmine, blue & ocher** (45,569,088)	.25	.20	❑❑❑❑❑
CM436	**1959. NATO Issue**			
4¢	**blue** (122,493,280)	.25	.20	❑❑❑❑❑
CM437	**1959. Arctic Explorations Issue**			
4¢	**turquoise blue** (131,260,200)	.25	.20	❑❑❑❑❑
CM438	**1959. Peace through Trade Issue**			
8¢	**brown purple** (47,125,200)	.25	.20	❑❑❑❑❑
CM439	**1959. Silver Centennial Issue**			
4¢	**black** (123,105,000)	.25	.20	❑❑❑❑❑
CM440	**1959. St. Lawrence Seaway Issue**			
4¢	**blue & red** (126,105,050)	.25	.20	❑❑❑❑❑
CM441	**1959. 49-Star Flag Issue**			
4¢	**deep blue & carmine** (209,170,000)	.25	.20	❑❑❑❑❑
CM442	**1959. Soil Conservation Issue**			
4¢	**blue green & yellow orange** (120,835,000)	.25	.20	❑❑❑❑❑
CM443	**1959. Petroleum Industry Centennial Issue**			
4¢	**brown** (115,715,000)	.25	.20	❑❑❑❑❑
CM444	**1959. Dental Health Issue**			
4¢	**dark green** (118,445,000)	.25	.20	❑❑❑❑❑
CM445	**1959. Ernst Reuter Issue**			
4¢	**black** (111,685,000)	.25	.20	❑❑❑❑❑
CM446	**1959. Ernst Reuter Issue**			
8¢	**carmine, blue & ocher** (43,099,200)	.25	.20	❑❑❑❑❑

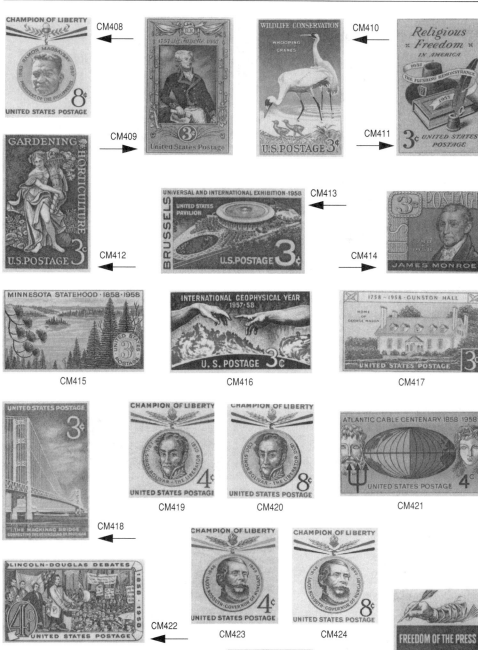

CM408

CM409

CM410

CM411

CM412

CM413

CM414

CM415

CM416

CM417

CM418

CM419

CM420

CM421

CM422

CM423

CM424

CM425

CM426

CM427

CM428

CM429

CM430

CM431

CM432

CM433

CM436

CM434

CM435

CM437

CM438

CM439

CM440

CM441

CM442

CM443

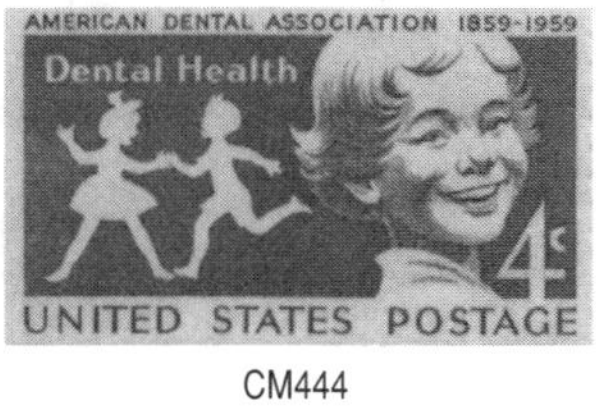

CM444

CM445

CM446

CM447

CM448

CM449

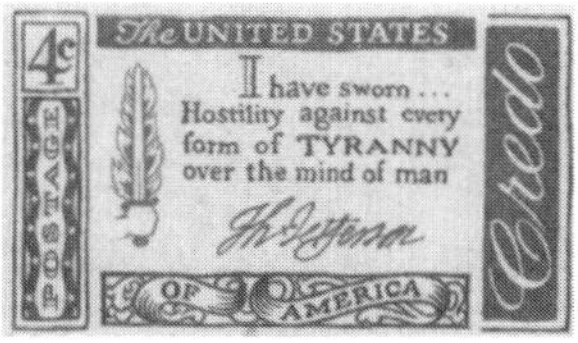

CM450

CM451

CM452

CM453

CM454

CM455

CM456

CM457

CM458

CM459

CM460

CM461

CM462

CM463

CM464

		MNHFVF	UseFVF
CM447	**1959. Ephraim McDowell Issue**		
4¢	**brown purple** (115,444,000)	.25	.20
CM448	**1960. George Washington Issue**		
4¢	**deep blue & carmine** (126,470,000)	.25	.20
CM449	**1960. Benjamin Franklin Issue**		
4¢	**brown bister & emerald** (124,460,000)	.25	.20
CM450	**1960. Thomas Jefferson Issue**		
4¢	**gray & scarlet** (115,445,000)	.25	.20
CM451	**1960. Francis Scott Key**		
4¢	**carmine red & deep blue** (122,060,000)	.25	.20
CM452	**1960. Abraham Lincoln Issue**		
4¢	**bright purple & green** (120,540,000)	.25	.20
CM453	**1960. Patrick Henry Issue**		
4¢	**green & brown** (113,075,000)	.25	.20
CM454	**1960. Boy Scout Issue**		
4¢	**red, deep blue & deep ocher** (139,325,000)	.25	.20
CM455	**1960. Winter Olympic Games Issue**		
4¢	**turquoise blue** (124,445,000)	.25	.20
CM456	**1960. Tomas G. Masaryk Issue**		
4¢	**blue** (113,792,000)	.25	.20
CM457			
8¢	**carmine, deep blue & ocher** (44,215,200)	.25	.20
CM458	**1960. World Refugee Year Issue**		
4¢	**gray black** (113,195,000)	.25	.20
CM459	**1960. Water Conservation Issue**		
4¢	**blue, green & orange brown** (120,570,000)	.25	.20
CM460	**1960. SEATO Issue**		
4¢	**blue** (115,353,000)	.25	.20
CM461	**1960. American Women Issue**		
4¢	**violet** (111,080,000)	.25	.20
CM462	**1960. 50-Star Flag Issue**		
4¢	**deep blue & scarlet** (153,025,000)	.25	.20
CM463	**1960. Pony Express Centenary Issue**		
4¢	**sepia** (119,665,000)	.25	.20
CM464	**1960. Employ the Handicapped Issue**		
4¢	**blue** (117,855,000)	.25	.20
CM465	**1960. Fifth World Forestry Congress Issue**		
4¢	**blue green** (118,185,000)	.25	.20
CM466	**1960. Mexican Independence Issue**		
4¢	**deep green & carmine red** (112,260,000)	.25	.20
CM467	**1960. United States of America-Japan Centennial Issue**		
4¢	**light blue & carmine** (125,010,000)	.25	.20
CM468	**1960. Ignace Jan Paderewski Issue**		
4¢	**blue** (119,798,000)	.25	.20
CM469			
8¢	**red, blue & ocher** (42,696,000)	.25	.20
CM470	**1960. Robert A. Taft Issue**		
4¢	**violet** (115,171,000)	.25	.20
CM471	**1960. Wheels of Freedom Issue**		
4¢	**blue** (109,695,000)	.25	.20
CM472	**1960. Boys' Club of America Issue**		
4¢	**deep blue, black & red** (123,690,000)	.25	.20
CM473	**1960. First Automated Post Office Issue**		
4¢	**deep blue & scarlet** (127,970,000)	.25	.20

CM465

CM466

CM467

CM468

CM469

CM470

CM471

CM472

CM473

CM474

CM475

CM476

CM477

CM478

CM479

CM480

CM481

CM482

CM483

CM484

CM485

		MNHFVF	UseFVF	
CM474	**1960. Baron Karl Gustaf Emil Mannerheim Issue**			
4¢	**blue** (124,796,000)	.25	.20	❑❑❑❑❑
CM475				
8¢	**red, blue & ocher** (42,076,800)	.25	.20	❑❑❑❑❑
CM476	**1960. Campfire Girls Issue**			
4¢	**blue & red** (116,215,000)	.25	.20	❑❑❑❑❑
CM477	**1960. Giuseppe Garibaldi Issue**			
4¢	**green** (126,252,000)	.25	.20	❑❑❑❑❑
CM478				
8¢	**red, blue & ocher** (42,746,400)	.25	.20	❑❑❑❑❑
CM479	**1960. Walter F. George Issue**			
4¢	**violet** (124,117,000)	.25	.20	❑❑❑❑❑
CM480	**1960. John Foster Dulles Issue**			
4¢	**violet** (177,187,000)	.20	.20	❑❑❑❑❑
CM481	**1960. Andrew Carnegie Issue**			
4¢	**claret** (119,840,000)	.20	.20	❑❑❑❑❑
CM482	**1960. Echo I Satellite Issue**			
4¢	**violet** (125,290,000)	.25	.20	❑❑❑❑❑
CM483	**1961. Mahatma Gandhi Issue**			
4¢	**red orange** (112,966,000)	.20	.20	❑❑❑❑❑
CM484				
8¢	**red, blue & ocher** (41,644,200)	.25	.20	❑❑❑❑❑
CM485	**1961. Range Conservation Issue**			
4¢	**blue, orange & indigo** (110,850,000)	.20	.20	❑❑❑❑❑
CM486	**1961. Horace Greeley Issue**			
4¢	**violet** (98,616,000)	.20	.20	❑❑❑❑❑
CM487	**1961. Fort Sumter Issue**			
4¢	**green** (101,125,000)	.25	.20	❑❑❑❑❑
CM488	**1962. Battle of Shiloh Issue**			
4¢	**black on pink** (124,865,000)	.25	.20	❑❑❑❑❑
CM489	**1963. Battle of Gettysburg Issue**			
5¢	**gray & blue** (79,905,000)	.25	.20	❑❑❑❑❑
CM490	**1964. Battle of the Wilderness Issue**			
5¢	**brown, purple & black** (125,410,000)	.25	.20	❑❑❑❑❑
CM491	**1965. Appomattox Issue**			
5¢	**blue & black** (112,845,000)	.25	.20	❑❑❑❑❑
CM492	**1961. Kansas Statehood Centennial Issue**			
4¢	**brown, lake & green** on yellow paper (106,210,000)	.20	.20	❑❑❑❑❑
CM493	**1961. George William Norris Issue**			
4¢	**blue green** (110,810,000)	.20	.20	❑❑❑❑❑
CM494	**1961. Naval Aviation Issue**			
4¢	**blue** (116,995,000)	.20	.20	❑❑❑❑❑
CM495	**1961. Workman's Compensation Issue**			
4¢	**ultramarine** on bluish paper (121,015,000)	.20	.20	❑❑❑❑❑
CM496	**1961. Frederic Remington Issue**			
4¢	**blue, red & yellow** (111,600,000)	.20	.20	❑❑❑❑❑
CM497	**1961. 50th Anniversary of the Republic of China Issue**			
4¢	**blue** (110,620,000)	.20	.20	❑❑❑❑❑
CM498	**1961. Naismith-Basketball Issue**			
4¢	**brown** (109,110,000)	.25	.20	❑❑❑❑❑
CM499	**1961. Nursing Issue**			
4¢	**blue, black, orange & flesh** (145,350,000)	.20	.20	❑❑❑❑❑
CM500	**1962. New Mexico Statehood Issue**			
4¢	**light blue, bister & brown purple** (112,870,000)	.20	.20	❑❑❑❑❑

CM486

CM487

CM488

CM489

CM490

CM491

CM492

CM493

CM494

CM495

CM496

CM497

CM498

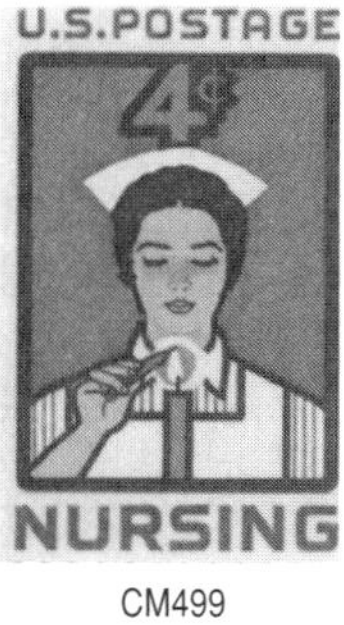

CM499

CM500

CM501

		MNHFVF	UseFVF	
CM501 ____________	**1962. Arizona Statehood Issue**			
4¢	**scarlet, deep blue & green** (121,820,000)	.20	.20	❑❑❑❑❑
CM502 ____________	**1962. Project Mercury Issue**			
4¢	**deep blue & yellow** (289,240,000)	.20	.20	❑❑❑❑❑
CM503 ____________	**1962. Malaria Eradication Issue**			
4¢	**blue & bister** (120,155,000)	.20	.20	❑❑❑❑❑
CM504 ____________	**1962. Charles Evans Hughes Issue**			
4¢	**black** on yellow paper (124,595,000)	.20	.20	❑❑❑❑❑
CM505 ____________	**1962. Seattle World's Fair Issue**			
4¢	**red & deep blue** (147,310,000)	.20	.20	❑❑❑❑❑
CM506 ____________	**1962. Louisiana Statehood Commemorative Issue**			
4¢	**gray green, blue & vermilion** (118,690,000)	.20	.20	❑❑❑❑❑
CM507 ____________	**1962. Homestead Act Issue**			
4¢	**slate blue** (122,730,000)	.20	.20	❑❑❑❑❑
CM508 ____________	**1962. Girl Scouts of America Issue**			
4¢	**red** (126,515,000)	.20	.20	❑❑❑❑❑
CM509 ____________	**1962. Brien McMahon Issue**			
4¢	**violet** (130,960,000)	.20	.20	❑❑❑❑❑
CM510 ____________	**1962. National Apprenticeship Issue**			
4¢	**black,** on buff (120,055,000)	.20	.20	❑❑❑❑❑
CM511 ____________	**1962. Sam Rayburn Issue**			
4¢	**brown & blue** (120,715,000)	.20	.20	❑❑❑❑❑
CM512 ____________	**1962. Dag Hammarskjöld Issue**			
4¢	**black, brown & yellow** (121,440,000)	.20	.20	❑❑❑❑❑
CM513 ____________	**1962. Dag Hammarskjöld Special Issue**			
4¢	**black, brown & yellow** (40,270,000)	.55	.25	❑❑❑❑❑
CM514 ____________	**1962. Higher Education Issue**			
4¢	**blue, green & black** (120,035,000)	.20	.20	❑❑❑❑❑
CM515 ____________	**1962. Winslow Homer Issue**			
4¢	**multicolored** (117,870,000)	.20	.20	❑❑❑❑❑
CM516 ____________	**1963. Carolina Charter Issue**			
5¢	**dark carmine & brown** (129,445,000)	.20	.20	❑❑❑❑❑
CM517 ____________	**1963. Food for Peace Issue**			
5¢	**green, yellow & red** (135,620,000)	.20	.20	❑❑❑❑❑
CM518 ____________	**1963. West Virginia Statehood Issue**			
5¢	**green, red & black** (137,540,000)	.20	.20	❑❑❑❑❑
CM519 ____________	**1963. Emancipation Proclamation Issue**			
5¢	**bright blue, scarlet & indigo** (132,435,000)	.20	.20	❑❑❑❑❑
CM520 ____________	**1963. Alliance for Progress Issue**			
5¢	**bright blue & green** (135,520,000)	.20	.20	❑❑❑❑❑
CM521 ____________	**1963. Cordell Hull Issue**			
5¢	**blue green** (131,420,000)	.20	.20	❑❑❑❑❑
CM522 ____________	**1963. Eleanor Roosevelt Issue**			
5¢	**purple** (133,170,000)	.20	.20	❑❑❑❑❑
CM523 ____________	**1963. National Academy of Science Issue**			
5¢	**turquoise, blue & black** (139,195,000)	.20	.20	❑❑❑❑❑
CM524 ____________	**1963. City Mail Delivery Issue**			
5¢	**red, gray & blue,** tagged (128,450,000)	.20	.20	❑❑❑❑❑
CM525 ____________	**1963. International Red Cross Issue**			
5¢	**deep gray & red** (116,665,000)	.20	.20	❑❑❑❑❑
CM526 ____________	**1963. John James Audubon Issue**			
5¢	**multicolored** (175,175,000)	.20	.20	❑❑❑❑❑
CM527 ____________	**1964. Sam Houston Issue**			
5¢	**black** (125,995,000)	.20	.20	❑❑❑❑❑

CM502

CM503

CM504

CM505

CM506

CM507

CM508

CM509

CM510

CM511

CM512

CM513

CM514

CM515

CM516

CM517

CM518

CM519

		MNHFVF	UseFVF
CM528	**1964. Charles M. Russell Issue**		
5¢	**multicolored** (128,025,000)	.20	.20
CM529	**1964. New York World's Fair Issue**		
5¢	**green** (145,700,000)	.20	.20
CM530	**1964. John Muir Issue**		
5¢	**brown, green, brownish gray & olive green** (120,310,000)	.20	.20
CM531	**1964. John F. Kennedy Memorial Issue**		
5¢	**gray blue** (500,000,000)	.20	.20
CM532	**1964. New Jersey Tercentenary Issue**		
5¢	**ultramarine** (123,845,000)	.20	.20
CM533	**1964. Nevada Statehood Issue**		
5¢	**multicolored** (122,825,000)	.20	.20
CM534	**1964. Register and Vote Issue**		
5¢	**blue & red** (325,000,000)	.20	.20
CM535	**1964. William Shakespeare Issue**		
5¢	**brown** on tan paper (123,245,000)	.20	.20
CM536	**1964. Doctors Mayo Issue**		
5¢	**green** (123,355,000)	.20	.20
CM537	**1964. American Music Issue**		
5¢	**red, gray & blue** on granite paper (126,370,000)	.20	.20
CM538	**1964. Homemakers Issue**		
5¢	**multicolored** on buff (121,250,000)	.20	.20
CM539	**1964. Verrazano-Narrows Bridge Issue**		
5¢	**green** (125,005,000)	.20	.20
CM540	**1964. Abstract Art Issue**		
5¢	**blue, black & red** (125,800,000)	.20	.20
CM541	**1964. Amateur Radio Operators Issue**		
5¢	**purple** (122,230,000)	.20	.20
CM542	**1965. Battle of New Orleans Issue**		
5¢	**carmine, blue & slate** (115,695,000)	.20	.20
CM543	**1965. Sokol Centennial - Physical Fitness Issue**		
5¢	**lake & deep slate** (115,095,000)	.20	.20
CM544	**1965. Crusade Against Cancer Issue**		
5¢	**reddish violet, black & red** (116,560,000)	.20	.20
CM545	**1965. Winston Churchill Memorial Issue**		
5¢	**black** (125,180,000)	.20	.20
CM546	**1965. Magna Carta Issue**		
5¢	**black, yellow & reddish-violet** (120,135,000)	.20	.20
CM547	**1965. UN International Cooperation Year Issue**		
5¢	**turquoise blue & slate** (115,405,000)	.20	.20
CM548	**1965. Salvation Army Issue**		
5¢	**red, black & deep blue** (115,855,000)	.20	.20
CM549	**1965. Dante Alighieri Issue**		
5¢	**carmine red** on light venetian red paper (115,340,000)	.20	.20
CM550	**1965. Herbert Hoover Issue**		
5¢	**red** (114,840,000)	.20	.20
CM551	**1965. Robert Fulton Issue**		
5¢	**blue & black** (116,140,000)	.20	.20
CM552	**1965. European Settlement Issue**		
5¢	**yellow, red & black** (116,900,000)	.20	.20
CM553	**1965. Traffic Safety Issue**		
5¢	**green, black & red** (114,085,000)	.20	.20
CM554	**1965. John Singleton Copley Issue**		
5¢	**black & tones of brown & olive** (114,880,000)	.20	.20

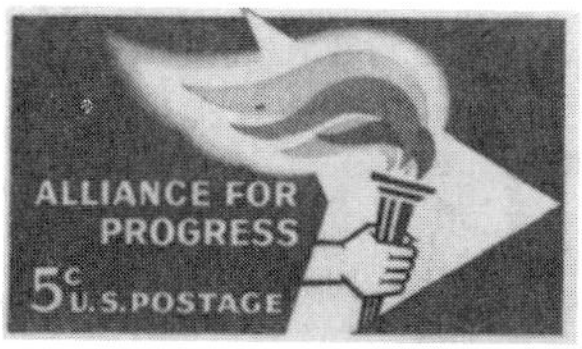

CM520

CM521

CM524

CM522

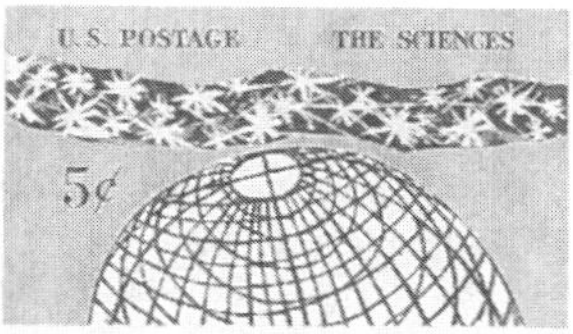

CM523

CM525

CM526

CM527

CM528

CM529

CM531

CM532

CM533

CM530

CM537

CM534

CM535

CM536

CM538

		MNHFVF	UseFVF	
CM555	**1965. International Telecommunication Union Issue**			
11¢	**yellow, red & black** (26,995,000)	.20	.20	❑❑❑❑❑
CM556	**1965. Adlai Stevenson Issue**			
5¢	**light blue gray, black, red & blue** (128,495,000)	.20	.20	❑❑❑❑❑
CM557	**1966. Migratory Bird Treaty Issue**			
5¢	**red, blue & light blue** (116,835,000)	.25	.20	❑❑❑❑❑
CM558	**1966. Humane Treatment of Animals Issue**			
5¢	**reddish brown & black** (117,470,000)	.25	.20	❑❑❑❑❑
CM559	**1966. Indiana Statehood Issue**			
5¢	**blue, yellow & brown** (123,770,000)	.25	.20	❑❑❑❑❑
CM560	**1966. American Circus Issue**			
5¢	**red, blue, pink & black** (131,270,000)	.25	.20	❑❑❑❑❑
CM561	**1966. Sixth International Philatelic Exhibition Issue**			
5¢	**multicolored** (122,285,000)	.25	.20	❑❑❑❑❑
CM562	**1966. SIPEX Souvenir Sheet**			
5¢	**multicolored** (14,680,000)	.30	.25	❑❑❑❑❑
CM563	**1966. Bill of Rights Issue**			
5¢	**red & blue** (114,160,000)	.25	.20	❑❑❑❑❑
CM564	**1966. Polish Millennium Issue**			
5¢	**red** (126,475,000)	.25	.20	❑❑❑❑❑
CM565	**1966. National Park Service Issue**			
5¢	**multicolored** (119,535,000)	.25	.20	❑❑❑❑❑
CM566	**1966. Marine Corps Reserve Issue**			
5¢	**black, olive, red & blue** (125,110,000)	.25	.20	❑❑❑❑❑
CM567	**1966. General Federation of Women's Clubs Issue**			
5¢	**pink, blue & black** (114,853,000)	.25	.20	❑❑❑❑❑
CM568	**1966. Johnny Appleseed Issue**			
5¢	**black, red & green** (124,290,000)	.25	.20	❑❑❑❑❑
CM569	**1966. Beautification of America Issue**			
5¢	**black, green & pink** (128,460,000)	.25	.20	❑❑❑❑❑
CM570	**1966. Great River Road Issue**			
5¢	**salmon, blue, olive yellow & yellow green** (127,585,000)	.25	.20	❑❑❑❑❑
CM571	**1966. U.S. Savings Bond Issue**			
5¢	**red, blue & black** (115,875,000)	.25	.20	❑❑❑❑❑
CM572	**1966. Mary Cassatt Issue**			
5¢	**multicolored** (114,015,000)	.25	.20	❑❑❑❑❑
CM573	**1967. National Grange Issue**			
5¢	**brownish orange, green, orange & black** (121,105,000)	.25	.20	❑❑❑❑❑
CM574	**1967. Canada Centennial Issue**			
5¢	**blue, green, dark blue & olive green,** tagged (132,045,000)	.25	.20	❑❑❑❑❑
CM575	**1967. Erie Canal Sesquicentennial Issue**			
5¢	**dark blue, light blue, black red,** tagged (118,780,000)	.25	.20	❑❑❑❑❑
CM576	**1967. Lions International Issue**			
5¢	**red, blue & black** on granite paper, tagged (121,985,000)	.25	.20	❑❑❑❑❑
CM577	**1967. Henry David Thoreau Issue**			
5¢	**red, black & green** tagged (111,850,000)	.25	.20	❑❑❑❑❑
CM578	**1967. Nebraska Statehood Issue**			
5¢	**yellow, green & brown** tagged (117,225,000)	.25	.20	❑❑❑❑❑
CM579	**1967. Voice of America Issue**			
5¢	**red, blue & black** tagged (111,515,000)	.25	.20	❑❑❑❑❑
CM580	**1967. Davy Crockett Issue**			
5¢	**green, black & yellow** tagged (114,270,000)	.25	.20	❑❑❑❑❑
CM581	**1967. Space Twins Issue**			
5¢	**dark blue, black & red** tagged (120,865,000)	1.00	.35	❑❑❑❑❑

CM540

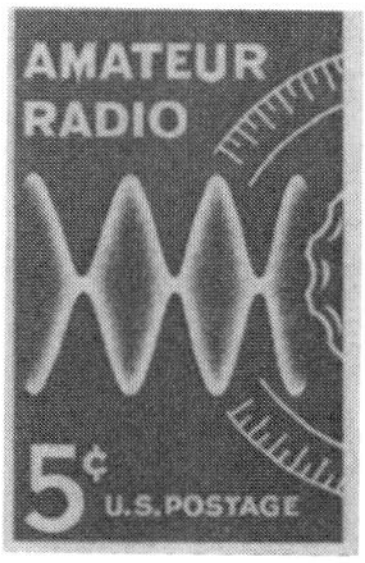

CM542

CM539 ←

CM541 →

CM546

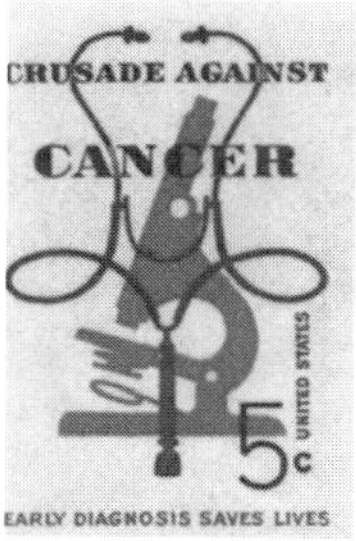

CM543

CM544

CM545

CM547

CM548

CM549

CM550

CM551

CM553

CM552 ←

CM554 →

CM556 →

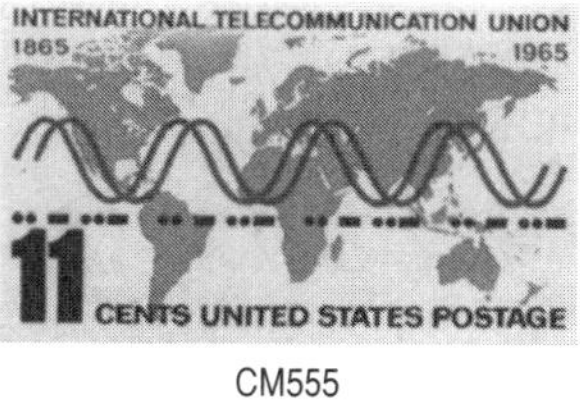

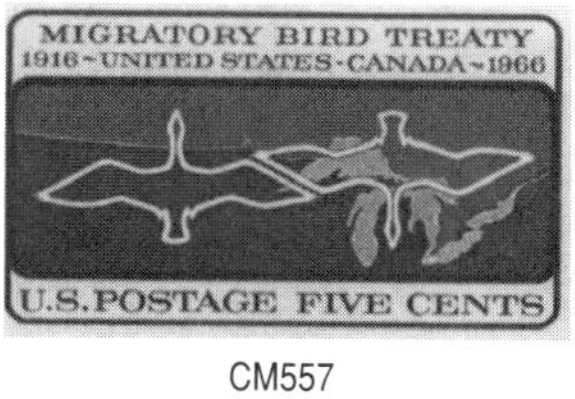

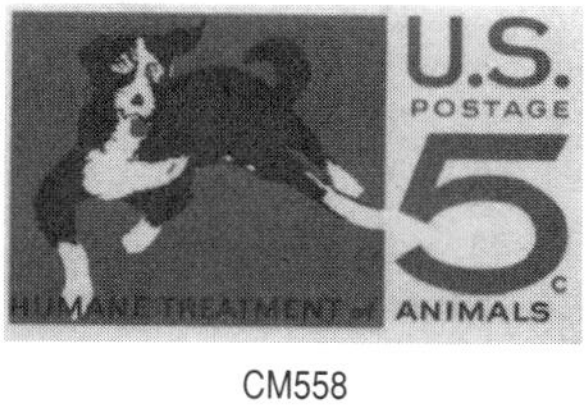

CM555

CM557

CM558

CM559

CM560

CM562

CM563

CM561

CM564

CM565

CM566

CM567

CM568

CM569

CM570

CM571

CM572

CM573

CM574

CM575

CM576

CM577

CM578

CM579

CM580

CM583

CM581-82

CM584

CM585

CM586

CM587

CM588

CM589

CM590

CM591

CM592

CM593

CM594

CM595

CM596

CM597

CM598

No.	Issue	Description	MNHFVF	UseFVF	
CM582		5¢ **dark blue, red & blue, green** tagged	1.00	.35	❑❑❑❑❑
CM583	**1967. Urban Planning Issue**	5¢ **dark blue, light blue & black** tagged (110,675,000)	.25	.20	❑❑❑❑❑
CM584	**1967. Finland Independence Issue**	5¢ **blue** tagged (110,670,000)	.25	.20	❑❑❑❑❑
CM585	**1967. Thomas Eakins Issue**	5¢ **gold & multicolored** tagged (113,825,000)	.25	.20	❑❑❑❑❑
CM586	**1967. Mississippi Statehood Issue**	5¢ **green blue, blue green & brown** tagged (113,330,000)	.25	.20	❑❑❑❑❑
CM587	**1968. Illinois Statehood Issue**	6¢ **multicolored** tagged (141,350,000)	.25	.20	❑❑❑❑❑
CM588	**1968. Hemisfair '68 Issue**	6¢ **blue, pink, & white** tagged (117,470,600)	.25	.20	❑❑❑❑❑
CM589	**1968. Support Our Youth Issue**	6¢ **red & blue** tagged (147,120,000)	.25	.20	❑❑❑❑❑
CM590	**1968. Law and Order Issue**	6¢ **red, blue & black** tagged (130,125,000)	.25	.20	❑❑❑❑❑
CM591	**1968. Register and Vote Issue**	6¢ **gold and black** tagged (158,070,000)	.25	.20	❑❑❑❑❑
CM592	**1968. Historic Flags Issue**	6¢ **blue** tagged (228,040,000)	.40	.30	❑❑❑❑❑
CM593		6¢ **red & blue** tagged	.40	.30	❑❑❑❑❑
CM594		6¢ **green & blue** tagged	.40	.30	❑❑❑❑❑
CM595		6¢ **red & blue** tagged	.40	.30	❑❑❑❑❑
CM596		6¢ **gold & blue** tagged	.40	.30	❑❑❑❑❑
CM597		6¢ **red & blue** tagged	.40	.30	❑❑❑❑❑
CM598		6¢ **red, green & blue** tagged	.40	.30	❑❑❑❑❑
CM599		6¢ **red & blue** tagged	.40	.30	❑❑❑❑❑
CM600		6¢ **multicolored** tagged	.40	.30	❑❑❑❑❑
CM601		6¢ **red, gold & blue** tagged	.40	.30	❑❑❑❑❑
CM602	**1968. Walt Disney Issue**	6¢ **multicolored** tagged (153,015,000)	.25	.20	❑❑❑❑❑
CM603	**1968. Father Jacques Marquette Issue**	6¢ **black, green & brown** tagged (132,560,000)	.25	.20	❑❑❑❑❑
CM604	**1968. Daniel Boone Issue**	6¢ **red brown, brown, yellow & black** tagged (130,385,000)	.25	.20	❑❑❑❑❑
CM605	**1968. Arkansas River Navigation Issue**	6¢ **blue, black & dark blue** tagged (132,265,000)	.25	.20	❑❑❑❑❑
CM606	**1968. Leif Erikson Issue**	6¢ **brown** (128,710,000)	.25	.20	❑❑❑❑❑
CM607	**1968. Cherokee Strip Issue**	6¢ **brown** tagged (124,775,000)	.25	.20	❑❑❑❑❑
CM608	**1968. John Trumbull Issue**	6¢ **multicolored** tagged (128,295,000)	.25	.20	❑❑❑❑❑

CM599

CM600

CM601

CM602

CM603

CM604

CM605

CM606

CM607

CM608

CM609

CM610

CM615

CM611-614

CM616

CM617

		MNHFVF	UseFVF
CM609____________	**1968. Waterfowl Conservation Issue**		
	6¢ **multicolored** (142,245,000)	.25	.20 ❑❑❑❑❑
CM610____________	**1968. Chief Joseph Issue**		
	6¢ **multicolored** tagged (125,100,000)	.25	.20 ❑❑❑❑❑
CM611____________	**1969. Beautification of America Issue**		
	6¢ **multicolored** tagged (102,570,000)	.30	.25 ❑❑❑❑❑
CM612____________			
	6¢ **multicolored** tagged	.30	.25 ❑❑❑❑❑
CM613____________			
	6¢ **multicolored** tagged	.30	.25 ❑❑❑❑❑
CM614____________			
	6¢ **multicolored** tagged	.30	.25 ❑❑❑❑❑
CM615____________	**1969. American Legion Issue**		
	6¢ **red, black & blue** tagged (148,770,000)	.25	.20 ❑❑❑❑❑
CM616____________	**1969. Grandma Moses Issue**		
	6¢ **multicolored** tagged (139,475,000)	.25	.20 ❑❑❑❑❑
CM617____________	**1969. Apollo 8 Issue**		
	6¢ **gray, deep blue & blue** tagged (187,165,000)	.25	.20 ❑❑❑❑❑
NOTE: Imperforate varieties, from printer's waste, exist.			
CM618____________	**1969. W.C. Handy Issue**		
	6¢ **multicolored** tagged (125,555,000)	.25	.20 ❑❑❑❑❑
CM619____________	**1969. Settlement of California Issue**		
	6¢ **multicolored** tagged (144,425,000)	.25	.20 ❑❑❑❑❑
CM620____________	**1969. John Wesley Powell Issue**		
	6¢ **multicolored** tagged (133,100,000)	.25	.20 ❑❑❑❑❑
CM621____________	**1969. Alabama Statehood Issue**		
	6¢ **multicolored** tagged (136,900,000)	.25	.20 ❑❑❑❑❑
CM622____________	**1969. 11th International Botanical Congress Issue**		
	6¢ **multicolored** tagged (158,695,000)	.30	.25 ❑❑❑❑❑
CM623____________			
	6¢ **multicolored** tagged	.30	.25 ❑❑❑❑❑
CM624____________			
	6¢ **multicolored** tagged	.30	.25 ❑❑❑❑❑
CM625____________			
	6¢ **multicolored** tagged	.30	.25 ❑❑❑❑❑
CM626____________	**1969. Dartmouth College Case Issue**		
	6¢ **green** tagged (124,075,000)	.25	.20 ❑❑❑❑❑
CM627____________	**1969. Professional Baseball Issue**		
	6¢ **yellow, red, black & green** tagged (129,925,000)	1.25	.20 ❑❑❑❑❑
CM628____________	**1969. Intercollegiate Football Issue**		
	6¢ **red & green** tagged (129,860,000)	.45	.20 ❑❑❑❑❑
NOTE: The intaglio portion of CM628 was printed on a rotary press normally used for currency.			
CM629____________	**1969. Dwight D. Eisenhower Issue**		
	6¢ **blue, black & reddish purple** tagged (138,976,000)	.25	.20 ❑❑❑❑❑
CM630____________	**1969. Hope for the Crippled Issue**		
	6¢ **multicolored** tagged (124,565,000)	.25	.20 ❑❑❑❑❑
CM631____________	**1969. William M. Harnett Issue**		
	6¢ **multicolored** tagged (124,729,000)	.25	.20 ❑❑❑❑❑
CM632____________	**1970. Natural History Issue**		
	6¢ **multicolored** tagged (201,794,600)	.25	.20 ❑❑❑❑❑
CM633____________			
	6¢ **multicolored** tagged	.25	.20 ❑❑❑❑❑
CM634____________			
	6¢ **multicolored** tagged	.25	.20 ❑❑❑❑❑

CM618

CM619

CM620

CM621

CM622-625

CM626

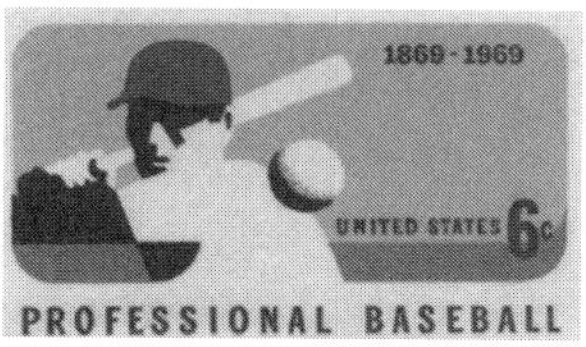

CM627

CM628

CM629

CM630

CM631

CM636

CM637

CM632-635

CM638

CM639

	MNHFVF	UseFVF	
CM635			
6¢ **multicolored** tagged	.25	.20	❑❑❑❑❑
CM636 **1970. Maine Statehood Issue**			
6¢ **multicolored** tagged (171,850,000)	.25	.20	❑❑❑❑❑
CM637 **1970. Wildlife Conservation Issue**			
6¢ **black** on tan (142,205,000)	.25	.20	❑❑❑❑❑
CM638 **1970. Edgar Lee Masters Issue**			
6¢ **black** tagged (137,660,000)	.25	.20	❑❑❑❑❑
CM639 **1970. The 50th Anniversary of Woman Suffrage Issue**			
6¢ **blue** tagged (135,125,000)	.25	.20	❑❑❑❑❑
CM640 **1970. South Carolina Issue**			
6¢ **brown, black & red** tagged (135,895,000)	.25	.20	❑❑❑❑❑
CM641 **1970. Stone Mountain Issue**			
6¢ **gray black** tagged (132,675,000)	.25	.20	❑❑❑❑❑
CM642 **1970. Fort Snelling Sesquicentennial Issue**			
6¢ **multicolored** tagged (134,795,000)	.25	.20	❑❑❑❑❑
CM643 **1970. Anti-Pollution Issue**			
6¢ **multicolored** tagged (161,600,000)	.25	.20	❑❑❑❑❑
CM644			
6¢ **multicolored** tagged	.25	.20	❑❑❑❑❑
CM645			
6¢ **multicolored** tagged	.25	.20	❑❑❑❑❑
CM646			
6¢ **multicolored** tagged	.25	.20	❑❑❑❑❑
CM647 **1970. United Nations Issue**			
6¢ **black, red & blue** tagged (127,610,000)	.25	.20	❑❑❑❑❑
CM648 **1970. Landing of the Pilgrims Issue**			
6¢ **multicolored** tagged (129,785,000)	.25	.20	❑❑❑❑❑
CM649 **1970. U.S. Servicemen Issue**			
6¢ **multicolored** tagged (134,380,000)	.25	.20	❑❑❑❑❑
CM650			
6¢ **dark blue, black & red** tagged	.25	.20	❑❑❑❑❑
CM651 **1971. American Wool Issue**			
6¢ **multicolored** tagged (135,305,000)	.25	.20	❑❑❑❑❑
CM652 **1971. Douglas MacArthur Issue**			
6¢ **red, blue & black** tagged (134,840,000)	.25	.20	❑❑❑❑❑
CM653 **1971. Blood Donors Issue**			
6¢ **red & blue** tagged (130,975,000)	.25	.20	❑❑❑❑❑
CM654 **1971. Missouri Statehood Issue**			
8¢ **multicolored** tagged (161,235,000)	.25	.20	❑❑❑❑❑
CM655 **1971. Wildlife Conservation Issue**			
8¢ **multicolored** tagged (175,680,000)	.25	.20	❑❑❑❑❑
CM656			
8¢ **multicolored** tagged	.25	.20	❑❑❑❑❑
CM657			
8¢ **multicolored** tagged	.25	.20	❑❑❑❑❑
CM658			
8¢ **multicolored** tagged	.25	.20	❑❑❑❑❑
CM659 **1971. Antarctic Treaty Issue**			
8¢ **red & dark blue** tagged (138,700,000)	.25	.20	❑❑❑❑❑
CM660 **1971. American Revolution Bicentennial Issue**			
8¢ **gray, red, blue & black** tagged (138,165,000)	.25	.20	❑❑❑❑❑
CM661 **1971. Space Achievements Decade Issue**			
8¢ **multicolored** tagged (176,295,000)	.25	.20	❑❑❑❑❑

CM640

CM641

CM642

CM643-646

CM647

CM648

CM649-650

CM651

CM652

CM660

CM653

CM654

CM659

CM655-658

CM663

CM664

		MNHFVF	UseFVF	
CM662				
8¢ **multicolored** tagged		.25	.20	❑❑❑❑❑
CM663	**1971. John Sloan Issue**			
8¢ **multicolored** tagged (152,125,000)		.25	.20	❑❑❑❑❑
CM664	**1971. Emily Dickinson Issue**			
8¢ **multicolored** tagged (142,845,000)		.25	.20	❑❑❑❑❑
CM665	**1971. San Juan Issue**			
8¢ **multicolored** tagged (148,755,000)		.25	.20	❑❑❑❑❑
CM666	**1971. Prevent Drug Abuse Issue**			
8¢ **blue, deep blue & black** tagged (139,080,000)		.25	.20	❑❑❑❑❑
CM667	**1971. CARE Issue**			
8¢ **black, blue, violet & red lilac** tagged (130,755,000)		.25	.20	❑❑❑❑❑
CM668	**1971. Historic Preservation Issue**			
8¢ **brown & dark beige** on buff, tagged (170,208,000)		.25	.20	❑❑❑❑❑
CM669				
8¢ **brown & dark beige** on buff, tagged		.25	.20	❑❑❑❑❑
CM670				
8¢ **brown & dark beige** on buff, tagged		.25	.20	❑❑❑❑❑
CM671				
8¢ **brown & dark beige** on buff, tagged		.25	.20	❑❑❑❑❑
CM672	**1972. American Poets Issue**			
8¢ **black, reddish brown & blue** tagged (137,355,000)		.25	.20	❑❑❑❑❑
CM673	**1972. Peace Corps Issue**			
8¢ **dark blue, light blue & red** tagged (150,400,000)		.25	.20	❑❑❑❑❑
CM674	**1972. Yellowstone Park Issue**			
8¢ **multicolored** tagged (164,096,000)		.25	.20	❑❑❑❑❑
CM675	**1972. Cape Hatteras Issue**			
2¢ **multicolored** tagged (172,730,000)		.25	.20	❑❑❑❑❑
CM676				
2¢ **multicolored** tagged		.25	.20	❑❑❑❑❑
CM677				
2¢ **multicolored** tagged		.25	.20	❑❑❑❑❑
CM678				
2¢ **multicolored** tagged		.25	.20	❑❑❑❑❑
CM679	**1972. Wolf Trap Farm Issue**			
6¢ **multicolored** tagged (104,090,000)		.25	.20	❑❑❑❑❑
CM680	**1972. Mount McKinley Issue**			
15¢ **multicolored** tagged (53,920,000)		.25	.20	❑❑❑❑❑
CM681	**1972. Family Planning Issue**			
8¢ **multicolored** tagged (153,025,000)		.25	.20	❑❑❑❑❑
CM682	**1972. Colonial Craftsmen Issue**			
8¢ **deep brown** on buff paper, tagged (201,890,000)		.25	.20	❑❑❑❑❑
CM683				
8¢ **deep brown** on buff paper, tagged		.25	.20	❑❑❑❑❑
CM684				
8¢ **deep brown** on buff paper, tagged		.25	.20	❑❑❑❑❑
CM685				
8¢ **deep brown** on buff paper, tagged		.25	.20	❑❑❑❑❑
CM686	**1972. Olympic Games Issue**			
6¢ **multicolored** tagged (67,335,000)		.25	.20	❑❑❑❑❑
CM687				
8¢ **multicolored** tagged (96,240,000)		.25	.20	❑❑❑❑❑
CM688				
15¢ **multicolored** tagged (46,340,000)		.25	.20	❑❑❑❑❑

CM661-662

CM665

CM666

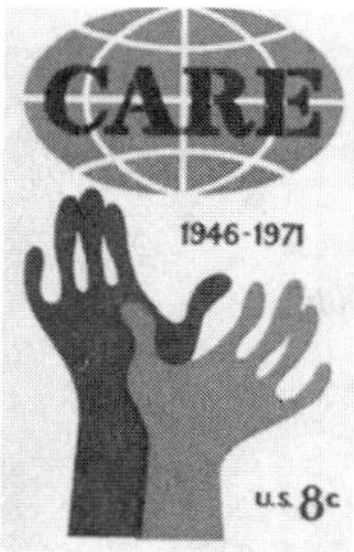

CM667

CM668-671

CM672

CM673

CM675-678

CM679

CM680

CM674

CM681

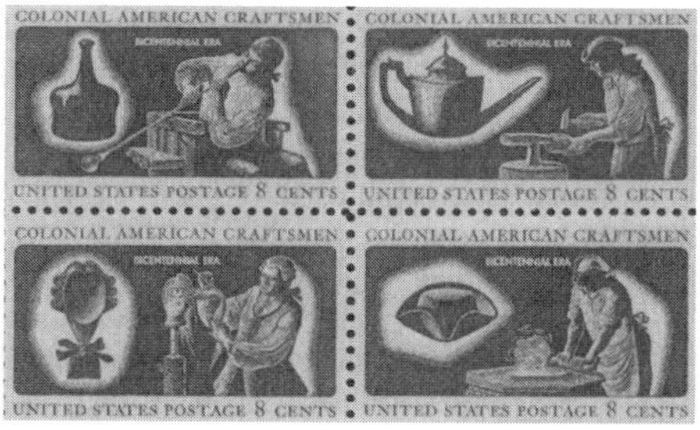

CM682-685

		MNHFVF	UseFVF
CM689	**1972. Parent Teacher Association Issue**		
8¢	**yellow & black** tagged (180,155,000)	.25	.20 ❑❑❑❑❑
CM690	**1972. Wildlife Conservation Issue**		
8¢	**multicolored** tagged (198,364,800)	.25	.20 ❑❑❑❑❑
CM691			
8¢	**multicolored** tagged	.25	.20 ❑❑❑❑❑
CM692			
8¢	**multicolored** tagged	.25	.20 ❑❑❑❑❑
CM693			
8¢	**multicolored** tagged	.25	.20 ❑❑❑❑❑
CM694	**1972. Mail Order Centennial Issue**		
8¢	**multicolored** tagged (185,490,000)	.25	.20 ❑❑❑❑❑

NOTE: Tagging on this issue typically consists of a vertical bar, 10mm wide.

		MNHFVF	UseFVF
CM695	**1972. Osteopathic Medicine Issue**		
8¢	**multicolored** tagged (162,335,000)	.25	.20 ❑❑❑❑❑
CM696	**1972. Tom Sawyer Issue**		
8¢	**multicolored** tagged (162,789,950)	.25	.20 ❑❑❑❑❑
CM697	**1972. Pharmacy Issue**		
8¢	**multicolored** tagged (165,895,000)	.25	.20 ❑❑❑❑❑
CM698	**1972. Stamp Collecting Issue**		
8¢	**multicolored** tagged (166,508,000)	.25	.20 ❑❑❑❑❑
CM699	**1973. Love Issue**		
8¢	**red, green, violet & blue** tagged (330,055,000)	.25	.20 ❑❑❑❑❑
CM700	**1973. Rise of the Spirit of Independence Issue**		
8¢	**blue, greenish black & red** tagged (166,005,000)	.25	.20 ❑❑❑❑❑
CM701			
8¢	**black, orange & ultramarine** tagged (163,050,000)	.25	.20 ❑❑❑❑❑
CM702			
8¢	**blue, black, red & green** tagged (159,005,000)	.25	.20 ❑❑❑❑❑
CM703			
8¢	**blue, black, yellow & red** tagged (147,295,000)	.25	.20 ❑❑❑❑❑
CM704	**1973. George Gershwin Issue**		
8¢	**multicolored** (139,152,000)	.25	.20 ❑❑❑❑❑
CM705	**1973. Nicolaus Copernicus Issue**		
8¢	**black & yellow** tagged (159,475,000)	.25	.20 ❑❑❑❑❑
CM706	**1973. Postal Service Employee Issue**		
8¢	**multicolored** tagged (486,020,000)	.25	.20 ❑❑❑❑❑
CM707			
8¢	**multicolored** tagged	.25	.20 ❑❑❑❑❑
CM708			
8¢	**multicolored** tagged	.25	.20 ❑❑❑❑❑
CM709			
8¢	**multicolored** tagged	.25	.20 ❑❑❑❑❑
CM710			
8¢	**multicolored** tagged	.25	.20 ❑❑❑❑❑
CM711			
8¢	**multicolored** tagged	.25	.20 ❑❑❑❑❑
CM712			
8¢	**multicolored** tagged	.25	.20 ❑❑❑❑❑
CM713			
8¢	**multicolored** tagged	.25	.20 ❑❑❑❑❑
CM714			
8¢	**multicolored** tagged	.25	.20 ❑❑❑❑❑

CM686

CM687

CM688

CM689

CM690-693

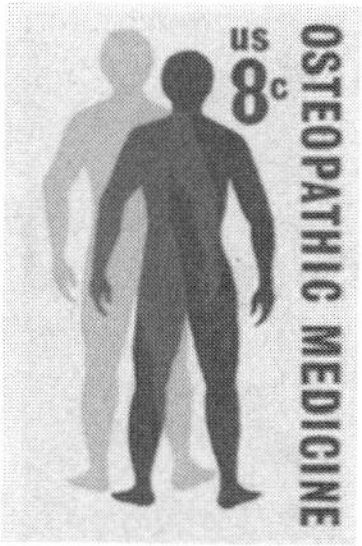

CM695

CM694

CM696

CM697

CM698

CM700

CM699

CM701

CM702

CM705

CM703

CM704

MNHFVF	UseFVF

CM715 _____
 8¢ **multicolored** tagged .25 .20 ☐☐☐☐☐

NOTE: Tagging consists of a 1/2 inch high horizontal band.
CM716 _____ **1973. Harry S. Truman Issue**
 8¢ **red, black & blue** tagged (157,052,800) .25 .25 ☐☐☐☐☐
CM717 _____ **1973. Boston Tea Party Issue**
 8¢ **multicolored** tagged (196,275,000) .25 .20 ☐☐☐☐☐
CM718 _____
 8¢ **multicolored** tagged .25 .20 ☐☐☐☐☐
CM719 _____
 8¢ **multicolored** tagged .25 .20 ☐☐☐☐☐
CM720 _____
 8¢ **multicolored** tagged .25 .20 ☐☐☐☐☐
CM721 _____ **1973. Progress in Electronics Issue**
 6¢ **multicolored** tagged (53,005,000) .25 .20 ☐☐☐☐☐
CM722 _____
 8¢ **multicolored** tagged (159,775,000) .25 .20 ☐☐☐☐☐
CM723 _____
 15¢ **multicolored** tagged (39,005,000) .25 .20 ☐☐☐☐☐
CM724 _____ **1973. Robinson Jeffers Issue**
 8¢ **multicolored** tagged (128,048,000) .25 .20 ☐☐☐☐☐
CM725 _____ **1973. Lyndon B. Johnson Issue**
 8¢ **multicolored** (152,624,000) .25 .20 ☐☐☐☐☐
CM726 _____ **1973. Henry O. Tanner Issue**
 8¢ **multicolored** tagged (146,008,000) .25 .20 ☐☐☐☐☐
CM727 _____ **1973. Willa Cather Issue**
 8¢ **multicolored** tagged (139,608,000) .25 .20 ☐☐☐☐☐
CM728 _____ **1973. Angus Cattle Issue**
 8¢ **multicolored** tagged (145,430,000) .25 .20 ☐☐☐☐☐
CM729 _____ **1974. Veterans of Foreign Wars Issue**
 10¢ **red & blue** tagged (145,430,000) .25 .20 ☐☐☐☐☐
CM730 _____ **1974. Robert Frost Issue**
 10¢ **black** tagged (145,235,000) .25 .20 ☐☐☐☐☐
CM731 _____ **1974. Expo 74 World's Fair Issue**
 10¢ **multicolored** tagged (135,052,000) .25 .20 ☐☐☐☐☐
CM732 _____ **1974. Horse Racing Issue**
 10¢ **multicolored** tagged (156,750,000) .25 .20 ☐☐☐☐☐
CM733 _____ **1974. Skylab Project Issue**
 10¢ **multicolored** tagged (164,670,000) .25 .20 ☐☐☐☐☐
CM734 _____ **1974. Universal Postal Union Issue**
 10¢ **multicolored** tagged (190,154,680) .25 .20 ☐☐☐☐☐
CM735 _____
 10¢ **multicolored** tagged .25 .20 ☐☐☐☐☐
CM736 _____
 10¢ **multicolored** tagged .25 .20 ☐☐☐☐☐
CM737 _____
 10¢ **multicolored** tagged .25 .20 ☐☐☐☐☐
CM738 _____
 10¢ **multicolored** tagged .25 .20 ☐☐☐☐☐
CM739 _____
 10¢ **multicolored** tagged .25 .20 ☐☐☐☐☐
CM740 _____
 10¢ **multicolored** tagged .25 .20 ☐☐☐☐☐
CM741 _____
 10¢ **multicolored** tagged .25 .20 ☐☐☐☐☐

CM706-715

CM716

CM717-720

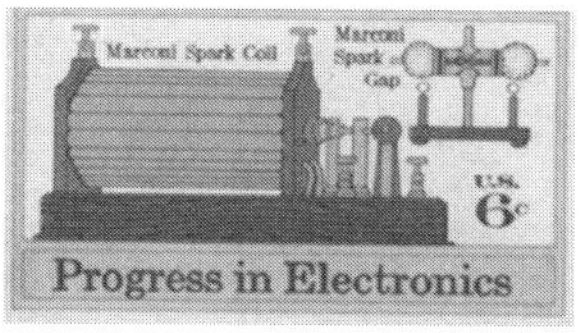

CM721

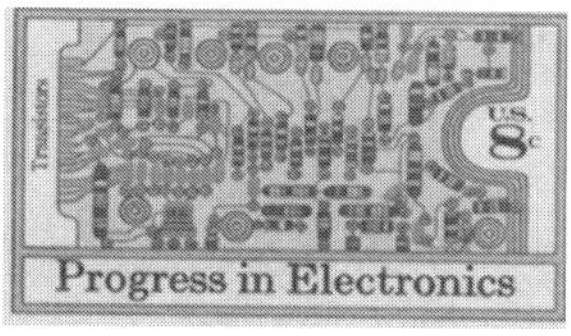

CM722

CM723

CM724

CM725

CM726

CM727

CM728

CM729

CM730

MNHFVF	UseFVF

CM742_____ **1974. Mineral Heritage Issue**
10¢ **multicolored** tagged (167,212,800) .25 .20 ☐☐☐☐☐

CM743_____
10¢ **multicolored** tagged .25 .20 ☐☐☐☐☐

CM744_____
10¢ **multicolored** tagged .25 .20 ☐☐☐☐☐

CM745_____
10¢ **multicolored** tagged .25 .20 ☐☐☐☐☐

CM746_____ **1974. Settlement of Kentucky Issue**
10¢ **multicolored** tagged (156,265,000) .25 .20 ☐☐☐☐☐

CM747_____ **1974. First Continental Congress Issue**
10¢ **dark blue & red** tagged (195,585,000) .25 .20 ☐☐☐☐☐

CM748_____
10¢ **red & dark blue** tagged .25 .20 ☐☐☐☐☐

CM749_____
10¢ **gray, dark blue & red** tagged .25 .20 ☐☐☐☐☐

CM750_____
10¢ **gray, dark blue & red** tagged .25 .20 ☐☐☐☐☐

CM751_____ **1974. Chautauqua Tent Issue**
10¢ **multicolored** tagged (151,335,000) .25 .20 ☐☐☐☐☐

CM731

CM732

CM733

CM734-741

CM742-745

CM746

CM751

CM752

CM753

CM754

CM747-750

CM757 →

CM755

CM756

CM758

CM759

CM760

CM761

CM762

		MNHFVF	UseFVF	
CM752__________	**1974. Winter Wheat and Train Issue**			
	10¢ **multicolored** tagged (141,085,000)	.25	.20	❑❑❑❑❑
CM753__________	**1974. Energy Conservation Issue**			
	10¢ **multicolored** tagged (148,850,000)	.25	.20	❑❑❑❑❑
CM754__________	**1974. Legend of Sleepy Hollow Issue**			
	10¢ **dark blue, black, orange, & yellow** tagged (157,270,000)	.25	.20	❑❑❑❑❑
CM755__________	**1974. Help for Retarded Children Issue**			
	10¢ **light & dark brown** tagged (150,245,000)	.25	.20	❑❑❑❑❑
CM756__________	**1975. Benjamin West Issue**			
	10¢ **multicolored** tagged (156,995,000)	.25	.20	❑❑❑❑❑
CM757__________	**1975. Pioneer Space Issue**			
	10¢ **dark blue, yellow & red** tagged (173,685,000)	.25	.20	❑❑❑❑❑
NOTE: Imperforate varieties came from printer's waste.				
CM758__________	**1975. Collective Bargaining Issue**			
	10¢ **multicolored** tagged (153,355,000)	.25	.20	❑❑❑❑❑
NOTE: Imperforate varieties came from printer's waste.				
CM759__________	**1975. Contributors to the Cause Issue**			
	10¢ **multicolored** tagged (63,205,000)	.25	.20	❑❑❑❑❑
CM760__________				
	10¢ **multicolored** tagged (157,865,000)	.25	.20	❑❑❑❑❑
CM761__________				
	10¢ **multicolored** tagged (166,810,000)	.25	.20	❑❑❑❑❑
CM762__________				
	18¢ **multicolored** tagged (44,825,000)	.25	.20	❑❑❑❑❑
CM763__________	**1975. Mariner Space Issue**			
	10¢ **black, red, ultramarine & bister** tagged (158,600,000)	.25	.20	❑❑❑❑❑
CM764__________	**1975. Lexington and Concord Issue**			
	10¢ **multicolored** tagged (114,028,000)	.25	.20	❑❑❑❑❑
CM765__________	**1975. Paul Laurence Dunbar Issue**			
	10¢ **multicolored** tagged (146,365,000)	.25	.20	❑❑❑❑❑
CM766__________	**1975. D.W. Griffith Issue**			
	10¢ **multicolored** tagged (148,805,000)	.25	.20	❑❑❑❑❑
CM767__________	**1975. Bunker Hill Issue**			
	10¢ **multicolored** tagged (139,928,000)	.25	.20	❑❑❑❑❑
CM768__________	**1975. Military Services Bicentennial Issue**			
	10¢ **multicolored** tagged (179,855,000)	.25	.20	❑❑❑❑❑
CM769__________				
	10¢ **multicolored** tagged	.25	.20	❑❑❑❑❑
CM770__________				
	10¢ **multicolored** tagged	.25	.20	❑❑❑❑❑
CM771__________				
	10¢ **multicolored** tagged	.25	.20	❑❑❑❑❑
CM772__________	**1975. Apollo Soyuz Issue**			
	10¢ **multicolored** tagged (161,863,200)	.25	.20	❑❑❑❑❑
CM773__________				
	10¢ **multicolored** tagged	.25	.20	❑❑❑❑❑
CM774__________	**1975. World Peace Through Law Issue**			
	10¢ **green, gray blue & brown** tagged (146,615,000)	.25	.20	❑❑❑❑❑
CM775__________	**1975. International Women's Year Issue**			
	10¢ **blue, orange & dark blue** tagged (145,640,000)	.25	.20	❑❑❑❑❑
CM776__________	**1975. U.S. Postal Service Bicentennial Issue**			
	10¢ **multicolored** tagged (168,655,000)	.25	.20	❑❑❑❑❑
CM777__________				
	10¢ **multicolored** tagged	.25	.20	❑❑❑❑❑

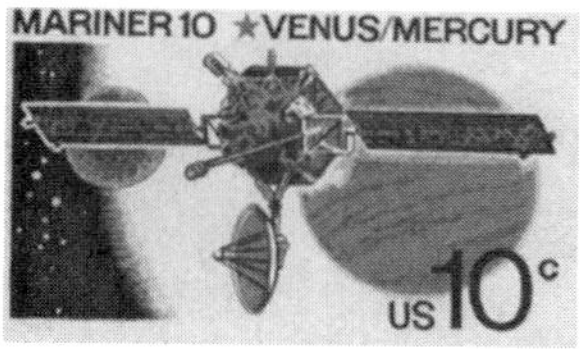

CM763

CM764

CM765

CM766

CM767

CM768-771

CM772-773

CM774

CM775

CM776-779

		MNHFVF	UseFVF	
CM778______				
10¢ **multicolored** tagged		.25	.20	❑❑❑❑❑
CM779______				
10¢ **multicolored** tagged		.25	.20	❑❑❑❑❑
CM780______	**1975. Banking and Commerce Issue**			
10¢ **multicolored** tagged (146,196,000)		.25	.20	❑❑❑❑❑
CM781______				
10¢ **multicolored** tagged		.25	.20	❑❑❑❑❑
CM782______	**1976. Spirit of 76 Issue**			
13¢ **multicolored** tagged (219,455,000)		.25	.20	❑❑❑❑❑
CM783______				
13¢ **multicolored** tagged		.25	.20	❑❑❑❑❑
CM784______				
13¢ **multicolored** tagged		.25	.20	❑❑❑❑❑
CM785______	**1976. INTERPHIL Issue**			
13¢ **blue, red & ultramarine** tagged (157,825,000)		.25	.20	❑❑❑❑❑
CM786______	**1976. 50-State Flag Issue**			
13¢ **Delaware,** tagged (436,005,000)		.55	.40	❑❑❑❑❑
CM787______				
13¢ **Pennsylvania,** tagged		.55	.40	❑❑❑❑❑
CM788______				
13¢ **New Jersey,** tagged		.55	.40	❑❑❑❑❑
CM789______				
13¢ **Georgia,** tagged		.55	.40	❑❑❑❑❑
CM790______				
13¢ **Connecticut,** tagged		.55	.40	❑❑❑❑❑
CM791______				
13¢ **Massachusetts,** tagged		.55	.40	❑❑❑❑❑
CM792______				
13¢ **Maryland,** tagged		.55	.40	❑❑❑❑❑
CM793______				
13¢ **South Carolina,** tagged		.55	.40	❑❑❑❑❑
CM794______				
13¢ **New Hampshire,** tagged		.55	.40	❑❑❑❑❑
CM795______				
13¢ **Virginia,** tagged		.55	.40	❑❑❑❑❑
CM796______				
13¢ **New York,** tagged		.55	.40	❑❑❑❑❑
CM797______				
13¢ **North Carolina,** tagged		.55	.40	❑❑❑❑❑
CM798______				
13¢ **Rhode Island,** tagged		.55	.40	❑❑❑❑❑
CM799______				
13¢ **Vermont,** tagged		.55	.40	❑❑❑❑❑
CM800______				
13¢ **Kentucky,** tagged		.55	.40	❑❑❑❑❑
CM801______				
13¢ **Tennessee,** tagged		.55	.40	❑❑❑❑❑
CM802______				
13¢ **Ohio,** tagged		.55	.40	❑❑❑❑❑
CM803______				
13¢ **Louisiana,** tagged		.55	.40	❑❑❑❑❑
CM804______				
13¢ **Indiana,** tagged		.55	.40	❑❑❑❑❑

CM780-781

CM782-784

CM785

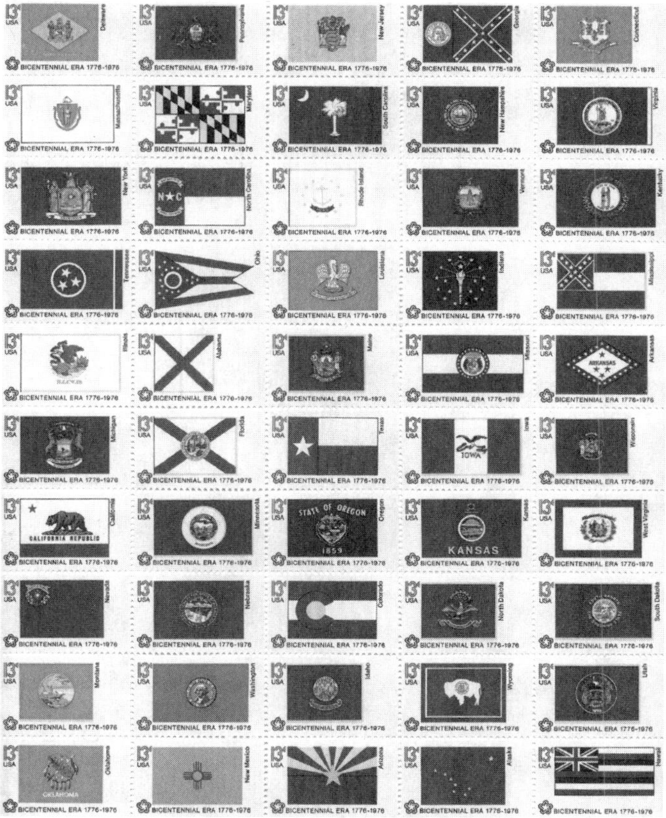

CM786-835

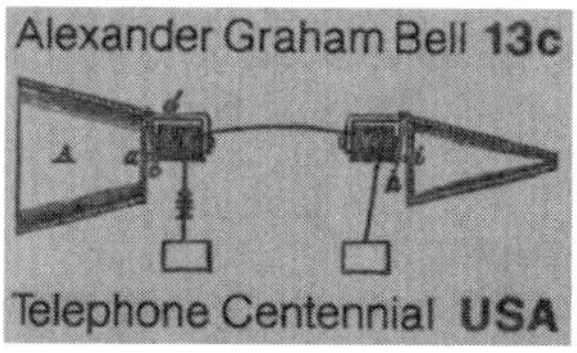

CM836

CM837

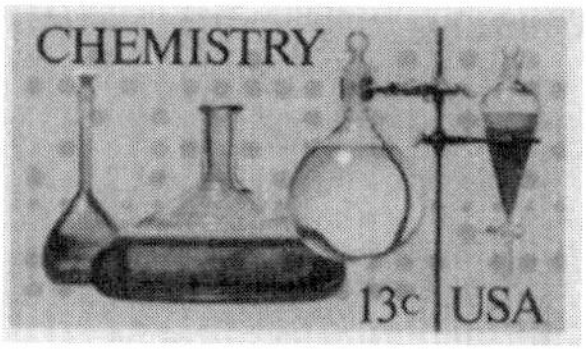

CM838

MNHFVF	UseFVF	

CM805 _____
 13¢ **Mississippi,** tagged .55 .40 ☐☐☐☐☐

CM806 _____
 13¢ **Illinois,** tagged .55 .40 ☐☐☐☐☐

CM807 _____
 13¢ **Alabama,** tagged .55 .40 ☐☐☐☐☐

CM808 _____
 13¢ **Maine,** tagged .55 .40 ☐☐☐☐☐

CM809 _____
 13¢ **Missouri,** tagged .55 .40 ☐☐☐☐☐

CM810 _____
 13¢ **Arkansas,** tagged .55 .40 ☐☐☐☐☐

CM811 _____
 13¢ **Michigan,** tagged .55 .40 ☐☐☐☐☐

CM812 _____
 13¢ **Florida,** tagged .55 .40 ☐☐☐☐☐

CM813 _____
 13¢ **Texas,** tagged .55 .40 ☐☐☐☐☐

CM814 _____
 13¢ **Iowa,** tagged .55 .40 ☐☐☐☐☐

CM815 _____
 13¢ **Wisconsin,** tagged .55 .40 ☐☐☐☐☐

CM816 _____
 13¢ **California,** tagged .55 .40 ☐☐☐☐☐

CM817 _____
 13¢ **Minnesota,** tagged .55 .40 ☐☐☐☐☐

CM818 _____
 13¢ **Oregon,** tagged .55 .40 ☐☐☐☐☐

CM819 _____
 13¢ **Kansas,** tagged .55 .40 ☐☐☐☐☐

CM820 _____
 13¢ **West Virginia,** tagged .55 .40 ☐☐☐☐☐

CM821 _____
 13¢ **Nevada,** tagged .55 .40 ☐☐☐☐☐

CM822 _____
 13¢ **Nebraska,** tagged .55 .40 ☐☐☐☐☐

CM823 _____
 13¢ **Colorado,** tagged .55 .40 ☐☐☐☐☐

CM824 _____
 13¢ **North Dakota,** tagged .55 .40 ☐☐☐☐☐

CM825 _____
 13¢ **South Dakota,** tagged .55 .40 ☐☐☐☐☐

CM826 _____
 13¢ **Montana,** tagged .55 .40 ☐☐☐☐☐

CM827 _____
 13¢ **Washington,** tagged .55 .40 ☐☐☐☐☐

CM828 _____
 13¢ **Idaho,** tagged .55 .40 ☐☐☐☐☐

CM829 _____
 13¢ **Wyoming,** tagged .55 .40 ☐☐☐☐☐

CM830 _____
 13¢ **Utah,** tagged .55 .40 ☐☐☐☐☐

CM831 _____
 13¢ **Oklahoma,** tagged .55 .40 ☐☐☐☐☐

CM839

CM840

CM841

CM842

CM843

CM844-847

CM848-851

CM852

CM853

			MNHFVF	UseFVF	
CM832 ________		13¢ **New Mexico,** tagged	.55	.40	❑❑❑❑❑
CM833 ________		13¢ **Arizona,** tagged	.55	.40	❑❑❑❑❑
CM834 ________		13¢ **Alaska,** tagged	.55	.40	❑❑❑❑❑
CM835 ________		13¢ **Hawaii,** tagged	.55	.40	❑❑❑❑❑
CM836 ________	**1976. Telephone Centennial Issue**	13¢ **black, purple & red,** on tan paper, tagged (159,915,000)	.25	.20	❑❑❑❑❑
CM837 ________	**1976. Commercial Aviation Issue**	13¢ **multicolored** tagged (156,960,000)	.25	.20	❑❑❑❑❑
CM838 ________	**1976. Chemistry Issue**	13¢ **multicolored** tagged (158,470,000)	.25	.20	❑❑❑❑❑
CM839 ________	**1976. Bicentennial Souvenir Sheets**	65¢ **multicolored** tagged (1,990,500)	4.75	4.50	❑❑❑❑❑
CM840 ________		90¢ **multicolored** tagged (1,983,000)	6.00	5.75	❑❑❑❑❑
CM841 ________		$1.20 **multicolored** tagged (1,953,000)	8.25	8.00	❑❑❑❑❑
CM842 ________		$1.55 **multicolored** tagged (1,903,000)	10.75	10.50	❑❑❑❑❑
CM843 ________	**1976. Benjamin Franklin Issue**	13¢ **multicolored** tagged (164,890,000)	.25	.20	❑❑❑❑❑
CM844 ________	**1976. Declaration of Independence Issue**	13¢ **multicolored** tagged (208,035,000)	.25	.20	❑❑❑❑❑
CM845 ________		13¢ **multicolored** tagged	.25	.20	❑❑❑❑❑
CM846 ________		13¢ **multicolored** tagged	.25	.20	❑❑❑❑❑
CM847 ________		13¢ **multicolored** tagged	.25	.20	❑❑❑❑❑
CM848 ________	**1976. Olympic Games Issue**	13¢ **multicolored** tagged (185,715,000)	.25	.20	❑❑❑❑❑
CM849 ________		13¢ **multicolored** tagged	.25	.20	❑❑❑❑❑
CM850 ________		13¢ **multicolored** tagged	.25	.20	❑❑❑❑❑
CM851 ________		13¢ **multicolored** tagged	.25	.20	❑❑❑❑❑
CM852 ________	**1976. Clara Maass Issue**	13¢ **multicolored** tagged (130,592,000)	.25	.20	❑❑❑❑❑
CM853 ________	**1976. Adolph S. Ochs Issue**	13¢ **gray & black** tagged (158,332,800)	.25	.20	❑❑❑❑❑
CM854 ________	**1977. Washington at Princeton Issue**	13¢ **multicolored** tagged (150,328,000)	.25	.20	❑❑❑❑❑
CM855 ________	**1977. Sound Recording Issue**	13¢ **multicolored** tagged (176,830,000)	.25	.20	❑❑❑❑❑
CM856 ________	**1977. Pueblo Indian Art Issue**	13¢ **multicolored** tagged (195,976,000)	.25	.20	❑❑❑❑❑
CM857 ________		13¢ **multicolored** tagged	.25	.20	❑❑❑❑❑
CM858 ________		13¢ **multicolored** tagged	.25	.20	❑❑❑❑❑

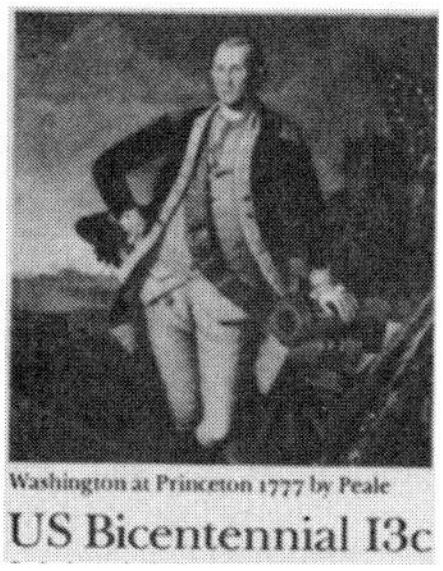
Washington at Princeton 1777 by Peale
US Bicentennial 13c

CM854

USA 13c
CENTENNIAL OF SOUND RECORDING

CM855

Hopi: Heard Museum Phoenix
Pueblo Art USA 13c
Acoma: School of American Research
Pueblo Art USA 13c
Zia: Museum of New Mexico
Pueblo Art USA 13c
San Ildefonso: Denver Art Museum
Pueblo Art USA 13c

CM856-859

USA·13c
50th Anniversary Solo Transatlantic Flight

CM860

COLORADO
13c usa
THE CENTENNIAL STATE

CM861

CM866

Lafayette
US Bicentennial 13c

Swallowtail
USA 13c Papilio oregonius
Checkerspot
USA 13c Euphydryas phaeton
Dogface
USA 13c Colias eurydice
Orange-Tip
USA 13c Anthocaris midea

CM862-865

CM871

United States & Canada
Peace Bridge 1927-77
USA 13c

the SEAMSTRESS
for INDEPENDENCE USA 13c
the BLACKSMITH
for INDEPENDENCE USA 13c
the WHEELWRIGHT
for INDEPENDENCE USA 13c
the LEATHERWORKER
for INDEPENDENCE USA 13c

CM867-870

CM872

Herkimer at Oriskany 1777 by Yohn
US Bicentennial 13cents

USA 13c
First Civil Settlement·Alta California·1777

CM873

Drafting the Articles of Confederation
York Town, Pennsylvania 1777 13c USA

CM874

13c USA
50th ANNIVERSARY YEAR OF TALKING PICTURES

CM875

		MNHFVF	UseFVF	
CM859__________				
13¢ **multicolored** tagged		.25	.20	❑❑❑❑❑
CM860__________	**1977. 50th Anniversary of Transatlantic Flight Issue**			
13¢ **multicolored** tagged (208,820,000)		.25	.20	❑❑❑❑❑
NOTE: Privately applied overprints on this stamp have no official status.				
CM861__________	**1977. Colorado Statehood Issue**			
13¢ **multicolored** tagged (190,005,000)		.25	.20	❑❑❑❑❑
CM862__________	**1977. Butterfly Issue**			
13¢ **multicolored** tagged (219,830,000)		.25	.20	❑❑❑❑❑
CM863__________				
13¢ **multicolored** tagged		.25	.20	❑❑❑❑❑
CM864__________				
13¢ **multicolored** tagged		.25	.20	❑❑❑❑❑
CM865__________				
13¢ **multicolored** tagged		.25	.20	❑❑❑❑❑
CM866__________	**1977. Lafayette Issue**			
13¢ **blue, black & red** (159,852,000)		.25	.20	❑❑❑❑❑
CM867__________	**1977. Skilled Hands of Independence Issue**			
13¢ **multicolored** tagged (188,310,000)		.25	.20	❑❑❑❑❑
CM868__________				
13¢ **multicolored** tagged		.25	.20	❑❑❑❑❑
CM869__________				
13¢ **multicolored** tagged		.25	.20	❑❑❑❑❑
CM870__________				
13¢ **multicolored**		.25	.20	❑❑❑❑❑
CM871__________	**1977. Peace Bridge Issue**			
13¢ **blue** tagged (163,625,000)		.25	.20	❑❑❑❑❑
CM872__________	**1977. Herkimer at Oriskany Issue**			
13¢ **multicolored** tagged (156,296,000)		.25	.20	❑❑❑❑❑
CM873__________	**1977. Alta California Issue**			
13¢ **multicolored** tagged (154,495,000)		.25	.20	❑❑❑❑❑
CM874__________	**1977. Articles of Confederation Issue**			
13¢ **red & dark brown** on cream paper, tagged (168,050,000)		.25	.20	❑❑❑❑❑
CM875__________	**1977. Talking Pictures Issue**			
13¢ **multicolored** tagged (156,810,000)		.25	.20	❑❑❑❑❑
CM876__________	**1977. Surrender at Saratoga**			
13¢ **multicolored** (153,736,000)		.25	.20	❑❑❑❑❑
CM876A __________	**1977. Energy Issue**			
13¢ **multicolored** tagged		.25	.20	❑❑❑❑❑
CM876B __________				
13¢ **multicolored** tagged		.25	.20	❑❑❑❑❑
CM877__________	**1978. Carl Sandburg Issue**			
13¢ **brown & black** tagged (156,560,000)		.25	.20	❑❑❑❑❑
CM878__________	**1978. Captain Cook Issue**			
13¢ **blue** tagged (202,155,000)		.25	.20	❑❑❑❑❑
CM879__________				
13¢ **green** tagged		.25	.20	❑❑❑❑❑
CM880__________	**1978. Harriet Tubman Issue**			
13¢ **multicolored** tagged (156,525,000)		.25	.20	❑❑❑❑❑
CM881__________	**1978. American Quilts Issue**			
13¢ **multicolored** tagged (165,182,000)		.25	.20	❑❑❑❑❑
CM882__________				
13¢ **multicolored** tagged		.25	.20	❑❑❑❑❑

CM876

CM876A-876B

CM877

CM878-879

CM880

CM881-884

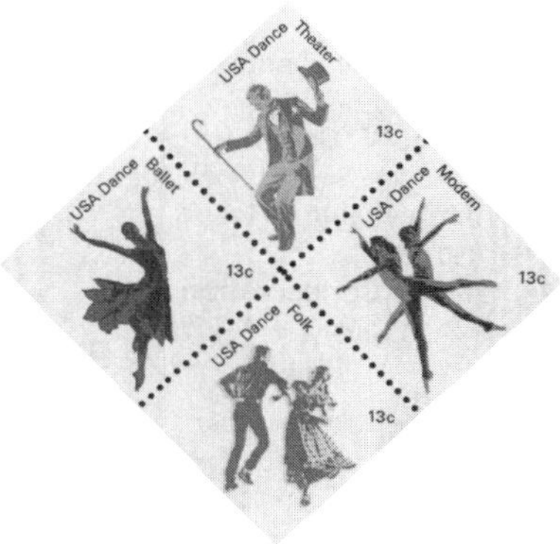

CM885-888

CM889

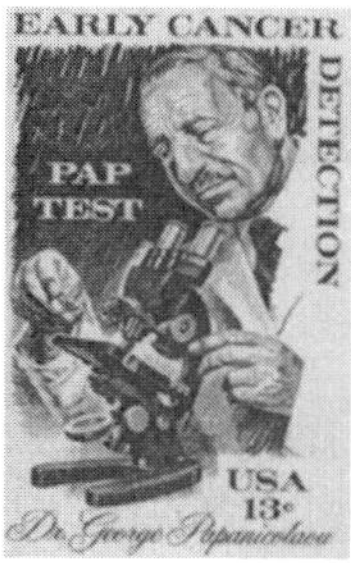

CM890

CM892

CM891

CM893

		MNHFVF	UseFVF	
CM883				
13¢ **multicolored** tagged		.25	.20	❑❑❑❑❑
CM884				
13¢ **multicolored** tagged		.25	.20	❑❑❑❑❑
CM885	**1978. American Dance Issue**			
13¢ **multicolored** tagged (157,598,400)		.25	.20	❑❑❑❑❑
CM886				
13¢ **multicolored** tagged		.25	.20	❑❑❑❑❑
CM887				
13¢ **multicolored** tagged		.25	.20	❑❑❑❑❑
CM888				
13¢ **multicolored** tagged		.25	.20	❑❑❑❑❑
CM889	**1978. French Alliance Issue**			
13¢ **blue, black, & red** tagged (102,856,000)		.25	.20	❑❑❑❑❑
CM890	**1978. George Papanicolaou Issue**			
13¢ **brown** tagged (152,270,000)		.25	.20	❑❑❑❑❑
CM891	**1978. Jimmie Rodgers Issue**			
13¢ **multicolored** tagged (94,600,000)		.25	.20	❑❑❑❑❑
CM892	**1978. Canadian International Philatelic Exhibition**			
$1.04 **multicolored** (10,400,000)		2.75	2.00	❑❑❑❑❑
CM893	**1978. Photography Issue**			
15¢ **multicolored** tagged (161,228,000)		.30	.20	❑❑❑❑❑
CM894	**1978. George M. Cohan Issue**			
15¢ **multicolored** tagged (151,570,000)		.30	.20	❑❑❑❑❑
CM895	**1978. Viking Missions Issue**			
15¢ **multicolored** tagged (158,880,000)		.30	.20	❑❑❑❑❑
CM896	**1978. Wildlife Conservation Issue**			
15¢ **Great Gray Owl,** tagged (186,550,000)		.30	.20	❑❑❑❑❑
CM897				
15¢ **Saw Whet Owl,** tagged		.30	.20	❑❑❑❑❑
CM898				
15¢ **Barred Owl,** tagged		.30	.20	❑❑❑❑❑
CM899				
15¢ **Great Horned Owl,** tagged		.30	.20	❑❑❑❑❑
CM900	**1978. American Trees Issue**			
15¢ **Giant Sequoia,** tagged (168,136,000)		.30	.20	❑❑❑❑❑
CM901				
15¢ **Eastern White Pine,** tagged		.30	.20	❑❑❑❑❑
CM902				
15¢ **White Oak,** tagged		.30	.20	❑❑❑❑❑
CM903				
15¢ **Gray Birch,** tagged		.30	.20	❑❑❑❑❑
CM904	**1979. Robert F. Kennedy Issue**			
15¢ **blue** tagged (159,297,000)		.30	.20	❑❑❑❑❑
CM905	**1979. Martin Luther King Jr. Issue**			
15¢ **multicolored** tagged (166,435,000)		.30	.20	❑❑❑❑❑
CM906	**1979. International Year of the Child Issue**			
15¢ **light & dark brown** tagged (162,535,000)		.30	.20	❑❑❑❑❑
CM907	**1979. John Steinbeck Issue**			
15¢ **dark blue** tagged (155,000,000)		.30	.20	❑❑❑❑❑
CM908	**1979. Albert Einstein Issue**			
15¢ **brown** tagged (157,310,000)		.30	.20	❑❑❑❑❑
CM909	**1979. Pennsylvania Toleware Issue**			
15¢ **Coffee pot with straight spout** (174,096,000)		.30	.20	❑❑❑❑❑

CM894

CM895

CM896-899

CM904

CM900-903

CM905

CM906

CM907

CM908

CM913-916

CM909-912

CM917-920

MNHFVF	UseFVF

CM910_____
15¢ **Tea caddy** .30 .20 ☐☐☐☐☐
CM911_____
15¢ **Sugar bowl with lid** .30 .20 ☐☐☐☐☐
CM912_____
15¢ **Coffee pot with gooseneck spout** .30 .20 ☐☐☐☐☐
CM913_____ **1979. American Architecture Issue**
15¢ **University of Virginia Rotunda,** tagged (164,793,000) .30 .20 ☐☐☐☐☐
CM914_____
15¢ **Baltimore Cathedral,** tagged .30 .20 ☐☐☐☐☐
CM915_____
15¢ **Boston State House,** tagged .30 .20 ☐☐☐☐☐
CM916_____
15¢ **Philadelphia Exchange,** tagged .30 .20 ☐☐☐☐☐
CM917_____ **1979. Endangered Flora Issue**
15¢ **Persistent Trillium,** tagged (163,055,000) .30 .20 ☐☐☐☐☐
CM918_____
15¢ **Hawaiian Wild Broadbean,** tagged .30 .20 ☐☐☐☐☐
CM919_____
15¢ **Contra Costa Wallflower,** tagged .30 .20 ☐☐☐☐☐
CM920_____
15¢ **Antioch Dunes Evening Primrose,** tagged .30 .20 ☐☐☐☐☐
CM921_____ **1979. Seeing Eye Dog Issue**
15¢ **multicolored** tagged (161,860,000) .30 .20 ☐☐☐☐☐
CM922_____ **1979. Special Olympics Issue**
15¢ **multicolored** tagged (165,775,000) .30 .20 ☐☐☐☐☐
CM923_____ **1979. Summer Games Issue**
10¢ **multicolored** tagged (67,195,000) .25 .25 ☐☐☐☐☐
CM924_____ **1979. John Paul Jones Issue**
15¢ **multicolored** tagged (160,000,000, all perforation types) .30 .20 ☐☐☐☐☐
NOTE: Imperforate errors are from printer's waste.
CM924A _____
15¢ **multicolored** tagged, perforated 11 .75 .25 ☐☐☐☐☐
CM924B _____
15¢ **multicolored** tagged, perforated 12 2,800.00 1,000.00 ☐☐☐☐☐
CM925_____ **1979. Summer Games Issue**
15¢ **Women runners,** tagged (186,905,000) .25 .20 ☐☐☐☐☐
CM926_____
15¢ **Women swimmers,** tagged .25 .20 ☐☐☐☐☐
CM927_____
15¢ **Pair of rowers,** tagged .25 .20 ☐☐☐☐☐
CM928_____
15¢ **Horse & Rider,** tagged .25 .20 ☐☐☐☐☐
CM929_____ **1979. Will Rogers Issue**
15¢ **multicolored** tagged (161,290,000) .30 .20 ☐☐☐☐☐
CM930_____ **1979. Vietnam Veterans Issue**
15¢ **multicolored** tagged (172,740,000) .30 .20 ☐☐☐☐☐
CM931_____ **1980. W.C. Fields Issue**
15¢ **multicolored** tagged (168,995,000) .30 .20 ☐☐☐☐☐
CM932_____ **1980. Winter Games Issue**
15¢ **Speed skater,** tagged (208,295,000) *(both perforation types)* .30 .20 ☐☐☐☐☐
CM933_____
15¢ **Ski jumper,** tagged .30 .20 ☐☐☐☐☐

CM921

CM922

CM923

CM924

CM925-928

CM929

CM930

CM931

CM932-935; CM932A-935A

CM936

CM909-912

CM943

CM944

	MNHFVF	UseFVF
CM934		
15¢ **Downhill skier,** tagged	.30	.20
CM935		
15¢ **Hockey goaltender,** tagged	.30	.20
CM935A		
15¢ **Speed Skater,** perforated 11, tagged	.80	.75
CM935B		
15¢ **Ski jumper,** perforated 11, tagged	.80	.75
CM935C		
15¢ **Downhill skier,** perforated 11, tagged	.80	.75
CM935D		
15¢ **Hockey goaltender,** perforated 11, tagged	.80	.75
CM936 **1980. Benjamin Banneker Issue**		
15¢ **multicolored** tagged (160,000,000)	.30	.20

NOTE: Imperforates with misregistered colors are from printers' waste, have been fraudulently perforated to simulate CM936v. Genuine examples of this error have colors correctly registered. Expert certification recommended.

	MNHFVF	UseFVF
CM937 **1980. National Letter Writing Issue**		
15¢ **"Letters Preserve Memories"** (232,134,000)	.30	.20
CM938		
15¢ **"Write Soon," (purple),** tagged	.30	.20
CM939		
15¢ **"Letters Lift Spirits,"** tagged	.30	.20
CM940		
15¢ **"Write Soon", (green),** tagged	.30	.20
CM941		
15¢ **"Letters Shape Opinions,"** tagged	.30	.20
CM942		
15¢ **"Write Soon," (red),** tagged	.30	.20
CM943 **1980. Frances Perkins Issue**		
15¢ **blue** tagged (163,510,000)	.30	.20
CM944 **1980. Emily Bissell Issue**		
15¢ **black & red** tagged (95,695,000)	.30	.20
CM945 **1980. Helen Keller and Anne Sullivan Issue**		
15¢ **multicolored** tagged (153,975,000)	.30	.20
CM946 **1980. Veterans Administration Issue**		
15¢ **red & dark blue** tagged (160,000,000)	.30	.20
CM947 **1980. Bernardo de Galvez Issue**		
15¢ **multicolored** tagged (103,850,000)	.30	.20
CM948 **1980. Coral Reefs Issue**		
15¢ **Brain Coral,** tagged (204,715,000)	.30	.20
CM949		
15¢ **Elkhorn Coral,** tagged	.30	.20
CM950		
15¢ **Chalice Coral,** tagged	.30	.20
CM951		
15¢ **Finger Coral,** tagged	.30	.20
CM952 **1980. Organized Labor Issue**		
15¢ **multicolored** tagged (166,545,000)	.30	.20
CM953 **1980. Edith Wharton Issue**		
15¢ **purple** tagged (163,310,000)	.30	.20
CM954 **1980. Education in America Issue**		
15¢ **multicolored** tagged (160,000,000)	.30	.20
CM955 **1980. Pacific Northwest Masks Issue**		
15¢ **Heiltsuk Bella Bella mask,** tagged (152,404,000)	.30	.20

CM945

CM946

CM947

CM948-951

CM952

CM953

CM954

CM955-958

CM959-962

CM963

CM964

CM965-968

		MNHFVF	UseFVF	
CM956				
	15¢ **Chikat Tlingit mask,** tagged	.30	.20	❑❑❑❑❑
CM957				
	15¢ **Tlingit mask,** tagged	.30	.20	❑❑❑❑❑
CM958				
	15¢ **Bella Coola mask,** tagged	.30	.20	❑❑❑❑❑
CM959	**1980. American Architecture Issue**			
	15¢ **Smithsonian Institution,** tagged (152,720,000)	.30	.20	❑❑❑❑❑
CM960				
	15¢ **Trinity Church,** tagged	.30	.20	❑❑❑❑❑
CM961				
	15¢ **Pennsylvania Academy of the Fine Arts,** tagged	.30	.20	❑❑❑❑❑
CM962				
	15¢ **Lyndhurst,** tagged	.30	.20	❑❑❑❑❑
CM963	**1981. Everett Dirksen Issue**			
	15¢ **gray** tagged (160,155,000)	.30	.20	❑❑❑❑❑
CM964	**1981. Whitney Moore Young Issue**			
	15¢ **multicolored** tagged (159,505,000)	.30	.20	❑❑❑❑❑
CM965	**1981. Flower Issue**			
	18¢ **Rose,** tagged (210,633,000)	.30	.20	❑❑❑❑❑
CM966				
	18¢ **Camellia,** tagged	.30	.20	❑❑❑❑❑
CM967				
	18¢ **Dahlia,** tagged	.30	.20	❑❑❑❑❑
CM968				
	18¢ **Lily,** tagged	.30	.20	❑❑❑❑❑
CM969	**1981. American Red Cross Issue**			
	18¢ **multicolored** tagged (165,175,000)	.30	.20	❑❑❑❑❑
CM970	**1981. Savings and Loan Issue**			
	18¢ **multicolored** tagged (107,240,000)	.30	.20	❑❑❑❑❑
CM971	**1981. Space Achievement Issue**			
	18¢ **Astronaut on Moon,** tagged (337,819,000)	.30	.20	❑❑❑❑❑
CM972				
	18¢ **Pioneer II & Saturn,** tagged	.30	.20	❑❑❑❑❑
CM973				
	18¢ **Skylab & Sun,** tagged	.30	.20	❑❑❑❑❑
CM974				
	18¢ **Hubble Space Telescope,** tagged	.30	.20	❑❑❑❑❑
CM975				
	18¢ **Space Shuttle in orbit,** tagged	.30	.20	❑❑❑❑❑
CM976				
	18¢ **Space Shuttle with arm deployed,** tagged	.30	.20	❑❑❑❑❑
CM977				
	18¢ **Space Shuttle at launch,** tagged	.30	.20	❑❑❑❑❑
CM978				
	18¢ **Space Shuttle at landing,** tagged	.30	.20	❑❑❑❑❑
CM979	**1981. Professional Management Issue**			
	18¢ **blue & black** tagged (99,420,000)	.30	.20	❑❑❑❑❑
CM980	**1981. Save Wildlife Habitats Issue**			
	18¢ **Blue heron,** tagged (178,930,000)	.30	.20	❑❑❑❑❑
CM981				
	18¢ **Badger,** tagged	.30	.20	❑❑❑❑❑
CM982				
	18¢ **Grizzly bear,** tagged	.30	.20	❑❑❑❑❑

CM969

CM970

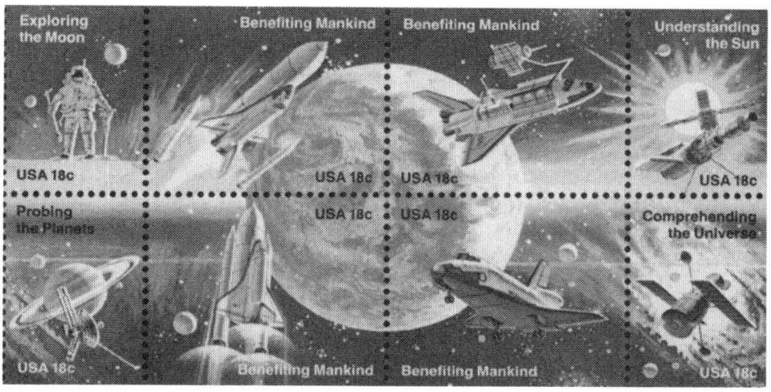

CM971-978

CM979

CM980-983

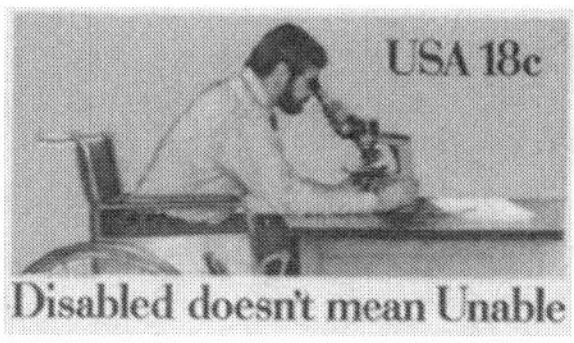

CM984

CM985

CM986

CM991

CM987-990

CM992

MNHFVF	UseFVF

CM983_____
18¢ **Ruffed grouse,** tagged .30 .20 ☐☐☐☐☐

CM984_____ **1981. Disabled Persons Issue**
18¢ **multicolored** tagged (100,265,000) .30 .20 ☐☐☐☐☐

CM985_____ **1981. Edna St. Vincent Millay Issue**
18¢ **multicolored** tagged (99,615,000) .30 .25 ☐☐☐☐☐

CM986_____ **1981. Beat Alcoholism Issue**
18¢ **blue & black** tagged (97,535,000) .65 .20 ☐☐☐☐☐

CM987_____ **1981. American Architecture Issue**
18¢ **N.Y. University Library,** tagged (167,308,000) .30 .20 ☐☐☐☐☐

CM988_____
18¢ **Biltmore House,** tagged .30 .20 ☐☐☐☐☐

CM989_____
18¢ **Palace of Arts,** tagged .30 .20 ☐☐☐☐☐

CM990_____
18¢ **National Farmers Bank Building,** tagged .30 .20 ☐☐☐☐☐

CM991_____ **1981. Bobby Jones Issue**
18¢ **green** tagged (99,170,000) .30 .20 ☐☐☐☐☐

CM992_____ **1981. (Mildred) Babe Zaharias Issue**
18¢ **light violet** tagged (101,625,000) .30 .20 ☐☐☐☐☐

CM993_____ **1981. Frederic Remington Issue**
18¢ **multicolored** tagged (101,155,000) .30 .20 ☐☐☐☐☐

CM994_____ **1981. James Hoban Issue**
18¢ **multicolored** tagged (101,200,000) .30 .20 ☐☐☐☐☐

CM995_____
20¢ **multicolored** tagged (167,360,000) .30 .20 ☐☐☐☐☐

CM996_____ **1981. Battle of Yorktown and the Virginia Capes Issue**
18¢ **multicolored** tagged (162,420,000) .30 .20 ☐☐☐☐☐

CM997_____
18¢ **multicolored** tagged .30 .20 ☐☐☐☐☐

CM998_____ **1981. John Hanson Issue**
20¢ **multicolored** tagged (167,130,000) .30 .20 ☐☐☐☐☐

CM999_____ **1981. Desert Plants Issue**
20¢ **Barrel cactus,** tagged (191,560,000) .35 .20 ☐☐☐☐☐

CM1000_____
20¢ **Agave,** tagged .35 .20 ☐☐☐☐☐

CM1001_____
20¢ **Beavertail cactus,** tagged .35 .20 ☐☐☐☐☐

CM1002_____
20¢ **Saguaro,** tagged .35 .20 ☐☐☐☐☐

CM1003_____ **1982. Franklin D. Roosevelt Issue**
20¢ **blue** tagged (163,939,200) .35 .20 ☐☐☐☐☐

CM1004_____ **1982. Love Issue**
20¢ **multicolored** tagged .35 .20 ☐☐☐☐☐

CM1004A _____
20¢ **multicolored** tagged, perforated 11 x 10 1/2 1.00 .25 ☐☐☐☐☐

CM1005_____ **1982. George Washington Issue**
20¢ **multicolored** tagged (180,700,000) .35 .20 ☐☐☐☐☐

CM1006_____ **1982. State Birds and Flowers**
20¢ **Alabama, multicolored,** tagged (666,950,000) 1.00 .50 ☐☐☐☐☐

CM1007_____
20¢ **Alaska, multicolored,** tagged 1.00 .50 ☐☐☐☐☐

CM1008_____
20¢ **Arizona, multicolored,** tagged 1.00 .50 ☐☐☐☐☐

	MNHFVF	UseFVF
CM1009___________		
20¢ **Arkansas, multicolored,** tagged	1.00	.50 ❑❑❑❑❑
CM1010___________		
20¢ **California, multicolored,** tagged	1.00	.50 ❑❑❑❑❑
CM1011___________		
20¢ **Colorado, multicolored,** tagged	1.00	.50 ❑❑❑❑❑
CM1012___________		
20¢ **Connecticut, multicolored,** tagged	1.00	.50 ❑❑❑❑❑
CM1013___________		
20¢ **Delaware, multicolored,** tagged	1.00	.50 ❑❑❑❑❑
CM1014___________		
20¢ **Florida, multicolored,** tagged	1.00	.50 ❑❑❑❑❑

CM993

CM994

CM995

CM996-997

CM998

CM999-1002

CM1003

CM1004

CM1005

	MNHFVF	UseFVF	
CM1015________			
20¢ **Georgia, multicolored,** tagged	1.00	.50	❑❑❑❑❑
CM1016________			
20¢ **Hawaii, multicolored,** tagged	1.00	.50	❑❑❑❑❑
CM1017________			
20¢ **Idaho, multicolored,** tagged	1.00	.50	❑❑❑❑❑
CM1018________			
20¢ **Illinois, multicolored,** tagged	1.00	.50	❑❑❑❑❑
CM1019________			
20¢ **Indiana, multicolored,** tagged	1.00	.50	❑❑❑❑❑
CM1020________			
20¢ **Iowa, multicolored,** tagged	1.00	.50	❑❑❑❑❑
CM1021________			
20¢ **Kansas, multicolored,** tagged	1.00	.50	❑❑❑❑❑
CM1022________			
20¢ **Kentucky, multicolored,** tagged	1.00	.50	❑❑❑❑❑
CM1023________			
20¢ **Louisiana, multicolored,** tagged	1.00	.50	❑❑❑❑❑
CM1024________			
20¢ **Maine, multicolored,** tagged	1.00	.50	❑❑❑❑❑
CM1025________			
20¢ **Maryland, multicolored,** tagged	1.00	.50	❑❑❑❑❑
CM1026________			
20¢ **Massachusetts, multicolored,** tagged	1.00	.50	❑❑❑❑❑
CM1027________			
20¢ **Michigan, multicolored,** tagged	1.00	.50	❑❑❑❑❑
CM1028________			
20¢ **Minnesota, multicolored,** tagged	1.00	.50	❑❑❑❑❑
CM1029________			
20¢ **Mississippi, multicolored,** tagged	1.00	.50	❑❑❑❑❑
CM1030________			
20¢ **Missouri, multicolored,** tagged	1.00	.50	❑❑❑❑❑
CM1031________			
20¢ **Montana, multicolored,** tagged	1.00	.50	❑❑❑❑❑
CM1032________			
20¢ **Nebraska, multicolored,** tagged	1.00	.50	❑❑❑❑❑
CM1033________			
20¢ **Nevada, multicolored,** tagged	1.00	.50	❑❑❑❑❑
CM1034________			
20¢ **New Hampshire, multicolored,** tagged	1.00	.50	❑❑❑❑❑
CM1035________			
20¢ **New Jersey, multicolored,** tagged	1.00	.50	❑❑❑❑❑
CM1036________			
20¢ **New Mexico, multicolored,** tagged	1.00	.50	❑❑❑❑❑
CM1037________			
20¢ **New York, multicolored,** tagged	1.00	.50	❑❑❑❑❑
CM1038________			
20¢ **North Carolina, multicolored,** tagged	1.00	.50	❑❑❑❑❑
CM1039________			
20¢ **North Dakota, multicolored,** tagged	1.00	.50	❑❑❑❑❑
CM1040________			
20¢ **Ohio, multicolored,** tagged	1.00	.50	❑❑❑❑❑
CM1041________			
20¢ **Oklahoma, multicolored,** tagged	1.00	.50	❑❑❑❑❑

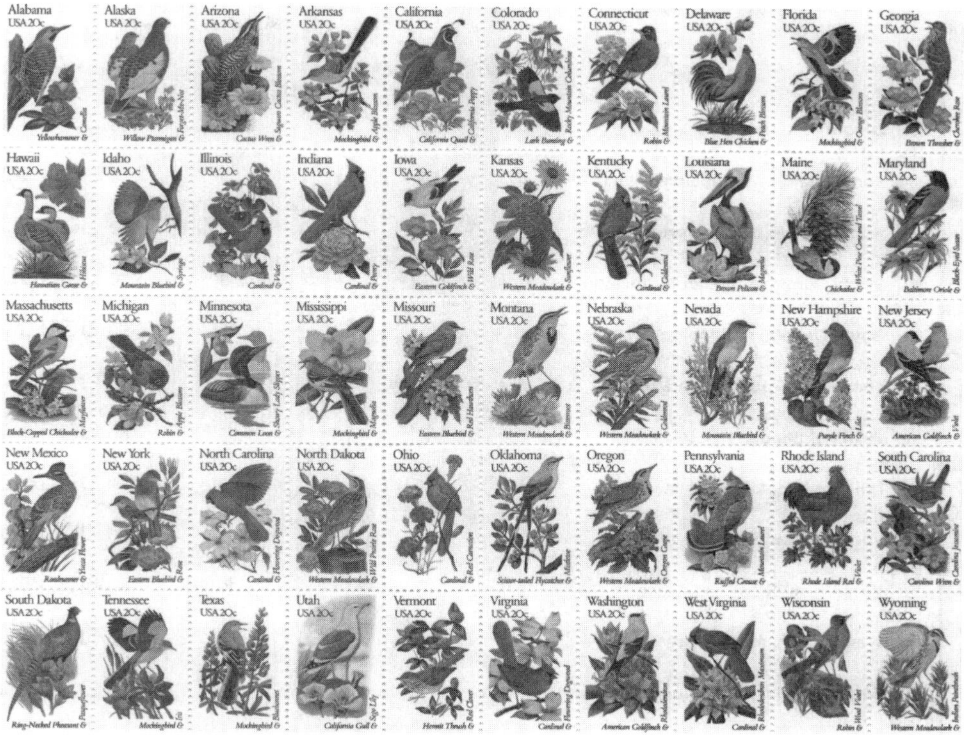

CM1006v-1055v

CM1056

CM1058-1061

CM1057

CM1062

CM1063

	MNHFVF	UseFVF	
CM1042__________			
20¢ **Oregon, multicolored,** tagged	1.00	.50	❑❑❑❑❑
CM1043__________			
20¢ **Pennsylvania, multicolored,** tagged	1.00	.50	❑❑❑❑❑
CM1044__________			
20¢ **Rhode Island, multicolored,** tagged	1.00	.50	❑❑❑❑❑
CM1045__________			
20¢ **South Carolina, multicolored,** tagged	1.00	.50	❑❑❑❑❑
CM1046__________			
20¢ **South Dakota, multicolored,** tagged	1.00	.50	❑❑❑❑❑
CM1047__________			
20¢ **Tennessee, multicolored,** tagged	1.00	.50	❑❑❑❑❑
CM1048__________			
20¢ **Texas multicolored,** tagged	1.00	.50	❑❑❑❑❑
CM1049__________			
20¢ **Utah, multicolored,** tagged	1.00	.50	❑❑❑❑❑
CM1050__________			
20¢ **Vermont, multicolored,** tagged	1.00	.50	❑❑❑❑❑
CM1051__________			
20¢ **Virginia, multicolored,** tagged	1.00	.50	❑❑❑❑❑
CM1052__________			
20¢ **Washington, multicolored,** tagged	1.00	.50	❑❑❑❑❑
CM1053__________			
20¢ **West Virginia, multicolored,** tagged	1.00	.50	❑❑❑❑❑
CM1054__________			
20¢ **Wisconsin, multicolored,** tagged	1.00	.50	❑❑❑❑❑
CM1055__________			
20¢ **Wyoming, multicolored,** tagged	1.00	.50	❑❑❑❑❑

NOTE: Because most plate block collectors consider that a plate block contains at least one copy of each stamp in the issue, a plate block of the State Birds and Flowers Issue is considered to be a full pane of 50 stamps.

CM1056__________ **1982. Netherlands Issue**			
20¢ **orange, red, blue & dark gray** tagged (109,245,000)	.35	.20	❑❑❑❑❑
CM1057__________ **1982. Library of Congress Issue**			
20¢ **black & red** tagged (112,535,000)	.35	.20	❑❑❑❑❑
CM1058__________ **1982. Knoxville World's Fair Issue**			
20¢ **Solar energy,** tagged (124,640,000)	.35	.20	❑❑❑❑❑
CM1059__________			
20¢ **Synthetic fuels,** tagged	.35	.20	❑❑❑❑❑
CM1060__________			
20¢ **Breeder reactor,** tagged	.35	.20	❑❑❑❑❑
CM1061__________			
20¢ **Fossil fuels,** tagged	.35	.20	❑❑❑❑❑
CM1062__________ **1982. Horatio Alger Issue**			
20¢ **red & black** on tan paper tagged (107,605,000)	.35	.20	❑❑❑❑❑
CM1063__________ **1982. Aging Together Issue**			
20¢ **brown** tagged (173,160,000)	.35	.20	❑❑❑❑❑
CM1064__________ **1982. Barrymore Family Issue**			
20¢ **multicolored** tagged (107,285,000)	.35	.20	❑❑❑❑❑
CM1065__________ **1982. Mary Walker Issue**			
20¢ **multicolored** tagged (109,040,000)	.35	.20	❑❑❑❑❑
CM1066__________ **1982. International Peace Garden Issue**			
20¢ **multicolored** tagged (183,270,000)	.35	.20	❑❑❑❑❑
CM1067__________ **1982. America's Libraries Issue**			
20¢ **red & black** tagged (169,495,000)	.35	.20	❑❑❑❑❑

		MNHFVF	UseFVF
CM1068__________	**1982. Jackie Robinson Issue**		
	20¢ **multicolored** tagged (164,235,000)	2.50	.20 ❑❑❑❑❑
CM1069__________	**1982. Touro Synagogue Issue**		
	20¢ **multicolored** tagged (110,130,000)	.35	.20 ❑❑❑❑❑
CM1070__________	**1982. Wolf Trap Farm Issue**		
	20¢ **multicolored** tagged (110,995,000)	.35	.20 ❑❑❑❑❑
CM1071__________	**1982. American Architecture Issue**		
	20¢ **Falling Water,** tagged (165,340,000)	.35	.20 ❑❑❑❑❑
CM1072__________			
	20¢ **Illinois Intitute of Technology,** tagged	.35	.20 ❑❑❑❑❑
CM1073__________			
	20¢ **Gropius House,** tagged	.35	.20 ❑❑❑❑❑
CM1074__________			
	20¢ **Washington International Airport,** tagged	.35	.20 ❑❑❑❑❑

CM1064

CM1065

CM1066

CM1067

CM1069

CM1071-1074

CM1068

CM1070

CM1075

CM1076

CM1077 →

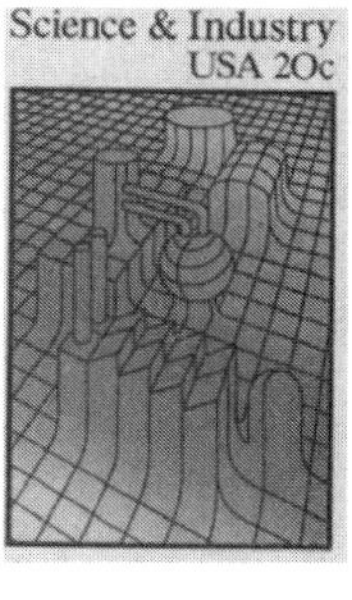

		MNHFVF	UseFVF	
CM1075 ____________	**1982. Francis of Assisi Issue**			
	20¢ **multicolored** tagged (174,180,000)	.35	.20	❑❑❑❑❑
CM1076 ____________	**1982. Ponce de Leon Issue**			
	20¢ **multicolored** tagged (110,261,000)	.35	.20	❑❑❑❑❑
CM1077 ____________	**1983. Science and Industry Issue**			
	20¢ **multicolored** tagged (118,555,000)	.35	.20	❑❑❑❑❑
CM1078 ____________	**1983. Sweden Issue**			
	20¢ **multicolored** tagged (118,225,000)	.30	.20	❑❑❑❑❑
CM1079 ____________	**1983. Ballooning Issue**			
	20¢ ***Intrepid,*** tagged (226,128,000)	.35	.20	❑❑❑❑❑
CM1080 ____________				
	20¢ **Hot air ballooning,** tagged	.35	.20	❑❑❑❑❑
CM1081 ____________				
	20¢ **Hot air ballooning,** tagged	.35	.20	❑❑❑❑❑
CM1082 ____________				
	20¢ ***Explorer II,*** tagged	.35	.20	❑❑❑❑❑
CM1083 ____________	**1983. Civilian Conservation Corps Issue**			
	20¢ **multicolored** tagged (114,290,000)	.35	.20	❑❑❑❑❑
CM1084 ____________	**1983. Joseph Priestly Issue**			
	20¢ **multicolored** tagged (165,000,000)	.35	.20	❑❑❑❑❑
CM1085 ____________	**1983. Volunteer Issue**			
	20¢ **red & black** tagged (120,430,000)	.35	.20	❑❑❑❑❑
CM1086 ____________	**1983. German Concord Issue**			
	20¢ **brown** tagged (117,025,000)	.35	.20	❑❑❑❑❑
CM1087 ____________	**1983. Physical Fitness Issue**			
	20¢ **multicolored** tagged (111,775,000)	.35	.20	❑❑❑❑❑
CM1088 ____________	**1983. Brooklyn Bridge Issue**			
	20¢ **blue** tagged (181,700,000)	.35	.20	❑❑❑❑❑
CM1089 ____________	**1983. Tennessee Valley Authority Issue**			
	20¢ **multicolored** tagged (114,250,000)	.35	.20	❑❑❑❑❑
CM1090 ____________	**1983. Medal of Honor Issue**			
	20¢ **multicolored** tagged (108,820,000)	.35	.20	❑❑❑❑❑
CM1091 ____________	**1983. Scott Joplin Issue**			
	20¢ **multicolored** tagged (115,200,000)	.35	.20	❑❑❑❑❑
CM1092 ____________	**1983. Babe Ruth Issue**			
	20¢ **blue** tagged (184,950,000)	.35	.20	❑❑❑❑❑
CM1093 ____________	**1983. Nathaniel Hawthorne Issue**			
	20¢ **multicolored** tagged (110,925,000)	.35	.20	❑❑❑❑❑
CM1094 ____________	**1983. 1984 Olympic Issue**			
	13¢ **Discus,** tagged (395,424,000)	.25	.20	❑❑❑❑❑
CM1095 ____________				
	13¢ **High jump,** tagged	.25	.20	❑❑❑❑❑
CM1096 ____________				
	13¢ **Archery,** tagged	.25	.20	❑❑❑❑❑
CM1097 ____________				
	13¢ **Boxing,** tagged	.25	.20	❑❑❑❑❑
CM1098 ____________	**1983. Treaty of Paris Issue**			
	20¢ **multicolored** tagged (104,340,000)	.35	.20	❑❑❑❑❑
CM1099 ____________	**1983. Civil Service Issue**			
	20¢ **beige, blue & red** tagged (114,725,000)	.35	.20	❑❑❑❑❑
CM1100 ____________	**1983. Metropolitan Opera Issue**			
	20¢ **dark carmine & yellow orange** tagged (112,525,000)	.35	.20	❑❑❑❑❑
CM1101 ____________	**1983. American Inventors Issue**			
	20¢ **Charles Steinmetz,** tagged (193,055,000)	.35	.20	❑❑❑❑❑

CM1078

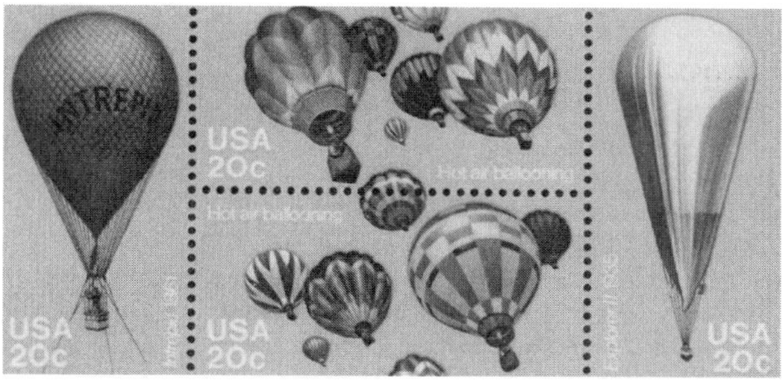

CM1079-1082

CM1083

CM1085

CM1086

CM1084

CM1087

CM1088

CM1089

CM1090

CM1091

CM1092

CM1093

CM1094-1097

		MNHFVF	UseFVF	
CM1102				
	20¢ **Edwin Armstrong,** tagged	.35	.20	❑❑❑❑❑
CM1103				
	20¢ **Nikola Tesla,** tagged	.35	.20	❑❑❑❑❑
CM1104				
	20¢ **Philo T. Farnsworth,** tagged	.35	.20	❑❑❑❑❑
CM1105	**1983. Streetcar Issue**			
	20¢ **NYC's First Horsecar,** tagged	.35	.20	❑❑❑❑❑
CM1106				
	20¢ **Montgomery electric,** tagged	.35	.20	❑❑❑❑❑
CM1107				
	20¢ **"Bobtail" Horse Car,** tagged	.35	.20	❑❑❑❑❑
CM1108				
	20¢ **St. Charles Streetcar,** tagged	.35	.20	❑❑❑❑❑
CM1109	**1983. Martin Luther Issue**			
	20¢ **multicolored** tagged (165,000,000)	.35	.20	❑❑❑❑❑
CM1110	**1984. Alaska Statehood Issue**			
	20¢ **multicolored** tagged (120,000,000)	.35	.20	❑❑❑❑❑
CM1111	**1984. Winter Olympics Issue**			
	20¢ **Ice dancing,** tagged (319,675,000)	.35	.20	❑❑❑❑❑
CM1112				
	20¢ **Alpine skiing,** tagged	.35	.20	❑❑❑❑❑
CM1113				
	20¢ **Cross-country skiing,** tagged	.35	.20	❑❑❑❑❑
CM1114				
	20¢ **Ice hockey,** tagged	.35	.20	❑❑❑❑❑
CM1115	**1984. Federal Deposit Insurance Corporation Issue**			
	20¢ **multicolored** tagged (103,975,000)	.35	.20	❑❑❑❑❑
CM1116	**1984. Love Issue**			
	20¢ **multicolored** tagged (554,675,000)	.35	.20	❑❑❑❑❑
CM1117	**1984. Carter G. Woodson Issue**			
	20¢ **multicolored** tagged (120,000,000)	.35	.20	❑❑❑❑❑
CM1118	**1984. Soil and Water Conservation Issue**			
	20¢ **multicolored** tagged (106,975,000)	.35	.20	❑❑❑❑❑
CM1119	**1984. Credit Union Act of 1934 Issue**			
	20¢ **multicolored** tagged (107,325,000)	.35	.20	❑❑❑❑❑
CM1120	**1984. Orchids Issue**			
	20¢ **Wild Pink Orchid,** tagged (306,912,000)	.35	.20	❑❑❑❑❑
CM1121				
	20¢ **Yellow Lady's-Slipper,** tagged	.35	.20	❑❑❑❑❑
CM1122				
	20¢ **Spreading Pogonia,** tagged	.35	.20	❑❑❑❑❑
CM1123				
	20¢ **Pacific Calypso Orchid,** tagged	.35	.20	❑❑❑❑❑
CM1124	**1984. Hawaii Statehood Issue**			
	20¢ **multicolored** tagged (120,000,000)	.35	.20	❑❑❑❑❑
CM1125	**1984. National Archives Issue**			
	20¢ **multicolored** tagged (108,000,000)	.35	.20	❑❑❑❑❑
CM1126	**1984. Summer Olympics Issue**			
	20¢ **Men's diving,** tagged (313,350,000)	.35	.20	❑❑❑❑❑
CM1127				
	20¢ **Women's long jump,** tagged	.35	.20	❑❑❑❑❑
CM1128				
	20¢ **Wrestling,** tagged	.35	.20	❑❑❑❑❑

CM1098

CM1099

CM1100

CM1101-1104

CM1109

CM1110

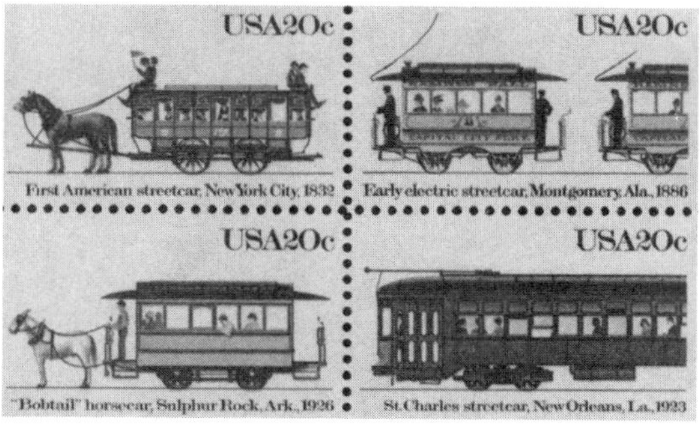

CM1105-1108

CM1111-1114

CM1115

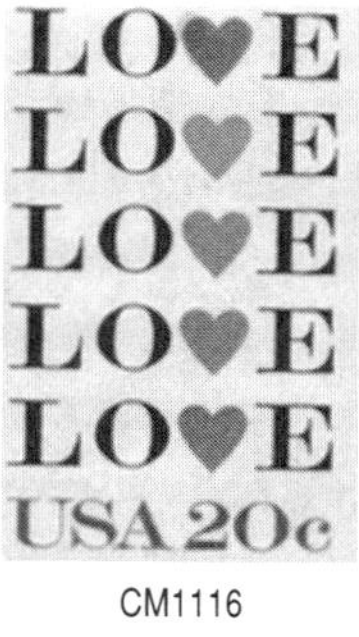

CM1116

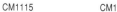

CM1117

	MNHFVF	UseFVF	
CM1129______			
20¢ **Women's kayacking,** tagged	.35	.20	❑❑❑❑❑
CM1130______ **1984. Louisiana World Exposition Issue**			
20¢ **multicolored** tagged (130,320,000)	.35	.20	❑❑❑❑❑
CM1131______ **1984. Health Research Issue**			
20¢ **multicolored** tagged (120,000,000)	.35	.20	❑❑❑❑❑
CM1132______ **1984. Douglas Fairbanks Issue**			
20¢ **multicolored** tagged (117,050,000)	.35	.20	❑❑❑❑❑
CM1133______ **1984. Jim Thorpe Issue**			
20¢ **dark brown** tagged (115,725,000)	.75	.20	❑❑❑❑❑
CM1134______ **1984. John McCormack Issue**			
20¢ **multicolored** tagged (116,600,000)	.35	.20	❑❑❑❑❑

CM1118

CM1119

CM1120-1123

CM1124

CM1125

CM1130

CM1132

CM1126-1129

CM1131

CM1133

CM1134

CM1135

CM1136

CM1137

CM1138

CM1142-1145

CM1139

CM1140

CM1141

CM1146

CM1147

CM1148

CM1149

CM1150

MNHFVF	UseFVF	

CM1135_____ **1984. St. Lawrence Seaway Issue**
20¢ **multicolored** tagged (120,000,000) — .35 — .20 ☐☐☐☐☐

CM1136_____ **1984. Wetlands Preservation Issue**
20¢ **blue** tagged (123,575,000) — .35 — .20 ☐☐☐☐☐

CM1137_____ **1984. Roanoke Voyages Issue**
20¢ **multicolored** tagged (120,000,000) — .35 — .20 ☐☐☐☐☐

CM1138_____ **1984. Herman Melville Issue**
20¢ **blue green** tagged (117,125,000) — .35 — .20 ☐☐☐☐☐

CM1139_____ **1984. Horace Moses Issue**
20¢ **orange & dark brown** tagged (117,225,000) — .35 — .20 ☐☐☐☐☐

CM1140_____ **1984. Smokey Bear Issue**
20¢ **multicolored** tagged (95,525,000) — .35 — .20 ☐☐☐☐☐

CM1141_____ **1984. Roberto Clemente Issue**
20¢ **multicolored** tagged (119,125,000) — 2.75 — .20 ☐☐☐☐☐

CM1142_____ **1984. American Dogs Issue**
20¢ **Beagle & Terrier,** tagged (216,260,000) — .35 — .20 ☐☐☐☐☐

CM1143_____
20¢ **Retriever & Cocker Spaniel,** tagged — .35 — .20 ☐☐☐☐☐

CM1144_____
20¢ **Malamute & Collie,** tagged — .35 — .20 ☐☐☐☐☐

CM1145_____
20¢ **Coonhound & Foxhound,** tagged — .35 — .20 ☐☐☐☐☐

CM1146_____ **1984. Crime Prevention Issue**
20¢ **multicolored** tagged (120,000,000) — .35 — .20 ☐☐☐☐☐

CM1147_____ **1984. Family Unity Issue**
20¢ **multicolored** tagged (117,625,000) — .35 — .20 ☐☐☐☐☐

CM1148_____ **1984. Eleanor Roosevelt Issue**
20¢ **blue** tagged (112,896,000) — .35 — .20 ☐☐☐☐☐

CM1149_____ **1984. Nation of Readers Issue**
20¢ **brown & dark red** tagged, (116,500,000) — .35 — .20 ☐☐☐☐☐

CM1150_____ **1984. Hispanic Americans Issue**
20¢ **multicolored** tagged (108,140,000) — .35 — .20 ☐☐☐☐☐

CM1151_____ **1984. Vietnam Veterans Memorial Issue**
20¢ **multicolored** tagged (105,300,000) — .35 — .20 ☐☐☐☐☐

CM1152_____ **1985. Jerome Kern Issue**
22¢ **multicolored** tagged (124,500,000) — .35 — .20 ☐☐☐☐☐

CM1153_____ **1985. Mary McLeod Bethune Issue**
22¢ **multicolored** tagged (120,000,000) — .35 — .20 ☐☐☐☐☐

CM1154_____ **1985. Duck Decoys Issue**
22¢ **Broadbill decoy,** tagged (300,000,000) — .40 — .20 ☐☐☐☐☐

CM1155_____
22¢ **Mallard decoy,** tagged — .40 — .20 ☐☐☐☐☐

CM1156_____
22¢ **Canvasback decoy,** tagged — .40 — .20 ☐☐☐☐☐

CM1157_____
22¢ **Redhead decoy,** tagged — .40 — .20 ☐☐☐☐☐

CM1158_____ **1985. Special Olympics Issue**
22¢ **multicolored** tagged (120,580,000) — .35 — .20 ☐☐☐☐☐

CM1159_____ **1985. Love Issue**
22¢ **multicolored** tagged (729,700,000) — .35 — .20 ☐☐☐☐☐

CM1160_____ **1985. Rural Electrification Administration Issue**
22¢ **multicolored** tagged (124,750,000) — .35 — .20 ☐☐☐☐☐

CM1161_____ **1985. Ameripex 86 Issue**
22¢ **multicolored** tagged (203,496,000) — .35 — .20 ☐☐☐☐☐

CM1151

CM1152

CM1153

CM1154-1157

CM1159

CM1160

CM1158

CM1163

CM1162

CM1161

CM1164

CM1165

CM1166

CM1167-1170

		MNHFVF	UseFVF	
CM1162______	**1985. Abigail Adams Issue**			
	22¢ **multicolored** tagged (126,325,000)	.35	.20	❑❑❑❑❑
CM1163______	**1985. Frederic Auguste Bartholdi Issue**			
	22¢ **multicolored** tagged (130,000,000)	.35	.20	❑❑❑❑❑
CM1164______	**1985. Korean War Veterans Issue**			
	22¢ **gray green & rose red** tagged (119,975,000)	.35	.20	❑❑❑❑❑
CM1165______	**1985. Social Security Act Issue**			
	22¢ **dark blue & light blue** tagged (120,000,000)	.35	.20	❑❑❑❑❑
CM1166______	**1985. World War I Veterans Issue**			
	22¢ **green & red** tagged (119,975,000)	.35	.20	❑❑❑❑❑
CM1167______	**1985. American Horses Issue**			
	22¢ **Quarter horse,** tagged (147,940,000)	2.75	.20	❑❑❑❑❑
CM1168______				
	22¢ **Morgan,** tagged	2.75	.20	❑❑❑❑❑
CM1169______				
	22¢ **Saddlebred,** tagged	2.75	.20	❑❑❑❑❑
CM1170______				
	22¢ **Appaloosa,** tagged	2.75	.20	❑❑❑❑❑
CM1171______	**1985. Public Education Issue**			
	22¢ **multicolored** tagged (120,000,000)	.35	.20	❑❑❑❑❑
CM1172______	**1985. International Youth Year Issue**			
	22¢ **YMCA youth camping,** tagged (130,000,000)	1.00	.20	❑❑❑❑❑
CM1173______				
	22¢ **Boy Scouts,** tagged	1.00	.20	❑❑❑❑❑
CM1174______				
	22¢ **Big Brothers/Sisters,** tagged	1.00	.20	❑❑❑❑❑
CM1175______				
	22¢ **Camp Fire,** tagged	1.00	.20	❑❑❑❑❑
CM1176______	**1985. Help End Hunger Issue**			
	22¢ **multicolored** tagged (129,000,000)	.35	.20	❑❑❑❑❑
CM1177______	**1986. Arkansas Statehood Issue**			
	22¢ **multicolored** tagged	.35	.20	❑❑❑❑❑
CM1178______	**1986. Stamp Collecting Booklet Issue**			
	22¢ **Covers & handstamp,** tagged (67,996,800)	.40	.20	❑❑❑❑❑
CM1179______				
	22¢ **Youth w/albums,** tagged	.40	.20	❑❑❑❑❑
CM1180______				
	22¢ **Magnifier & stamp,** tagged	.40	.20	❑❑❑❑❑
CM1181______				
	22¢ **AMERIPEX '86 souvenir sheet,** tagged	.40	.20	❑❑❑❑❑
CM1182______	**1986. Love Stamp Issue**			
	22¢ **multicolored** tagged (947,450,000)	.35	.20	❑❑❑❑❑
CM1183______	**1986. Sojourner Truth Issue**			
	22¢ **multicolored** tagged (130,000,000)	.35	.20	❑❑❑❑❑
CM1184______	**1986. Republic of Texas Issue**			
	22¢ **dark blue, dark red & dark gray** tagged (136,500,000)	.35	.20	❑❑❑❑❑
CM1185______	**1986. Fish Booklet Issue**			
	22¢ **Muskellunge,** tagged (219,990,000)	1.75	.20	❑❑❑❑❑
CM1186______				
	22¢ **Atlantic cod,** tagged	1.75	.20	❑❑❑❑❑
CM1187______				
	22¢ **Largemouth bass,** tagged	1.75	.20	❑❑❑❑❑
CM1188______				
	22¢ **Bluefin tuna,** tagged	1.75	.20	❑❑❑❑❑

CM1171

CM1172-1175

CM1176

CM1178-1181

CM1177

CM1185-1189

CM1182

CM1183

CM1184

CM1190

CM1191

		MNHFVF	UseFVF
CM1189__________			
22¢ **Catfish,** tagged		1.75	.20 ❑❑❑❑❑
CM1190__________	**1986. Public Hospitals Issue**		
22¢ **multicolored** tagged (130,000,000)		.35	.20 ❑❑❑❑❑
CM1191__________	**1986. Duke Ellington Issue**		
22¢ **multicolored** tagged (130,000,000)		.35	.20 ❑❑❑❑❑
CM1192__________	**1986. Presidents Souvenir Sheets**		
$1.98 **Souvenir sheet of 9** (5,825,050)		5.25	4.50 ❑❑❑❑❑
CM1193__________	**1986. Presidents Souvenir Sheets**		
$1.98 **Souvenir sheet of 9** (5,825,050)		5.25	4.50 ❑❑❑❑❑
CM1194__________	**1986. Presidents Souvenir Sheets**		
$1.98 **Souvenir sheet of 9** (5,825,050)		5.25	4.50 ❑❑❑❑❑
CM1195__________	**1986. Presidents Souvenir Sheets**		
$1.98 **Souvenir sheet of 9** (5,825,050)		5.25	4.50 ❑❑❑❑❑
CM1196__________	**1986. Arctic Explorers Issue**		
22¢ **E.K. Kane,** (130,000,000)		1.10	.20 ❑❑❑❑❑
CM1197__________			
22¢ **A.W. Greely**		1.10	.20 ❑❑❑❑❑
CM1198__________			
22¢ **V. Stefansson**		1.10	.20 ❑❑❑❑❑
CM1199__________			
22¢ **R.E. Peary & M. Henson**		1.10	.20 ❑❑❑❑❑
CM1200__________	**1986. Statue of Liberty Issue**		
22¢ **red & blue** (220,725,000)		.35	.20 ❑❑❑❑❑
CM1201__________	**1986. Navajo Art Issue**		
22¢ **multicolored** (240,525,000)		.40	.20 ❑❑❑❑❑
CM1202__________			
22¢ **multicolored**		.40	.20 ❑❑❑❑❑
CM1203__________			
22¢ **multicolored**		.40	.20 ❑❑❑❑❑
CM1204__________			
22¢ **multicolored**		.40	.20 ❑❑❑❑❑
CM1205__________	**1986. T.S. Eliot Issue**		
22¢ **copper red** (131,700,000)		.35	.20 ❑❑❑❑❑
CM1206__________	**1986. Woodcarved Figurines Issue**		
22¢ **Highlander figure,** tagged (240,000,000)		.40	.20 ❑❑❑❑❑
CM1207__________			
22¢ **Ship figurehead,** tagged		.40	.20 ❑❑❑❑❑
CM1208__________			
22¢ **Nautical figure,** tagged		.40	.20 ❑❑❑❑❑
CM1209__________			
22¢ **Cigar Store figure,** tagged		.40	.20 ❑❑❑❑❑
CM1210__________	**1987. Michigan Statehood Issue**		
22¢ **multicolored** tagged (167,430,000)		.35	.20 ❑❑❑❑❑
CM1211__________	**1987. Pan-American Games Issue**		
22¢ **multicolored** tagged (166,555,000)		.35	.20 ❑❑❑❑❑
CM1212__________	**1987. Love Stamp Issue**		
22¢ **multicolored** tagged (811,560,000)		.35	.20 ❑❑❑❑❑
CM1213__________	**1987. Jean-Baptiste du Sable Issue**		
22¢ **multicolored** tagged (142,905,000)		.35	.20 ❑❑❑❑❑
CM1214__________	**1987. Enrico Caruso Issue**		
22¢ **multicolored** tagged (130,000,000)		.35	.20 ❑❑❑❑❑

CM1192

Presidents of
the United States: I
AMERIPEX 86
International
Stamp Show
Chicago, Illinois
May 22-June 1, 1986

CM1193

Presidents of
the United States: II
AMERIPEX 86
International
Stamp Show
Chicago, Illinois
May 22-June 1, 1986

CM1194

Presidents of
the United States: III
AMERIPEX 86
International
Stamp Show
Chicago, Illinois
May 22-June 1, 1986

CM1195

Presidents of
the United States: IV
AMERIPEX 86
International
Stamp Show
Chicago, Illinois
May 22-June 1, 1986

	MNHFVF	UseFVF	
CM1215 **1987. Girl Scouts Issue**			
22¢ **multicolored** tagged (149,980,000)	.35	.20	❑❑❑❑❑
CM1216 **1987. Special Occasions Issue**			
22¢ **Congratulations,** tagged (610,425,000)	1.75	.40	❑❑❑❑❑
CM1217			
22¢ **Get Well,** tagged	1.75	.40	❑❑❑❑❑
CM1218			
22¢ **Thank You,** tagged	1.75	.40	❑❑❑❑❑
CM1219			
22¢ **Love You, Dad,** tagged	1.75	.40	❑❑❑❑❑
CM1220			
22¢ **Best Wishes,** tagged	1.75	.40	❑❑❑❑❑
CM1221			
22¢ **Happy Birthday,** tagged	1.75	.40	❑❑❑❑❑
CM1222			
22¢ **Love You, Mother,** tagged	1.75	.40	❑❑❑❑❑
CM1223			
22¢ **Keep in Touch,** tagged	1.75	.40	❑❑❑❑❑
NOTE: Nos. CM1224 and CM1225 are not assigned.			
CM1226 **1987. United Way Issue**			
22¢ **multicolored** tagged (156,995,000)	.35	.20	❑❑❑❑❑
CM1227 **1987. American Wildlife Issue**			
22¢ **Barn Swallow,** tagged	1.50	.55	❑❑❑❑❑
CM1228			
22¢ **Monarch Butterfly,** tagged	1.50	.55	❑❑❑❑❑
CM1229			
22¢ **Bighorn Sheep,** tagged	1.50	.55	❑❑❑❑❑
CM1230			
22¢ **Broad-tailed Hummingbird,** tagged	1.50	.55	❑❑❑❑❑
CM1231			
22¢ **Cottontail,** tagged	1.50	.55	❑❑❑❑❑
CM1232			
22¢ **Osprey,** tagged	1.50	.55	❑❑❑❑❑
CM1233			
22¢ **Mountain Lion,** tagged	1.50	.55	❑❑❑❑❑
CM1234			
22¢ **Luna Moth,** tagged	1.50	.55	❑❑❑❑❑
CM1235			
22¢ **Mule Deer,** tagged	1.50	.55	❑❑❑❑❑
CM1236			
22¢ **Gray Squirrel,** tagged	1.50	.55	❑❑❑❑❑
CM1237			
22¢ **Armadillo,** tagged	1.50	.55	❑❑❑❑❑
CM1238			
22¢ **Eastern Chipmunk,** tagged	1.50	.55	❑❑❑❑❑
CM1239			
22¢ **Moose,** tagged	1.50	.55	❑❑❑❑❑
CM1240			
22¢ **Black Bear,** tagged	1.50	.55	❑❑❑❑❑
CM1241			
22¢ **Tiger Swallowtail,** tagged	1.50	.55	❑❑❑❑❑
CM1242			
22¢ **Bobwhite,** tagged	1.50	.55	❑❑❑❑❑

CM1196-1199

CM1200

CM1201-1204

CM1205

CM1206-1209

CM1210

CM1211

CM1212

CM1213

CM1214

CM1215

CM1216-1223

	MNHFVF	UseFVF	
CM1243 ___________			
22¢ **Ringtail,** tagged	1.50	.55	❑❑❑❑❑
CM1244 ___________			
22¢ **Red-winged Blackbird,** tagged	1.50	.55	❑❑❑❑❑
CM1245 ___________			
22¢ **American Lobster,** tagged	1.50	.55	❑❑❑❑❑
CM1246 ___________			
22¢ **Black-tailed Jack Rabbit, Rabbit,** tagged	1.50	.55	❑❑❑❑❑
CM1247 ___________			
22¢ **Scarlet Tanager,** tagged	1.50	.55	❑❑❑❑❑
CM1248 ___________			
22¢ **Woodchuck,** tagged	1.50	.55	❑❑❑❑❑
CM1249 ___________			
22¢ **Roseate Spoonbill,** tagged	1.50	.55	❑❑❑❑❑
CM1250 ___________			
22¢ **Bald Eagle,** tagged	1.50	.55	❑❑❑❑❑
CM1251 ___________			
22¢ **Alaskan Brown Bear,** tagged	1.50	.55	❑❑❑❑❑
CM1252 ___________			
22¢ **Iiwi,** tagged	1.50	.55	❑❑❑❑❑
CM1253 ___________			
22¢ **Badger,** tagged	1.50	.55	❑❑❑❑❑
CM1254 ___________			
22¢ **Pronghorn,** tagged	1.50	.55	❑❑❑❑❑
CM1255 ___________			
22¢ **River Otter,** tagged	1.50	.55	❑❑❑❑❑
CM1256 ___________			
22¢ **Ladybug,** tagged	1.50	.55	❑❑❑❑❑
CM1257 ___________			
22¢ **Beaver,** tagged	1.50	.55	❑❑❑❑❑
CM1258 ___________			
22¢ **White-tailed Deer,** tagged	1.50	.55	❑❑❑❑❑
CM1259 ___________			
22¢ **Blue Jay,** tagged	1.50	.55	❑❑❑❑❑
CM1260 ___________			
22¢ **Pika,** tagged	1.50	.55	❑❑❑❑❑
CM1261 ___________			
22¢ **Bison,** tagged	1.50	.55	❑❑❑❑❑
CM1262 ___________			
22¢ **Snowy Egret,** tagged	1.50	.55	❑❑❑❑❑
CM1263 ___________			
22¢ **Gray Wolf,** tagged	1.50	.55	❑❑❑❑❑
CM1264 ___________			
22¢ **Mountain Goat,** tagged	1.50	.55	❑❑❑❑❑
CM1265 ___________			
22¢ **Deer Mouse,** tagged	1.50	.55	❑❑❑❑❑
CM1266 ___________			
22¢ **Black-tailed Prairie Dog,** tagged	1.50	.55	❑❑❑❑❑
CM1267 ___________			
22¢ **Box Turtle,** tagged	1.50	.55	❑❑❑❑❑
CM1268 ___________			
22¢ **Wolverine,** tagged	1.50	.55	❑❑❑❑❑
CM1269 ___________			
22¢ **American Elk,** tagged	1.50	.55	❑❑❑❑❑

		MNHFVF	UseFVF	
CM1270	22¢ **California Sea Lion,** tagged	1.50	.55	❑❑❑❑❑
CM1271	22¢ **Mockingbird,** tagged	1.50	.55	❑❑❑❑❑
CM1272	22¢ **Raccoon,** tagged	1.50	.55	❑❑❑❑❑
CM1273	22¢ **Bobcat,** tagged	1.50	.55	❑❑❑❑❑
CM1274	22¢ **Black-footed Ferret,** tagged	1.50	.55	❑❑❑❑❑
CM1275	22¢ **Canada Goose,** tagged	1.50	.55	❑❑❑❑❑
CM1276	22¢ **Red Fox,** tagged	1.50	.55	❑❑❑❑❑
CM1277	**1987. Delaware Statehood Issue**			
	22¢ **multicolored** tagged (166,725,000)	.35	.20	❑❑❑❑❑
CM1278	**1987. Friendship with Morocco Issue**			
	22¢ **red & black** tagged (157,475,000)	.35	.20	❑❑❑❑❑
CM1279	**1987. William Faulkner Issue**			
	22¢ **green** tagged (156,225,000)	.35	.20	❑❑❑❑❑
	NOTE: Imperforate singles are untagged and from printer's waste.			
CM1280	**1987. Lacemaking Issue**			
	22¢ **Squash blossoms,** tagged (163,980,000)	.40	.20	❑❑❑❑❑
CM1281	22¢ **Floral design,** tagged	.40	.20	❑❑❑❑❑
CM1282	22¢ **Floral lace design,** tagged	.40	.20	❑❑❑❑❑
CM1283	22¢ **Dogwood blossoms,** tagged	.40	.20	❑❑❑❑❑
CM1284	**1987. Pennsylvania Statehood Issue**			
	22¢ **multicolored** tagged (186,575,000)	.35	.20	❑❑❑❑❑
CM1285	**1987. Constitution Bicentennial Issue**			
	22¢ **The Bicentennial...,** tagged (584,340,000)	.75	.25	❑❑❑❑❑
CM1286	22¢ **We the people...,** tagged	.75	.25	❑❑❑❑❑
CM1287	22¢ **Establish justice...,** tagged	.75	.25	❑❑❑❑❑
CM1288	22¢ **And secure... liberty...,** tagged	.75	.25	❑❑❑❑❑
CM1289	22¢ **Do ordain...,** tagged	.75	.25	❑❑❑❑❑
CM1290	**1987. New Jersey Statehood Issue**			
	22¢ **multicolored** tagged (184,325,000)	.35	.20	❑❑❑❑❑
CM1291	**1987. Constitution Bicentennial Issue**			
	22¢ **multicolored** tagged (168,995,000)	.35	.20	❑❑❑❑❑
CM1292	**1987. Certified Public Accountants Issue**			
	22¢ **multicolored** tagged (163,120,000)	.35	.20	❑❑❑❑❑
CM1293	**1987. Steam Locomotive Issue**			
	22¢ ***Stourbridge Lion,*** tagged	.75	.25	❑❑❑❑❑
CM1294	22¢ ***Best Friend of Charleston,*** tagged	.75	.25	❑❑❑❑❑
CM1295	22¢ ***John Bull,*** tagged	.75	.25	❑❑❑❑❑

		MNHFVF	UseFVF	
CM1296___________				
22¢ ***Brother Jonathan,*** tagged		.75	.25	❑❑❑❑❑
CM1297___________				
22¢ ***Gowan & Marx,*** tagged		.75	.25	❑❑❑❑❑
CM1298___________	**1988. Georgia Statehood Issue**			
22¢ **multicolored** tagged (165,845,000)		.35	.20	❑❑❑❑❑
CM1299___________	**1988. Connecticut Statehood Issue**			
22¢ **multicolored** tagged (155,170,000)		.35	.20	❑❑❑❑❑
CM1300___________	**1988. Winter Olympics Issue**			
22¢ **multicolored** tagged (158,870,000)		.35	.20	❑❑❑❑❑
CM1301___________	**1988. Australia Bicentennial Issue**			
22¢ **multicolored** tagged (145,560,000)		.35	.20	❑❑❑❑❑
CM1302___________	**1988. James Weldon Johnson Issue**			
22¢ **multicolored** tagged (97,300,000)		.35	.20	❑❑❑❑❑
CM1303___________	**1988. Cats Issue**			
22¢ **Siamese, Exotic Shorthair,** tagged (158,556,000)		1.00	.20	❑❑❑❑❑
CM1304___________				
22¢ **Abyssinian, Himalayan,** tagged		1.00	.20	❑❑❑❑❑
CM1305___________				
22¢ **Maine Coon Cat, Burmese,** tagged		1.00	.20	❑❑❑❑❑
CM1306___________				
22¢ **American Shorthair, Persian,** tagged		1.00	.20	❑❑❑❑❑
CM1307___________	**1988. Massachusetts Statehood Issue**			
22¢ **dark blue & dark red** tagged (102,100,000)		.35	.20	❑❑❑❑❑
CM1308___________	**1988. Maryland Statehood Issue**			
22¢ **multicolored** tagged (103,325,000)		.35	.20	❑❑❑❑❑
CM1309___________	**1988. Knute Rockne Issue**			
22¢ **multicolored** tagged (97,300,000)		.35	.20	❑❑❑❑❑
CM1310___________	**1988. South Carolina Statehood Issue**			
25¢ **multicolored** tagged (162,045,000)		.40	.20	❑❑❑❑❑
CM1311___________	**1988. Francis Ouimet Issue**			
25¢ **multicolored** tagged (153,045,000)		.40	.20	❑❑❑❑❑
CM1312___________	**1988. New Hampshire Statehood Issue**			
25¢ **multicolored** tagged (153,295,000)		.40	.20	❑❑❑❑❑
CM1313___________	**1988. Virginia Statehood Issue**			
25¢ **multicolored** tagged (153,295,000)		.40	.20	❑❑❑❑❑
CM1314___________	**1988. Love Issue**			
25¢ **multicolored** tagged (841,240,000)		.40	.20	❑❑❑❑❑
CM1315___________	**1988. New York Statehood Issue**			
25¢ **multicolored** tagged (183,290,000)		.40	.20	❑❑❑❑❑
CM1316___________	**1988. Love Issue**			
45¢ **multicolored** tagged (169,765,000)		1.35	.20	❑❑❑❑❑
CM1317___________	**1988. Summer Olympic Games Issue**			
25¢ **multicolored** tagged (157,215,000)		.40	.20	❑❑❑❑❑
CM1318___________	**1988. Classic Cars Issue**			
25¢ **Locomobile,** tagged (635,238,000)		2.00	.50	❑❑❑❑❑
CM1319___________				
25¢ **Pierce-Arrow,** tagged		2.00	.50	❑❑❑❑❑
CM1320___________				
25¢ **Cord,** tagged		2.00	.50	❑❑❑❑❑
CM1321___________				
25¢ **Packard,** tagged		2.00	.50	❑❑❑❑❑
CM1322___________				
25¢ **Duesenberg,** tagged		2.00	.50	❑❑❑❑❑

CM1227-1276

CM1226

CM1277

CM1278

CM1279

CM1280-1283

CM1284

CM1285-1289

		MNHFVF	UseFVF	
CM1323__________	**1988. Antarctic Explorers Issue**			
	25¢ **Nathaniel Palmer,** tagged (162,142,500)	1.00	.20	❑❑❑❑❑
CM1324__________				
	25¢ **Lt. Charles Wilkes,** tagged	1.00	.20	❑❑❑❑❑
CM1325__________				
	25¢ **Richard E. Byrd,** tagged	1.00	.20	❑❑❑❑❑
CM1326__________				
	25¢ **Lincoln Ellsworth,** tagged	1.00	.20	❑❑❑❑❑
CM1327__________	**1988. Carousel Animal Issue**			
	25¢ **Deer,** tagged (305,015,000)	1.00	.20	❑❑❑❑❑
CM1328__________				
	25¢ **Horse,** tagged	1.00	.20	❑❑❑❑❑
CM1329__________				
	25¢ **Camel,** tagged	1.00	.20	❑❑❑❑❑
CM1330__________				
	25¢ **Goat,** tagged	1.00	.20	❑❑❑❑❑
CM1331__________	**1988. Special Occasions Issue**			
	25¢ **multicolored** tagged (480,000,000)	1.00	.20	❑❑❑❑❑
CM1332__________				
	25¢ **multicolored** tagged	1.00	.20	❑❑❑❑❑
CM1333__________				
	25¢ **multicolored** tagged	1.00	.20	❑❑❑❑❑
CM1334__________				
	25¢ **multicolored** tagged	1.00	.20	❑❑❑❑❑
CM1335__________	**1989. Montana Statehood Issue**			
	25¢ **multicolored** tagged	.40	.20	❑❑❑❑❑
CM1336__________	**1989. A. Philip Randolph Issue**			
	25¢ **multicolored** tagged (151,675,000)	.40	.20	❑❑❑❑❑
CM1337__________	**1989. North Dakota Statehood Issue**			
	25¢ **multicolored** tagged (163,000,000)	.40	.20	❑❑❑❑❑
CM1338__________	**1989. Washington Statehood Issue**			
	25¢ **multicolored** tagged (264,625,000)	.40	.20	❑❑❑❑❑
CM1339__________	**1989. Steamboats Issue**			
	25¢ ***Experiment,*** tagged (204,984,000)	.75	.20	❑❑❑❑❑
CM1340__________				
	25¢ ***Phoenix,*** tagged	.75	.20	❑❑❑❑❑
CM1341__________				
	25¢ ***New Orleans,*** tagged	.75	.20	❑❑❑❑❑
CM1342__________				
	25¢ ***Washington,*** tagged	.75	.20	❑❑❑❑❑
CM1343__________				
	25¢ ***Walk in the Water,*** tagged	.75	.20	❑❑❑❑❑
CM1344__________	**1989. World Stamp Expo 89 Issue**			
	25¢ **red, gray & black** (103,835,000)	.40	.20	❑❑❑❑❑
CM1345__________	**1989. Arturo Toscanini Issue**			
	25¢ **multicolored** tagged (152,250,000)	.40	.20	❑❑❑❑❑
CM1346__________	**1989. House of Representatives Issue**			
	25¢ **multicolored** tagged (138,760,000)	.40	.20	❑❑❑❑❑
CM1347__________	**1989. Senate Issue**			
	25¢ **multicolored** tagged (137,985,000)	.40	.20	❑❑❑❑❑
CM1348__________	**1989. Executive Branch Issue**			
	25¢ **multicolored** tagged (138,580,000)	.40	.20	❑❑❑❑❑
CM1349__________	**1989. South Dakota Statehood Issue**			
	25¢ **multicolored** tagged (164,680,000)	.40	.20	❑❑❑❑❑

CM1290

CM1291

CM1292

CM1293-1297

CM1298

CM1299

CM1300

CM1301

CM1302

CM1307

CM1308

CM1303-1306

CM1309

CM1310

		MNHFVF	UseFVF	
CM1350	**1989. Lou Gehrig Issue**			
	25¢ **multicolored** tagged (138,760,000)	1.10	.20	❑❑❑❑❑
CM1351	**1989. Ernest Hemingway Issue**			
	25¢ **multicolored** tagged (191,755,000)	.40	.20	❑❑❑❑❑
CM1352	**1989. Moon Landing Anniversary Issue**			
	$2.40 **multicolored** tagged	6.00	2.25	❑❑❑❑❑
CM1353	**1989. North Carolina Statehood Issue**			
	25¢ **multicolored** tagged (179,800,000)	.40	.20	❑❑❑❑❑
CM1354	**1989. Letter Carriers Issue**			
	25¢ **multicolored** tagged (188,400,000)	.40	.20	❑❑❑❑❑
CM1355	**1989. Bill of Rights Issue**			
	25¢ **multicolored** tagged (191,860,000)	.40	.20	❑❑❑❑❑
CM1356	**1989. Dinosaurs Issue**			
	25¢ **Tyrannosaurus,** tagged	1.25	.20	❑❑❑❑❑
CM1357				
	25¢ **Pteranodon,** tagged	1.25	.20	❑❑❑❑❑
CM1358				
	25¢ **Stegosaurus,** tagged	1.25	.20	❑❑❑❑❑
CM1359				
	25¢ **Apatosaurus,** tagged	1.25	.20	❑❑❑❑❑
CM1360	**1989. America Issue**			
	25¢ **multicolored** tagged (137,410,000)	.40	.20	❑❑❑❑❑
CM1361	**1989. World Stamp Expo 89 Souvenir Sheet**			
	$3.60 **Souvenir sheet of 4** (2,017,225)	20.00	13.50	❑❑❑❑❑
CM1362	**1989. Classic Mail Transportation Issue**			
	25¢ **Stagecoach,** tagged (163,824,000)	.75	.20	❑❑❑❑❑
CM1363				
	25¢ **Steamboat,** tagged	.75	.20	❑❑❑❑❑
CM1364				
	25¢ **Biplane,** tagged	.75	.20	❑❑❑❑❑
CM1365				
	25¢ **Early automobile,** tagged	.75	.20	❑❑❑❑❑
CM1366	**1989. Classic Mail Transportation Souvenir Sheet Issue**			
	$1 **multicolored Souvenir sheet,** tagged	5.00	4.00	❑❑❑❑❑
CM1367	**1990. Idaho Statehood Issue**			
	25¢ **multicolored** tagged	.40	.20	❑❑❑❑❑
CM1368	**1990. Love Issue**			
	25¢ **multicolored** tagged perforated 12 1/2 x 13	.40	.20	❑❑❑❑❑
CM1369				
	25¢ **multicolored** tagged perforated 11 1/2 on 2 or 3 sides	.40	.20	❑❑❑❑❑
CM1370	**1990. Ida B. Wells Issue**			
	25¢ **multicolored** tagged	.40	.20	❑❑❑❑❑
CM1371	**1990. Supreme Court Issue**			
	25¢ **multicolored** tagged	.40	.20	❑❑❑❑❑
CM1372	**1990. Wyoming Statehood Issue**			
	25¢ **multicolored** tagged	.40	.20	❑❑❑❑❑
CM1373	**1990. Classic Films Issue**			
	25¢ ***Wizard of Oz,*** tagged	2.00	.20	❑❑❑❑❑
CM1374				
	25¢ ***Gone with The Wind,*** tagged	2.00	.20	❑❑❑❑❑
CM1375				
	25¢ ***Beau Geste,*** tagged	2.00	.20	❑❑❑❑❑
CM1376				
	25¢ ***Stagecoach,*** tagged	2.00	.20	❑❑❑❑❑

CM1311

CM1312

CM1313

CM1314

CM1318-1322

CM11315

CM1316

CM11317

CM1323-1326

CM1327-1330

CM1331

CM1333

CM1332

CM1334

		MNHFVF	UseFVF	
CM1377	**1990. Marianne Moore Issue**			
	25¢ **multicolored** tagged	.40	.20	❑❑❑❑❑
CM1378	**1990. American Lighthouses Issue**			
	25¢ **Admiralty Head,** tagged	.40	.20	❑❑❑❑❑
CM1379				
	25¢ **Cape Hatteras,** tagged	.40	.20	❑❑❑❑❑
CM1380				
	25¢ **West Quoddy Head,** tagged	.40	.20	❑❑❑❑❑
CM1381				
	25¢ **American Shoals,** tagged	.40	.20	❑❑❑❑❑
CM1382				
	25¢ **Sandy Hook,** tagged	.40	.20	❑❑❑❑❑
CM1383	**1990. Rhode Island Statehood Issue**			
	25¢ **multicolored** tagged	.40	.20	❑❑❑❑❑
CM1384	**1990. Olympic Athletes Issue**			
	25¢ **Jesse Owens,** tagged	.40	.20	❑❑❑❑❑
CM1385				
	25¢ **Ray Ewry,** tagged	.40	.20	❑❑❑❑❑
CM1386				
	25¢ **Hazel Wightman,** tagged	.40	.20	❑❑❑❑❑
CM1387				
	25¢ **Eddie Eagan,** tagged	.40	.20	❑❑❑❑❑
CM1388				
	25¢ **Helene Madison,** tagged	.40	.20	❑❑❑❑❑
CM1389	**1990. American Indian Headdresses Issue**			
	25¢ **Assiniboine,** tagged	.40	.20	❑❑❑❑❑
CM1390				
	25¢ **Cheyenne,** tagged	.40	.20	❑❑❑❑❑
CM1391				
	25¢ **Commanche,** tagged	.40	.20	❑❑❑❑❑
CM1392				
	25¢ **Flathead,** tagged	.40	.20	❑❑❑❑❑
CM1393				
	25¢ **Shoshone,** tagged	.40	.20	❑❑❑❑❑
CM1394	**1990. Micronesia and Marshall Islands Issue**			
	25¢ **Micronesia,** tagged	.40	.20	❑❑❑❑❑
CM1395				
	25¢ **Marshall Islands,** tagged	.40	.20	❑❑❑❑❑
CM1396	**1990. Sea Mammals Issue**			
	25¢ **Killer Whale,** tagged (278,264,000)	.75	.20	❑❑❑❑❑
CM1397				
	25¢ **Northern Sea Lion,** tagged	.75	.20	❑❑❑❑❑
CM1398				
	25¢ **Sea Otter,** tagged	.75	.20	❑❑❑❑❑
CM1399				
	25¢ **Dolphin,** tagged	.75	.20	❑❑❑❑❑
CM1400	**1990. America Issue**			
	25¢ **multicolored** tagged (143,995,000)	.40	.20	❑❑❑❑❑
CM1401	**1990. Dwight D. Eisenhower Issue**			
	25¢ **multicolored** tagged (142,692,000)	.45	.20	❑❑❑❑❑
CM1402	**1991. Switzerland 700th Anniversary Issue**			
	50¢ **multicolored** tagged (103,648,000)	.75	.35	❑❑❑❑❑
CM1403	**1991. Vermont Statehood Issue**			
	29¢ **multicolored** tagged (179,990,000)	.45	.20	❑❑❑❑❑

CM1335

CM1336

CM1337

CM1338

CM1344

CM1345

CM1339-1343

CM1346

CM1347

CM1348

CM1349

CM1350

CM1351

CM1352

CM1353

		MNHFVF	UseFVF
CM1404	**1991. U.S. Savings Bond Issue**		
	29¢ **multicolored** tagged (150,560,000)	.45	.20 ❑❑❑❑❑
CM1405	**1991. Love Issue**		
	29¢ **multicolored** tagged, perforated 12 1/2 x 13	.45	.20 ❑❑❑❑❑
CM1405A			
	29¢ **multicolored** tagged, perforated 11	.45	.20 ❑❑❑❑❑
CM1406			
	29¢ **multicolored** tagged, perforated 11 on 2 or 3 sides	.45	.20 ❑❑❑❑❑
CM1407			
	52¢ **multicolored** tagged, perforated 11	.75	.35 ❑❑❑❑❑
CM1408	**1991. William Saroyan Issue**		
	29¢ **multicolored** tagged (161,498,000)	.45	.20 ❑❑❑❑❑
CM1409	**1991. Fishing Flies Issue**		
	29¢ **Royal Wulff,** tagged (744,918,000)	.45	.20 ❑❑❑❑❑
CM1410			
	29¢ **Jack Scott,** tagged	.45	.20 ❑❑❑❑❑

CM1354

CM1355

CM1356-1359

CM1360

WORLD STAMP EXPO'89
The classic 1869 U.S. Abraham Lincoln stamp is reborn in these four larger versions commemorating World Stamp Expo'89, held in Washington, D.C. during the 20th Universal Postal Congress of the UPU. These stamps show the issued colors and three of the trial proof color combinations.

CM1361

CM1362, 1366a (upper left)
CM1363, 1366b (upper right)
CM1364, 1366c (lower left)
CM1365, 1366d (lower right)

20th Universal Postal Congress
A review of historical methods of delivering the mail in the United States is the theme of these four stamps issued in commemoration of the convening of the 20th Universal Postal Congress in Washington, D.C. from November 13 through December 14, 1989. The United States, as host nation to the Congress for the first time in ninety-two years, welcomed more than 1,000 delegates from most of the member nations of the Universal Postal Union to the major international event.
USA 25
20th Universal Postal Congress

CM1366

CM1367

CM1368-1369

CM1372

CM1370

CM1371

CM1373-1376

CM1377

CM1383

CM1378-1382

CM1384-1388

CM1389-1393

		MNHFVF	UseFVF	
CM1411				
	29¢ **Apte Tarpon,** tagged	.45	.20	❑❑❑❑❑
CM1412				
	29¢ **Lefty's Deceiver,** tagged	.45	.20	❑❑❑❑❑
CM1413				
	29¢ **Muddler Minnow,** tagged	.45	.20	❑❑❑❑❑
CM1414	**1991. Cole Porter Issue**			
	29¢ **multicolored** tagged (149,848,000)	.45	.20	❑❑❑❑❑
CM1415	**1991. Desert Shield-Desert Storm Issue**			
	29¢ **multicolored** tagged (200,003,000)	.45	.20	❑❑❑❑❑
CM1416	**1991. Desert Shield-Desert Storm Booklet Issue**			
	29¢ **multicolored** tagged (200,000,000)	.45	.20	❑❑❑❑❑
CM1417	**1991. Olympic Track and Field Issue**			
	29¢ **Pole vault,** tagged (170,025,000)	.45	.20	❑❑❑❑❑
CM1418				
	29¢ **Discus,** tagged	.45	.20	❑❑❑❑❑
CM1419				
	29¢ **Women's sprint,** tagged	.45	.20	❑❑❑❑❑
CM1420				
	29¢ **Javelin,** tagged	.45	.20	❑❑❑❑❑
CM1421				
	29¢ **Women's hurdles,** tagged	.45	.20	❑❑❑❑❑
CM1422	**1991. Numismatics Issue**			
	29¢ **multicolored** tagged (150,310,000)	.45	.20	❑❑❑❑❑
CM1423	**1991. Basketball Centennial Issue**			
	29¢ **multicolored** tagged (149,810,000)	.45	.20	❑❑❑❑❑
CM1424	**1991. American Comedians Issue**			
	29¢ **Laurel & Hardy,** tagged (699,978,000)	.45	.20	❑❑❑❑❑
CM1425				
	29¢ **Bergen & McCarthy,** tagged	.45	.20	❑❑❑❑❑
CM1426				
	29¢ **Jack Benny,** tagged	.45	.20	❑❑❑❑❑
CM1427				
	29¢ **Fanny Brice,** tagged	.45	.20	❑❑❑❑❑
CM1428				
	29¢ **Abbott & Costello,** tagged	.45	.20	❑❑❑❑❑
CM1429	**1991. 1941: A World At War Issue**			
	$2.90 **Commemorative pane of 10**	9.00	5.00	❑❑❑❑❑
CM1430	**1991. District of Columbia Bicentennial Issue**			
	29¢ **multicolored** tagged (699,978,000)	.45	.20	❑❑❑❑❑
CM1431	**1991. Jan E. Matzeliger Issue**			
	29¢ **multicolored** tagged (148,973,000)	.45	.20	❑❑❑❑❑
CM1432	**1991. Space Exploration Issue**			
	29¢ **Mercury,** tagged (333,948,000)	.45	.20	❑❑❑❑❑
CM1433				
	29¢ **Venus,** tagged	.45	.20	❑❑❑❑❑
CM1434				
	29¢ **Earth,** tagged	.45	.20	❑❑❑❑❑
CM1435				
	29¢ **Moon,** tagged	.45	.20	❑❑❑❑❑
CM1436				
	29¢ **Mars,** tagged	.45	.20	❑❑❑❑❑
CM1437				
	29¢ **Jupiter,** tagged	.45	.20	❑❑❑❑❑

CM1394-1395

CM1396-1399

CM1400

CM1401

CM1402

CM1403

CM1404

CM1405-1406

CM1407

CM1409-1413

CM1422

CM1408

CM1423

CM1414

CM1415-1416

CM1417-1421

No.	Issue / Description	MNHFVF	UseFVF
CM1438	29¢ **Saturn,** tagged	.45	.20
CM1439	29¢ **Uranus,** tagged	.45	.20
CM1440	29¢ **Neptune,** tagged	.45	.20
CM1441	29¢ **Pluto,** tagged	.45	.20
CM1442	**1992. Winter Olympics Issue**		
	29¢ **multicolored** tagged	.45	.20
CM1443	29¢ **multicolored** tagged	.45	.20
CM1444	29¢ **multicolored** tagged	.45	.20
CM1445	29¢ **multicolored** tagged	.45	.20
CM1446	29¢ **multicolored** tagged	.45	.20
CM1447	**1992. World Columbian Stamp Expo '92 Issue**		
	29¢ **multicolored** tagged	.45	.20
CM1448	**1992. W.E.B. Du Bois Issue**		
	29¢ **multicolored** tagged	.45	.20
CM1449	**1992. Love Issue**		
	29¢ **multicolored** tagged	.45	.20
CM1450	**1992. Olympic Baseball Issue**		
	29¢ **multicolored** tagged	1.00	.20
CM1451	**1992. Voyage of Columbus Issue**		
	29¢ **Seeking Support,** tagged	1.00	.20
CM1452	29¢ **Atlantic Crossing,** tagged	1.00	.20
CM1453	29¢ **Approaching Land,** tagged	1.00	.20
CM1454	29¢ **Coming Ashore,** tagged	1.00	.20
CM1455	**1992. New York Stock Exchange Issue**		
	29¢ **multicolored** tagged	.45	.20
CM1456	**1992. Columbian Souvenir Sheets**		
	85¢ **Sheet of three**	3.00	

NOTE: Imperforate Columbian souvenir sheets are very probably the result of printer's waste.

No.	Issue / Description	MNHFVF	UseFVF
CM1457	**1992. Columbian Souvenir Sheets**		
	$1.05 **Sheet of three**	2.50	
CM1458	**1992. Columbian Souvenir Sheets**		
	$2.25 **Sheet of three**	5.00	
CM1459	**1992. Columbian Souvenir Sheets**		
	$3.14 **Sheet of three**	8.50	
CM1460	**1992. Columbian Souvenir Sheets**		
	$4.05 **Sheet of three**	9.00	
CM1461	**1992. Columbian Souvenir Sheets**		
	$5 **Sheet of one, black** like CM15	12.00	8.50
CM1462	**1992. Space Achievements Issue**		
	29¢ **Space Shuttle,** tagged	1.00	.20
CM1463	29¢ **Space station,** tagged	1.00	.20

LAUREL & HARDY
USA 29
BERGEN & McCARTHY
USA 29
JACK BENNY
USA 29
USA 29
FANNY BRICE
ABBOTT & COSTELLO
USA 29

CM1424-1428

District of Columbia Bicentennial
USA 29
Pennsylvania Avenue, circa 1903

CM1430

29 USA
Burma Road, 717-mile lifeline to China
29 USA
America's first peacetime draft, 1940
29 USA
U.S. supports allies with Lend-Lease Act
29 USA
Atlantic Charter sets war aims of allies
29 USA
America becomes "arsenal of democracy"
ASIA
Burma Road helps supply China's ongoing war with Japan.
CHINA
CHUNGKING
TOKYO
PACIFIC
HONG KONG
WAKE I.
GUAM
PHILIPPINES
HONOLULU
SINGAPORE
Japan invades Philippines, Borneo, Thailand, Burma, Malaya, Shanghai (December).
Guam and Wake Island, U.S. outposts, fall to Japanese (December).
Japanese carrier planes attack U.S. fleet at anchor in Pearl Harbor; 2,343 Americans die (December 7, 1941).
EQUATOR
OCEAN
AUSTRALIA
CANADA
OTTAWA
UNITED STATES
WASHINGTON
F.D.R. and Churchill sign Atlantic Charter at Placentia Bay, Newfoundland.
H.M.S. Hood sunk May 24.
U.S. occupies Iceland.
U.S.S. Reuben James sunk while escorting supply convoys to Iceland.
Bismarck sunk May 27.
ATLANTIC
SOUTH AMERICA
OCEAN
LENINGRAD
LONDON
PARIS
BERLIN
ROME
MOSCOW
U.S.S.R.
Germany breaks 1939 pact, invades U.S.S.R. in June, blitzkrieg almost reaches Moscow.
Germany takes Yugoslavia and Greece (April).
British seize Vichy Syria and pro-Nazi Iraq.
British fight Italians, Germans in Libyan desert.
AFRICA
INDIA
British liberate Ethiopia, Eritrea, and Somalia from Italian control.
INDIAN OCEAN
1941: A World at War
29 USA
Destroyer Reuben James sunk October 31
29 USA
Civil Defense mobilizes Americans at home
29 USA
First Liberty ship delivered December 30
29 USA
Japanese bomb Pearl Harbor, December 7
29 USA
U.S. declares war on Japan, December 8

CM1429

Jan E. Matzeliger
29
Black Heritage USA

CM1431

29
USA

CM1442

29
USA

CM1443

MERCURY MARINER 10 29USA
VENUS MARINER 2 29USA
EARTH LANDSAT 29USA
MOON LUNAR ORBITER 29USA
MARS VIKING ORBITER 29USA
JUPITER PIONEER 11 29USA
SATURN VOYAGER 2 29USA
URANUS VOYAGER 2 29USA
NEPTUNE VOYAGER 2 29USA
PLUTO NOT YET EXPLORED 29USA

CM1432-1441

		MNHFVF	UseFVF	
CM1464				
	29¢ **Apollo & Vostok craft,** tagged	1.00	.20	❑❑❑❑❑
CM1465				
	29¢ **Soyuz, Mercury & Gemini craft,** tagged	1.00	.20	❑❑❑❑❑
CM1466	**1992. Alaska Highway Issue**			
	29¢ **multicolored** tagged	.45	.20	❑❑❑❑❑
CM1467	**1992. Kentucky Statehood Issue**			
	29¢ **multicolored** tagged	.45	.20	❑❑❑❑❑
CM1468	**1992. Summer Olympic Games Issue**			
	29¢ **Soccer,** tagged	.45	.20	❑❑❑❑❑
CM1469				
	29¢ **Gymnastics,** tagged	.45	.20	❑❑❑❑❑
CM1470				
	29¢ **Vollyball,** tagged	.45	.20	❑❑❑❑❑
CM1471				
	29¢ **Boxing,** tagged	.45	.20	❑❑❑❑❑
CM1472				
	29¢ **Swimming,** tagged	.45	.20	❑❑❑❑❑
CM1473	**1992. Hummingbirds Issue**			
	29¢ **Ruby-throated,** tagged	.45	.20	❑❑❑❑❑
CM1474				
	29¢ **Broad-billed,** tagged	.45	.20	❑❑❑❑❑
CM1475				
	29¢ **Costa's,** tagged	.45	.20	❑❑❑❑❑
CM1476				
	29¢ **Rufous,** tagged	.45	.20	❑❑❑❑❑
CM1477				
	29¢ **Calliope,** tagged	.45	.20	❑❑❑❑❑
CM1478	**1992. Wildflowers Issue**			
	29¢ **Indian Paintbrush,** tagged	.95	.60	❑❑❑❑❑
CM1479				
	29¢ **Fragrant Water Lily,** tagged	.95	.60	❑❑❑❑❑

CM1444

CM1445

CM1446

CM1447

CM1448

CM1449

CM1450

CM1451-1454

CM1455

CM1456

CM1457

CM1458

CM1459

The Voyages of Columbus
Claiming a New World
© USPS 1991

CM1460

Christopher Columbus
The United States Postal Service celebrates the 500th anniversary of the voyages of Christopher Columbus. This set is based on the first U.S. stamps in commemorative format, engraved a century ago.
© USPS 1991

CM1461

	MNHFVF	UseFVF	
CM1480__________ 29¢ **Meadow Beauty,** tagged	.95	.60	❑❑❑❑❑
CM1481__________ 29¢ **Jack-in-the-Pulpit,** tagged	.95	.60	❑❑❑❑❑
CM1482__________ 29¢ **California Poppy,** tagged	.95	.60	❑❑❑❑❑
CM1483__________ 29¢ **Large-Flowered Trillium,** tagged	.95	.60	❑❑❑❑❑
CM1484__________ 29¢ **Tickseed,** tagged	.95	.60	❑❑❑❑❑
CM1485__________ 29¢ **Shooting Star,** tagged	.95	.60	❑❑❑❑❑
CM1486__________ 29¢ **Stream Violet,** tagged	.95	.60	❑❑❑❑❑
CM1487__________ 29¢ **Bluets,** tagged	.95	.60	❑❑❑❑❑
CM1488__________ 29¢ **Herb Robert,** tagged	.95	.60	❑❑❑❑❑
CM1489__________ 29¢ **Marsh Marigold,** tagged	.95	.60	❑❑❑❑❑
CM1490__________ 29¢ **Sweet White Violet,** tagged	.95	.60	❑❑❑❑❑
CM1491__________ 29¢ **Claret Cup Cactus,** tagged	.95	.60	❑❑❑❑❑
CM1492__________ 29¢ **White Mountain Avens,** tagged	.95	.60	❑❑❑❑❑
CM1493__________ 29¢ **Sessile Bellwort,** tagged	.95	.60	❑❑❑❑❑
CM1494__________ 29¢ **Blue Flag,** tagged	.95	.60	❑❑❑❑❑
CM1495__________ 29¢ **Harlequin Lupine,** tagged	.95	.60	❑❑❑❑❑
CM1496__________ 29¢ **Twinflower,** tagged	.95	.60	❑❑❑❑❑
CM1497__________ 29¢ **Common Sunflower,** tagged	.95	.60	❑❑❑❑❑
CM1498__________ 29¢ **Sego Lily,** tagged	.95	.60	❑❑❑❑❑
CM1499__________ 29¢ **Virginia Bluebells,** tagged	.95	.60	❑❑❑❑❑
CM1500__________ 29¢ **Ohi'a Lehua,** tagged	.95	.60	❑❑❑❑❑
CM1501__________ 29¢ **Rosebud Orchid,** tagged	.95	.60	❑❑❑❑❑
CM1502__________ 29¢ **Showy Evening Primrose,** tagged	.95	.60	❑❑❑❑❑
CM1503__________ 29¢ **Fringed Gentian,** tagged	.95	.60	❑❑❑❑❑
CM1504__________ 29¢ **Yellow Lady's Slipper,** tagged	.95	.60	❑❑❑❑❑
CM1505__________ 29¢ **Passionflower,** tagged	.95	.60	❑❑❑❑❑
CM1506__________ 29¢ **Bunchberry,** tagged	.95	.60	❑❑❑❑❑

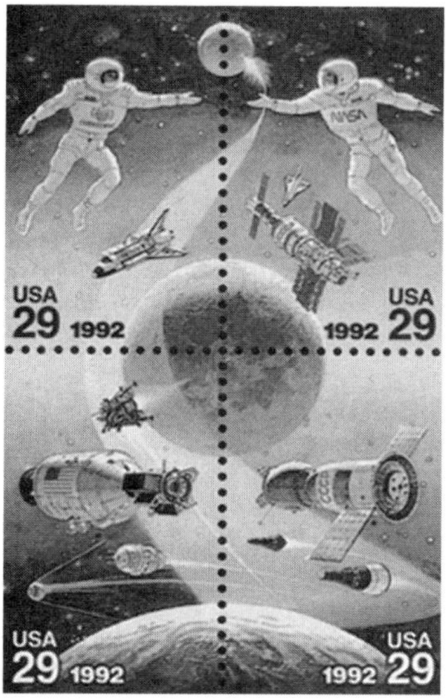

CM1462-1465

CM1466

CM1467

CM1473-1477

CM1468-1472

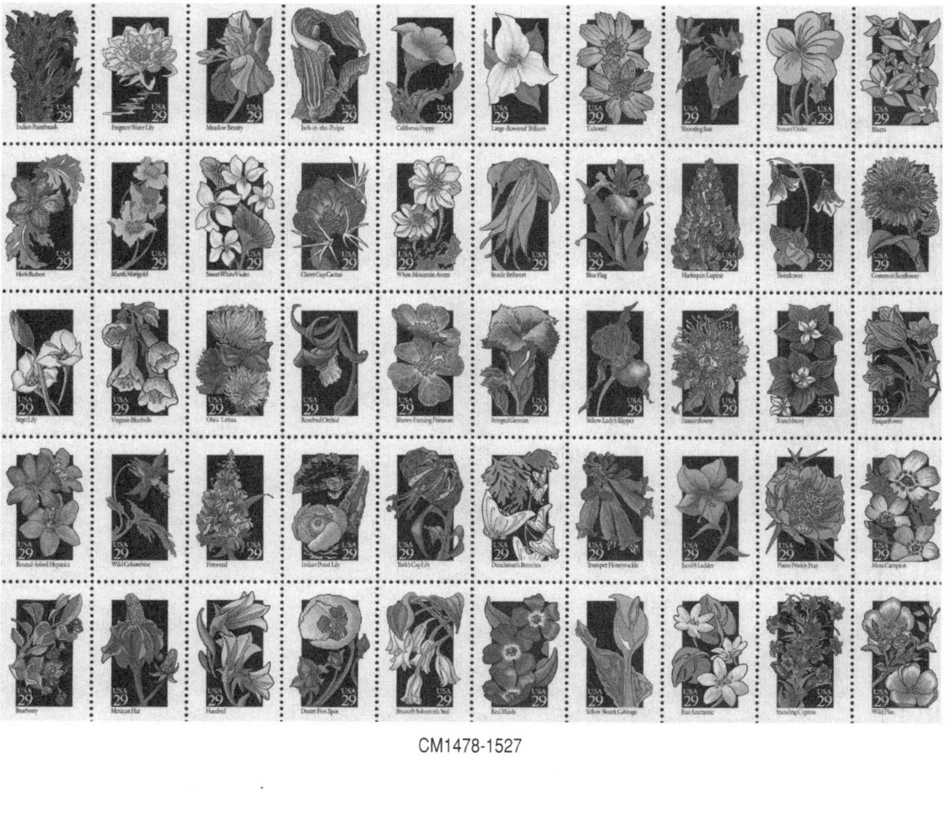

CM1478-1527

	MNHFVF	UseFVF	
CM1507			
29¢ **Pasqueflower,** tagged	.95	.60	❑❑❑❑❑
CM1508			
29¢ **Round-Lobed Hepatica,** tagged	.95	.60	❑❑❑❑❑
CM1509			
29¢ **Wild Columbine,** tagged	.95	.60	❑❑❑❑❑
CM1510			
29¢ **Fireweed,** tagged	.95	.60	❑❑❑❑❑
CM1511			
29¢ **Indian Pond Lily,** tagged	.95	.60	❑❑❑❑❑
CM1512			
29¢ **Turk's Cap Lily,** tagged	.95	.60	❑❑❑❑❑
CM1513			
29¢ **Dutchman's Breeches,** tagged	.95	.60	❑❑❑❑❑
CM1514			
29¢ **Trumpet Honeysuckle,** tagged	.95	.60	❑❑❑❑❑
CM1515			
29¢ **Jacob's Ladder,** tagged	.95	.60	❑❑❑❑❑
CM1516			
29¢ **Plains Prickly Pear,** tagged	.95	.60	❑❑❑❑❑
CM1517			
29¢ **Moss Campion,** tagged	.95	.60	❑❑❑❑❑
CM1518			
29¢ **Bearberry,** tagged	.95	.60	❑❑❑❑❑
CM1519			
29¢ **Mexican Hat,** tagged	.95	.60	❑❑❑❑❑
CM1520			
29¢ **Harebell,** tagged	.95	.60	❑❑❑❑❑
CM1521			
29¢ **Desert Five Spot,** tagged	.95	.60	❑❑❑❑❑
CM1522			
29¢ **Smooth Solomon's Seal,** tagged	.95	.60	❑❑❑❑❑
CM1523			
29¢ **Red Maids,** tagged	.95	.60	❑❑❑❑❑
CM1524			
29¢ **Yellow Skunk Cabbage,** tagged	.95	.60	❑❑❑❑❑
CM1525			
29¢ **Rue Anemone,** tagged	.95	.60	❑❑❑❑❑
CM1526			
29¢ **Standing Cypress,** tagged	.95	.60	❑❑❑❑❑
CM1527			
29¢ **Wild Flax,** tagged	.95	.60	❑❑❑❑❑
CM1528 **1992. 1942: Into The Battle Issue**			
$2.90 **Commemorative pane of 10**	9.00	5.00	❑❑❑❑❑
CM1529 **1992. Dorothy Parker Issue**			
29¢ **multicolored** tagged	.45	.20	❑❑❑❑❑
CM1530 **1992. Theodore von Kármán Issue**			
29¢ **multicolored** tagged	.45	.20	❑❑❑❑❑
CM1531 **1992. Minerals Issue**			
29¢ **Azurite,** tagged	.45	.20	❑❑❑❑❑
CM1532			
29¢ **Copper,** tagged	.45	.20	❑❑❑❑❑
CM1533			
29¢ **Variscite,** tagged	.45	.20	❑❑❑❑❑

	MNHFVF	UseFVF	
CM1534__________			
29¢ **Wulfenite,** tagged	.45	.20	❑❑❑❑❑
CM1535__________ **1992. Juan Rodríguez Cabrillo Issue**			
29¢ **multicolored** tagged	.45	.20	❑❑❑❑❑
CM1536__________ **1992. Wild Animals Issue**			
29¢ **Giraffe,** tagged	.45	.20	❑❑❑❑❑
CM1537__________			
29¢ **Giant Panda,** tagged	.45	.20	❑❑❑❑❑
CM1538__________			
29¢ **Flamingo,** tagged	.45	.20	❑❑❑❑❑
CM1539__________			
29¢ **King Penquins,** tagged	.45	.20	❑❑❑❑❑
CM1540__________			
29¢ **White Bengal Tiger,** tagged	.45	.20	❑❑❑❑❑
CM1541__________ **1992. New Year Issue**			
29¢ **multicolored** tagged	.45	.20	❑❑❑❑❑
CM1542__________ **1993. Elvis Presley Issue**			
29¢ **multicolored** tagged	.45	.20	❑❑❑❑❑
CM1543__________ **1993. Space Fantasy Issue**			
29¢ **Saturn Rings,** tagged	.45	.20	❑❑❑❑❑
CM1544__________			
29¢ **Two oval crafts,** tagged	.45	.20	❑❑❑❑❑
CM1545__________			
29¢ **Spacemen & Jet Pack,** tagged	.45	.20	❑❑❑❑❑
CM1546__________			
29¢ **Craft & lights,** tagged	.45	.20	❑❑❑❑❑
CM1547__________			
29¢ **Three craft,** tagged	.45	.20	❑❑❑❑❑

29 USA
B-25s take off to raid Tokyo April 18, 1942
Food and other commodities rationed, 1942
U.S. wins Battle of the Coral Sea May 1942
Corregidor falls to Japanese May 6, 1942
Japan invades Aleutian Islands June 194
ASIA
CHINA
PACIFIC
CANADA
UNITED STATES
ATLANTIC OCEAN
SOUTH AMERICA
AFRICA
INDIAN OCEAN
AUSTRALIA
U.S.S.R.
INDIA
1942: Into the Battle
Note: Red areas controlled by enemy.
Allies decipher secret enemy codes, 1942
Yorktown lost, U.S. wins at Midway, 1942
Millions of women join war effort, 1942
Marines land on Guadalcanal Aug. 7, 1942
Allies land in North Africa November 194
CM1528

MNHFVF	UseFVF	

CM1548_____ **1993. Percy Lavon Julian Issue**
29¢ **multicolored** tagged .45 .20 ☐☐☐☐☐

CM1549_____ **1993. Oregon Trail Issue**
29¢ **multicolored** tagged .45 .20 ☐☐☐☐☐
NOTE: The official first day city was Salem, Ore., but the stamp was available Feb. 12 at 36 cities along the Trail.

CM1550_____ **1993. World University Games Issue**
29¢ **multicolored** tagged .45 .20 ☐☐☐☐☐

CM1551_____ **1993. Grace Kelly Issue**
29¢ **blue** tagged .45 .20 ☐☐☐☐☐

CM1552_____ **1993. Oklahoma! Issue**
29¢ **multicolored** tagged .45 .20 ☐☐☐☐☐

CM1553_____ **1993. Circus Issue**
29¢ **Trapeze Artist,** tagged .45 .20 ☐☐☐☐☐

CM1554_____
29¢ **Elephant,** tagged .45 .20 ☐☐☐☐☐

CM1555_____
29¢ **Clown,** tagged .45 .20 ☐☐☐☐☐

CM1556_____
29¢ **Ringmaster,** tagged .45 .20 ☐☐☐☐☐

CM1557_____ **1993. Cherokee Strip Land Run Centennial Issue**
29¢ **multicolored** tagged .45 .20 ☐☐☐☐☐

CM1558_____ **1993. Dean Acheson Issue**
29¢ **green** tagged .45 .20 ☐☐☐☐☐

CM1559_____ **1993. Sporting Horses Issue**
29¢ **Steeplechase,** tagged .45 .20 ☐☐☐☐☐

CM1560_____
29¢ **Thoroughbred racing,** tagged .45 .20 ☐☐☐☐☐

CM1561_____
29¢ **Harness racing,** tagged .45 .20 ☐☐☐☐☐

CM1562_____
29¢ **Polo,** tagged .45 .20 ☐☐☐☐☐

CM1563_____ **1993. Garden Flowers Issue**
29¢ **Hyacinth,** tagged .45 .20 ☐☐☐☐☐

CM1564_____
29¢ **Daffodil,** tagged .45 .20 ☐☐☐☐☐

CM1565_____
29¢ **Tulip,** tagged .45 .20 ☐☐☐☐☐

CM1566_____
29¢ **Iris,** tagged .45 .20 ☐☐☐☐☐

CM1567_____
29¢ **Lilac,** tagged .45 .20 ☐☐☐☐☐

CM1568_____ **1993. 1943: Turning The Tide Issue**
$2.90 **Commemorative pane of 10** 8.75 7.00 ☐☐☐☐☐

CM1569_____ **1993. Hank Williams Issue**
29¢ **multicolored** tagged .45 .20 ☐☐☐☐☐

CM1570_____ **1993. Rock 'n Roll - Rhythm & Blues Issue**
29¢ **Elvis Presley,** tagged .45 .20 ☐☐☐☐☐

CM1571_____
29¢ **Buddy Holly,** tagged .45 .20 ☐☐☐☐☐

CM1572_____
29¢ **Richie Valens,** tagged .45 .20 ☐☐☐☐☐

CM1573_____
29¢ **Bill Haley,** tagged .45 .20 ☐☐☐☐☐

CM1574_____
29¢ **Dinah Washington,** tagged .45 .20 ☐☐☐☐☐

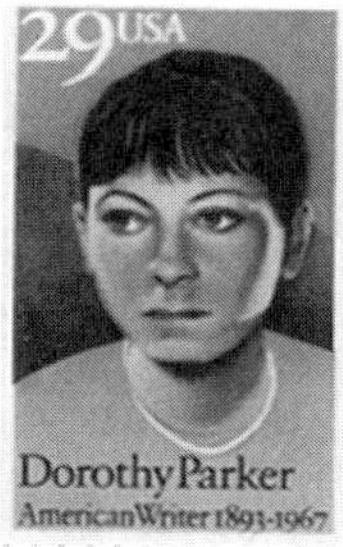

CM1529

CM1530

CM1531-1534

CM1535

CM1536-1540

CM1541

CM1542

CM1543-1547

CM1548

CM1549

CM1550

CM1551

CM1552

MNHFVF	UseFVF	

CM1575_____
29¢ **Otis Redding,** tagged .45 .20 ☐☐☐☐☐

CM1576_____
29¢ **Clyde McPhatter,** tagged .45 .20 ☐☐☐☐☐

CM1577_____
29¢ **multicolored** tagged .45 .20 ☐☐☐☐☐

CM1578_____
29¢ **multicolored** tagged .45 .20 ☐☐☐☐☐

CM1579_____
29¢ **multicolored** tagged .45 .20 ☐☐☐☐☐

CM1580_____
29¢ **multicolored** tagged .45 .20 ☐☐☐☐☐

CM1581_____
29¢ **multicolored** tagged .45 .20 ☐☐☐☐☐

CM1582_____
29¢ **multicolored** tagged .45 .20 ☐☐☐☐☐

CM1583_____
29¢ **multicolored** tagged .45 .20 ☐☐☐☐☐

NOTE: The vertically oriented pane of eight consists of the following stamps, from top to bottom: CM1577, CM1578, CM1579, CM1580, CM1581, CM1582, CM1583, CM1577. The vertically oriented pane of four consists of the following stamps, from top to bottom: CM1581, CM1582, CM1583, CM1584. A complete booklet consists of two panes of eight and one pane of four. CM1583n1 without tab is indistinguishable from a strip of the bottom four stamps of CM1583n.

CM1584_____ **1993. Joe Louis Issue**
29¢ **multicolored** tagged .45 .20 ☐☐☐☐☐

CM1585_____ **1993. Broadway Musicals Issue**
29¢ *Show Boat,* tagged .45 .20 ☐☐☐☐☐

CM1586_____
29¢ *Porgy & Bess,* tagged .45 .20 ☐☐☐☐☐

CM1587_____
29¢ *Oklahoma!,* tagged .45 .20 ☐☐☐☐☐

CM1588_____
29¢ *My Fair Lady,* tagged .45 .20 ☐☐☐☐☐

CM1589_____ **1993. National Postal Museum Issue**
29¢ **Benjamin Franklin,** tagged .45 .20 ☐☐☐☐☐

CM1590_____
29¢ **Civil War soldier writing letter** .45 .20 ☐☐☐☐☐

CM1591_____
29¢ **Charles Lindbergh,** tagged .45 .20 ☐☐☐☐☐

CM1592_____
29¢ **Letters & date stamp,** tagged .45 .20 ☐☐☐☐☐

CM1593_____ **1993. Recognizing Deafness/American Sign Language Issue**
29¢ **Mother and child,** tagged .45 .20 ☐☐☐☐☐

CM1594_____
29¢ **Sign "I love you"** .45 .20 ☐☐☐☐☐

CM1595_____ **1993. Country Music Issue**
29¢ **Hank Williams,** tagged .45 .20 ☐☐☐☐☐

CM1596_____
29¢ **The Carter Family,** tagged .45 .20 ☐☐☐☐☐

CM1597_____
29¢ **Patsy Cline,** tagged .45 .20 ☐☐☐☐☐

CM1598_____
29¢ **Bob Wills,** tagged .45 .20 ☐☐☐☐☐

NOTE: Gravure by American Bank Note Co., perforated 11 on 1 or 2 sides, from booklet panes.

CM1599_____
29¢ **Hank Williams,** tagged .45 .20 ☐☐☐☐☐

USA 29
CIRCUS
USA 29
CIRCUS
USA 29
CIRCUS
USA 29
CIRCUS

CM1553-1556

29 USA
Cherokee Strip Land Run 1893

CM1557

Dean Acheson
1893-1971
STATESMAN
USA 29

CM1558

USA29
USA29
USA29
USA29

CM1559-1562

CM1563-1567

29 USA Hyacinth
29 USA Daffodil
29 USA Tulip
29 USA Iris
29 USA Lilac

29
USA
HANK
WILLIAMS

CM1569

29 USA
Allied forces battle German U-boats, 1943
29 USA
Military medics treat the wounded, 1943
29 USA
Sicily attacked by Allied forces, July 1943
29 USA
B-24s hit Ploesti refineries, August 1943
29 USA
V-mail delivers letters from home, 1943
ASIA
CHINA
AUSTRALIA
PACIFIC
OCEAN
CANADA
UNITED STATES
ATLANTIC
OCEAN
SOUTH AMERICA
AFRICA
INDIAN OCEAN
INDIA
U.S.S.R.
Allies invade Sicily in July, and Italy in September. German counterattack repulsed at Salerno.
Roosevelt and Churchill demand "unconditional surrender" at Casablanca in January.
North Africa cleared of Axis forces when Germans surrender in Tunis in May.
Stalin, Roosevelt, Churchill meet in Teheran November 28.
U.S. hits Gilbert Islands, November 20. Marines take Tarawa, Army takes Makin.
Allies go on the offensive in the Solomons, New Britain and New Guinea.
Note: Red areas controlled by enemy.
1943: Turning the Tide
29 USA
Italy invaded by Allies, September 1943
29 USA
Bonds and stamps help war effort, 1943
29 USA
"Willie and Joe" keep spirits high, 1943
29 USA
Gold Stars mark World War II losses, 1943
29 USA
Marines assault Tarawa, November 1943

CM1568

		MNHFVF	UseFVF	
CM1600________				
29¢ **The Carter Family,** tagged		.45	.20	❑❑❑❑❑
CM1601________				
29¢ **Patsy Cline,** tagged		.45	.20	❑❑❑❑❑
CM1602________				
29¢ **Bob Wills,** tagged		.45	.20	❑❑❑❑❑
CM1603________	**1993. Youth Classics Issue**			
29¢ ***Rebecca,*** block tagged		.45	.20	❑❑❑❑❑
CM1604________				
29¢ ***Little House***		.60	.20	❑❑❑❑❑
CM1605________				
29¢ ***Huck Finn***		.60	.20	❑❑❑❑❑
CM1606________				
29¢ ***Little Women,*** block tagged		.45	.20	❑❑❑❑❑
CM1607________	**1993. Commonwealth of the Northern Mariana Islands Issue**			
29¢ **multicolored** tagged		.45	.20	❑❑❑❑❑
CM1608________	**1993. Columbus Landing in Puerto Rico Issue**			
29¢ **multicolored** tagged		.45	.20	❑❑❑❑❑
CM1609________	**1993. AIDS Awareness Issue**			
29¢ **red & black** tagged, perforated 11 1/4		.45	.20	❑❑❑❑❑
CM1609A ________				
29¢ **red & black** tagged, perforated 11 vertically on 1 or 2 sides		.75	.25	❑❑❑❑❑
CM1610________	**1994. Winter Olympics Issue**			
29¢ **Downhill skiing,** tagged		.45	.20	❑❑❑❑❑
CM1611________				
29¢ **Luge,** tagged		.45	.20	❑❑❑❑❑
CM1612________				
29¢ **Figure skating,** tagged		.45	.20	❑❑❑❑❑
CM1613________				
29¢ **Cross-country skiing,** tagged		.45	.20	❑❑❑❑❑
CM1614________				
29¢ **Hockey,** tagged		.45	.20	❑❑❑❑❑
CM1615________	**1994. Edward R. Murrow Issue**			
29¢ **brown** tagged		.45	.20	❑❑❑❑❑
CM1616________	**1994. Love Issue**			
29¢ **multicolored** tagged		.45	.20	❑❑❑❑❑
CM1617________	**1994. Dr. Allison Davis Issue**			
29¢ **red brown & brown** tagged		.45	.20	❑❑❑❑❑
CM1618________	**1994. New Year Issue**			
29¢ **multicolored** tagged		.45	.20	❑❑❑❑❑
CM1619________	**1994. Love Issues**			
29¢ **multicolored** tagged		.45	.20	❑❑❑❑❑
CM1620________				
52¢ **multicolored** tagged		1.50	.35	❑❑❑❑❑
CM1621________	**1994. Buffalo Soldiers Issue**			
29¢ **multicolored** tagged		.45	.20	❑❑❑❑❑
CM1622________	**1994. Silent Screen Stars Issue**			
29¢ **Rudolph Valentino,** tagged		.45	.20	❑❑❑❑❑
CM1623________				
29¢ **Clara Bow,** tagged		.45	.20	❑❑❑❑❑
CM1624________				
29¢ **Charlie Chaplin,** tagged		.45	.20	❑❑❑❑❑
CM1625________				
29¢ **Lon Chaney,** tagged		.45	.20	❑❑❑❑❑

CM1584

CM1570, CM1577 (first stamp)
CM1571, CM1582 (second stamp)
CM1572, CM1580 (third stamp)
CM1573, CM1578 (fourth stamp)
CM1574, CM1583 (fifth stamp)
CM1575, CM1581 (sixth stamp)
CM1576. CM1579 (seventh stamp)

CM1585-1588 →

CM1595, CM1599 (first stamp)
CM1596, CM1600 (second stamp)
CM1597, CM1601 (third stamp)
CM1598, CM1602 (fourth stamp)

← CM1589-1592

CM1603-1606 →

CM1593-1594 ↓

			MNHFVF	UseFVF
CM1626		29¢ **John Gilbert,** tagged	.45	.20
CM1627		29¢ **Zasu Pitts,** tagged	.45	.20
CM1628		29¢ **Harold Lloyd,** tagged	.45	.20
CM1629		29¢ **Keystone Cops,** tagged	.45	.20
CM1630		29¢ **Theda Bara,** tagged	.45	.20
CM1631		29¢ **Buster Keaton,** tagged	.45	.20
CM1632	**1994. Garden Flowers Issue**	29¢ **multicolored** tagged	.45	.20
CM1633		29¢ **multicolored** tagged	.45	.20
CM1634		29¢ **multicolored** tagged	.45	.20
CM1635		29¢ **multicolored** tagged	.45	.20
CM1636		29¢ **multicolored** tagged	.45	.20
CM1637	**1994. World Cup Soccer Championship Issue**	29¢ **multicolored** phosphored paper	.75	.20
CM1638		40¢ **multicolored** phosphored paper	1.00	.35
CM1639		50¢ **multicolored** phosphored paper	1.50	.50
CM1640		$1.19 **Souvenir Sheet**	3.75	3.00
CM1641	**1994. 1944: Road to Victory Issue**	$2.90 **Commemorative pane of 10,** tagged	8.75	7.00
CM1642	**1994. Love Issue**	29¢ **multicolored** tagged	.50	.20
CM1643	**1994. Norman Rockwell Issue**	29¢ **multicolored** tagged	.50	.20
CM1644		$2 **multicolored** tagged	6.00	5.00
CM1645	**1994. Moon Landing Anniversary Issue**	29¢ **multicolored** tagged	.50	.25
CM1646	**1994. Locomotives Issue**	29¢ **Hudson's General,** tagged	.75	.50
CM1647		29¢ **McQueen's Jupiter,** tagged	.75	.50
CM1648		29¢ **Eddy's No. 242,** tagged	.75	.50
CM1649		29¢ **Ely's No. 10,** tagged	.75	.50
CM1650		29¢ **Buchannan's No. 999,** tagged	.75	.50
CM1651	**1994. George Meany Issue**	29¢ **blue** tagged	.50	.20
CM1652	**1994. Popular Singers Issue**	29¢ **Al Jolson,** tagged	.75	.50

	MNHFVF	UseFVF	
CM1653			
29¢ **Bing Crosby,** tagged	.75	.50	☐☐☐☐☐
CM1654			
29¢ **Ethel Waters,** tagged	.75	.50	☐☐☐☐☐

CM1607

CM1608

CM1609

CM1615

CM1610-1614

CM1616

CM1617

CM1618

CM1619

CM1620

CM1621

CM1622-1631

	MNHFVF	UseFVF
CM1655__________		
29¢ **Nat "King" Cole,** tagged	.47	.50 ❑❑❑❑❑
CM1656__________		
29¢ **Ethel Merman,** tagged	.75	.50 ❑❑❑❑❑
CM1657__________ **1994. James Thurber Issue**		
29¢ **multicolored** tagged	.50	.20 ❑❑❑❑❑
CM1658__________ **1994. Blues and Jazz Singers Issue**		
29¢ **Bessie Smith,** tagged	.50	.25 ❑❑❑❑❑
CM1659__________		
29¢ **Muddy Waters,** tagged	.50	.25 ❑❑❑❑❑
CM1660__________		
29¢ **Billie Holiday,** tagged	.50	.25 ❑❑❑❑❑
CM1661__________		
29¢ **Robert Johnson,** tagged	.50	.25 ❑❑❑❑❑
CM1662__________		
29¢ **Jimmy Rushing,** tagged	.50	.25 ❑❑❑❑❑
CM1663__________		
29¢ **"Ma" Rainy,** tagged	.50	.25 ❑❑❑❑❑
CM1664__________		
29¢ **Mildred Bailey,** tagged	.50	.25 ❑❑❑❑❑
CM1665__________		
29¢ **Howlin' Wolf,** tagged	.50	.25 ❑❑❑❑❑

29 USA Lily
29 USA Zinnia
29 USA Gladiola
29 USA Marigold
29 USA Rose

CM1632-1636

CM1642

LOVE
29 USA

CM1643

29 USA
Norman Rockwell

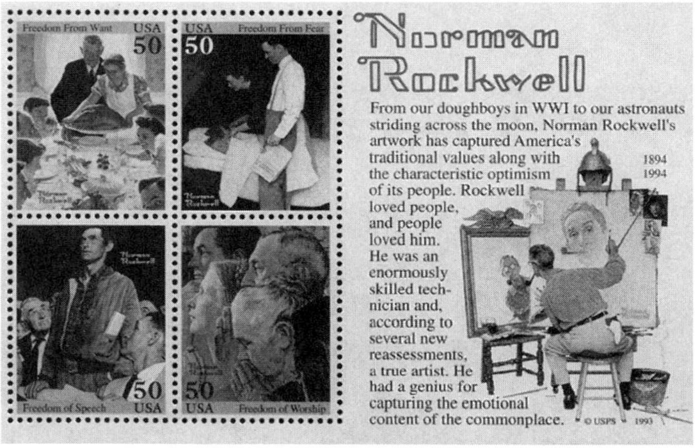
Freedom From Want USA 50
USA 50 Freedom From Fear
50 Freedom of Speech USA
50 USA Freedom of Worship
Norman Rockwell
From our doughboys in WWI to our astronauts striding across the moon, Norman Rockwell's artwork has captured America's traditional values along with the characteristic optimism of its people. Rockwell loved people, and people loved him. He was an enormously skilled technician and, according to several new reassessments, a true artist. He had a genius for capturing the emotional content of the commonplace.
1894
1994
© USPS 1993

CM1644a-1644d

CM1645

USA 29
First Moon Landing, 1969

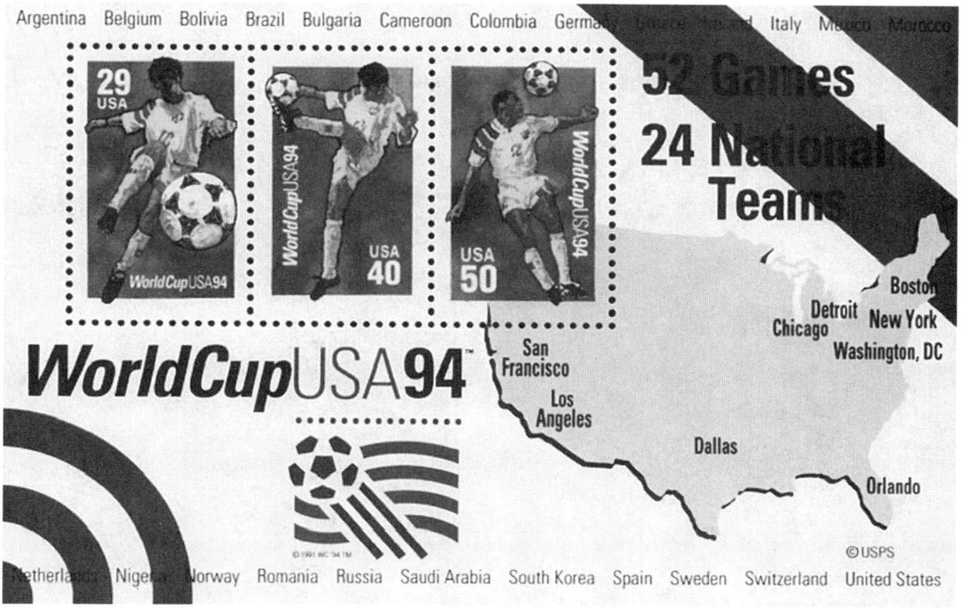
Argentina Belgium Bolivia Brazil Bulgaria Cameroon Colombia Italy
29 USA
WorldCupUSA94
USA 40
WorldCupUSA94
USA 50
WorldCupUSA94
24 National
Teams
WorldCupUSA94
San Francisco
Los Angeles
Dallas
Chicago
Detroit
New York
Washington, DC
Orlando
©USPS
Norway Romania Russia Saudi Arabia South Korea Spain Sweden Switzerland United States

CM1637-1640

29 USA
Allied forces retake New Guinea, 1944
29 USA
P-51s escort B-17s on bombing raids, 1944
29 USA
Allies in Normandy, D-Day, June 6, 1944
29 USA
Airborne units spearhead attacks, 1944
29 USA
Submarines shorten war in Pacific, 1944
ASIA
U.S. Navy fliers deal mortal blow to Japanese naval aviation in Philippine Sea in June. Battle becomes known as "the Marianas Turkey Shoot."
Extent of Japanese control at end of 1944.
PACIFIC
U.S. Marines and Army troops take Saipan, Tinian and Guam in fierce fighting in June, July and August.
U.S. aircraft and ship production hit wartime peak.
CANADA
UNITED STATES
WASHINGTON
CHINA
TOKYO
HONOLULU
SAIPAN
TINIAN
GUAM
PHILIPPINES
NEW GUINEA
President Roosevelt signs the "GI Bill of Rights," landmark legislation that will provide college and vocational training, housing and other benefits to millions of returning veterans.
EQUATOR
Supplies flown from India to China over "the Hump" rise sharply in late 1944 as U.S.-led Allied forces regain territory in Burma.
Biggest fleet action in history, the Battle for Leyte Gulf in October, all but destroys Japanese naval power.
OCEAN
Note: Red areas controlled by enemy. (Several enemy bases and islands are not shown)
Extent of German control at end of 1944.
Landings in Normandy and in Southern France result in liberation of France.
Advancing GIs enter Germany in September, seizing Aachen and breaching the Siegfried Line.
LONDON
PARIS
BERLIN
ROME
MOSCOW
U.S.S.R.
American heavy bombers, escorted by long-range fighters, batter German industry.
Leningrad's 900-day siege ends in January.
Advancing Soviet armies drive Germans from Baltic nations, Byelorussia, Ukraine and Balkans.
Allied troops free Rome June 4.
INDIA
ATLANTIC
OCEAN
SOUTH AMERICA
AFRICA
INDIAN OCEAN
1944: Road to Victory
29 USA
Allies free Rome, June 4; Paris, Aug. 25, 1944
29 USA
U.S. troops clear Saipan bunkers, 1944
29 USA
Red Ball Express speeds vital supplies, 1944
29 USA
Battle for Leyte Gulf, October 23-26, 1944
29 USA
Bastogne and Battle of the Bulge, Dec. 1944

CM1641

	MNHFVF	UseFVF	
CM1666__________ **1994. Wonders of the Seas Issue**			
29¢ **Porcupine fish,** tagged	.75	.25	❑❑❑❑❑
CM1667__________			
29¢ **Dolphin,** tagged	.75	.25	❑❑❑❑❑
CM1668__________			
29¢ **Nautilus & ship's wheel,** tagged	.75	.25	❑❑❑❑❑
CM1669__________			
29¢ **Fish & coral,** tagged	.75	.25	❑❑❑❑❑

CM1646-1650

CM1651

CM1657

CM1658-1665

CM1666-1669

		MNHFVF	UseFVF	
CM1670__________	**1994. Cranes Issue**			
	29¢ **Black-necked crane,** tagged	.45	.20	❑❑❑❑❑
CM1671__________				
	29¢ **Whooping crane,** tagged	.45	.20	❑❑❑❑❑
CM1671A ________	**1993-1994. Legends of the West Issue**			
	$5.80 **Legends of the West commemorative pane,** tagged, *(earliest known use Dec. 14, 1993)*	195.00		❑❑❑❑❑
CM1672__________	**1994. Revised Legends of the West Issue**			
	29¢ **Home on the Range,** tagged	.45	.20	❑❑❑❑❑
CM1673__________				
	29¢ **Buffalo Bill,** tagged	.45	.20	❑❑❑❑❑

CM1670-1671

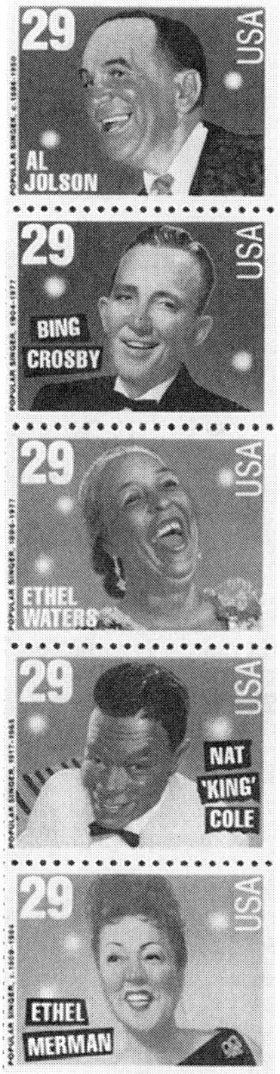

CM1652-1656

CM1671A

		MNHFVF	UseFVF	
CM1674________				
	29¢ **Jim Bridger,** tagged	.45	.20	❑❑❑❑❑
CM1675________				
	29¢ **Annie Oakley,** tagged	.45	.20	❑❑❑❑❑
CM1676________				
	29¢ **Native American Culture,** tagged	.45	.20	❑❑❑❑❑
CM1677________				
	29¢ **Chief Joseph,** tagged	.45	.20	❑❑❑❑❑
CM1678________				
	29¢ **Bill Pickett,** tagged	.45	.20	❑❑❑❑❑
CM1679________				
	29¢ **Bat Masterson,** tagged	.45	.20	❑❑❑❑❑
CM1680________				
	29¢ **John Fremont,** tagged	.45	.20	❑❑❑❑❑
CM1681________				
	29¢ **Wyatt Earp,** tagged	.45	.20	❑❑❑❑❑
CM1682________				
	29¢ **Nellie Cashman,** tagged	.45	.20	❑❑❑❑❑
CM1683________				
	29¢ **Charles Goodnight,** tagged	.45	.20	❑❑❑❑❑
CM1684________				
	29¢ **Geronimo,** tagged	.45	.20	❑❑❑❑❑
CM1685________				
	29¢ **Kit Carson,** tagged	.45	.20	❑❑❑❑❑
CM1686________				
	29¢ **Wild Bill Hickok,** tagged	.45	.20	❑❑❑❑❑
CM1687________				
	29¢ **Western Wildlife,** tagged	.45	.20	❑❑❑❑❑
CM1688________				
	29¢ **Jim Beckwourth,** tagged	.45	.20	❑❑❑❑❑
CM1689________				
	29¢ **Bill Tilghman,** tagged	.45	.20	❑❑❑❑❑
CM1690________				
	29¢ **Sacagawea,** tagged	.45	.20	❑❑❑❑❑
CM1691________				
	29¢ **Overland Mail,** tagged	.45	.20	❑❑❑❑❑

NOTE: Because this issue also was made available to collectors in full six-pane printing sheets, gutter pairs and blocks and cross-gutter multiples also exist.

CM1692________	**1994. Bureau of Engraving and Printing Centennial Souvenir Issue**			
	$8 **multicolored** tagged *(Nov. 3, 1994)*	20.00	14.50	❑❑❑❑❑

NOTE: Listings for minor double transfers refer to any of approximately 10 different ones that are known.

CM1693________	**1994. New Year Issue**			
	29¢ **multicolored** tagged	.50	.20	❑❑❑❑❑
CM1694________	**1995. Love Cherub Issue**			
	32¢ **multicolored** phosphored paper	.50	.20	❑❑❑❑❑

NOTE: Self-adhesive booklet, offset and intaglio by Banknote Corp. of America, imperforate (die cut).

CM1695________				
	32¢ **multicolored** phosphored paper	.50	.20	❑❑❑❑❑
CM1696________	**1995. Florida Sesquicentennial Issue**			
	32¢ **multicolored** phosphored paper	.50	.20	❑❑❑❑❑
CM1697________	**1995. Earth Day Issue**			
	32¢ **Clean Earth,** phosphored paper	.50	.20	❑❑❑❑❑
CM1698________				
	32¢ **Solar Power,** phosphored paper	.50	.20	❑❑❑❑❑

CM1691y

CM1693

CM1694

CM1695

CM1692

CM1697-1700

CM1696

CM1701

CM1702

MNHFVF	UseFVF	

CM1699_____
32¢ **Tree Planting,** phosphored paper .50 .20 ☐☐☐☐☐

CM1700_____
32¢ **Clean Beaches,** phosphored paper .50 .20 ☐☐☐☐☐

CM1701_____ **1995. Richard M. Nixon Issue**
32¢ **multicolored** phosphored paper .50 .20 ☐☐☐☐☐

CM1702_____ **1995. Bessie Coleman Issue**
32¢ **red & black** phosphored paper .50 .20 ☐☐☐☐☐

CM1703_____ **1995. Love Cherub Issue**
32¢ **multicolored** phosphored paper .50 .20 ☐☐☐☐☐

CM1704_____ **1995. Love Cherub Booklet Issue**
32¢ **multicolored** phosphored paper .50 .20 ☐☐☐☐☐

CM1705_____
55¢ **multicolored** phosphored paper 1.00 .35 ☐☐☐☐☐

CM1706_____ **1995. Love Cherub Self-Adhesive Booklet Issue**
55¢ **multicolored** phosphored paper 1.00 .35 ☐☐☐☐☐

CM1707_____ **1995. Recreational Sports Issue**
32¢ **Bowling,** phosphored paper .50 .20 ☐☐☐☐☐

CM1708_____
32¢ **Tennis,** phosphored paper .50 .20 ☐☐☐☐☐

CM1709_____
32¢ **Golf,** phosphored paper .50 .20 ☐☐☐☐☐

CM1710_____
32¢ **Volleyball,** phosphored paper .50 .20 ☐☐☐☐☐

CM1711_____
32¢ **Baseball,** phosphored paper .50 .20 ☐☐☐☐☐

CM1712_____ **1995. POW & MIA Issue**
32¢ **multicolored** phosphored paper .50 .20 ☐☐☐☐☐

CM1713_____ **1995. Marilyn Monroe Issue**
32¢ **multicolored** block tagged .75 .20 ☐☐☐☐☐

NOTE: Because this issue also was made available to collectors in full six-pane printing sheets, gutter pairs and blocks and cross-gutter multiples also exist.

CM1714_____ **1995. Texas Sesquicentennial Issue**
32¢ **multicolored** phosphored paper .50 .20 ☐☐☐☐☐

CM1715_____ **1995. Lighthouses Issue**
32¢ **Split Rock,** phosphored paper .50 .20 ☐☐☐☐☐

CM1716_____
32¢ **St. Joseph,** phosphored paper .50 .20 ☐☐☐☐☐

CM1717_____
32¢ **Spectacle Reef,** phosphored paper .50 .20 ☐☐☐☐☐

CM1718_____
32¢ **Marblehead,** phosphored paper .50 .20 ☐☐☐☐☐

CM1719_____
32¢ **Thirty Mile Point,** phosphored paper .50 .20 ☐☐☐☐☐

CM1720_____ **1995. United Nations Issue**
32¢ **blue** phosphored paper .50 .20 ☐☐☐☐☐

CM1721_____ **1995. Civil War Issue**
32¢ *Monitor and Virginia* .75 .50 ☐☐☐☐☐

CM1722_____
32¢ **Robert E. Lee** .75 .50 ☐☐☐☐☐

CM1723_____
32¢ **Clara Barton** .75 .50 ☐☐☐☐☐

CM1724_____
32¢ **Ulysses S. Grant** .75 .50 ☐☐☐☐☐

CM1703

CM1704

CM1705

CM1706

CM1707-1711

CM1712

CM1714

CM1715-1719

CM1721-1740

CM1713

CM1720

MNHFVF	UseFVF	

CM1725_____
32¢ **Battle of Shiloh** — .75 .50 ☐☐☐☐☐

CM1726_____
32¢ **Jefferson Davis** — .75 .50 ☐☐☐☐☐

CM1727_____
32¢ **David Farragut** — .75 .50 ☐☐☐☐☐

CM1728_____
32¢ **Frederick Douglass** — .75 .50 ☐☐☐☐☐

CM1729_____
32¢ **Raphael Semmes** — .75 .50 ☐☐☐☐☐

CM1730_____
32¢ **Abraham Lincoln** — .75 .50 ☐☐☐☐☐

CM1731_____
32¢ **Harriet Tubman** — .75 .50 ☐☐☐☐☐

CM1732_____
32¢ **Stand Watie** — .75 .50 ☐☐☐☐☐

CM1733_____
32¢ **Joseph E. Johnston** — .75 .50 ☐☐☐☐☐

CM1734_____
32¢ **Winfield Hancock** — .75 .50 ☐☐☐☐☐

CM1735_____
32¢ **Mary Chesnut** — .75 .50 ☐☐☐☐☐

CM1736_____
32¢ **Battle of Chancellorsville** — .75 .50 ☐☐☐☐☐

CM1737_____
32¢ **William T. Sherman** — .75 .50 ☐☐☐☐☐

CM1738_____
32¢ **Phoebe Pember** — .75 .50 ☐☐☐☐☐

CM1739_____
32¢ **"Stonewall" Jackson** — .75 .50 ☐☐☐☐☐

CM1740_____
32¢ **Battle of Gettysburg** — .75 .50 ☐☐☐☐☐

NOTE: Because this issue also was made available to collectors in full six-pane printing sheets, gutter pairs and blocks and cross-gutter multiples also exist.

CM1741_____ **1995. Carousel Horses Issue**
32¢ **Golden horse,** phosphored paper — .50 .20 ☐☐☐☐☐

CM1742_____
32¢ **Black horse,** phosphored paper — .50 .20 ☐☐☐☐☐

CM1743_____
32¢ **Armored horse,** phosphored paper — .50 .20 ☐☐☐☐☐

CM1744_____
32¢ **Brown horse,** phosphored paper — .50 .20 ☐☐☐☐☐

CM1745_____ **1995. Woman Suffrage Issue**
32¢ **multicolored,** phosphored paper — .50 .20 ☐☐☐☐☐

CM1746_____ **1995. Louis Armstrong Issue**
32¢ **multicolored,** phosphored paper — .50 .20 ☐☐☐☐☐

NOTE: For a similar design with "32" in black, see CM1749.

CM1747_____ **1995. 1945: Victory at Last Issue**
$3.20 **Commemorative pane of 10,** overall tagged — 9.00 8.00 ☐☐☐☐☐

CM1748_____ **1995. Jazz Musicians Issue**
32¢ **Coleman Hawkins,** phosphored paper — .50 .20 ☐☐☐☐☐

CM1749_____
32¢ **Louis Armstrong,** phosphored paper — .50 .20 ☐☐☐☐☐

	MNHFVF	UseFVF	
CM1750			
32¢ **James P. Johnson,** phosphored paper	.50	.20	❑❑❑❑❑
CM1751			
32¢ **"Jelly Roll" Morton,** phosphored paper	.50	.20	❑❑❑❑❑
CM1752			
32¢ **Charles Parker,** phosphored paper	.50	.20	❑❑❑❑❑
CM1753			
32¢ **Eubie Blake,** phosphored paper	.50	.20	❑❑❑❑❑
CM1754			
32¢ **Charlie Mingus,** phosphored paper	.50	.20	❑❑❑❑❑

CM1745

CM1746

CM1741-1744

CM1747

MNHFVF	UseFVF	

CM1755_____
 32¢ **Thelonious Monk,** phosphored paper .50 .20 ☐☐☐☐☐

CM1756_____
 32¢ **John Coltrane,** phosphored paper .50 .20 ☐☐☐☐☐

CM1757_____
 32¢ **Erroll Garner,** phosphored paper .50 .20 ☐☐☐☐☐

CM1758_____ **1995. Garden Flowers Issue**
 32¢ **Aster,** overall tagged .50 .20 ☐☐☐☐☐

CM1759_____
 32¢ **Chrysanthemum,** overall tagged .50 .20 ☐☐☐☐☐

CM1760_____
 32¢ **Dahlia,** overall tagged .50 .20 ☐☐☐☐☐

CM1761_____
 32¢ **Hydrangea,** overall tagged .50 .20 ☐☐☐☐☐

CM1762_____
 32¢ **Rudbeckia,** overall tagged .50 .20 ☐☐☐☐☐

CM1763_____ **1995. Republic of Palau Issue**
 32¢ **multicolored** phosphored paper .50 .20 ☐☐☐☐☐

CM1764_____ **1995. Comic Strip Classics Issue**
 32¢ **The Yellow Kid** .75 .50 ☐☐☐☐☐

CM1765_____
 32¢ **Katzenjammer Kids** .75 .50 ☐☐☐☐☐

CM1748-1757

CM1758-1762

CM1763

CM1764-1783

CM1784

CM1785

	MNHFVF	UseFVF	
CM1766 ____________ 32¢ **Little Nemo in Slumberland**	.75	.50	❑❑❑❑❑
CM1767 ____________ 32¢ **Bringing Up Father**	.75	.50	❑❑❑❑❑
CM1768 ____________ 32¢ **Krazy Kat**	.75	.50	❑❑❑❑❑
CM1769 ____________ 32¢ **Rube Goldberg's Inventions**	.75	.50	❑❑❑❑❑
CM1770 ____________ 32¢ **Toonerville Folks**	.75	.50	❑❑❑❑❑
CM1771 ____________ 32¢ **Gasoline Alley**	.75	.50	❑❑❑❑❑
CM1772 ____________ 32¢ **Barney Google**	.75	.50	❑❑❑❑❑
CM1773 ____________ 32¢ **Little Orphan Annie**	.75	.50	❑❑❑❑❑
CM1774 ____________ 32¢ **Popeye**	.75	.50	❑❑❑❑❑
CM1775 ____________ 32¢ **Blondie**	.75	.50	❑❑❑❑❑
CM1776 ____________ 32¢ **Dick Tracy**	.75	.50	❑❑❑❑❑
CM1777 ____________ 32¢ **Alley Oop**	.75	.50	❑❑❑❑❑
CM1778 ____________ 32¢ **Nancy**	.75	.50	❑❑❑❑❑
CM1779 ____________ 32¢ **Flash Gordon**	.75	.50	❑❑❑❑❑
CM1780 ____________ 32¢ **Li'l Abner**	.75	.50	❑❑❑❑❑
CM1781 ____________ 32¢ **Terry & the Pirates**	.75	.50	❑❑❑❑❑
CM1782 ____________ 32¢ **Prince Valiant**	.75	.50	❑❑❑❑❑
CM1783 ____________ 32¢ **Brenda Starr**	.75	.50	❑❑❑❑❑

NOTE: Because this issue also was made available to collectors in full six-pane printing sheets, gutter pairs and blocks and cross-gutter multiples also exist.

	MNHFVF	UseFVF	
CM1784 ____________ **1995. U.S. Naval Academy Issue**			
32¢ **multicolored** phosphored paper	.50	.20	❑❑❑❑❑
CM1785 ____________ **1995. Tennessee Williams Issue**			
32¢ **multicolored** phosphored paper	.50	.20	❑❑❑❑❑
CM1786 ____________ **1995. James K. Polk Issue**			
32¢ **reddish brown** phosphored paper	.50	.20	❑❑❑❑❑
CM1787 ____________ **1995. Antique Automobiles Issue**			
32¢ **Duryea,** phosphored paper	.75	.50	❑❑❑❑❑
CM1788 ____________ 32¢ **Haynes,** phosphored paper	.75	.50	❑❑❑❑❑
CM1789 ____________ 32¢ **Columbia,** phosphored paper	.75	.50	❑❑❑❑❑
CM1790 ____________ 32¢ **Winton,** phosphored paper	.75	.50	❑❑❑❑❑
CM1791 ____________ 32¢ **White,** phosphored paper	.75	.50	❑❑❑❑❑

MNHFVF	UseFVF

CM1792_____ **1996. Utah Centennial Issue**

32¢ **multicolored** tagged (120,000,000) .50 .20 ☐☐☐☐☐

CM1793_____ **1996. Garden Flowers Issue**

32¢ **Crocus,** phosphored paper (160,000,000) .50 .20 ☐☐☐☐☐

CM1794_____

32¢ **Winter Aconite,** phosphored paper .50 .20 ☐☐☐☐☐

CM1795_____

32¢ **Pansy,** phosphored paper .50 .20 ☐☐☐☐☐

CM1796_____

32¢ **Snowdrop,** phosphored paper .50 .20 ☐☐☐☐☐

CM1797_____

32¢ **Anemone,** phosphored paper .50 .20 ☐☐☐☐☐

CM1798_____ **1996. Love Cherub Issue**

32¢ **multicolored** tagged (2,550,000,000) .50 .20 ☐☐☐☐☐

CM1799_____ **1996. Ernest E. Just Issue**

32¢ **black & gray** tagged (92,100,000) .50 .20 ☐☐☐☐☐

CM1786 ◄

CM1792

CM1798

CM1799

CM1787-1791

CM1793-1797

CM1800

CM11801

	MNHFVF	UseFVF	
CM1800___________ **1996. Smithsonian Institution Sesquicentennial Issue**			
32¢ **multicolored** tagged (115,600,000)	.50	.20	❑❑❑❑❑
CM1801___________ **1996. New Years Issue**			
32¢ **multicolored** tagged (93,150,000)	.50	.20	❑❑❑❑❑
CM1802___________ **1996. Pioneers of Communications Issue**			
32¢ **Eadweard Muybridge,** phosphored paper (23,292,500)	.50	.20	❑❑❑❑❑
CM1803___________			
32¢ **Ottmar Mergenthaler,** phosphored paper	.50	.20	❑❑❑❑❑
CM1804___________			
32¢ **Frederic E. Ives,** phosphored paper	.50	.20	❑❑❑❑❑
CM1805___________			
32¢ **William Dickson,** phosphored paper	.50	.20	❑❑❑❑❑
CM1806___________ **1996. Fulbright Scholarships Issue**			
32¢ **multicolored** tagged (111,000,000)	.50	.20	❑❑❑❑❑
CM1807___________ **1996. Marathon Issue**			
32¢ **multicolored** tagged (209,450,000)	.50	.20	❑❑❑❑❑
CM1808___________ **1996. Atlanta 1996 Centennial Olympic Games Issue**			
32¢ **Javelin**	.75	.50	❑❑❑❑❑
CM1809___________			
32¢ **Whitewater canoeing**	.75	.50	❑❑❑❑❑
CM1810___________			
32¢ **Women's running**	.75	.50	❑❑❑❑❑
CM1811___________			
32¢ **Women's platform diving**	.75	.50	❑❑❑❑❑
CM1812___________			
32¢ **Men's cycling**	.75	.50	❑❑❑❑❑
CM1813___________			
32¢ **Freestyle wrestling**	.75	.50	❑❑❑❑❑
CM1814___________			
32¢ **Women's gymnastics**	.75	.50	❑❑❑❑❑
CM1815___________			
32¢ **Women's sailboarding**	.75	.50	❑❑❑❑❑
CM1816___________			
32¢ **Men's shot put**	.75	.50	❑❑❑❑❑
CM1817___________			
32¢ **Women's soccer**	.75	.50	❑❑❑❑❑
CM1818___________			
32¢ **Beach volleyball**	.75	.50	❑❑❑❑❑
CM1819___________			
32¢ **Men's rowing**	.75	.50	❑❑❑❑❑
CM1820___________			
32¢ **Men's sprinting events**	.75	.50	❑❑❑❑❑
CM1821___________			
32¢ **Women's swimming**	.75	.50	❑❑❑❑❑
CM1822___________			
32¢ **Women's softball**	.75	.50	❑❑❑❑❑
CM1823___________			
32¢ **Men's hurdles**	.75	.50	❑❑❑❑❑
CM1824___________			
32¢ **Men's swimming (backstroke)**	.75	.50	❑❑❑❑❑
CM1825___________			
32¢ **Men's gymnastics (pommel Horse)**	.75	.50	❑❑❑❑❑
CM1826___________			
32¢ **Equestrian events**	.75	.50	❑❑❑❑❑

CM1802-1805

CM1806

CM1807

CM1808-1827

MNHFVF	UseFVF	

CM1827_____
 32¢ **Men's basketball** .75 .50 ☐☐☐☐☐

NOTE: Because this issue also was made available to collectors in full six-pane printing sheets, gutter pairs and blocks and cross-gutter multiples also exist.

CM1828_____ **1996. Georgia O'Keeffe Issue**
 32¢ **multicolored** tagged (156,300,000) .50 .20 ☐☐☐☐☐

CM1829_____ **1996. Tennessee Bicentennial Issue**
 32¢ **multicolored** tagged (100,000,000) .50 .20 ☐☐☐☐☐

CM1830_____ **1996. Tennessee Bicentennial Booklet Issue**
 32¢ **multicolored** tagged (60,120,000) .75 .20 ☐☐☐☐☐

CM1831_____ **1996. American Indian Dances Issue**
 32¢ **Fancy Dance,** tagged (27,850,000) .75 .50 ☐☐☐☐☐

CM1832_____
 32¢ **Butterfly Dance,** tagged .75 .50 ☐☐☐☐☐

CM1833_____
 32¢ **Traditional Dance,** tagged .75 .50 ☐☐☐☐☐

CM1834_____
 32¢ **Raven Dance,** tagged .75 .50 ☐☐☐☐☐

CM1835_____
 32¢ **Hoop Dance,** tagged .75 .50 ☐☐☐☐☐

CM1836_____ **1996. Prehistoric Animals Issue**
 32¢ **Eohippus,** tagged (22,218,000) .75 .50 ☐☐☐☐☐

CM1837_____
 32¢ **Woolly Mammoth,** tagged .75 .50 ☐☐☐☐☐

CM1838_____
 32¢ **Mastodon,** tagged .75 .50 ☐☐☐☐☐

CM1839_____
 32¢ **Saber-tooth Cat,** tagged .75 .50 ☐☐☐☐☐

CM1840_____ **1996. Breast Cancer Awareness Issue**
 32¢ **multicolored** tagged (95,600,000) .50 .20 ☐☐☐☐☐

CM1841_____ **1996. James Dean Issue**
 32¢ **multicolored** tagged (300,000,000) .50 .20 ☐☐☐☐☐

NOTE: Because this issue also was made available to collectors in full six-pane printing sheets, gutter pairs and blocks and cross-gutter multiples also exist.

CM1842_____ **1996. Folk Heroes Issue**
 32¢ **Mighty Casey,** tagged (23,681,250) .50 .20 ☐☐☐☐☐

CM1843_____
 32¢ **Paul Bunyan,** tagged .50 .20 ☐☐☐☐☐

CM1844_____
 32¢ **John Henry,** tagged .50 .20 ☐☐☐☐☐

CM1845_____
 32¢ **Pecos Bill,** tagged .50 .20 ☐☐☐☐☐

CM1846_____ **1996. Olympic Games Centennial Issue**
 32¢ **brown** tagged (133,613,000) .50 .20 ☐☐☐☐☐

CM1847_____ **1996. Iowa Sesquicentennial Issue**
 32¢ **multicolored** tagged (103,400,000) .50 .20 ☐☐☐☐☐

CM1848_____ **1996. Iowa Sesquicentennial Self Adhesive Issue**
 32¢ **multicolored** tagged (60,000,000) .75 .30 ☐☐☐☐☐

CM1849_____ **1996. Rural Free Delivery Centennial Issue**
 32¢ **multicolored** tagged (134,000,000) .50 .20 ☐☐☐☐☐

CM1850_____ **1996. Riverboats Issue**
 32¢ *Robt. E. Lee,* tagged (32,000,000) .75 .50 ☐☐☐☐☐

CM1851_____
 32¢ *Sylvan Dell,* tagged .75 .50 ☐☐☐☐☐

CM1828

CM1829-1830

CM1836-1839

CM1831-1835

CM1840

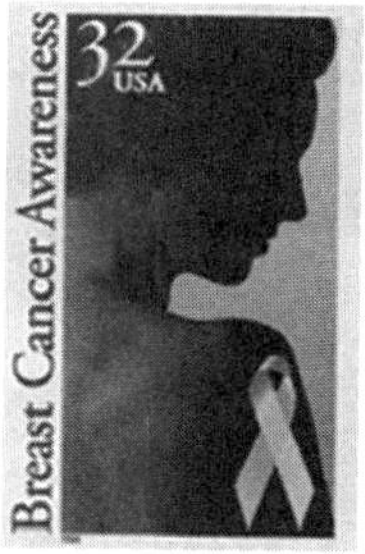

CM1841

CM1842-1845

CM1846

CM1847, CM1848

CM1849

CM1850-1854

		MNHFVF	UseFVF
CM1852__________	32¢ ***Far West,*** tagged	.75	.50 ❑❑❑❑❑
CM1853__________	32¢ ***Rebecca Everingham,*** tagged	.75	.50 ❑❑❑❑❑
CM1854__________	32¢ ***Bailey Gatzert,*** tagged	.75	.50 ❑❑❑❑❑
CM1855__________ **1996. Big Band Leaders Issue**	32¢ **Count Basie,** tagged (23,025,000)	.50	.20 ❑❑❑❑❑
CM1856__________	32¢ **Tommy & Jimmy Dorsey,** tagged	.50	.20 ❑❑❑❑❑
CM1857__________	32¢ **Glenn Miller,** tagged	.50	.20 ❑❑❑❑❑
CM1858__________	32¢ **Benny Goodman,** tagged	.50	.20 ❑❑❑❑❑
CM1859__________ **1996. Songwriters Issue**	32¢ **Harold Arlen,** tagged (23,025,000)	.50	.20 ❑❑❑❑❑
CM1860__________	32¢ **Johhny Mercer,** tagged	.50	.20 ❑❑❑❑❑

CM1855-1858

CM1859-1862

	MNHFVF	UseFVF	
CM1861__________			
32¢ **Dorothy Fields,** tagged	.50	.20	❑❑❑❑❑
CM1862__________			
32¢ **Hoagy Carmichael,** tagged	.50	.20	❑❑❑❑❑
CM1863__________ **1996. F. Scott Fitzgerald Issue**			
23¢ **multicolored** tagged (300,000,000)	.50	.20	❑❑❑❑❑
CM1864__________ **1996. Endangered Species Issue**			
32¢ **Black-footed ferret**	.50	.20	❑❑❑❑❑
CM1865__________			
32¢ **Thick-billed parrot**	.50	.20	❑❑❑❑❑
CM1866__________			
32¢ **Hawaiian Monk seal**	.50	.20	❑❑❑❑❑

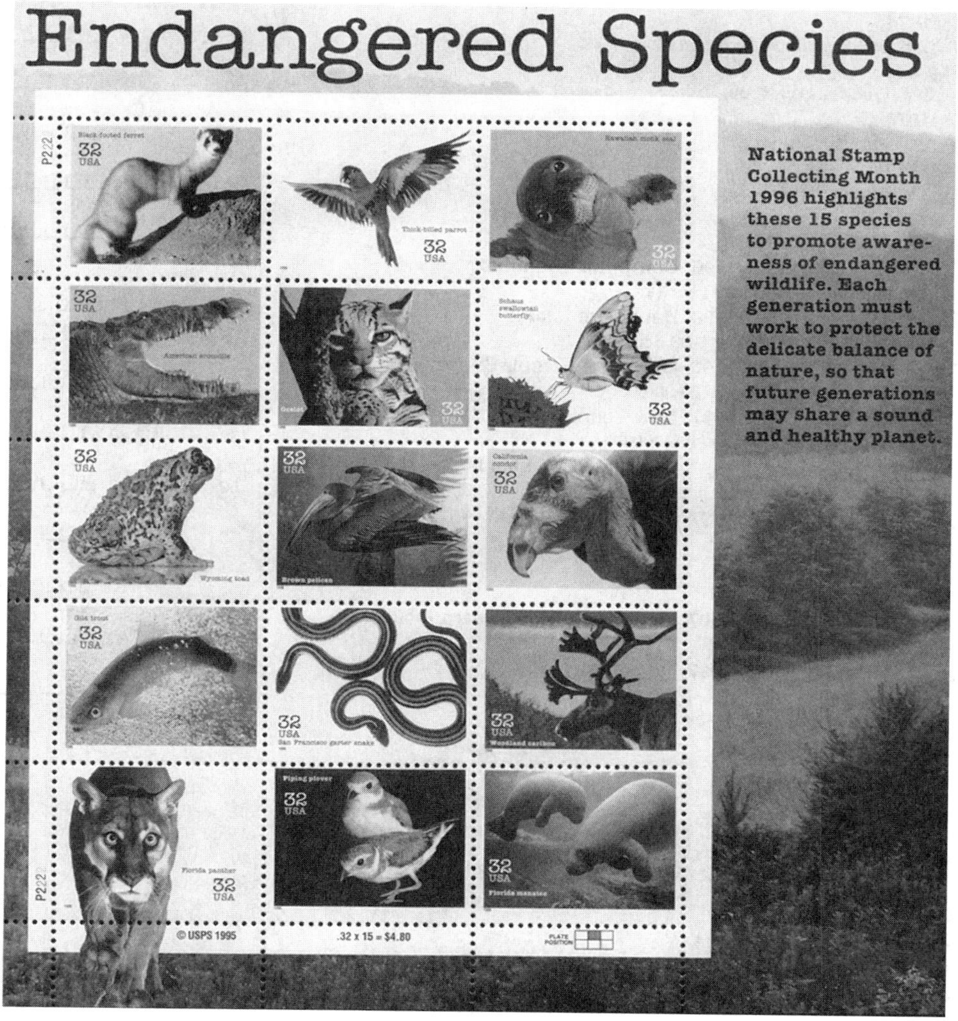

Endangered Species
National Stamp Collecting Month 1996 highlights these 15 species to promote awareness of endangered wildlife. Each generation must work to protect the delicate balance of nature, so that future generations may share a sound and healthy planet.
© USPS 1995
.32 x 15 = $4.80

CM1864-1878

MNHFVF	UseFVF	

CM1867_____
32¢ **American crocodile** .50 .20 ☐☐☐☐☐

CM1868_____
32¢ **Ocelot** .50 .20 ☐☐☐☐☐

CM1869_____
32¢ **Schaus swallowtail butterfly** .50 .20 ☐☐☐☐☐

CM1870_____
32¢ **Wyoming toad** .50 .20 ☐☐☐☐☐

CM1871_____
32¢ **Brown pelican** .50 .20 ☐☐☐☐☐

CM1872_____
32¢ **California condor** .50 .20 ☐☐☐☐☐

CM1873_____
32¢ **Gila trout** .50 .20 ☐☐☐☐☐

CM1874_____
32¢ **San Francisco garter snake** .50 .20 ☐☐☐☐☐

CM1875_____
32¢ **Woodland caribou** .50 .20 ☐☐☐☐☐

CM1876_____
32¢ **Florida panther** .50 .20 ☐☐☐☐☐

CM1877_____
32¢ **Piping plover** .50 .20 ☐☐☐☐☐

CM1878_____
32¢ **Florida manatee** .50 .20 ☐☐☐☐☐

CM1879_____ **1996. Computer Technology Issue**
32¢ **multicolored** tagged (93,612,000) .50 .20 ☐☐☐☐☐

CM1880_____ **1996. Hanukkah Issue**
32¢ **multicolored** tagged (103,520,000) .75 .20 ☐☐☐☐☐

CM1881_____ **1996. Cycling Souvenir Sheet**
50¢ **multicolored** tagged (20,000,000) 2.50 1.00 ☐☐☐☐☐

CM1882_____ **1997. New Years Issue**
32¢ **multicolored** tagged (160,000,000) .50 .20 ☐☐☐☐☐

CM1883_____ **1997. Benjamin O. Davis Issue**
32¢ **gray, green & black** phosphored paper (112,000,000) .50 .20 ☐☐☐☐☐

CM1884_____ **1997. Love Issue**
32¢ **multicolored** tagged .50 .20 ☐☐☐☐☐

CM1885_____
55¢ **multicolored** tagged 1.00 .30 ☐☐☐☐☐

CM1886_____ **1997. Helping Children Learn Issue**
32¢ **multicolored** tagged .50 .20 ☐☐☐☐☐

CM1887_____ **1997. Pacific 97 Issue**
32¢ **red** phosphored paper (65,000,000) .50 .20 ☐☐☐☐☐

CM1863

CM1879

CM1880

		MNHFVF	UseFVF	
CM1888				
	32¢ **blue** phosphored paper	.50	.20	❑❑❑❑❑

NOTE: Because this issue also was made available in full 96-subject printing sheets of six 16-stamp panes, gutter pairs and blocks and cross-gutter multiples also exist.

CM1889	**1997. Thornton Wilder Issue**			
	32¢ **multicolored** tagged (97,500,000)	.50	.20	❑❑❑❑❑
CM1890	**1997. Raoul Wallenberg Issue**			
	32¢ **multicolored** tagged (96,000,000)	.50	.20	❑❑❑❑❑

CM1881

CM1883

CM1882

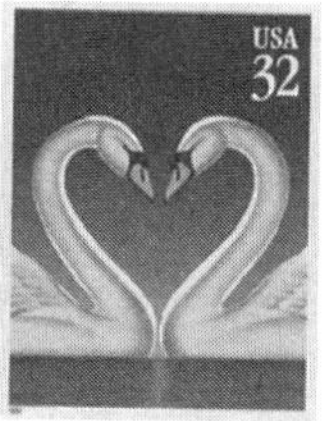

CM1884

CM1885

CM1886

CM1887

CM1888

	MNHFVF	UseFVF
CM1891 **1997. The World of Dinosaurs Issue**		
$4.80 **Sheet of 15,** tagged (14,600,000)	15.00	9.50
CM1892 **1997. Bugs Bunny Issue**		
$3.20 **Pane of 10,** tagged	7.50	

NOTE: Serpentine die cut 11 through stamps and backing.

	MNHFVF	UseFVF
CM1893		
$3.20 **Pane of 10,** tagged	200.00	

NOTE: This issue also was made available in top and bottom half printing sheets of six 10-stamp panes each. A single plate number, trimmed away on individual panes, appears adjacent to the bottom-left pane in the bottom half of the printing sheet only. Value of plate number half is $225.

A gummed, non-denominated, untagged item similar to CM1893n on the same backing paper as the normal stamps lacks Bugs' "autograph" and single stamp, the latter of which is replaced by "32 USA" as on the issued stamp. Though printed for the USPS, this item was an advertising piece and was not postally valid.

CM1889

CM1890

CM1892

CM1891

CM1894

CM1896

CM1895

MNHFVF	UseFVF	

CM1894＿＿＿＿＿＿ **1997. Pacific 97 U.S. Stamp Sesquicentennial Issue**
$6 **Pane of 12,** tagged 11.50 9.00 ☐☐☐☐☐
CM1895＿＿＿＿＿＿ **1997. Pacific 97 U.S. Stamp Sesquicentennial Issue**
$7.20 **Pane of 12,** tagged 12.50 10.00 ☐☐☐☐☐

NOTE: Because this issue also was made available to collectors in full six-pane printing sheets, gutter pairs and blocks and cross-gutter multiples also exist.

CM1896＿＿＿＿＿＿ **1997. Marshall Plan 50th Anniversary Issue**
32¢ **multicolored** tagged (45,250,000) .50 .20 ☐☐☐☐☐
CM1897＿＿＿＿＿＿ **1997. Classic American Aircraft Issue**
32¢ **North American P-51 Mustang fighter** .75 .50 ☐☐☐☐☐
CM1898＿＿＿＿＿＿
32¢ **Wright Model B Flyer** .75 .50 ☐☐☐☐☐
CM1899＿＿＿＿＿＿
32¢ **Piper J-3 Cub** .75 .50 ☐☐☐☐☐
CM1900＿＿＿＿＿＿
32¢ **Lockheed Vega** .75 .50 ☐☐☐☐☐
CM1901＿＿＿＿＿＿
32¢ *Northrop Alpha* .75 .50 ☐☐☐☐☐
CM1902＿＿＿＿＿＿
32¢ **Martin B-10 bomber** .75 .50 ☐☐☐☐☐

CM1897-1916

MNHFVF	UseFVF	

CM1903_____
 32¢ **Chance Vought Corsair F4U fighter** .75 .50 ☐☐☐☐☐
CM1904_____
 32¢ **Boeing B-47 Stratojet bomber** .75 .50 ☐☐☐☐☐
CM1905_____
 32¢ **Gee Bee Super-Sportster** .75 .50 ☐☐☐☐☐
CM1906_____
 32¢ **Beech Model C17L Staggerwing** .75 .50 ☐☐☐☐☐
CM1907_____
 32¢ **Boeing B-17 Flying Fortress bomber** .75 .50 ☐☐☐☐☐
CM1908_____
 32¢ **Stearman PT-13 training aircraft** .75 .50 ☐☐☐☐☐
CM1909_____
 32¢ **Lockheed Constellation** .75 .50 ☐☐☐☐☐
CM1910_____
 32¢ **Lockheed P-38 Lightning fighter** .75 .50 ☐☐☐☐☐
CM1911_____
 32¢ **Boeing P-26 Peashooter fighter** .75 .50 ☐☐☐☐☐
CM1912_____
 32¢ **Ford Tri-Motor** .75 .50 ☐☐☐☐☐
CM1913_____
 32¢ **Douglas DC-3 passenger plane** .75 .50 ☐☐☐☐☐
CM1914_____
 32¢ **Boeing 314 Clipper flying boat** .75 .50 ☐☐☐☐☐
CM1915_____
 32¢ **Curtiss JN-4 Jenny training aircraft** .75 .50 ☐☐☐☐☐
CM1916_____
 32¢ **Grumman F4F Wildcat fighter** .75 .50 ☐☐☐☐☐

NOTE: Because this issue also was made available to collectors in full six-pane printing sheets, gutter pairs and blocks and cross-gutter multiples also exist.

CM1917_____ **1997. Legendary Football Coaches Issue**
 32¢ **Paul "Bear" Bryant,** tagged (22,500,000) .50 .20 ☐☐☐☐☐
CM1918_____
 32¢ **Glen "Pop" Warner,** tagged .50 .20 ☐☐☐☐☐
CM1919_____
 32¢ **Vince Lombardi,** tagged .50 .20 ☐☐☐☐☐
CM1920_____
 32¢ **George Halas,** tagged .50 .20 ☐☐☐☐☐

CM1917-1920

	MNHFVF	UseFVF	
CM1921 ________ **1997. Classic American Dolls Issue**			
32¢ **"Alabama Baby" and Martha Chase Doll**	.75	.50	❑❑❑❑❑
CM1922 ________			
32¢ **Rutta Sisters "The Columbian Doll"**	.75	.50	❑❑❑❑❑
CM1923 ________			
32¢ **Johnny Gruelle's "Raggedy Ann"**	.75	.50	❑❑❑❑❑
CM1924 ________			
32¢ **Martha Chase Cloth Doll**	.75	.50	❑❑❑❑❑
CM1925 ________			
32¢ **Effanbee Doll Co. "American Child"**	.75	.50	❑❑❑❑❑
CM1926 ________			
32¢ **Ideal Novelty & Toy Co. "Baby Coos"**	.75	.50	❑❑❑❑❑
CM1927 ________			
32¢ **Plains Indian Doll 1920s**	.75	.50	❑❑❑❑❑
CM1928 ________			
32¢ **Izannah Walker Oil-Painted Cloth Doll**	.75	.50	❑❑❑❑❑
CM1929 ________			
32¢ **All-Cloth "Babyland Rag" Doll**	.75	.50	❑❑❑❑❑
CM1930 ________			
32¢ **Rose O'Neill "Scootles" Doll**	.75	.50	❑❑❑❑❑

CM1921-1935

MNHFVF	UseFVF	

CM1931_____
 32¢ **Ludwig Greiner First U.S. Patent Doll** .75 .50 ☐☐☐☐☐
CM1932_____
 32¢ **"Betsy McCall" American Character Doll** .75 .50 ☐☐☐☐☐
CM1933_____
 32¢ **Percy Crosby's "Skippy"** .75 .50 ☐☐☐☐☐
CM1934_____
 32¢ **Alexander Doll Co. "Maggie Mix-up"** .75 .50 ☐☐☐☐☐
CM1935_____
 32¢ **Schoenut "All Word Perfection Art Dolls"** .75 .50 ☐☐☐☐☐
CM1936_____ **1997. Humphrey Bogart Issue**
 32¢ **multicolored** tagged (195,000,000) .50 .20 ☐☐☐☐☐
NOTE: Because this issue also was made available to collectors in full six-pane printing sheets, gutter pairs and blocks and cross-gutter multiples also exist.
CM1937_____ **1997. Vince Lombardi Issue**
 32¢ **multicolored** tagged (20,000,000) .50 .20 ☐☐☐☐☐
CM1938_____ **1997. Paul "Bear" Bryant Issue**
 32¢ **multicolored** tagged (20,000,000) .50 .20 ☐☐☐☐☐
CM1939_____ **1997. Glen "Pop" Warner Issue**
 32¢ **multicolored** tagged (10,000,000) .50 .20 ☐☐☐☐☐
CM1940_____ **1997. George Halas Issue**
 32¢ **multicolored** tagged (10,000,000) .50 .20 ☐☐☐☐☐
CM1941_____ **1997. "The Stars And Stripes Forever" Issue**
 32¢ **multicolored** tagged (323,000,000) .50 .20 ☐☐☐☐☐

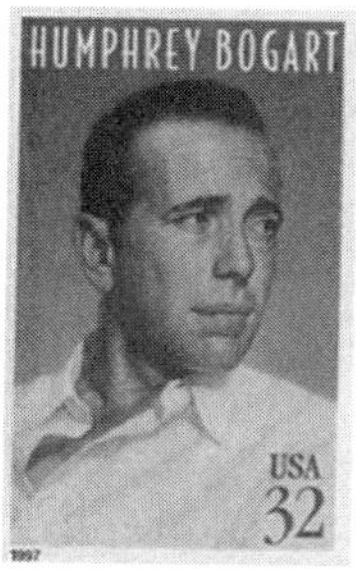

CM1936

CM1937

CM1938

CM1939

CM1940

CM1942-1945

CM1941

CM1954

		MNHFVF	UseFVF	
CM1942___________	**1997. Opera Singers Issue**			
	32¢ **Lily Pons,** tagged (21,500,000)	.50	.20	❑❑❑❑❑
CM1943___________				
	32¢ **Richard Tucker,** tagged	.50	.20	❑❑❑❑❑
CM1944___________				
	32¢ **Lawrence Tibbett,** tagged	.50	.20	❑❑❑❑❑
CM1945___________				
	32¢ **Rosa Ponselle,** tagged	.50	.20	❑❑❑❑❑
CM1946___________	**1997. Classical Composers and Conductors Issue**			
	32¢ **Leopold Stokowski,** tagged (4,300,000) 20-stamp panes	.50	.20	❑❑❑❑❑
CM1947___________				
	32¢ **Arthur Fiedler,** tagged	.50	.20	❑❑❑❑❑
CM1948___________				
	32¢ **George Szell,** tagged	.50	.20	❑❑❑❑❑
CM1949___________				
	32¢ **Eugene Ormandy,** tagged	.50	.20	❑❑❑❑❑
CM1950___________				
	32¢ **Samuel Barber,** tagged	.50	.20	❑❑❑❑❑
CM1951___________				
	32¢ **Ferde Grofe,** tagged	.50	.20	❑❑❑❑❑
CM1952___________				
	32¢ **Charles Ives,** tagged	.50	.20	❑❑❑❑❑
CM1953___________				
	32¢ **Louis Moreau Gottschalk,** tagged	.50	.20	❑❑❑❑❑
CM1954___________	**1997. Padre Felix Varela Issue**			
	32¢ **purple** tagged (25,250,000)	.50	.20	❑❑❑❑❑
CM1955___________	**1997. U.S. Department of the Air Force Issue**			
	32¢ **multicolored** tagged (45,250,000)	.50	.20	❑❑❑❑❑
CM1956___________	**1997. Classic Movie Monsters Issue**			
	32¢ **Lon Chaney, as Phantom of the Opera,** (29,000,000)	.50	.20	❑❑❑❑❑
CM1957___________				
	32¢ **Bela Lugosi, as Dracula,** tagged	.50	.20	❑❑❑❑❑
CM1958___________				
	32¢ **Boris Karloff, in Frankenstein,** tagged	.50	.20	❑❑❑❑❑

CM1946-1953

CM1955

CM1956-1960

CM1961

MNHFVF	UseFVF

CM1959_____

32¢ **Boris Karloff, as The Mummy,** tagged .50 .20 ☐☐☐☐☐

CM1960_____

32¢ **Lon Chaney Jr., as The Wolf Man,** tagged .50 .20 ☐☐☐☐☐

NOTE: Because this issue also was made available to collectors in full nine-pane printing sheets, gutter pairs and blocks and cross-gutter multiples also exist.

CM1961_____ **1997. First Supersonic Flight Issue**

32¢ **multicolored** tagged (173,000,000) .50 .20 ☐☐☐☐☐

CM1962_____ **1997. Women in Military Service Issue**

32¢ **multicolored** tagged (37,000,000) .50 .20 ☐☐☐☐☐

CM1963_____ **1997. Kwanzaa Issue**

32¢ **multicolored** tagged (133,000,000) .50 .20 ☐☐☐☐☐

NOTE: Because this issue also was made available to collectors in full six-pane printing sheets, gutter pairs and blocks and cross-gutter multiples also exist.

CM1964_____ **1998. Year of The Tiger New Year Issue**

32¢ **multicolored** tagged .50 .20 ☐☐☐☐☐

CM1965_____ **1998. Winter Sports Issue**

32¢ **multicolored** tagged .50 .20 ☐☐☐☐☐

CM1966_____ **1998. Madam C.J. Walker Issue**

32¢ **multicolored** tagged .50 .20 ☐☐☐☐☐

CM1967_____ **1998. Celebrate the Century 1900s Issue**

$4.80 **Pane of 15,** tagged 12.50 9.50 ☐☐☐☐☐

CM1968_____ **1998. Celebrate the Century 1910s Issue**

$4.80 **Pane of 15,** tagged 12.50 9.50 ☐☐☐☐☐

CM1969_____ **1998. Spanish American War Issue**

32¢ **red & black** tagged .50 .20 ☐☐☐☐☐

CM1970_____ **1998. Flowering Trees Issue**

32¢ **Southern Magnolia,** tagged .50 .20 ☐☐☐☐☐

CM1971_____

32¢ **Blue Paloverde,** tagged .50 .20 ☐☐☐☐☐

CM1972_____

32¢ **Yellow Poplar,** tagged .50 .20 ☐☐☐☐☐

CM1962

CM1963

CM1964

CM1965

CM1966

CM1967

CM1968

	MNHFVF	UseFVF	
CM1973			
32¢ **Prairie Crab Apple,** tagged	.50	.20	❑❑❑❑❑
CM1974			
32¢ **Pacific Dogwood,** tagged	.50	.20	❑❑❑❑❑
CM1975 **1998. Alexander Calder Issue**			
32¢ **Black Cascade, 13 verticals,** tagged	.50	.20	❑❑❑❑❑
CM1976			
32¢ **Untitled,** tagged	.50	.20	❑❑❑❑❑
CM1977			
32¢ **Rearing Stallion,** tagged	.50	.20	❑❑❑❑❑
CM1978			
32¢ **Portrait of a young man,** tagged	.50	.20	❑❑❑❑❑
CM1979			
32¢ **Un Effet du Japonais,** tagged	.50	.20	❑❑❑❑❑
CM1980 **1998. Cinco de Mayo Issue**			
32¢ **multicolored**	.50	.20	❑❑❑❑❑
CM1981 **1998. Sylvester and Tweety Issue**			
$3.20 **Pane of 10,** tagged	5.00		❑❑❑❑❑

CM1969

CM1970-1974

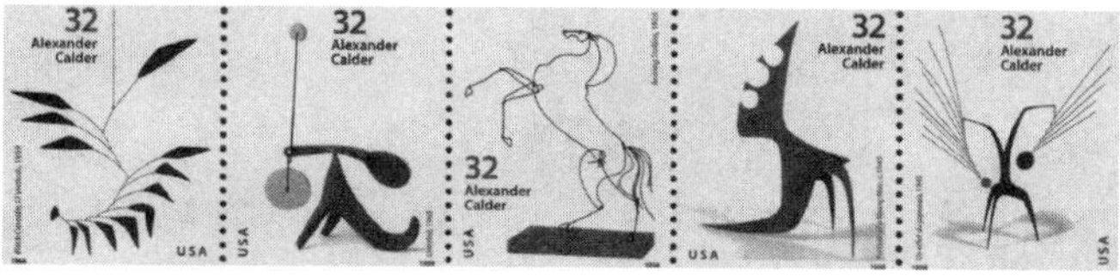

CM1975-1979

CM1980

CM1981-1982

CSP1

MNHFVF	UseFVF

CM1982_____ 1998. Sylvester and Tweety Issue

$3.20 **Pane of 10,** tagged 5.00 ☐☐☐☐☐

NOTE: This issue also was made available in top- and bottom-half printing sheets of six 10-stamp panes each. Vertical rouletting between the two panes is missing on these half sheets. A plate number, trimmed away or individual panes, appears adjacent to the bottom-left pane in the bottom half of the printing sheet only.

CM1983_____ 1998. Celebrate the Century, 1920s Issue

$4.80 **Sheetlet of 15,** tagged 15.00 9.50 ☐☐☐☐☐

CM1984_____ 1998. Wisconsin Statehood Sesquicentennial Issue

32¢ **multicolored** .50 .20 ☐☐☐☐☐

CM1985_____ 1998. Trans-Mississippi Color Issue

$3.80 **Pane of 9** 7.50 3.50 ☐☐☐☐☐

CM1986_____ 1998. Trans-Mississippi Color Issue

$9 **Pane,** 9 examples of CM1985h 15.00 ☐☐☐☐☐

CM1987_____ 1998. Berlin Airlift Issue

32¢ **multicolored** .50 .20 ☐☐☐☐☐

CM1988_____ 1998. Folk Musicians Issue

32¢ **Woody Guthrie,** tagged .50 .20 ☐☐☐☐☐

CM1989_____

32¢ **Sonny Terry,** tagged .50 .20 ☐☐☐☐☐

CM1990_____

32¢ **Huddie "Leadbelly" Ledbetter** .50 .20 ☐☐☐☐☐

CM1991_____

32¢ **Josh White** .50 .20 ☐☐☐☐☐

CM1983

CM1984

		MNHFVF	UseFVF	
CM1992	**1998. Spanish Settlement of the Southwest Issue**			
	32¢ **multicolored**	.50	.20	❑❑❑❑❑
CM1993	**1998. Gospel Singers Issue**			
	32¢ **Mahalia Jackson**	.50	2.00	❑❑❑❑❑
CM1994				
	32¢ **Roberta Martin**	.50	.20	❑❑❑❑❑
CM1995				
	32¢ **Clara Ward**	.50	.20	❑❑❑❑❑
CM1996				
	32¢ **Sister Rosetta Tharpe**	.50	.20	❑❑❑❑❑
CM1997	**1998. Stephen Vincent Benét Issue**			
	32¢ **multicolored**	.50	.20	❑❑❑❑❑
CMSP1	**1998. Breast Cancer Research Semipostal Issue**			
	40¢ **multicolored**	.75	.20	❑❑❑❑❑
CM1998	**1998. Tropical Birds Issue**			
	32¢ **Antillean Euphonia**	.50	.20	❑❑❑❑❑
CM1999				
	32¢ **Green-throated Carib**	.50	.20	❑❑❑❑❑

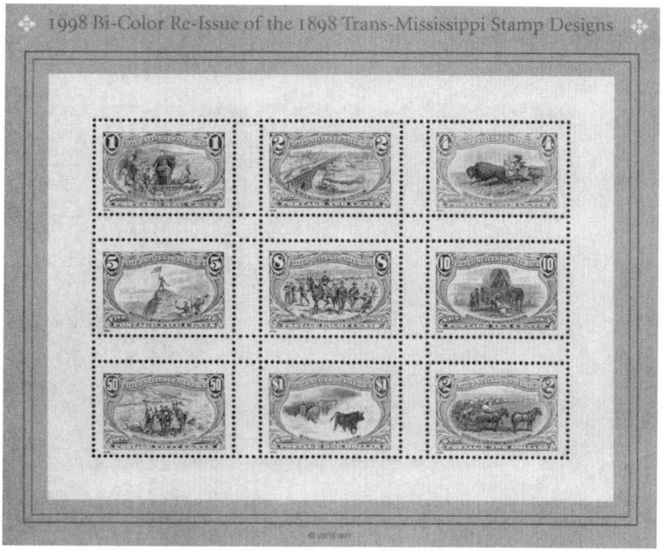

CM1985 (CM1986 is a pane of 9 examples of the $1 stamp)

CM1987

CM1992

CM1997

CM1988-1991

CM1993-1996

MNHFVF	UseFVF

CM2000_____
 32¢ **Crested Honeycreeper** — .50 — .20 ☐☐☐☐☐
CM2001_____
 32¢ **Cardinal Honeyeater** — .50 — .20 ☐☐☐☐☐
CM2002_____ **1998. Alfred Hitchcock Issue**
 32¢ **black & gray** — .75 — .20 ☐☐☐☐☐
CM2003_____ **1998. Organ & Tissue Donation Issue**
 32¢ **multicolored** — .50 — .20 ☐☐☐☐☐
CM2004_____ **1998. Bright Eyes Pet Issue**
 32¢ **Dog,** tagged — .50 — .20 ☐☐☐☐☐
CM2005_____
 32¢ **Goldfish,** tagged — .50 — .20 ☐☐☐☐☐
CM2006_____
 32¢ **Cat,** tagged — .50 — .20 ☐☐☐☐☐
CM2007_____
 32¢ **Parakeet,** tagged — .50 — .20 ☐☐☐☐☐
CM2008_____
 32¢ **Hamster,** tagged — .50 — .20 ☐☐☐☐☐
CM2009_____ **1998. Klondike Gold Rush Issue**
 32¢ **multicolored** tagged — .50 — .20 ☐☐☐☐☐
CM2010_____ **1998. American Art Issue**
 32¢ **John Foster** — .50 — .20 ☐☐☐☐☐
CM2011_____
 32¢ **The Freake Limner** — .50 — .20 ☐☐☐☐☐
CM2012_____
 32¢ **Ammi Phillips** — .50 — .20 ☐☐☐☐☐
CM2013_____
 32¢ **Rembrandt Peale** — .50 — .20 ☐☐☐☐☐
CM2014_____
 32¢ **John J. Audubon** — .50 — .20 ☐☐☐☐☐

CM1998-2001

CM2004-2008

CM2002

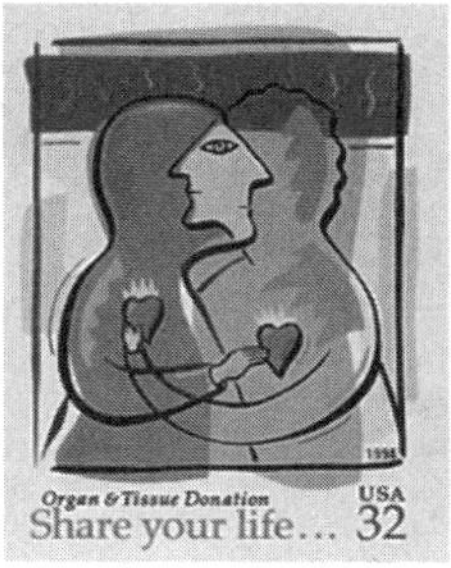

CM2003

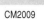

CM2009

	MNHFVF	UseFVF	
CM2015			
32¢ **George Caleb Bingham**	.50	.20	❑❑❑❑❑
CM2016			
32¢ **Asher B. Durand**	.50	.20	❑❑❑❑❑
CM2017			
32¢ **Joshua Johnson**	.50	.20	❑❑❑❑❑
CM2018			
32¢ **William M. Harnett**	.50	.20	❑❑❑❑❑
CM2019			
32¢ **Winslow Homer**	.50	.20	❑❑❑❑❑
CM2020			
32¢ **George Catlin**	.50	.20	❑❑❑❑❑
CM2021			
32¢ **Thomas Moran**	.50	.20	❑❑❑❑❑
CM2022			
32¢ **Albert Bierstadt**	.50	.20	❑❑❑❑❑
CM2023			
32¢ **Frederic Edwin Church**	.50	.20	❑❑❑❑❑
CM2024			
32¢ **Mary Cassatt**	.50	.20	❑❑❑❑❑
CM2025			
32¢ **Edward Hopper**	.50	.20	❑❑❑❑❑

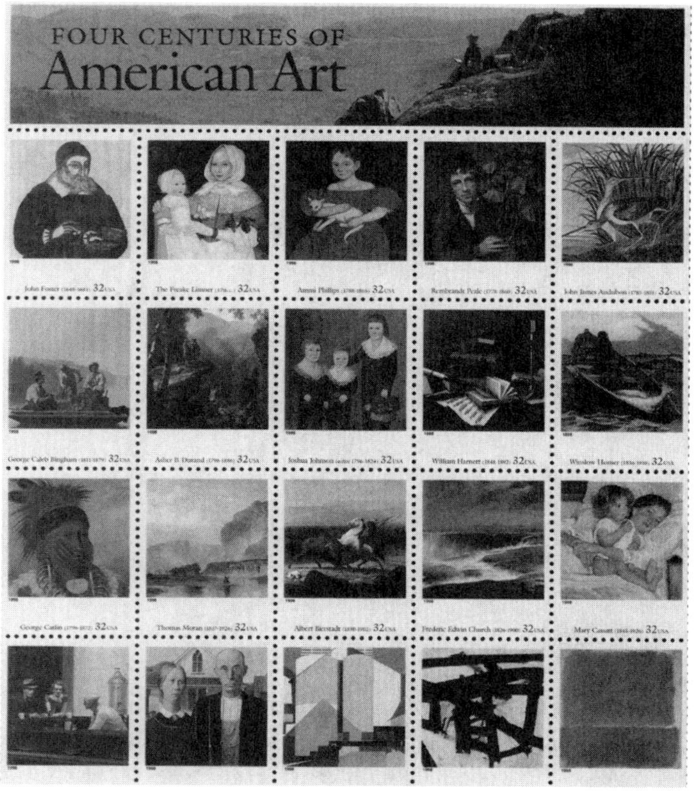

CM2010-2029

MNHFVF	UseFVF	
CM2026_____			
32¢ **Grant Wood**	.50	.20	☐☐☐☐☐
CM2027_____			
32¢ **Charles Sheeler**	.50	.20	☐☐☐☐☐
CM2028_____			
32¢ **Franny Kline**	.50	.20	☐☐☐☐☐
CM2029_____			
32¢ **Mark Rothko**	.50	.20	☐☐☐☐☐
CM2030_____ **1998. Celebrate the Century, 1930s Issue**			
$4.80 **Sheetlet of 15,** tagged	10.00	7.50	☐☐☐☐☐
CM2031_____ **1998. Ballet Issue**			
32¢ **multicolored**	.50	.20	☐☐☐☐☐
CM2032_____ **1998. Space Discovery Issue**			
32¢ **Land craft**	.50	.20	☐☐☐☐☐
CM2033_____			
32¢ **Space ship**	.50	.20	☐☐☐☐☐
CM2034_____			
32¢ **Figure**	.50	.20	☐☐☐☐☐
CM2035_____			
32¢ **Jagged hills**	.50	.20	☐☐☐☐☐
CM2036_____			
32¢ **Moon**	.50	.20	☐☐☐☐☐

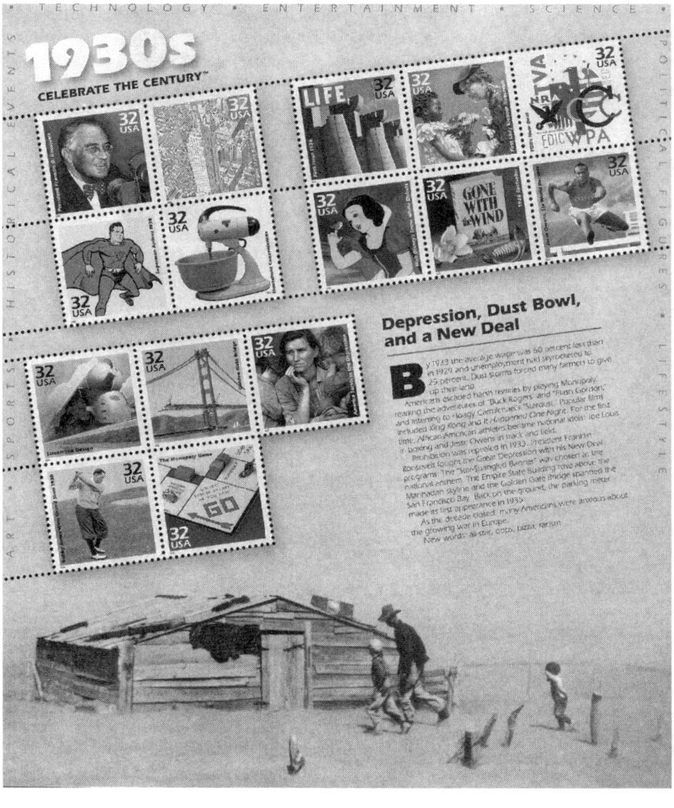

CM2030

MNHFVF	UseFVF	

CM2037_____ **1998. Giving & Sharing Issue**
32¢ **multicolored** .50 .20 ☐☐☐☐☐

CM2038_____ **1999. Year of the Hare Issue**
33¢ **multicolored** tagged .50 .20 ☐☐☐☐☐

CM2039_____ **1999. Malcolm X Issue**
33¢ **multicolored** .50 .20 ☐☐☐☐☐

CM2040_____ **1999. Victorian Hearts Issue**
33¢ **multicolored** .50 .20 ☐☐☐☐☐

CM2041_____ **1999. Victorian Hearts Issue**
55¢ **multicolored** .85 .25 ☐☐☐☐☐

CM2042_____ **1999. Hospice Care Issue**
33¢ **multicolored** phosphored paper .50 .20 ☐☐☐☐☐

CM2043_____ **1999. Celebrate the Century 1940s Issue**
$4.95 **Commemorative pane of 15, multicolored** tagged 10.00 7.50 ☐☐☐☐☐

CM2044_____ **1999. Irish Immigration Issue**
33¢ **multicolored** .50 .20 ☐☐☐☐☐

CM2045_____ **1999. Alfred Lunt and Lynn Fontanne Issue**
33¢ **multicolored** .50 .20 ☐☐☐☐☐

CM2046_____ **1999. Arctic Animals Issue**
33¢ **Arctic Hare, multicolored** .60 .20 ☐☐☐☐☐

CM2047_____
33¢ **Arctic Fox, multicolored** .60 .20 ☐☐☐☐☐

CM2048_____
33¢ **Snowy Owl, multicolored** .60 .20 ☐☐☐☐☐

CM2049_____
33¢ **Polar Bear, multicolored** .60 .20 ☐☐☐☐☐

CM2050_____
33¢ **Gray Wolf, multicolored** .60 .20 ☐☐☐☐☐

CM2031 ◀

CM2032-2036 ▶

CM2037

CM2038

CM2039

CM2040

CM2041

CM2042 ◀

MNHFVF	UseFVF	

CM2051_____ **1999. Sonoran Desert Issue**

$3.30 **multicolored Sheetlet of 10,** blocked tagged 7.50 3.00 ☐☐☐☐☐

CM2052_____ **1999. Daffy Duck Issue**

$3.30 **Pane of 10,** tagged 7.50 ☐☐☐☐☐

NOTE: This issue also was made available in top- and bottom-half printing sheets of six 10-stamp panes each. Vertical rouletting between the two panes is missing on these half sheets. A single plate number, trimmed away on individual panes, appears adjacent to the bottom-left pane in the bottom half of the printing sheet only.

CM2053_____ **1999. Daffy Duck Issue**

$3.30 **Pane of 10,** tagged 7.50 ☐☐☐☐☐

CM2054_____ **1999. Ayn Rand Issue**

33¢ **multicolored** .50 .20 ☐☐☐☐☐

CM2055_____ **1999. Cinco de Mayo Issue**

33¢ **multicolored** .50 .20 ☐☐☐☐☐

CM2043
←

CM2044

CM2045

CM2046-2050

CM2051

CM2054

CM2055

CM2056-2059

CM2052-2053

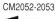

CM2060

MNHFVF	UseFVF

CM2056_____ **1999. Tropical Flowers Issue**
 33¢ **Bird of paradise, multicolored** .50 .20 ☐☐☐☐☐
CM2057_____
 33¢ **Royal poinciana, multicolored** .50 .20 ☐☐☐☐☐
CM2058_____
 33¢ **Gloriosa lily, multicolored** .50 .20 ☐☐☐☐☐
CM2059_____
 33¢ **Chinese hibiscus, multicolored** .50 .20 ☐☐☐☐☐
CM2060_____ **1999. John & William Bartram Issue**
 33¢ **multicolored** .60 .20 ☐☐☐☐☐
CM2061_____ **1999. Celebrate the Century 1950s Issue**
 $4.95 **Commemorative page of 15, multicolored** tagged 10.00 7.50 ☐☐☐☐☐
CM2062_____ **1999. Prostate Cancer Awareness Issue**
 33¢ **multicolored** .50 .20 ☐☐☐☐☐
CM2063_____ **1999. California Gold Rush Issue**
 33¢ **multicolored** .50 .20 ☐☐☐☐☐
CM2064_____ **1999. Aquarium Fish Issue**
 33¢ **Black-and-white fish** .50 .20 ☐☐☐☐☐
CM2065_____
 33¢ **Thermometer** .50 .20 ☐☐☐☐☐
CM2066_____
 33¢ **Blue-and-yellow fish** .50 .20 ☐☐☐☐☐

CM2061

CM2062

CM2063

MNHFVF	UseFVF	

CM2067_____
　　33¢ **red-and-white fish**　　　　　　　.50　　.20 ☐☐☐☐☐
NOTE: This issue was also made available in press sheets.
CM2068_____　**1999. Xtreme Sports Issue**
　　33¢ **Skateboarding**　　　　　　　　　.50　　.20 ☐☐☐☐☐
CM2069_____
　　33¢ **BMX biking**　　　　　　　　　　.50　　.20 ☐☐☐☐☐
CM2070_____
　　33¢ **Snowboarding**　　　　　　　　　.50　　.20 ☐☐☐☐☐
CM2071_____
　　33¢ **In-line skating**　　　　　　　　.50　　.20 ☐☐☐☐☐
CM2072_____　**1999. American Glass Issue**
　　33¢ **Freeblown glass**　　　　　　　　.50　　.20 ☐☐☐☐☐
CM2073_____
　　33¢ **Mold-blown glass**　　　　　　　.50　　.20 ☐☐☐☐☐
CM2074_____
　　33¢ **Pressed glass**　　　　　　　　　.50　　.20 ☐☐☐☐☐
CM2075_____
　　33¢ **Art glass**　　　　　　　　　　　.50　　.20 ☐☐☐☐☐
CM2076_____　**1999. James Cagney Issue**
　　33¢ **multicolored**　　　　　　　　　.50　　.20 ☐☐☐☐☐
CM2077_____　**1999. Honoring Those Who Served Issue**
　　33¢ **multicolored**　　　　　　　　　.50　　.20 ☐☐☐☐☐

CM2064-2067

CM2068-2071

CM2076

CM2072-2075

		MNHFVF	UseFVF	
CM2078	**1999. Universal Postal Union Issue**			
45¢ **multicolored**		.90	.40	❑❑❑❑❑
CM2079	**1999. All Aboard! Issue**			
33¢ **multicolored**		.50	.20	❑❑❑❑❑
CM2080				
33¢ **multicolored**		.50	.20	❑❑❑❑❑
CM2081				
33¢ **multicolored**		.50	.20	❑❑❑❑❑
CM2082				
33¢ **multicolored**		.50	.20	❑❑❑❑❑
CM2083				
33¢ **multicolored**		.50	.20	❑❑❑❑❑
CM2084	**1999. Frederic Law Olmsted Issue**			
33¢ **multicolored**		.50	.20	❑❑❑❑❑
CM2085	**1999. Hollywood Composers Issue**			
33¢ **multicolored**		.50	.20	❑❑❑❑❑
CM2086				
33¢ **multicolored**		.50	.20	❑❑❑❑❑
CM2087				
33¢ **multicolored**		.50	.20	❑❑❑❑❑
CM2088				
33¢ **multicolored**		.50	.20	❑❑❑❑❑
CM2089				
33¢ **multicolored**		.50	.20	❑❑❑❑❑
CM2090				
33¢ **multicolored**				❑❑❑❑❑
CM2091	**1999. Celebrate the Century 1960s Issue**			
$4.95 **Commemorative pane of 15, multicolored,** tagged		10.00	7.50	❑❑❑❑❑

CM2077

CM2078

CM2084

CM2085-2090

		MNHFVF	UseFVF	
CM2092	**1999. Broadway Songwriters Issue**			
	33¢ **multicolored**	.50	.20	❑❑❑❑❑
CM2093				
	33¢ **multicolored**	.50	.20	❑❑❑❑❑
CM2094				
	33¢ **multicolored**	.50	.20	❑❑❑❑❑
CM2095				
	33¢ **multicolored**	.50	.20	❑❑❑❑❑
CM2096				
	33¢ **multicolored**	.50	.20	❑❑❑❑❑
CM2097				
	33¢ **multicolored**	.50	.20	❑❑❑❑❑
CM2098	**1999. Insects and Spiders Issue**			
	33¢ **Pane of 20, multicolored**	10.00	.50	❑❑❑❑❑
CM2099	**1999. Hanukkah Issue**			
	33¢ **multicolored**	.50	.20	❑❑❑❑❑
CM2100	**1999. North Atlantic Treaty Organization Issue**			
	33¢ **multicolored**	.50	.20	❑❑❑❑❑
CM2101	**1999. Kwanzaa Issue**			
	33¢ **multicolored**	.50	.20	❑❑❑❑❑
CM2102	**1999. Celebrate the Century 1970s Issue**			
	$4.95 **Sheetlet of 15,** tagged	10.00	7.00	❑❑❑❑❑

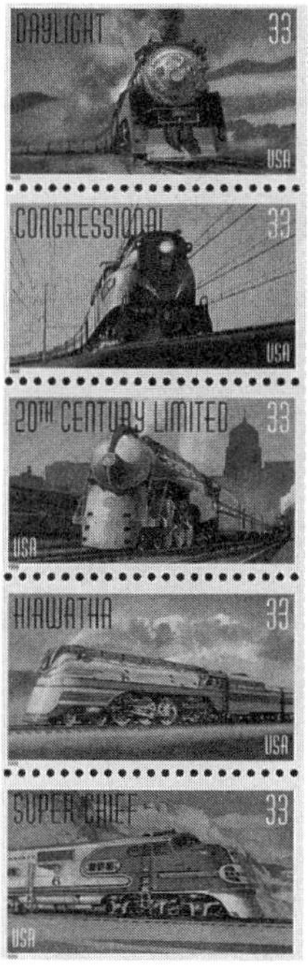

CM2079-2083

CM2091

		MNHFVF	UseFVF	
CM2103	**1999. Year 2000 Issue**			
	33¢ **multicolored**	.50	.20	❑❑❑❑❑
CM2104	**2000. Year of the Dragon Issue**			
	33¢ **multicolored**	.50	.20	❑❑❑❑❑
CM2105	**2000. Celebrate the Century 1980s Issue**			
	33¢ **Commemorative pane of 15, multicolored,** tagged	10.00	7.00	❑❑❑❑❑
CM2106	**2000. Patricia Roberts Harris Issue**			
	33¢ **multicolored**	.50	.20	❑❑❑❑❑
CM2107	**2000. U.S. Navy Submarines Issue**			
	60¢ **USS *Holland***	1.20	1.00	❑❑❑❑❑
CM2108				
	22¢ **S Class submarine**	.40	.30	❑❑❑❑❑
CM2109				
	$3.20 ***Gato*-class submarine**	6.00	2.50	❑❑❑❑❑
CM2110				
	33¢ ***Los Angeles*-class attack submarine**	.60	.30	❑❑❑❑❑
CM2111				
	55¢ **Ohio-*class ICBM submarine***	1.00	1.00	❑❑❑❑❑

NOTE: CM2111n was issued with two different descriptive texts.

		MNHFVF	UseFVF	
CM2112	**2000. Los Angeles Class Submarine Issue**			
	33¢ **multicolored**	.50	.20	❑❑❑❑❑
CM2113	**2000. Pacific Coast Rain Forest Issue**			
	33¢ **multicolored,** pane of 10	7.50	—	❑❑❑❑❑
CM2114	**2000. Louise Nevelson Issue**			
	33¢ **multicolored**	.50	.20	❑❑❑❑❑
CM2115				
	33¢ **multicolored**	.50	.20	❑❑❑❑❑

CM2092-2097

CM2099

CM2100

CM2101

CM2098

CM2103

CM2104

CM2102

CM2106

TECHNOLOGY • ENTERTAINMENT • SCIENCE
HISTORICAL EVENTS
POLITICAL FIGURES • LIFESTYLE
ART • SPORTS
1980s
CELEBRATE THE CENTURY®
33 USA
Space Shuttle Launched, Berlin Wall Falls
The space shuttle Columbia, the first reusable spacecraft, was originally launched April 12, 1981. Sandra Day O'Connor became the first female justice on the U.S. Supreme Court, and Sally Ride became the first American woman in space. The Iran-Contra hearings made headlines.
Several events signaled the easing of international tensions. In December 1987 President Ronald Reagan and Soviet leader Mikhail Gorbachev signed a nuclear arms reduction treaty. The fall of the Berlin Wall in November 1989 presaged the end of the Cold War.
The Vietnam Veterans Memorial was dedicated November 13, 1982. A new national holiday, Martin Luther King Day, was first celebrated in January 1986.
The growth of cable television, video games, and compact discs had a major impact on home entertainment. Dallas and The Cosby Show topped TV ratings. Hip-hop culture and music videos gained popularity.
New Words: yuppie, infomercial, biodiversity

CM2105

USS HOLLAND
USA 60
S CLASS
USA 22
GATO CLASS
USA $3.20
LOS ANGELES CLASS
USA 33
OHIO CLASS
USA 55

CM2107-2111

LOS ANGELES CLASS
USA 33

CM2112

	MNHFVF	UseFVF	
CM2116________			
33¢ **multicolored**	.50	.20	❑❑❑❑❑
CM2117________			
33¢ **multicolored**	.50	.20	❑❑❑❑❑
CM2118________			
33¢ **multicolored**	.50	.20	❑❑❑❑❑
CM2119________ **2000. Edwin Powell Hubble Issue**			
33¢ **Eagle Nebula**	.50	.20	❑❑❑❑❑
CM2120________			
33¢ **Ring Nebula**	.50	.20	❑❑❑❑❑
CM2121________			
33¢ **Lagoon Nebula**	.50	.20	❑❑❑❑❑
CM2122________			
33¢ **Egg Nebula**	.50	.20	❑❑❑❑❑
CM2123________			
33¢ **Galaxy NGC 1316**	.50	.20	❑❑❑❑❑

CM2113

CM2114-2118

		MNHFVF	UseFVF
CM2124	**2000. American Samoa Issue**		
33¢ **multicolored**		.50	.20 ❑❑❑❑❑
CM2125	**2000. Library of Congress Issue**		
33¢ **multicolored**		.50	.20 ❑❑❑❑❑
CM2126	**2000. Celebrate the Century 1990-1999 Issue**		
33¢ **Commemorative pane of 15, multicolored,** tagged		10.00	7.00 ❑❑❑❑❑
CM2127	**2000. Wile E. Coyote & Road Runner Issue**		
33¢ **multicolored**		7.50	❑❑❑❑❑
CM2128			
33¢ **multicolored**		7.50	❑❑❑❑❑

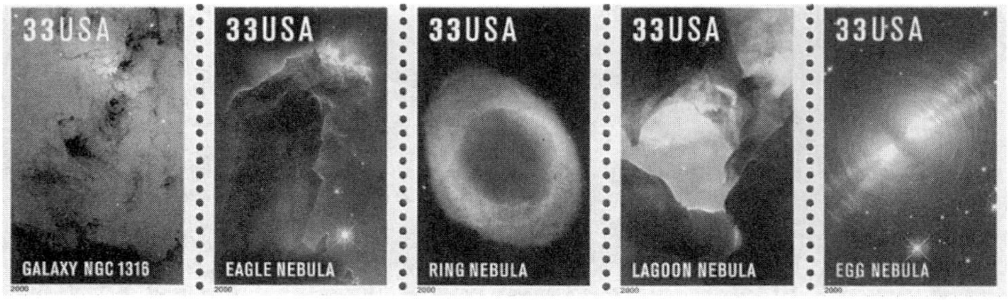

CM2119-2123

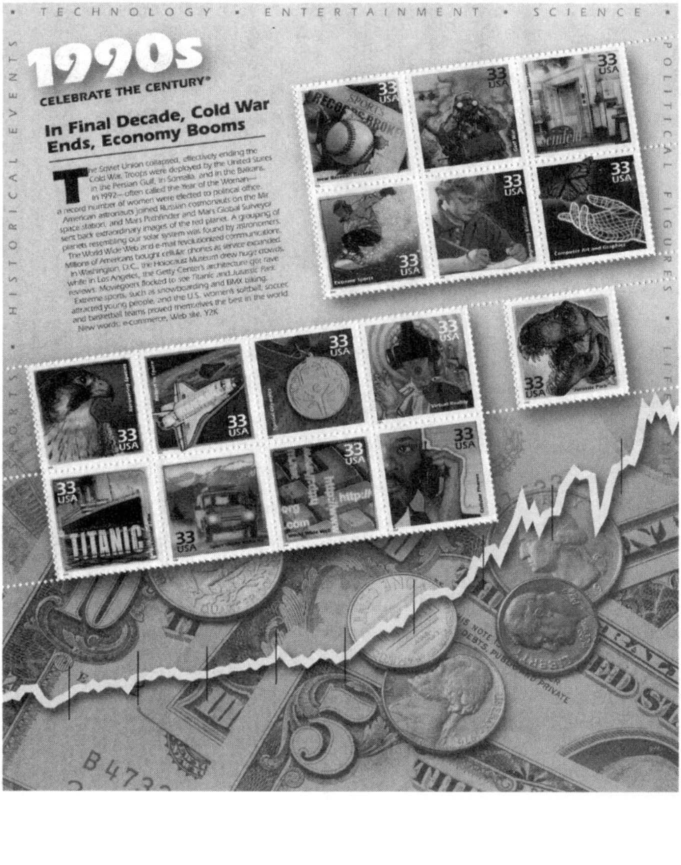

CM2124

CM2125

CM2126
←

		MNHFVF	UseFVF
CM2129__________	**2000. Distinguished Soldiers Issue**		
33¢ **multicolored**		.50	.20 ❑❑❑❑❑
CM2130__________			
33¢ **multicolored**		.50	.20 ❑❑❑❑❑
CM2131__________			
33¢ **multicolored**		.50	.20 ❑❑❑❑❑
CM2132__________			
33¢ **multicolored**		.50	.20 ❑❑❑❑❑
CM2133__________	**2000. Summer Sports Issue**		
33¢ **multicolored**		.50	.20 ❑❑❑❑❑
CM2134__________	**2000. Adoption Issue**		
33¢ **multicolored**		.50	.20 ❑❑❑❑❑
CM2135__________	**2000. Youth Team Sports Issue**		
33¢ **multicolored**		.50	.20 ❑❑❑❑❑
CM2136__________			
33¢ **multicolored**		.50	.20 ❑❑❑❑❑
CM2137__________			
33¢ **multicolored**		.50	.20 ❑❑❑❑❑
CM2138__________			
33¢ **multicolored**		.50	.20 ❑❑❑❑❑

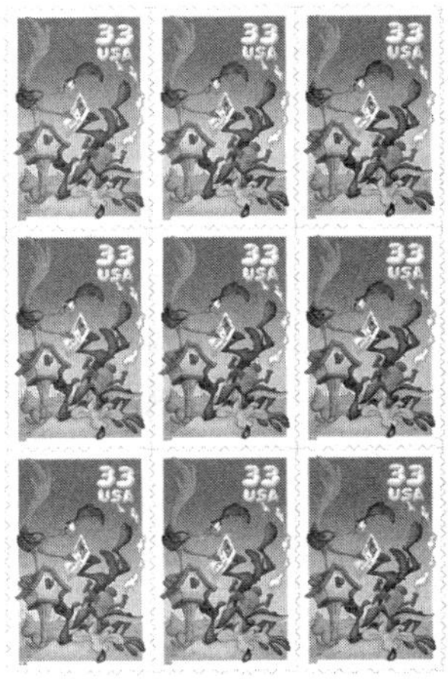

CM2127-2128

CM2133

CM2129-2132

CM2134

MNHFVF	UseFVF	
CM2139_____	**2000. Stars and Stripes Issue**			
33¢ **multicolored**		.50	.20	☐☐☐☐☐
CM2140_____				
33¢ **multicolored**		.50	.20	☐☐☐☐☐
CM2141_____				
33¢ **multicolored**		.50	.20	☐☐☐☐☐
CM2142_____				
33¢ **multicolored**		.50	.20	☐☐☐☐☐
CM2143_____				
33¢ **multicolored**		.50	.20	☐☐☐☐☐
CM2144_____				
33¢ **multicolored**		.50	.20	☐☐☐☐☐
CM2145_____				
33¢ **multicolored**		.50	.20	☐☐☐☐☐
CM2146_____				
33¢ **multicolored**		.50	.20	☐☐☐☐☐
CM2147_____				
33¢ **multicolored**		.50	.20	☐☐☐☐☐
CM2148_____				
33¢ **multicolored**		.50	.20	☐☐☐☐☐
CM2149_____				
33¢ **multicolored**		.50	.20	☐☐☐☐☐
CM2150_____				
33¢ **multicolored**		.50	.20	☐☐☐☐☐
CM2151_____				
33¢ **multicolored**		.50	.20	☐☐☐☐☐
CM2152_____				
33¢ **multicolored**		.50	.20	☐☐☐☐☐

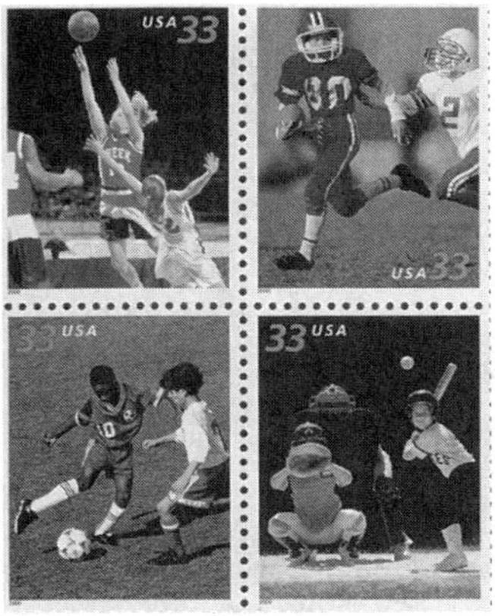

CM2135-2138

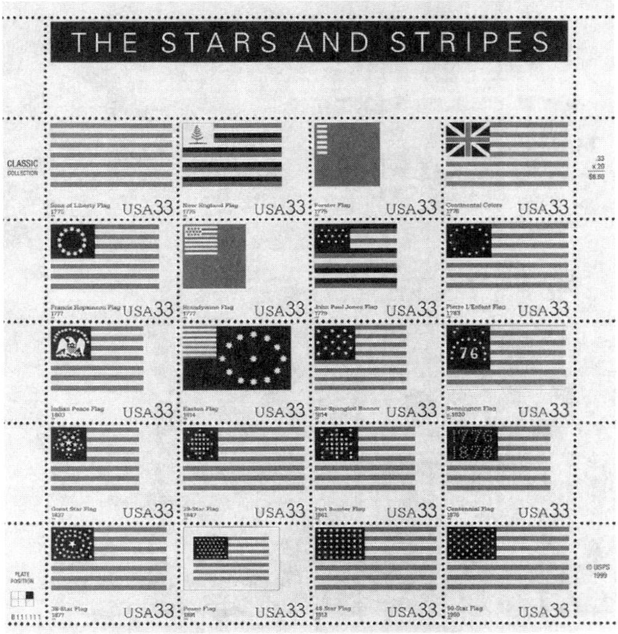

CM2139-2158

		MNHFVF	UseFVF	
CM2153				
33¢ **multicolored**		.50	.20	❑❑❑❑❑
CM2154				
33¢ **multicolored**		.50	.20	❑❑❑❑❑
CM2155				
33¢ **multicolored**		.50	.20	❑❑❑❑❑
CM2156				
33¢ **multicolored**		.50	.20	❑❑❑❑❑
CM2157				
33¢ **multicolored**		.50	.20	❑❑❑❑❑
CM2158				
33¢ **multicolored**		.50	.20	❑❑❑❑❑
CM2159	**2000. Legends of Baseball Issue**			
33¢ **multicolored**		.50	.20	❑❑❑❑❑
CM2160				
33¢ **multicolored**		.50	.20	❑❑❑❑❑
CM2161				
33¢ **multicolored**		.50	.20	❑❑❑❑❑

CM2159-2178

		MNHFVF	UseFVF	
CM2162				
33¢ **multicolored**		.50	.20	❑❑❑❑❑
CM2163				
33¢ **multicolored**		.50	.20	❑❑❑❑❑
CM2164				
33¢ **multicolored**		.50	.20	❑❑❑❑❑
CM2165				
33¢ **multicolored**		.50	.20	❑❑❑❑❑
CM2166				
33¢ **multicolored**		.50	.20	❑❑❑❑❑
CM2167				
33¢ **multicolored**		.50	.20	❑❑❑❑❑
CM2168				
33¢ **multicolored**		.50	.20	❑❑❑❑❑
CM2169				
33¢ **multicolored**		.50	.20	❑❑❑❑❑
CM2170				
33¢ **multicolored**		.50	.20	❑❑❑❑❑
CM2171				
33¢ **multicolored**		.50	.20	❑❑❑❑❑
CM2172				
33¢ **multicolored**		.50	.20	❑❑❑❑❑
CM2173				
33¢ **multicolored**		.50	.20	❑❑❑❑❑
CM2174				
33¢ **multicolored**		.50	.20	❑❑❑❑❑
CM2175				
33¢ **multicolored**		.50	.20	❑❑❑❑❑
CM2176				
33¢ **multicolored**		.50	.20	❑❑❑❑❑
CM2177				
33¢ **multicolored**		.50	.20	❑❑❑❑❑
CM2178				
33¢ **multicolored**		.50	.20	❑❑❑❑❑
CM2179	**2000. Space Achievement and Exploration Issue**			
$11.75 **multicolored**		22.00	10.00	❑❑❑❑❑
NOTE: The foil hologram is affixed with water-soluble adhesive and may release from the stamp while soaking.				
CM2180	**2000. Landing on the Moon Issue**			
$11.75 **multicolored**		22.00	10.00	❑❑❑❑❑
NOTE: The foil hologram is affixed with water-soluble adhesive and may release from the stamp while soaking.				
CM2181	**2000. Escaping the Gravity of Earth Issue**			
$3.20 **multicolored**		6.50	3.00	❑❑❑❑❑
NOTE: The foil holograms are affixed with water-soluble adhesive and may release from the stamps while soaking.				
CM2182				
$3.20 **multicolored**		6.50	3.00	❑❑❑❑❑
CM2183	**2000. Probing the Vastness of Space Issue**			
60¢ **multicolored**		1.10	.60	❑❑❑❑❑
CM2184				
60¢ **multicolored**		1.10	.60	❑❑❑❑❑
CM2185				
60¢ **multicolored**		1.10	.60	❑❑❑❑❑
CM2186				
60¢ **multicolored**		1.10	.60	❑❑❑❑❑
CM2187				
60¢ **multicolored**		1.10	.60	❑❑❑❑❑

CM2179

CM2180

CM2181-2182

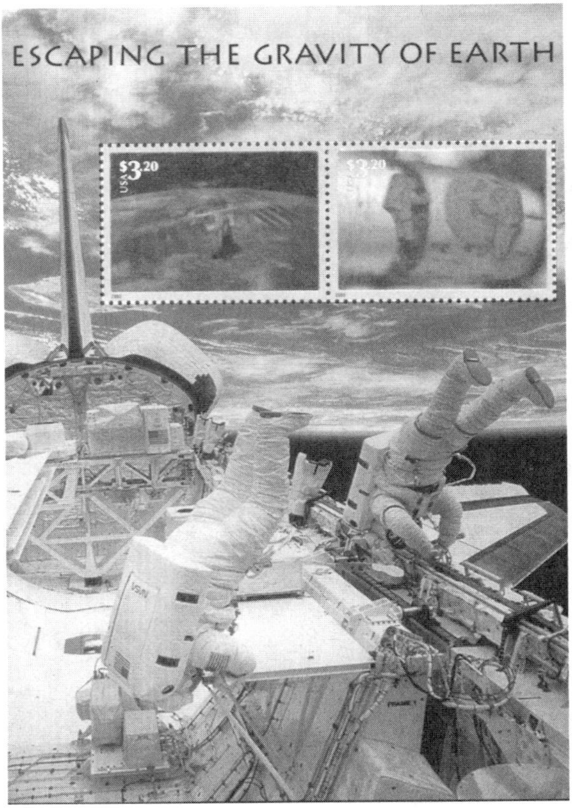

CM2183-2188

		MNHFVF	UseFVF	
CM2188	60¢ **multicolored**	1.10	.60	❑❑❑❑❑

2000. Exploring the Solar System Issue

		MNHFVF	UseFVF	
CM2189	$1 **multicolored**	2.00	1.00	❑❑❑❑❑
CM2190	$1 **multicolored**	2.00	1.00	❑❑❑❑❑
CM2191	$1 **multicolored**	2.00	1.00	❑❑❑❑❑
CM2192	$1 **multicolored**	2.00	1.00	❑❑❑❑❑
CM2193	$1 **multicolored**	2.00	1.00	❑❑❑❑❑

2000. Stampin' the Future Issue

		MNHFVF	UseFVF	
CM2194	33¢ **multicolored**	.50	.20	❑❑❑❑❑
CM2195	33¢ **multicolored**	.50	.20	❑❑❑❑❑
CM2196	33¢ **multicolored**	.50	.20	❑❑❑❑❑
CM2197	33¢ **multicolored**	.50	.20	❑❑❑❑❑

2000. California Statehood Issue

		MNHFVF	UseFVF	
CM2198	33¢ **multicolored**	.50	.20	❑❑❑❑❑

CM2189-2193

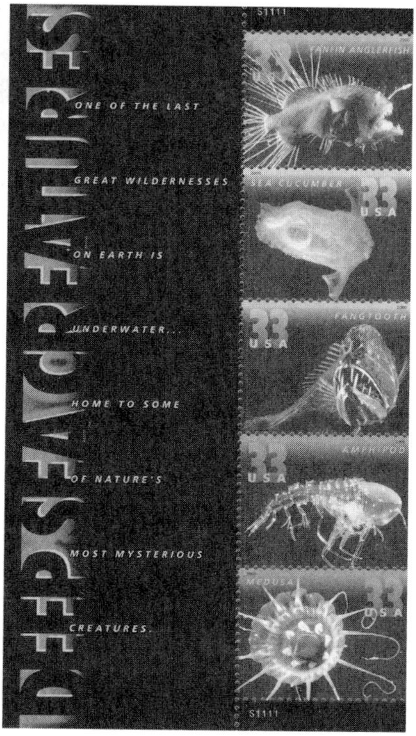

CM2199-2203

		MNHFVF	UseFVF	
CM2199 33¢ **Fanfin anglerfish**	**2000. Deep-Sea Creatures Issue**	.50	.20	❑❑❑❑❑
CM2200 33¢ **Sea cucumber**		.50	.20	❑❑❑❑❑
CM2201 33¢ **Fangtooth**		.50	.20	❑❑❑❑❑
CM2202 33¢ **Amphipod**		.50	.20	❑❑❑❑❑
CM2203 33¢ **Medusa**		.50	.20	❑❑❑❑❑
CM2204 33¢ **multicolored**	**2000. Thomas Wolfe Issue**	.50	.20	❑❑❑❑❑
CM2205 33¢ **multicolored**	**2000. The White House Issue**	.50	.20	❑❑❑❑❑
CM2206 33¢ **multicolored**	**2000. Edward G. Robinson Issue**	.50	.20	❑❑❑❑❑
CM2207 (34¢) **multicolored**	**2001. Rose and Love Letter Issue**	.70	.20	❑❑❑❑❑
CM2208 34¢ **multicolored**	**2001. Year of the Snake Issue**	.75	.25	❑❑❑❑❑
CM2209 34¢ **multicolored**	**2001. Roy Wilkins Issue**	.75	.25	❑❑❑❑❑

CM2194-2197

CM2206 →

← CM2198

CM2204

CM2205

CM2208 →

CM2209

CM2207

CM2230

CM2231

CM2232 (CM2271 is 57¢)

	MNHFVF	UseFVF
CM2210 **2001. American Illustrators Issue**		
34¢ **multicolored,** tagged (single)	.75	.25 ❑❑❑❑❑
CM2211		
34¢ **multicolored,** tagged (single)	.75	.25 ❑❑❑❑❑
CM2212		
34¢ **multicolored,** tagged (single)	.75	.25 ❑❑❑❑❑
CM2213		
34¢ **multicolored,** tagged (single)	.75	.25 ❑❑❑❑❑
CM2214		
34¢ **multicolored,** tagged (single)	.75	.25 ❑❑❑❑❑
CM2215		
34¢ **multicolored,** tagged (single)	.75	.25 ❑❑❑❑❑
CM2216		
34¢ **multicolored,** tagged (single)	.75	.25 ❑❑❑❑❑
CM2217		
34¢ **multicolored,** tagged (single)	.75	.25 ❑❑❑❑❑
CM2218		
34¢ **multicolored,** tagged (single)	.75	.25 ❑❑❑❑❑

CM2210-2229

MNHFVF	UseFVF	

CM2219_____
34¢ **multicolored,** tagged (single) — .75 .25 ☐☐☐☐☐

CM2220_____
34¢ **multicolored,** tagged (single) — .75 .25 ☐☐☐☐☐

CM2221_____
34¢ **multicolored,** tagged (single) — .75 .25 ☐☐☐☐☐

CM2222_____
34¢ **multicolored,** tagged (single) — .75 .25 ☐☐☐☐☐

CM2223_____
34¢ **multicolored,** tagged (single) — .75 .25 ☐☐☐☐☐

CM2224_____
34¢ **multicolored,** tagged (single) — .75 .25 ☐☐☐☐☐

CM2225_____
34¢ **multicolored,** tagged (single) — .75 .25 ☐☐☐☐☐

CM2226_____
34¢ **multicolored,** tagged (single) — .75 .25 ☐☐☐☐☐

CM2227_____
34¢ **multicolored,** tagged (single) — .75 .25 ☐☐☐☐☐

CM2228_____
34¢ **multicolored,** tagged (single) — .75 .25 ☐☐☐☐☐

CM2229_____
34¢ **multicolored,** tagged (single) — .75 .25 ☐☐☐☐☐

CM2230_____ **2001. Rose and Love Letter Issue**
34¢ **multicolored** — .70 .20 ☐☐☐☐☐

CM2231_____
34¢ **multicolored** — .70 .20 ☐☐☐☐☐

CM2232_____
55¢ **multicolored** — 1.00 .40 ☐☐☐☐☐

CM2233_____ **2001. Diabetes Issue**
34¢ **multicolored** — .70 .20 ☐☐☐☐☐

CM2234_____ **2001. Nobel Prize Centennial Issue**
34¢ **multicolored** — .65 .20 ☐☐☐☐☐

CM2235_____ **2001. Pan-American Exposition Centennial Issue**
1¢ **green & black** — .20 .20 ☐☐☐☐☐

CM2236_____
2¢ **carmine & black** — .20 .20 ☐☐☐☐☐

CM2237_____
4¢ **red brown & black** — .20 .20 ☐☐☐☐☐

CM2238_____
80¢ **red & blue** — 1.60 .40 ☐☐☐☐☐

CM2239_____ **2001. Great Plains Prairie Issue**
34¢ **multicolored,** — .65 .20 ☐☐☐☐☐

CM2240_____ **2001. Peanuts Issue**
34¢ **multicolored** — .65 .30 ☐☐☐☐☐

CM2241_____ **2001. Veterans Continuing To Serve Issue**
34¢ **multicolored** — .65 .20 ☐☐☐☐☐

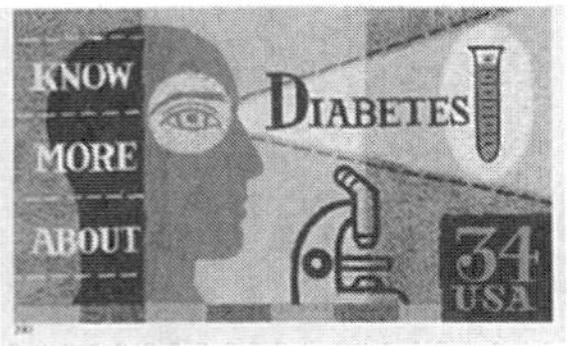

CM2233

CM2234

CM2240

CM2235-2238

CM2243-2252

CM2239

Stamp	Description	Issue	MNHFVF	UseFVF	
CM2242	34¢ **multicolored**	**2001. Frida Kahlo Issue**	.65	.20	□□□□□
CM2243	34¢ **multicolored**	**2001. Baseball's Legendary Playing Fields Issue**	.65	.20	□□□□□
CM2244	34¢ **multicolored**		.65	.20	□□□□□
CM2245	34¢ **multicolored**		.65	.20	□□□□□
CM2246	34¢ **multicolored**		.65	.20	□□□□□
CM2247	34¢ **multicolored**		.65	.20	□□□□□
CM2248	34¢ **multicolored**		.65	.20	□□□□□
CM2249	34¢ **multicolored**		.65	.20	□□□□□
CM2250	34¢ **multicolored**		.65	.20	□□□□□
CM2251	34¢ **multicolored**		.65	.20	□□□□□
CM2252	34¢ **multicolored**		.65	.20	□□□□□
CM2253	34¢ **multicolored**	**2001. Leonard Bernstein Issue**	.65	.20	□□□□□
CM2254	34¢ **multicolored**	**2001. Lucille Ball Issue**	.65	.20	□□□□□
CM2255	34¢ **multicolored**	**2001. Amish Quilts Issue**	.65	.20	□□□□□

CM2241

CM2242

CM2253

CM2254

CM2255-2258

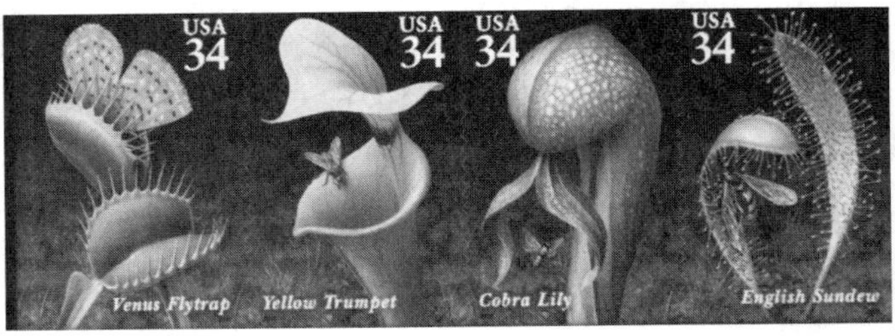

CM2259-2262

Number	Description	Issue	MNHFVF	UseFVF
CM2256	34¢ multicolored		.65	.20
CM2257	34¢ multicolored		.65	.20
CM2258	34¢ multicolored		.65	.20
CM2259	34¢ multicolored	2001. Carnivorous Plants Issue	.65	.20
CM2260	34¢ multicolored		.65	.20
CM2261	34¢ multicolored		.65	.20
CM2262	34¢ multicolored		.65	.20
CM2263	34¢ blue & gold	2001. Eid Issue	.65	.20
CM2264	34¢ multicolored	2001. Enrico Fermi Issue	.65	.20
CM2265	34¢ multicolored	2001. Porky Pig ("That's all, folks")	.65	.20
CM2266	34¢ multicolored	2001. Porky Pig ("That's all, folks" Special Die Cut Issue)	.65	.20
CM2267	34¢ multicolored	2001. James Madison Issue	.65	.20

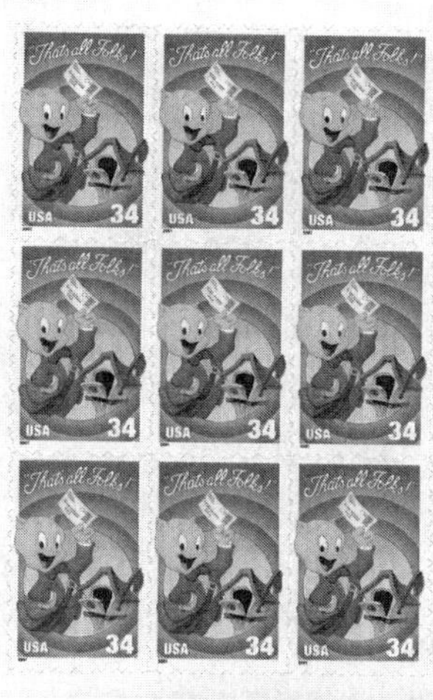

CM2265-2266

CM2263

CM2264

CM2267

CM2268

CM2269

MNHFVF	UseFVF	

CM2268_____ **2001. We Give Thanks Issue**
 34¢ **multicolored** .65 .20 ☐☐☐☐☐
CM2269_____ **2001. Hanukkah Issue**
 34¢ **multicolored** .65 .20 ☐☐☐☐☐
CM2270_____ **2001. Kwanzaa Issue**
 34¢ **multicolored** 1.20 .30 ☐☐☐☐☐
CM2271_____ **2001. Love Letter Issue**
 57¢ **multicolored** .65 .20 ☐☐☐☐☐
CM2272_____ **2002. Winter Sports Issue**
 34¢ **multicolored** .65 .20 ☐☐☐☐☐
CM2273_____
 34¢ **multicolored** .65 .20 ☐☐☐☐☐
CM2274_____
 34¢ **multicolored** .65 .20 ☐☐☐☐☐
CM2275_____
 34¢ **multicolored** .65 .20 ☐☐☐☐☐
CM2276_____ **2002. Mentoring a Child Issue**
 34¢ **multicolored** .65 .20 ☐☐☐☐☐
CM2277_____ **2002. Year of the Horse Issue**
 34¢ **multicolored** .65 .20 ☐☐☐☐☐
CM2278_____ **2002. Langston Hughes Issue**
 34¢ **multicolored** .65 .20 ☐☐☐☐☐
CM2279_____ **2002. Happy Birthday Issue**
 34¢ **multicolored** .65 .20 ☐☐☐☐☐

CM2270

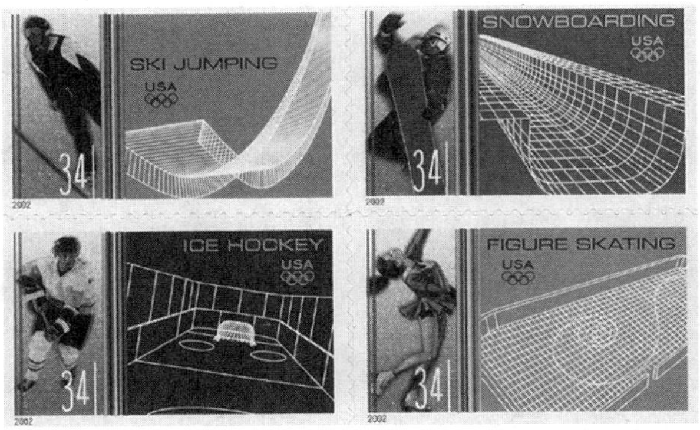

CM2272-2275

CM2276

CM2277

CM2278

CM2279

UnFVF UseFVF

Airmail

A1 ______ **1918. Curtiss Biplane Issue**

6¢ **red orange** (3,395,854) 75.00 30.00 ❑❑❑❑❑

A2 ______

16¢ **green** (3,793,887) 90.00 40.00 ❑❑❑❑❑

A3 ______

24¢ **carmine red & blue** (2,134,888) 90.00 45.00 ❑❑❑❑❑

NOTE: One sheet of 100 stamps with the blue vignette of the airplane upside down was purchased in a post office at Washington, D.C., by William T. Robey, who sold it to Eugene Klein of Philadelphia, who in turn sold it to Col. Edward H.R. Green. Green retained some of the errors, including the position pieces, and through Klein disposed of the rest. No. A3v is one of the most famous post office finds in U.S. stamp history.

A4 ______ **1923. The Second Airmail Series Issue**

8¢ **green** (6,414,576) 25.00 15.00 ❑❑❑❑❑

A5 ______

16¢ **indigo** (5,309,275) 85.00 30.00 ❑❑❑❑❑

A6 ______

24¢ **carmine** (5,285,775) 95.00 30.00 ❑❑❑❑❑

A7 ______ **1926-27. Map Issue**

10¢ **blue** (42,092,800) 3.00 .45 ❑❑❑❑❑

A8 ______

15¢ **olive brown** (15,597,307) 3.75 2.50 ❑❑❑❑❑

A9 ______

20¢ **yellow green** (17,616,350) 9.00 2.00 ❑❑❑❑❑

A10 ______ **1927. Lindbergh Airmail Issue**

10¢ **indigo** (20,379,179) 8.00 2.00 ❑❑❑❑❑

NOTE: First-day covers for No. A10 are from Washington, D.C., Little Falls, Minn. (where Lindbergh grew up), St. Louis, Mo., and Detroit, Mich. (his birthplace). FDCs for No. A10n are from Washington, D.C., and Cleveland, Ohio.

A11 ______ **1928. Air Mail Beacon Issue**

5¢ **carmine red & blue** (106,887,675) 4.50 .75 ❑❑❑❑❑

A12 ______ **1930. Winged Globe Issue**

5¢ **purple** (97,641,200) 10.00 .50 ❑❑❑❑❑

A13 ______ **1930. Graf Zeppelin Issue**

65¢ **green** (93,536) 325.00 240.00 ❑❑❑❑❑

A14 ______

$1.30 **yellow brown** (72,428) 650.00 450.00 ❑❑❑❑❑

A15 ______

$2.60 **blue** (61,296) 975.00 700.00 ❑❑❑❑❑

A16 ______ **1931-34. Winged Globe Issue**

5¢ **reddish violet** (57,340,000) 5.50 .60 ❑❑❑❑❑

A17 ______

6¢ **orange** (302,205,100) 2.50 .35 ❑❑❑❑❑

A18 ______

8¢ **yellow olive** (76,648,803) 2.50 .35 ❑❑❑❑❑

A19 ______ **1933. Century of Progress Zeppelin Issue**

50¢ **green** (324,070) 90.00 75.00 ❑❑❑❑❑

A20 ______ **1935-37. China Clipper Over Pacific Issue**

20¢ **green** (12,794,600) 10.00 1.50 ❑❑❑❑❑

A21 ______

25¢ **blue** (10,205,400) 1.50 1.00 ❑❑❑❑❑

A22 ______

50¢ **carmine** (9,285,300) 10.00 4.50 ❑❑❑❑❑

A23 ______ **1938. Eagle and Shield Issue**

6¢ **indigo & carmine** (349,946,500) .50 .20 ❑❑❑❑❑

A1

A2

A3

A3v

A4

A5

A6

A7-A9

A10

A11

A12

A13

A14

A15

A16-A18

A19

A33-A34

A20

A23

A24

A25

A32

A35

		UnFVF	UseFVF
A24 ______	**1939. Transatlantic Issue**		
30¢	**slate blue** (19,768,150)	9.00	1.50 ❑❑❑❑❑
		MNHFVF	UseFVF
A25 ______			
6¢	**rose red** (4,746,527,700)	.25	.20 ❑❑❑❑❑
A26 ______			
8¢	**light olive green** (1,744,878,650)	.30	.20 ❑❑❑❑❑
A27 ______			
10¢	**violet** (67,117,400)	1.40	.20 ❑❑❑❑❑
A28 ______			
15¢	**brown carmine** (78,434,800)	2.75	.40 ❑❑❑❑❑
A29 ______			
20¢	**emerald** (42,359,850)	2.75	.40 ❑❑❑❑❑
A30 ______			
30¢	**light blue** (59,880,850)	2.75	.50 ❑❑❑❑❑
A31 ______			
50¢	**orange** (11,160,600)	14.00	4.00 ❑❑❑❑❑
A32 ______	**1946. Skymaster Issue**		
5¢	**carmine** (864,753,100)	.25	.20 ❑❑❑❑❑
A33 ______	**1947. Small 5¢ Skymaster Issue**		
5¢	**carmine** (971,903,700)	.25	.20 ❑❑❑❑❑
A34 ______	**1947. Small 5¢ Skymaster Coil Issue**		
5¢	**carmine** (33,244,500)	1.00	1.00 ❑❑❑❑❑
A35 ______	**1947. Pictorial Airmail Issue**		
10¢	**black** (207,976,550)	.40	.20 ❑❑❑❑❑
A36 ______			
15¢	**blue green** (756,186,350)	.50	.20 ❑❑❑❑❑
A37 ______			
25¢	**blue** (132,956,100)	1.25	.20 ❑❑❑❑❑
A38 ______	**1948. New York City Issue**		
5¢	**carmine red** (38,449,100)	.25	.20 ❑❑❑❑❑
A39 ______	**1949. Small 6¢ Skymaster Issue**		
6¢	**carmine** (5,070,095,200)	.25	.20 ❑❑❑❑❑
A40 ______	**1949. Small 6¢ Skymaster Coil Issue**		
6¢	**carmine**	3.50	.20 ❑❑❑❑❑
A41 ______	**1949. Alexandria Bicentennial Issue**		
6¢	**carmine** (75,085,000)	.20	.20 ❑❑❑❑❑
A42 ______	**1949. Universal Postal Union Issue**		
10¢	**violet** (21,061,300)	.40	.30 ❑❑❑❑❑
A43 ______			
15¢	**cobalt** (36,613,100)	.50	.40 ❑❑❑❑❑
A44 ______			
25¢	**carmine** (16,217,100)	.85	.60 ❑❑❑❑❑
A45 ______	**1949. Wright Brothers Issue**		
6¢	**carmine purple** (80,405,000)	.30	.20 ❑❑❑❑❑
A46 ______	**1952. Hawaii Airmail Issue**		
80¢	**bright purple** (18,876,800)	6.00	1.50 ❑❑❑❑❑
A47 ______	**1953. Powered Flight Issue**		
6¢	**carmine** (78,415,000)	.25	.20 ❑❑❑❑❑
A48 ______	**1954. Eagle Issue**		
4¢	**blue** (40,483,600)	.25	.20 ❑❑❑❑❑
A49 ______	**1957. Air Force Issue**		
6¢	**bright Prussian blue** (63,185,000)	.25	.20 ❑❑❑❑❑

A36

A37

A38

A39-A40

A41

A42

A43

A44

A45

A46

A47

A48, 50

A49

A51-A52, A60-A61

A53

A54

A55

A56

A57

A58

A59

A62

A63

		MNHFVF	UseFVF	
A50 ______________	**1958. Eagle Issue**			
5¢	**carmine red** (72,480,000)	.25	.20	❑❑❑❑❑
A51 ______________	**1958. Jet Silhouette Issue**			
7¢	**blue** (1,326,960,000)	.25	.20	❑❑❑❑❑
A52 ______________	**1958. Jet Silhouette Coil Issue**			
7¢	**blue** (157,035,000)	2.00	.20	❑❑❑❑❑
A53 ______________	**1959. Alaska Statehood Issue**			
7¢	**deep blue** (90,055,200)	.30	.20	❑❑❑❑❑
A54 ______________	**1959. Balloon Jupiter Issue**			
7¢	**deep blue & scarlet** (79,290,000)	.30	.20	❑❑❑❑❑
A55 ______________	**1959. Pan American Games Issue**			
10¢	**deep blue & scarlet** (38,770,000)	.35	.30	❑❑❑❑❑
A56 ______________	**1959. Hawaii Statehood Issue**			
7¢	**dull scarlet** (84,815,000)	.30	.20	❑❑❑❑❑
A57 ______________	**1960. Liberty Bell Issue**			
10¢	**black & green** (39,960,000)	1.75	.80	❑❑❑❑❑
A58 ______________	**1959. Statue of Liberty Issue**			
15¢	**black & orange** (98,160,000)	.50	.20	❑❑❑❑❑
A59 ______________	**1966. Abraham Lincoln Issue**			
25¢	**black & brown purple**	.75	.20	❑❑❑❑❑
A60 ______________	**1960. Jet Silhouette Issue**			
7¢	**bright red** (1,289,460,000)	.25	.20	❑❑❑❑❑
A61 ______________	**1960. Jet Silhouette Coil Issue**			
7¢	**bright red** (87,140,000)	4.50	.40	❑❑❑❑❑
A62 ______________	**1961. Statue of Liberty Issue**			
15¢	**black & orange**	.50	.20	❑❑❑❑❑
A63 ______________	**1961. Liberty Bell Issue**			
13¢	**black & scarlet**	.50	.20	❑❑❑❑❑
A64 ______________	**1962. Airliner Over Capitol Issue**			
8¢	**carmine**	.30	.20	❑❑❑❑❑

NOTE: Type I tagging: mat tagging, using four separate mats that did not cover entire sheet of 400 stamps (untagged areas identify the variety). Stamps from the four corners of a pane have two untagged margins.

Type II tagging: roll tagging, where continuous rolls replaced the tagging mats. Only the plate number selvage margin is partially tagged.

		MNHFVF	UseFVF	
A65 ______________	**1962. Airliner Over Capitol Coil Issue**			
8¢	**carmine**	.60	.20	❑❑❑❑❑
A66 ______________	**1963. Montgomery Blair Issue**			
15¢	**red, maroon & blue** (42,245,000)	.75	.60	❑❑❑❑❑
A67 ______________	**1963. Bald Eagle Issue**			
6¢	**carmine**	.25	.20	❑❑❑❑❑
A68 ______________	**1963. Amelia Earhart Issue**			
8¢	**carmine red & brown purple** (63,890,000)	.35	.20	❑❑❑❑❑
A69 ______________	**1964. Robert H. Goddard Issue**			
8¢	**multicolored** (65,170,000)	.45	.20	❑❑❑❑❑
A70 ______________	**1967. Alaska Purchase Issue**			
8¢	**brown & light brown** (64,710,000)	.40	.20	❑❑❑❑❑
A71 ______________	**1967. Columbia Jays Issue**			
20¢	**blue, brown & yellow,** tagged (165,430,000)	1.25	.20	❑❑❑❑❑
A72 ______________	**1968. Star Runway Issue**			
10¢	**red** tagged	.40	.20	❑❑❑❑❑
A73 ______________	**1968. Star Runway Coil Issue**			
10¢	**red**	.40	.20	❑❑❑❑❑
A74 ______________	**1968. Airmail Service Issue**			
10¢	**black, red & blue** (74,180,000)	.40	.20	❑❑❑❑❑

A64-A65

A66

A67

A68

A69

A70

A71

A72-A73

A74

A75 (A81 has "21¢")

A76

A77

A78-A79

A80

A82

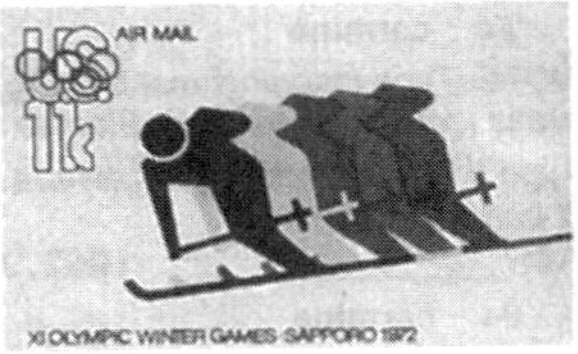

A83

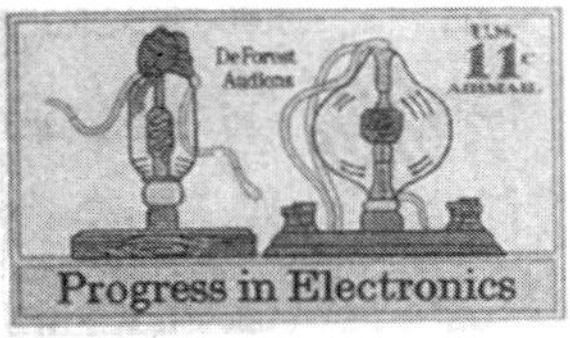

A84

A85, A86

A87

A88

A89

A90

		MNHFVF	UseFVF	
A75 ______________	**1968. USA and Jet Issue**			
	20¢ **multicolored**	.75	.20	❑❑❑❑❑
A76 ______________	**1969. Moon Landing Issue**			
	10¢ **multicolored** (152,364,800)	.40	.20	❑❑❑❑❑

NOTE: No. A76v must have missing red from the entire design, including the dots on top of the yellow area as well as the astronaut's shoulder patch. Stamps with any red present are worth far less than the true red-omitted error.

		MNHFVF	UseFVF	
A77 ______________	**1971. Delta Wing Silhouette Issue**			
	9¢ **red** (25,830,000)	.30	.20	❑❑❑❑❑
A78 ______________	**1971. Jet Silhouette Issue**			
	11¢ **red** tagged (317,810,000)	.40	.20	❑❑❑❑❑
A79 ______________	**1971. Jet Silhouette Coil Issue**			
	11¢ **red**	.40	.20	❑❑❑❑❑
A80 ______________	**1971. Head of Liberty Issue**			
	17¢ **multicolored** tagged	.60	.20	❑❑❑❑❑
A81 ______________	**1971. Jet and "USA" Issue**			
	21¢ **multicolored** tagged (49,815,000)	.75	.20	❑❑❑❑❑
A82 ______________	**1972. National Park Issue**			
	11¢ **multicolored** (78,210,000)	.35	.20	❑❑❑❑❑
A83 ______________	**1972. Olympic Issue**			
	11¢ **multicolored** (92,710,000)	.40	.20	❑❑❑❑❑
A84 ______________	**1973. Progress in Electronics Issue**			
	11¢ **multicolored** tagged (56,000,000)	.30	.20	❑❑❑❑❑
A85 ______________	**1973. Winged Envelope Issue**			
	13¢ **red** tagged	.40	.20	❑❑❑❑❑
A86 ______________	**1973. Winged Envelope Coil Issue**			
	13¢ **red**	.50	.20	❑❑❑❑❑
A87 ______________	**1974. Statue of Liberty Issue**			
	18¢ **multicolored** tagged	.60	.50	❑❑❑❑❑
A88 ______________	**1974. Mount Rushmore Issue**			
	26¢ **multicolored** tagged	.75	.20	❑❑❑❑❑
A89 ______________	**1976. Plane and Globes Issue**			
	25¢ **multicolored** tagged	.75	.20	❑❑❑❑❑
A90 ______________				
	31¢ **multicolored** tagged	.90	.20	❑❑❑❑❑
A91 ______________	**1978. Orville and Wilbur Wright Issue**			
	31¢ **multicolored large portraits & biplane**	1.75	1.50	❑❑❑❑❑
A92 ______________				
	31¢ **multicolored, small portraits, biplane and hangar**	1.75	1.50	❑❑❑❑❑
A93 ______________	**1978. Octave Chanute Issue**			
	21¢ **multicolored, large portrait**	1.75	1.50	❑❑❑❑❑
A94 ______________				
	21¢ **multicolored, small portrait**	1.75	1.50	❑❑❑❑❑
A95 ______________	**1979. High Jumper Issue**			
	31¢ **multicolored** tagged	1.00	.35	❑❑❑❑❑
A96 ______________	**1979. Wiley Post Issue**			
	25¢ **multicolored, large portrait,** tagged	3.00	2.00	❑❑❑❑❑
A97 ______________				
	25¢ **multicolored, small portrait,** tagged	3.00	2.00	❑❑❑❑❑
A98 ______________	**1982. Philip Mazzei Issue**			
	40¢ **multicolored** tagged	1.25	.25	❑❑❑❑❑
A99 ______________	**1980. Blanche Stuart Scott Issue**			
	28¢ **multicolored** tagged	.90	.25	❑❑❑❑❑
A100 ______________	**1980. Glenn Curtiss Issue**			
	35¢ **multicolored** tagged	1.00	.25	❑❑❑❑❑

A91, A92

A93, A94

A95

A99

A96, A97

A98

A100

A101, A102, A103, A104

A105, A106, A107, A108

A109, A110, A111, A112

A113

A114

A115

A116

A117

A118

		MNHFVF	UseFVF	
A101	**1983. Olympic Issues**			
	40¢ **Men's shot put,** tagged	1.25	.25	❑❑❑❑❑
A102				
	40¢ **Men's gymnastics,** tagged	1.25	.25	❑❑❑❑❑
A103				
	40¢ **Women's swimming,** tagged	1.25	.25	❑❑❑❑❑
A104				
	40¢ **Men's weight lifting,** tagged	1.25	.25	❑❑❑❑❑
A105	**1983. Olympics Second Issue**			
	28¢ **Women's gymnastics,** tagged	1.25	.25	❑❑❑❑❑
A106				
	28¢ **Men's hurdles,** tagged	1.25	.25	❑❑❑❑❑
A107				
	28¢ **Women's basketball,** tagged	1.25	.25	❑❑❑❑❑
A108				
	28¢ **Soccer,** tagged	1.25	.25	❑❑❑❑❑
A109	**1983. Olympics Third Issue**			
	35¢ **Fencing,** tagged	1.25	.25	❑❑❑❑❑
A110				
	35¢ **Cycling,** tagged	1.25	.25	❑❑❑❑❑
A111				
	35¢ **Women's volleyball,** tagged	1.25	.25	❑❑❑❑❑
A112				
	35¢ **Pole vaulting,** tagged	1.25	.25	❑❑❑❑❑
A113	**1985. Alfred V. Verville Issue**			
	33¢ **multicolored** tagged	1.00	.30	❑❑❑❑❑
A114	**1985. Lawrence and Elmer Sperry Issue**			
	39¢ **multicolored** tagged	1.25	.40	❑❑❑❑❑
A115	**1986. Transpacific Airmail Issue**			
	44¢ **multicolored** tagged	1.25	.40	❑❑❑❑❑
A116	**1985. Junipero Serra Issue**			
	44¢ **multicolored** tagged	1.75	.60	❑❑❑❑❑
A117	**1988. Settlement of New Sweden Issue**			
	44¢ **multicolored** tagged (22,975,000)	1.40	.50	❑❑❑❑❑
A118	**1988. Samuel P. Langley Issue**			
	45¢ **multicolored** tagged	1.40	.30	❑❑❑❑❑
A119	**1988. Igor Sikorsky Issue**			
	36¢ **multicolored** tagged	1.25	.40	❑❑❑❑❑
	NOTE: Traces of red have been detected in all copies of a so-called "red-omitted" error of this stamp. Such stamps, on which even minute traces of red are present, are worth far less than a genuine color-omitted error would be.			
A120	**1989. French Revolution Bicentennial Issue**			
	45¢ **multicolored** tagged (38,532,000)	1.40	.40	❑❑❑❑❑
A121	**1989. America Issue**			
	45¢ **multicolored** tagged (39,325,000)	1.50	.30	❑❑❑❑❑
A122	**1989. Future Mail Transportation Souvenir Sheet**			
	$1.80 **multicolored,** souvenir sheet, tagged (1,944,000)	7.00	5.00	❑❑❑❑❑
A123	**1989. Future Mail Transportation Issue**			
	45¢ **Hypersonic airliner,** tagged	1.25	.25	❑❑❑❑❑
A124				
	45¢ **Hovercraft,** tagged	1.25	.25	❑❑❑❑❑
A125				
	45¢ **Service rover,** tagged	1.25	.25	❑❑❑❑❑
A126				
	45¢ **Space Shuttle,** tagged	1.25	.25	❑❑❑❑❑

		MNHFVF	UseFVF	
A127 ____________	**1990. America Issue**			
45¢ **multicolored** tagged		1.50	.50	❑❑❑❑❑
A128 ____________	**1991. Harriet Quimby Issue**			
50¢ **multicolored** tagged		1.50	.50	❑❑❑❑❑
A129 ____________	**1991. William T. Piper Issue**			
40¢ **multicolored** tagged		1.40	.50	❑❑❑❑❑
A130 ____________	**1991. Antarctic Treaty Issue**			
50¢ **multicolored** tagged		1.50	.60	❑❑❑❑❑
A131 ____________	**1991. America Issue**			
50¢ **multicolored** tagged		1.50	.50	❑❑❑❑❑
A132 ____________	**1993. William T. Piper Issue**			
40¢ **multicolored,** tagged		1.50	.50	❑❑❑❑❑

36 USAirmail
Igor Sikorsky
A119

1789
French Revolution • USAirmail 45
A120

USAirmail 45
AMERICA
A121

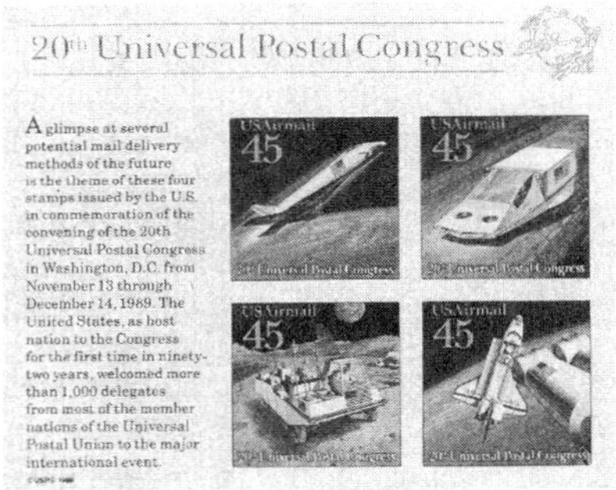
20th Universal Postal Congress
A glimpse at several potential mail delivery methods of the future is the theme of these four stamps issued by the U.S. in commemoration of the convening of the 20th Universal Postal Congress in Washington, D.C. from November 13 through December 14, 1989. The United States, as host nation to the Congress for the first time in ninety-two years, welcomed more than 1,000 delegates from most of the member nations of the Universal Postal Union to the major international event.
A122

A123, A124, A125, A126

USAirmail 45
20th Universal Postal Congress

AMERICA USAirmail 45
A127

Harriet Quimby
Pioneer Pilot
USAirmail
50
A128

William T. Piper
Aviation Pioneer
USAirmail
40
A129

USAirmail 50
1961 Antarctic Treaty
A130

THE FIRST AMERICANS CROSSED OVER FROM ASIA
USAirmail 50
AMERICA
A131

William T. Piper
Aviation Pioneer
USAirmail
40
A132

Special Delivery Stamps

No.	Denomination / Color	Issue	UnFVF	UseFVF
SD1	10¢ Prussian blue	1885. Messenger, First Issue	115.00	22.50
SD2	10¢ Prussian blue	1888. Messenger, Second Issue	120.00	7.00
SD3	10¢ orange yellow	1893. Messenger, Third Issue	75.00	10.00
SD4	10¢ deep blue	1894. Messenger Issue	300.00	20.00
SD5	10¢ blue	1895. Messenger Issue	65.00	1.75
SD6	10¢ ultramarine	1902. Messenger on Bicycle Issue	75.00	3.00
SD7	10¢ green	1908. Helmet of Mercury Issue	50.00	30.00
SD8	10¢ ultramarine	1911. Messenger on Bicycle Issue	75.00	4.50
SD9	10¢ ultramarine	1914. Messenger on Bicycle Issue	140.00	5.00
SD10	10¢ pale ultramarine	1916. Messenger on Bicycle Issue	225.00	22.50
SD11	10¢ ultramarine	1917. Messenger on Bicycle Issue	14.50	.50
SD12	10¢ gray blue	1922. Messenger and Motorcycle Issue	22.50	.25
SD13	15¢ red orange		19.00	1.00
SD14	20¢ black	1925. Post Office Delivery Truck Issue	2.25	1.50
SD15	10¢ dark lilac	1927. Messenger and Motorcycle Issue	1.00	.20
			MNHFVF	UseFVF
SD16	13¢ blue	1944. Messenger and Motorcycle Issue	1.00	.20
SD17	15¢ yellow orange	1931. Messenger and Motorcycle Issue	.75	.20
SD18	17¢ yellow	1944. Messenger and Motorcycle Issue	3.50	3.00
SD19	20¢ black	1951. Post Office Delivery Truck Issue	17.50	.20
SD20	20¢ gray blue	1954. Letter and Hands Issue	.75	.20
SD21	30¢ maroon	1957. Letter and Hands Issue	.75	.20
SD22	45¢ carmine & violet blue	1969. Dual Arrows Issue	1.50	.50
SD23	60¢ violet blue & carmine	1971. Dual Arrows Issue	1.50	.25

SD1

SD2, SD3

SD4, SD5

SD6

SD7

SD8-SD11

SD12, SD13, SD15-SD18

SD14, SD19

SD20, SD21

SD22, SD23

UnFVF UseFVF

Airmail/Special Delivery

ASD1 ______ 1934. Blue Airmail Special Delivery Stamp Issue

16¢ **Prussian blue** (9,215,750) .90 .75 ❑❑❑❑❑

NOTE: An imperforate, ungummed version of the blue airmail special delivery issue, CM161, is listed with other so-called Farley Series stamps among the commemorative listings.

ASD2 ______ 1936. Red and Blue Airmail Special Delivery Stamp Issue

16¢ **carmine & blue** .60 .30 ❑❑❑❑❑

ASD1

ASD2

Parcel Post Stamps

		UnFVF	UseFVF	
PP1 ______	**1912. Parcel Post Stamps**			
1¢	**carmine** (209,691,094)	3.00	1.25	❑❑❑❑❑
PP2 ______				
2¢	**carmine** (206,417,253)	3.50	1.00	❑❑❑❑❑
PP3 ______				
3¢	**carmine** (29,027,433)	6.50	4.50	❑❑❑❑❑
PP4 ______				
4¢	**carmine** (76,743,813)	17.50	2.50	❑❑❑❑❑
PP5 ______				
5¢	**carmine** (108,153,993)	17.50	1.75	❑❑❑❑❑
PP6 ______				
10¢	**carmine** (56,896,653)	30.00	2.50	❑❑❑❑❑
PP7 ______				
15¢	**carmine** (21,147,033)	45.00	8.00	❑❑❑❑❑
PP8 ______				
20¢	**carmine** (17,142,393)	85.00	16.00	❑❑❑❑❑
PP9 ______				
25¢	**carmine** (21,940,653)	42.50	5.00	❑❑❑❑❑
PP10 ______				
50¢	**carmine** (2,117,793)	190.00	32.50	❑❑❑❑❑
PP11 ______				
75¢	**carmine** (2,772,615)	55.00	25.00	❑❑❑❑❑
PP12 ______				
$1	**carmine** (1,053,273)	250.00	20.00	❑❑❑❑❑

Parcel Post/Postage Due Stamps

PPD1 ______	**1912. Parcel Post Postage Due Stamps**			
1¢	**green** (7,322,400)	6.00	3.50	❑❑❑❑❑
PPD2 ______				
2¢	**green** (3,132,000)	55.00	15.00	❑❑❑❑❑
PPD3 ______				
5¢	**green** (5,840,100)	9.00	3.50	❑❑❑❑❑
PPD4 ______				
10¢	**green** (2,124,540)	125.00	40.00	❑❑❑❑❑
PPD5 ______				
25¢	**green** (2,117,700)	65.00	3.75	❑❑❑❑❑

Special Handling Stamps

SH1 ______	**1925-29. Issue**			
25¢	**green**	22.50	5.50	❑❑❑❑❑
SH2 ______				
10¢	**yellow green**	2.25	1.00	❑❑❑❑❑
SH3 ______				
15¢	**yellow green**	2.25	1.00	❑❑❑❑❑
SH4 ______				
20¢	**yellow green**	3.00	1.75	❑❑❑❑❑
SH5 ______				
25¢	**yellow green** *(1929)*	17.50	7.50	❑❑❑❑❑

	UnFVF	UseFVF

Registration Stamp

REG1 1911. Registration Stamp		
10¢ **bright blue**	65.00	5.00 ❑❑❑❑❑

	MNHFVF	UseFVF

Certified Mail Stamp

CER1 1955. Certified Mail Stamp		
15¢ **red**	.50	.35 ❑❑❑❑❑

PP1

PP2

PP3

PP4

PP5

PP6

PP7

PP8

PP9

PP10

PP11

PP12

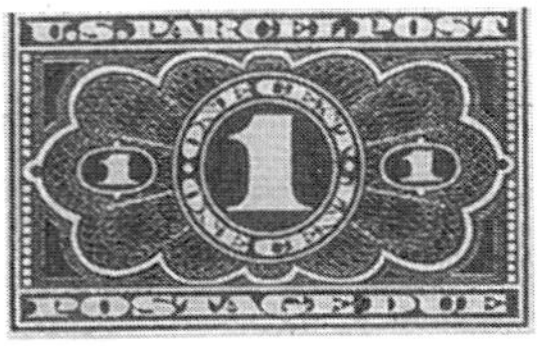

PPD1-5

SH1-SH5

REG1

CER1 →

POSTAGE DUE

First Printing

			UnFVF	UseFVF	
PD1 ______		**1879. Postage Due Stamps Issue**			
1¢	**yellow brown**		40.00	8.00	❑❑❑❑❑
PD2 ______		**1879. Postage Due Stamps Issue**			
2¢	**yellow brown**		250.00	6.50	❑❑❑❑❑
PD3 ______		**1879. Postage Due Stamps Issue**			
3¢	**yellow brown**		35.00	5.00	❑❑❑❑❑
PD4 ______		**1879. Postage Due Stamps Issue**			
5¢	**yellow brown**		400.00	38.00	❑❑❑❑❑
PD5 ______		**1879. Postage Due Stamps Issue**			
10¢	**yellow brown**		450.00	30.00	❑❑❑❑❑
PD6 ______		**1879. Postage Due Stamps Issue**			
30¢	**yellow brown**		200.00	47.50	❑❑❑❑❑
PD7 ______		**1879. Postage Due Stamps Issue**			
50¢	**yellow brown**		350.00	55.00	❑❑❑❑❑

Later Printings

PD8 ______		**1879. Postage Due Stamps Issue**			
1¢	**brown**		40.00	8.00	❑❑❑❑❑
PD9 ______					
2¢	**brown**		250.00	5.00	❑❑❑❑❑
PD10 ______					
3¢	**brown**		35.00	5.00	❑❑❑❑❑
PD11 ______					
5¢	**brown**		400.00	18.00	❑❑❑❑❑
PD12 ______					
10¢	**brown**		450.00	30.00	❑❑❑❑❑
PD13 ______					
30¢	**brown**		200.00	50.00	❑❑❑❑❑
PD14 ______					
50¢	**brown**		350.00	55.00	❑❑❑❑❑

1887. *Previous designs in changed colors.*

PD15 ______					
1¢	**brown red**		40.00	5.00	❑❑❑❑❑
PD16 ______					
2¢	**brown red**		50.00	5.00	❑❑❑❑❑
PD17 ______					
3¢	**brown red**		700.00	150.00	❑❑❑❑❑
PD18 ______					
5¢	**brown red**		350.00	20.00	❑❑❑❑❑
PD19 ______					
10¢	**brown red**		350.00	15.00	❑❑❑❑❑
PD20 ______					
20¢	**brown red**		175.00	50.00	❑❑❑❑❑

PD1

		UnFVF	UseFVF	
PD21	50¢ **brown red**	1,225.00	175.00	❑❑❑❑❑

1891. *Previous designs in changed colors. Imperforate varieties of PD22-28 exist, but they were not regularly issued.*

		UnFVF	UseFVF	
PD22	1¢ **claret**	20.00	1.00	❑❑❑❑❑
PD23	2¢ **claret**	25.00	1.00	❑❑❑❑❑
PD24	3¢ **claret**	50.00	8.00	❑❑❑❑❑
PD25	5¢ **claret**	60.00	8.00	❑❑❑❑❑
PD26	10¢ **claret**	100.00	17.50	❑❑❑❑❑
PD27	30¢ **claret**	350.00	150.00	❑❑❑❑❑
PD28	50¢ **claret**	375.00	150.00	❑❑❑❑❑
SPD1 **1879. Special Printings**	1¢ **brown** (4420)	5,000.00		❑❑❑❑❑
SPD2 **1879. Special Printings**	2¢ **brown** (1361)	3,500.00		❑❑❑❑❑
SPD3 **1879. Special Printings**	3¢ **brown** (436)	2,500.00		❑❑❑❑❑
SPD4 **1879. Special Printings**	5¢ **brown** (249)	1,750.00		❑❑❑❑❑
SPD5 **1879. Special Printings**	10¢ **brown** (174)	1,750.00		❑❑❑❑❑
SPD6 **1879. Special Printings**	30¢ **brown** (179)	1,750.00		❑❑❑❑❑
SPD7 **1879. Special Printings**	50¢ **brown** (179)	1,750.00		❑❑❑❑❑
PD29 **1894. New Designs Issue**	1¢ **vermilion** *(1894)*	1,300.00	300.00	❑❑❑❑❑
PD30	1¢ **brown carmine** *(Aug. 14, 1894)*	32.50	5.50	❑❑❑❑❑
PD31	2¢ **vermilion** *(1894)*	550.00	130.00	❑❑❑❑❑
PD32	2¢ **brown carmine** *(July 20, 1894)*	35.00	4.00	❑❑❑❑❑
PD33	3¢ **brown carmine** *(April 27, 1895)*	130.00	26.00	❑❑❑❑❑
PD34	5¢ **brown carmine** *(April 27, 1895)*	200.00	27.50	❑❑❑❑❑

PD28

PD29

	UnFVF	UseFVF	
PD35 ____________			
10¢ **brown carmine** *(Sept. 24, 1894)*	200.00	25.00	❑❑❑❑❑
PD36 ____________			
30¢ **brown carmine** *(April 27, 1895)*	350.00	90.00	❑❑❑❑❑
PD37 ____________			
50¢ **brown carmine** *(April 27, 1895)*	900.00	250.00	❑❑❑❑❑
***1895.** Same as previous designs. Double-line USPS watermark.*			
PD38 ____________			
1¢ **brown carmine** *(Aug. 29, 1895)*	7.50	.75	❑❑❑❑❑
PD39 ____________			
2¢ **brown carmine** *(Sept. 14, 1895)*	7.50	.70	❑❑❑❑❑
PD40 ____________			
3¢ **brown carmine** *(Oct. 30, 1895)*	47.50	1.50	❑❑❑❑❑
PD41 ____________			
5¢ **brown carmine** *(Oct. 15, 1895)*	50.00	1.50	❑❑❑❑❑
PD42 ____________			
10¢ **brown carmine** *(Sept. 14, 1895)*	47.50	3.50	❑❑❑❑❑
PD43 ____________			
30¢ **brown carmine** *(Aug. 21, 1897)*	450.00	50.00	❑❑❑❑❑
PD44 ____________			
50¢ **brown carmine** *(March 17, 1896)*	275.00	35.00	❑❑❑❑❑
***1910.** Same as previous designs. Single-line USPS watermark.*			
PD45 ____________			
1¢ **brown carmine** *(Aug. 30, 1910)*	27.50	2.75	❑❑❑❑❑
PD46 ____________			
2¢ **brown carmine** *(Nov. 25, 1910)*	27.50	1.25	❑❑❑❑❑
PD47 ____________			
3¢ **brown carmine** *(Aug. 31, 1910)*	450.00	30.00	❑❑❑❑❑
PD48 ____________			
5¢ **brown carmine** *(Aug. 31, 1910)*	75.00	6.25	❑❑❑❑❑
PD49 ____________			
10¢ **brown carmine** *(Aug. 31, 1910)*	95.00	12.50	❑❑❑❑❑
PD50 ____________			
50¢ **brown carmine** *(Sept. 23, 1912)*	750.00	120.00	❑❑❑❑❑
***1914.** Same as previous designs. Perforated 10.*			
PD51 ____________			
1¢ **rose red**	50.00	11.00	❑❑❑❑❑
PD52 ____________			
2¢ **vermilion**	45.00	.30	❑❑❑❑❑
PD53 ____________			
2¢ **rose red**	45.00	.30	❑❑❑❑❑
PD54 ____________			
3¢ **rose red**	750.00	38.00	❑❑❑❑❑
PD55 ____________			
5¢ **rose red**	32.00	2.50	❑❑❑❑❑
PD56 ____________			
10¢ **rose red**	50.00	2.00	❑❑❑❑❑
PD57 ____________			
30¢ **rose red**	200.00	16.00	❑❑❑❑❑
PD58 ____________			
50¢ **rose red**	8,200.00	650.00	❑❑❑❑❑
***1916.** Same as previous designs. Unwatermarked.*			
PD59 ____________			
1¢ **rose red**	2,000.00	300.00	❑❑❑❑❑

UnFVF	UseFVF	

PD60 _____
2¢ **rose red** 125.00 20.00 ☐☐☐☐☐

1917-25. *Same as previous designs. Perforated 11.*
PD61 _____
1/2¢ **carmine** *(April 13, 1925)* 1.00 .25 ☐☐☐☐☐
PD62 _____
1¢ **carmine** 2.25 .25 ☐☐☐☐☐
PD63 _____
2¢ **carmine** 2.25 .25 ☐☐☐☐☐
PD64 _____
3¢ **carmine** 10.00 .25 ☐☐☐☐☐
PD65 _____
5¢ **carmine** 10.00 .25 ☐☐☐☐☐
PD66 _____
10¢ **carmine** 15.00 .30 ☐☐☐☐☐
PD67 _____
30¢ **carmine** 80.00 .75 ☐☐☐☐☐
PD68 _____
50¢ **carmine** 10.00 .30 ☐☐☐☐☐
PD69 _____ **1930. New Designs Issue**
1/2¢ **carmine** 4.00 1.25 ☐☐☐☐☐
PD70 _____
1¢ **carmine** 2.50 .25 ☐☐☐☐☐
PD71 _____
2¢ **carmine** 3.50 .25 ☐☐☐☐☐
PD72 _____
3¢ **carmine** 20.00 1.50 ☐☐☐☐☐
PD73 _____
5¢ **carmine** 20.00 2.50 ☐☐☐☐☐
PD74 _____
10¢ **carmine** 40.00 1.00 ☐☐☐☐☐
PD75 _____
30¢ **carmine** 110.00 2.00 ☐☐☐☐☐
PD76 _____
50¢ **carmine** 140.00 .75 ☐☐☐☐☐
PD77 _____
$1 **carmine** 25.00 .25 ☐☐☐☐☐
PD78 _____
$5 **carmine** 40.00 .25 ☐☐☐☐☐

1931. *Same as previous design. Rotary press printing, perforated 11 x 10 1/2.*
PD79 _____
1/2¢ **vermilion** 1.00 .20 ☐☐☐☐☐
PD80 _____
1¢ **vermilion** .20 .20 ☐☐☐☐☐
PD81 _____
2¢ **vermilion** .20 .20 ☐☐☐☐☐

PD68 PD69, PD79 PD76 PD77, PD87 PD78

No.	Value	Color	UnFVF	UseFVF
PD82	3¢	**vermilion**	.25	.20 ❑❑❑❑❑
PD83	5¢	**vermilion**	.40	.20 ❑❑❑❑❑
PD84	10¢	**vermilion**	1.00	.20 ❑❑❑❑❑
PD85	30¢	**vermilion**	8.00	.25 ❑❑❑❑❑
PD86	50¢	**vermilion**	10.00	.25 ❑❑❑❑❑

1956. *Perforated 10 1/2 x 11.*

No.	Value	Color	UnFVF	UseFVF
PD87	$1	**vermilion**	35.00	.25 ❑❑❑❑❑

1959-85. New Designs Issue

No.	Value	Color	UnFVF	UseFVF
PD88	1/2¢	**red & black** *(June 19, 1959)*	1.25	1.00 ❑❑❑❑❑
PD89	1¢	**red & black** *(June 19, 1959)*	.20	.20 ❑❑❑❑❑
PD90	2¢	**red & black** *(June 19, 1959)*	.20	.20 ❑❑❑❑❑
PD91	3¢	**red & black** *(June 19, 1959)*	.20	.20 ❑❑❑❑❑
PD92	4¢	**red & black** *(June 19, 1959)*	.20	.20 ❑❑❑❑❑
PD93	5¢	**red & black** *(June 19, 1959)*	.20	.20 ❑❑❑❑❑
PD94	6¢	**red & black** *(June 19, 1959)*	.20	.20 ❑❑❑❑❑
PD95	7¢	**red & black** *(June 19, 1959)*	.20	.20 ❑❑❑❑❑
PD96	8¢	**red & black** *(June 19, 1959)*	.20	.20 ❑❑❑❑❑
PD97	10¢	**red & black** *(June 19, 1959)*	.20	.20 ❑❑❑❑❑
PD98	30¢	**red & black** *(June 19, 1959)*	.75	.20 ❑❑❑❑❑
PD99	50¢	**red & black** *(June 19, 1959)*	1.00	.20 ❑❑❑❑❑
PD100	$1	**red & black** *(June 19, 1959)*	1.75	.20 ❑❑❑❑❑
PD101	$5	**red & black**	9.00	.20 ❑❑❑❑❑
PD102	11¢	**red & black** *(Jan. 2, 1978)*	.25	.20 ❑❑❑❑❑
PD103	13¢	**red & black** *(Jan. 2, 1978)*	.25	.20 ❑❑❑❑❑
PD104	17¢	**red & black** *(June 10, 1985)*	.40	.30 ❑❑❑❑❑

PD88

PD89

PD101

MIGRATORY BIRD HUNTING PERMIT

		UnFVF	UseFVF
RH1	1934. Mallard Issue		
$1 blue		575.00	115.00 ☐☐☐☐☐
RH2	1935. Canvasback Duck Issue		
$1 crimson		525.00	135.00 ☐☐☐☐☐
RH3	1936. Canada Geese Issue		
$1 brown black		300.00	65.00 ☐☐☐☐☐
RH4	1937. Scaup Ducks Issue		
$1 dull green		250.00	45.00 ☐☐☐☐☐
RH5	1938. Pintail Duck Issue		
$1 violet		250.00	45.00 ☐☐☐☐☐
RH6	1939. Green-Winged Teal Issue		
$1 sepia		140.00	40.00 ☐☐☐☐☐

		MNHFVF	UseFVF
RH7	1940. Black Mallard Issue		
$1 black brown		140.00	40.00 ☐☐☐☐☐
RH8	1941. Ruddy Ducks Issue		
$1 red brown		140.00	35.00 ☐☐☐☐☐
RH9	1942. Baldpates Issue		
$1 sepia		140.00	35.00 ☐☐☐☐☐
RH10	1943. Wood Duck Issue		
$1 carmine red		60.00	35.00 ☐☐☐☐☐
RH11	1944. White-Fronted Geese Issue		
$1 red orange		60.00	25.00 ☐☐☐☐☐
RH12	1945. Shoveller Ducks Issue		
$1 black		45.00	18.00 ☐☐☐☐☐
RH13	1946. Redhead Ducks Issue		
$1 chestnut brown		35.00	13.50 ☐☐☐☐☐
RH14	1947. Snow Geese Issue		
$1 black		35.00	13.50 ☐☐☐☐☐
RH15	1948. Bufflehead Ducks Issue		
$1 light blue		45.00	13.50 ☐☐☐☐☐
RH16	1949. Goldeneye Ducks Issue		
$2 emerald		50.00	13.50 ☐☐☐☐☐
RH17	1950. Trumpeter Swans Issue		
$2 violet		60.00	10.00 ☐☐☐☐☐
RH18	1951. Gadwall Ducks Issue		
$2 gray black		60.00	10.00 ☐☐☐☐☐
RH19	1952. Harlequin Ducks Issue		
$2 deep ultramarine		60.00	10.00 ☐☐☐☐☐
RH20	1953. Blue-Winged Teal Issue		
$2 lavender brown		60.00	12.00 ☐☐☐☐☐
RH21	1954. Ring-Necked Ducks Issue		
$2 black		60.00	8.00 ☐☐☐☐☐
RH22	1955. Blue Geese Issue		
$2 deep blue		60.00	8.00 ☐☐☐☐☐
RH23	1956. American Merganser Issue		
$2 black		60.00	8.00 ☐☐☐☐☐
RH24	1957. American Eider Issue		
$2 yellow emerald		60.00	8.00 ☐☐☐☐☐
RH25	1958. Canada Geese Issue		
$2 black		60.00	8.00 ☐☐☐☐☐

RH1

RH2

RH3

RH4

RH5

RH6

RH7

RH8

RH9

RH10

RH11

RH12

RH13

RH14

RH15

RH16

RH17

RH18

		UnFVF	UseFVF	
RH26	**1959. Retriever Carrying Mallard Issue**			
$3	**blue, orange brown & black**	85.00	8.00	❑❑❑❑❑
RH27	**1960. Redhead Ducks Issue**			
$3	**multicolored**	65.00	8.00	❑❑❑❑❑
RH28	**1961. Mallards Issue**			
$3	**blue, brown & yellow brown**	70.00	8.00	❑❑❑❑❑
RH29	**1962. Pintails Issue**			
$3	**multicolored**	70.00	8.00	❑❑❑❑❑
RH30	**1963. Pacific Brant Issue**			
$3	**multicolored**	70.00	8.00	❑❑❑❑❑
RH31	**1964. Nene Geese Issue**			
$3	**multicolored**	70.00	8.00	❑❑❑❑❑
RH32	**1965. Canvasbacks Issue**			
$3	**multicolored**	70.00	8.00	❑❑❑❑❑
RH33	**1966. Whistling Swans Issue**			
$3	**deep green, black & blue**	70.00	8.00	❑❑❑❑❑
RH34	**1967. Old Squaw Ducks Issue**			
$3	**multicolored**	70.00	8.00	❑❑❑❑❑
RH35	**1968. Hooded Mergansers Issue**			
$3	**multicolored**	55.00	8.00	❑❑❑❑❑
RH36	**1969. White-Winged Scoters Issue**			
$3	**multicolored**	40.00	7.00	❑❑❑❑❑
RH37	**1970. Ross' Geese Issue**			
$3	**multicolored**	40.00	7.00	❑❑❑❑❑

RH19

RH20

RH21

RH22

RH23

RH24

RH25

RH26

RH27

RH28

82%

113%

RH29

RH30

RH31

RH32

RH33

RH34

RH35

RH36

RH37

RH38

RH39

RH40

RH41

RH42

RH43

RH44

RH45

		UnFVF	UseFVF	
RH38 $3 multicolored	**1971. Cinnamon Teal Issue**	35.00	7.00	❑❑❑❑❑
RH39 $5 multicolored	**1972. Emperor Geese Issue**	22.50	7.00	❑❑❑❑❑
RH40 $5 multicolored	**1973. Steller's Eider Issue**	20.00	7.00	❑❑❑❑❑
RH41 $5 multicolored	**1974. Wood Ducks Issue**	18.00	7.00	❑❑❑❑❑
RH42 $5 multicolored	**1975. Canvasbacks Issue**	14.00	7.00	❑❑❑❑❑
RH43 $5 green & black	**1976. Canada Geese Issue**	14.00	7.00	❑❑❑❑❑
RH44 $5 multicolored	**1977. Ross' Geese Issue**	14.00	7.00	❑❑❑❑❑
RH45 $5 multicolored	**1978. Hooded Merganser Issue**	14.00	7.00	❑❑❑❑❑
RH46 $7.50 multicolored	**1979. Green-Winged Teal Issue**	17.50	7.00	❑❑❑❑❑
RH47 $7.50 multicolored	**1980. Mallards Issue**	17.50	7.00	❑❑❑❑❑
RH48 $7.50 multicolored	**1981. Ruddy Ducks Issue**	17.50	7.00	❑❑❑❑❑
RH49 $7.50 multicolored	**1982. Canvasbacks Issue**	17.50	7.00	❑❑❑❑❑
RH50 $7.50 multicolored	**1983. Pintails Issue**	17.50	7.00	❑❑❑❑❑
RH51 $7.50 multicolored	**1984. Widgeons Issue**	17.50	7.00	❑❑❑❑❑

NOTE: After No. RH51's period of use had expired, 15 uncut sheets of 120 (four panes of 30 stamps per sheet, separated by gutters) were overprinted "1934-84" and "50th Anniversary" along the margins. These sheets were auctioned off by the U.S. Fish and Wildlife Service, beginning Sept. 1, 1985, with a minimum acceptable bid for each sheet of $2,000. Face value of the sheets, when valid for use, was $900. Fourteen sheets were sold, and one was donated to the Smithsonian Institution. Individual stamps of the sheet cannot be differentiated from normal copies of No. RH51. Various configurations were formed from the sheets and sold to collectors: horizontal and vertical pairs with a gutter between, cross-gutter blocks of four, and margin blocks. Sheets were submitted to The Philatelic Foundation for certification prior to being broken up, and each stamp from each of the sheets has a mark of the expertizer on the reverse. With such marks in place, individual stamps not attached to a margin were sold along with configurations noted above.

RH46

RH47

RH48

RH49

RH50

RH51

UnFVF	UseFVF	

RH51a _____ **1984. Special Commemorative Issue**

$7.50 **Special Commemorative Issue**
(All examples must have P.F. certificates)

RH52 _____ **1985. Cinnamon Teal Issue**

$7.50 **multicolored** 17.50 7.00 ☐☐☐☐☐

RH53 _____ **1986. Fulvous Whistling Duck Issue**

$7.50 **multicolored** 17.50 7.00 ☐☐☐☐☐

RH54 _____ **1987. Redhead Issue**

$10 **multicolored** 20.00 10.00 ☐☐☐☐☐

RH55 _____ **1988. Snow Goose Issue**

$10 **multicolored** 20.00 7.00 ☐☐☐☐☐

RH56 _____ **1989. Lesser Scaup Issue**

$12.50 **multicolored** 22.50 7.00 ☐☐☐☐☐

RH57 _____ **1990. Black-Bellied Whistling Duck Issue**

$12.50 **multicolored** 22.50 7.00 ☐☐☐☐☐

NOTE: printing on back of stamp normally is on top of gum. No. RH57v can exist only unused. Beware of copies with gum removed.

RH58 _____ **1991. King Eiders Issue**

$15 **multicolored** 27.50 12.50 ☐☐☐☐☐

RH59 _____ **1992. Spectacled Eider Issue**

$15 **multicolored** 27.50 12.50 ☐☐☐☐☐

RH60 _____ **1993. Canvasback issue**

$15 **multicolored** 27.50 12.50 ☐☐☐☐☐

RH61 _____ **1994. Red-breasted Mergansers Issue**

$15 **multicolored** 25.00 10.00 ☐☐☐☐☐

RH52

RH53

RH54

RH55

RH56

RH57

RH58

RH59

RH60

		UnFVF	UseFVF	
RH62	**1995. Mallard Issue**			
$15 **multicolored**		25.00	10.00	☐☐☐☐☐
RH63	**1996. Surf Scoter Issue**			
$15 **multicolored**		25.00	10.00	☐☐☐☐☐
RH64	**1997. Canada Goose Issue**			
$15 **multicolored**		25.00	10.00	☐☐☐☐☐
RH65	**1998. Barrow's Goldeneye Issue**			
$15 **multicolored**		25.00	10.00	☐☐☐☐☐
RH66	**1998. Barrow's Goldeneye Self-adhesive Issue**			
$15 **multicolored**		30.00	15.00	☐☐☐☐☐
RH67	**1999. Greater Scaup Issue**			
$15 **multicolored**		30.00	15.00	☐☐☐☐☐
RH68	**1999. Greater Scaup Issue**			
$15 **multicolored**		30.00	15.00	☐☐☐☐☐
RH69	**2000. Mottled Duck Issue**			
$15 **multicolored**		25.00	15.00	☐☐☐☐☐
RH70	**2000. Mottled Duck Issue**			
$15 **multicolored**		25.00	15.00	☐☐☐☐☐
RH71	**2001. Northern Pintail Issue**			
$15 **multicolored**		25.00	15.00	☐☐☐☐☐
RH72	**2001. Northern Pintail Issue**			
$15 **multicolored**		25.00	15.00	☐☐☐☐☐

RH61

RH62

RH63

RH64

RH65

RH66

RH67

RH68

RH69

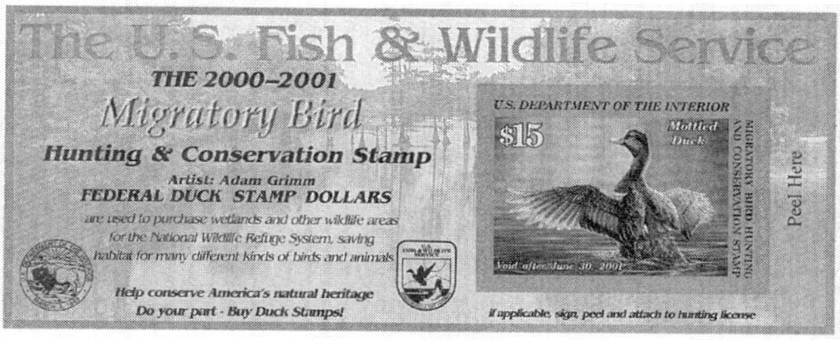

RH70

RH71

RH72